Shigemitsu
and Togo
and Their Time

Shigemitsu and Togo

and Their Time

Okazaki Hisahiko

Translated by Noda Makito

Japan Publishing Industry Foundation for Culture

TRANSLATION NOTE
All Japanese names appearing in this book are written with surname first and given name last. In addition, all Japanese words and names have been romanized in accordance with the Hepburn system, and macrons have been applied to indicate long vowels wherever deemed appropriate.

Shigemitsu and Togo and Their Time
Okazaki Hisahiko. Translated by Noda Makito
Published by Japan Publishing Industry Foundation for Culture (JPIC)
3-12-3 Kanda-Jinbocho, Chiyoda-ku, Tokyo 101-0051, Japan
First English edition: March 2019
© Okazaki Hisahiko, Okazaki Akiko, 2003.
English translation © The Japan Institute of International Affairs (JIIA)

This book is the result of a collaborative effort between The Japan Institute of International Affairs (JIIA) and Japan Publishing Industry Foundation for Culture (JPIC)
Photo: Kyodo News for pages 11(top), 30, 73, 102, 118, 249, 257, 274, 301
Photo: Kingendai PL/Afloo for front cover (right), page 11 (bottom)
Photo: Diplomatic Archives of the Ministry of Foreign Affairs of Japan for the front cover (left)
All other photographs: Kingendai Photo Library

Originally published in Japanese under the titles of *Shigemitsu/Tōgō to sono jidai*
by PHP Institute, Inc. in 2003.
Jacket & cover design: Miki Kazuhiko, Ampersand Works
All rights reserved.

Printed in Japan
ISBN 978-4-86658-071-5
http://www.jpic.or.jp/

CONTENTS

CHAPTER 16

This War Must End
—Fifty Years of Glory Perish Like a Bubble—   355

Shigemitsu Mamoru

Tōgō Shigenori

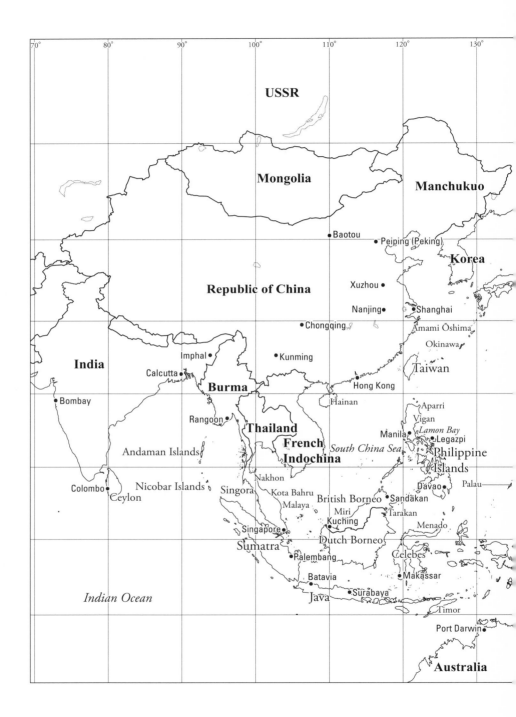

70°	80°	90°	100°	110°	120°	130°	

USSR

Mongolia

Manchukuo

• Baotou
• Peiping (Peking)

Korea

Xuzhou •

Republic of China

Nanjing • ○ • Shanghai

• Chongqing

Amami Ōshima

Okinawa

Imphal •

• Kunming

Taiwan

India

Calcutta •

• Hong Kong

Burma

• Bombay

Hainan

Aparri

Rangoon •

Vigan

Thailand

Lamon Bay

French

Manila • • Legazpi

Andaman Islands

South China Sea

Indochina

Philippine

Islands

Nakhon

Davao •

Palau

Colombo •

Nicobar Islands

Singora

Kota Bahru

British Borneo • Sandakan

Ceylon

Malaya

Miri • Tarakan

Kuching

Menado

Singapore •

Dutch Borneo

Sumatra

Celebes

• Palembang

• Makassar

• Batavia

• Surabaya

Timor

Indian Ocean

Java

Port Darwin •

Australia

Asian Theater as of 1941

150°   160°   170°   180°   170°   160°

Kamchatka

Aleutian Islands

Attsu   Kiska   Dutch Harbor

50°

Chishima Islands

Etorofu
Hitokappu Bay

Ōminato   40°

Tokyo

30°

Ogasawara Islands   · Midway
Hahajima

Iwo Jima   · Minami Torishima   *Pacific Ocean*   Hawaiian Islands

Oahu

· Waki   20°

Mariana Islands
Saipan

Guam

Marshall Islands   10°

Truck Islands   Kwajalein

Makin
Tarawa

0°

Bismarck Archipelago   Gilbert Islands·

New Guinea ·Rabaul
Lae   Solomon Islands
Buna
Guadalcanal   10°
Port Moresby·

Samoan Islands

Coral Sea

Fiji Islands

China, 1935

USSR

Heilongjiang
○ Qiqihar
Ne River

Mongolia

Manchukuo
○ Harbin

Jilin
○ Jilin

Changchun ○

Chahars

Jehol (2)

Liaoning (3)
○ Mukden
(Fengtian)

Duolun ○

Suiyuan
○ Dehua

Chengde ○
Jinzhou

Ningxia
○ Suiyuan

Peiping (4) ○ ○ Tongzhou

○ Dailian
Lushun

Sea of Japan

Tianjin ○

Hebei (1)

Taiyuan ○

Korea

Shanxi

○ Jinan

Gansu

Yanan ○

Shandong
○ Qingdao

Yellow Sea

Shaanxi
○ Luoyang

○ Haeju

Xian ○ *Yellow River
(Huang Ho)*

○ Xuzhou

Henan

Jiangsu

Anhui ○ Nanjings

Sichuan

Hubei

Huaining
○

Hankou ○
Wuchang

Chongqing ○

*Chang Jiang
(Yangtze River)*

Hunan
Changsha ○

○ Shanghai

Hangzhou ○

○ Ningbo

Mt. Lu ▲ ○ Jiujiang

Zhejiang

○ Nanchang

East China Sea

○ Zunyi

Guizhou
○ Guiyang

Mt. Jinggang ▲

Jiangxi

Ruijin ○

Fujian

○ Yangzhou

○ Guilin

Guanxi

Guangdong

Nanning ○

○ Guangzhou
○ Hong Kong

○ Amoy

Taiwan

French
Indochina

Hainan

Philippines

(1) Hebei Province (Zhili Province until 1928)
(2) Jehol Province (established 1928)
(3) Liaoning Province (Fengtian Province until 1929)
(4) Peking until 1928 (now spelled Beijing)

PROLOGUE

The Truth of History

—Judge History Not on Contemporary Values Alone—

So far I have written as a series of the Japanese edition for Mutstu Munemitsu (陸奥宗光) Komura Jutarō (小村寿太郎) , and Shidehara Kijūrō (幣原喜重郎) through the Japan's political and diplomatic history. I realize that I am at a loss. The reason is that I cannot continue to interpret the modern Japanese history through the lens of someone's biography. Ever since the time of Shidehara's resignation as foreign minister in the Manchurian Incident until Japan's defeat in World War II, there is no single individual who I deem qualified to be called a leader of Japan's diplomacy.

This situation cannot be attributed to a popular, simplistic explanation such as a deficiency of outstanding personalities in Shōwa Japan, compared with Meiji. In the background was the drastic transformation of Japanese society.

From the time of its opening to the outside world up until the Taishō era, Japan had to leave diplomacy to the preciously exceptional handful of people who had been privileged enough to know the world firsthand. In the Shōwa era, those days were gone. It was no longer the era when people could simply leave diplomacy to the likes of Shidehara.

By the 1930s, Japanese people in all walks of life had travelled abroad, including elite military officers who were given opportunities to study overseas or assume duties as military attachés. Politicians in these days benefitted from organizational support on foreign affairs by bureaucrats, while the skills of interpreters also became highly advanced. Thus, diplomacy did not necessarily call for those who were knowledgeable about foreign countries.

Also, as the education system and the national bureaucracy became increasingly well organized, competent human resources were produced one after another. Thus, it was no longer necessary, for example, for one outstanding person to monopolize for long periods the position of vice-minister or minister for foreign affairs. These positions came to be selected by order of seniority.

Shidehara passed the Foreign Service Examination in 1896 immediately after the First Sino-Japanese War. He consistently stayed at the center of Japan's diplomacy for 35 years until his retirement in 1931, serving as vice minister for foreign affairs in 1915, ambassador to the United States in 1919, and foreign minister in 1924. After Shidehara, nobody was as good.

Career diplomats who became foreign minister after Shidehara included Yoshizawa Kenkichi (芳澤謙吉) and Uchida Kōsai (内田康哉), who both served briefly. After these two, the foreign ministry entered a new era of diplomats who were some ten years younger than Shidehara.

This new generation entered the foreign ministry around the time of the Russo-Japanese War (1904–05), an era of crisis when a sense of nationhood was heightened. The new generation of diplomats included Matsuoka Yōsuke (松岡洋右, who passed the Foreign Service Examination in 1904), Satō Naotake (佐藤尚武), Saburi Sadao (佐分利貞男, a young hopeful of the foreign ministry who passed the Foreign Service Examination in 1905 but met a mysterious death in 1929), and Hirota Kōki (広田弘毅) and Yoshida Shigeru (吉田茂) who, after passing the examination in 1906, became good rivals in later years.

Entering the foreign ministry a little after the above five, when the Great Empire of Japan was at its zenith, having annexed the Korean peninsula, were Arita Hachirō (有田八郎, 1909), Saitō Hiroshi (斎藤博, who joined the foreign ministry in 1910, and became highly reputed as an outstanding ambassador to the United States, where he passed away from disease), Shigemitsu Mamoru (重光葵, 1911), Ashida Hitoshi (芦田均, 1911), Tōgō Shigenori (東郷茂徳, 1912), and Tani Masayuki (谷正之, 1913). During World War II, Tōgō and Shigemitsu each took a turn as Japan's foreign minister. Hence the title of this book, *Shigemitsu and Tōgō and Their Time*.

All of these foreign ministers had been legendary prodigies in their respective hometowns, with their futures promised. They were also endowed with the necessary insights to serve as foreign ministers.

Had one or two of the above remained responsible for Japan's foreign policy singlehandedly for 14 years between the Manchurian Incident and the defeat in World War II, Japan would probably not have been drawn into a war on the Chinese continent without a long-term strategy or an assessment of the situation. In fact, Japan did not need a genius at the time. If only a man with ordinary common sense had been at the steering wheel of Japan's diplomacy, it would have been unbearable for him to watch Japan go down the drain. As it turned out, however, all the foreign ministers in this period succeeded their respective predecessors' faits accomplis and passed the baton to their respective successors halfway through their terms despite their efforts to break free from their situations. Horiba Kazuo (堀場一雄) was quite right when he said in his *Shina Jihen Senso Shidō-shi* (History of Leadership during the Second Sino-Japanese War) that a dearth of human resources during the war was further aggravated by frequent routine personnel changes.

Furthermore, they were not endowed with enough political clout to realize their ideals. In retrospect, the statesmen I have written about so far did have this political clout, which they used in pursuit of their respective foreign policies. Mutsu was backed up by his personal friendship with Itō Hirobumi (伊藤博文) and the political power of Tosa's *Jiyūtō*, while Komura cashed in on the strong nationalistic trend among Meiji's second generation represented by Katsura Tarō (桂太郎). Based on the great principle of parliamentary democracy, Shidehara relied on *Minseitō*'s power of the majority that it had obtained through legitimate elections.

In contrast, none of the legislatures or diplomats of the early Shōwa period were equipped with comparable political clout. To put it another way, nobody had the political power to restrict the arbitrary conduct of the military.

During the Taishō Democracy, the political party had succeeded in taking power away from the *han*-clique at long last, but power was soon snatched from it by the military. As I have written in the past two volumes (*Komura Jutarō and His Time* and *Shidehara Kijūrō and His Time*), of the original Japanese edition since the Taishō Democracy was Japan's first attempt at democratic government, people in Japan naturally did not have the experience or the flexibility in their minds to accept Winston Churchill's famous observation that "Democracy is the worst form of government, except for all those other forms that have been tried from time to time." Thus, people became disillusioned by the "worst" aspects of party politics—that is, intra/inter-party feuds and corruption—leading them to expect more from the alternative options, particularly the military.

Since the real power in the early Shōwa period had lain not in the elder statesmen, nor in the bureaucracy or parliament, but in the military, Japanese history in this period would have been better if the military had been endowed with excellent human resources.

To be sure, the military did have a few outstanding generals and officers who were contemporaries of and comparable to the likes of the foreign ministry's Tōgō and Shigemitsu. But even they could not restrict both the arbitrary conduct and the defiant behavior of junior officers. This was a uniquely Japanese phenomenon absent in other fascist states like Germany or Italy.

The military was indeed a high hope for the Japanese people. It seems undeniable that the Japanese people in those days had favorable images of young, gallant military officers leading the nation in place of politicians tarnished by party strife and corruption.

Seen in this light, it seems undeniable that there is a lot of truth in the judgment, as discussed in the previous book, that letting those who had been involved in the assassination of Zhang Zuolin (張作霖) go unpunished planted the root of later problems in all Shōwa politics, contributing to the rise of the trend of defiant junior officers.

Theoretically, there still was a chance to prevent Japan from destroying itself not only at the end of the Manchurian Incident in 1931 but even after the Marco Polo Bridge Incident in 1937. Now that nobody could restrict the arbitrary conduct of young military officers, however, any insightful diplomatic judgment or a national strategy based on these judgments became meaningless.

Leaving aside the post-World War II ethic of anti-colonialism, to "stop at Manchuria" might have been a correct judgment from the viewpoint of Japan's national strategy regarding the international situation of the time. But when the Japanese government could not restrict the military, the issue of the correctness of a national strategy was of no significance. Japan was comparable to a gambler who, after eventually losing heavily, lamented that he should have left the casino when he made his biggest win. When a gambler refuses to return home after being told it was high time to do so, there is no room for any strategy. Unless he takes over the entire casino—in this case, the entire China mainland—a consummately wild fantasy, he would end up playing the game until he loses every penny. "The house always wins," goes the saying.

And if that was indeed the case, it could lead to a conclusion that it was wrong to be at the casino in the first place. And this logic could be easily converted to a simplistic historical view that it was wrong for Japan to have possessed a military in the first place.

In fact, this was the mainstream historical view in post–World War II Japan. This phenomenon was at least partially attributable to the Communist propaganda during the Cold War. Because the ultimate objective of the Communist propaganda was to make it easier to conquer Japan by reducing Japan's defense capability, it was only natural for the Communists to agitate anti-war, anti-military sentiment.

Thus, a synergy of the historical lessons after World War II and the anti-military sentiment provoked by the Communist propaganda generated a simplistic historical view that became the mainstream in postwar Japan.

It would be sad if the only historical lesson the Japanese had learned from the World War II to which the entire nation devoted everything was this simplistic historical view. In fact, Prime Minister Shidehara once proposed to establish a panel to review the entire process of the "Greater East Asian War" with the participation of the former military. But it was opposed by the occupation authorities as an attempt to start a war again.

The postwar Japanese people themselves refused to learn strategic lessons from the war. They tried to justify themselves by claiming that nothing would have made any difference unless they could control the military.

I once commented that if Japan had refrained from attacking Pearl Harbor and, instead, publicized the Hull note and declared that it would enter into war with the United States unless the latter lifted the embargo on oil within 48 hours, the United States could have either not started the war or, if it did start the war, would not have been able to continue it due to opposition in Congress and public opinion, especially after it lost 20,000 Marines on Iwo Jima. In response to this comment of mine, even some of the more sensible people criticized me, saying, "That may be so, but termination of the war in that way would have encouraged the military to remain big-headed, would it not?"

Against this psychological background, which adamantly refuses to learn any strategic lessons from the war, it is not an easy task to document the history and discuss the people of the time. When one narrates on that time along this line of argument, he will end up with a historical view which regards those who catered to or did not resist any conduct of the military as those who misled the nation, while those who at least attempted to resist the military in vain were admired as men of conscience and tragic heroes.

Because the devastation of the war and the defeat of the Japanese people was so immense, it might be unavoidable to judge the rights and wrongs of the people concerned based only on whether they sided with the military during the war. In fact, almost all the postwar books on Shōwa history have reiterated the issue. The present book may also not be free from this theme, depending on the time and place.

But is it really a good history for foreign readers and Japanese readers of future generations to judge it only from the angle of whether they resisted the military or not?

In addition, the extremely peculiar issues in post–World War II Japan, i.e., the "apology" issue and the textbook issue, are of particular note.

Contrary to the popular notion, these issues have by no means been left unresolved for fifty years after the end of the war.

Usually, love and hate caused by a war perish after one generation, say, 30 years. While Napoleon Bonaparte had been harshly criticized in the period of "reaction" immediately after his defeat at Waterloo in 1815, his positive evaluation as a hero who brought glory to France had been firmly established within France around the time of the Revolution of 1848.

In Japan, also, by the late 1970s, thirty years after the end of World War II, historical issues had been non-existent. While I gave replies in the Diet more than 300 times as government testimonies between 1978 and 1981, such issues as the Nanjing Massacre, the comfort women issue, and the apology issue had never been mentioned in the Diet. Neither had there been any concept of taking into consideration reactions of Asian neighbors when building up Japan's national defense. Neither the Diet nor the mass media and, consequently, foreign governments/institutions, took up these issues at all. This can be verified by closely studying the newspapers and magazines in those two to three years.

It was the so-called textbook issue of 1982, which in itself was a product of erroneous reporting, that triggered the digging up of a chain of historical incidents that had long been forgotten. Issues that were thus artificially created in Japan were exported overseas one after another, and some of them in fact became international political issues. This was an unprecedented phenomenon in the history of the world.

The difficulty of this problem lies in the very fact that it was historically unprecedented. Should we consider that these issues would soon die away again because all of them were artificially revived and, therefore, necessarily transient? Or are these problems here to stay considering that, in Japan, they had already been artificially implanted in school textbooks and, in China, those views had already been embedded in people's sentiment through the suppression of the post-Tiananmen Incident democratization movement and the subsequent drive to inspire people with patriotism? There is no knowing which will be the case.

I have consistently predicted that these issues would vanish into thin air as soon as their advocates within Japan ceased to be vocal, because the issues had been dragged up in Japan first. I am convinced that China will stop complaining as soon as all the Japanese in unison criticize China's interference with Japan's domestic affairs. After all, the Chinese government pursues its diplomacy in order to enhance national and people's interests. It is natural that the government will stop saying something which is detrimental to these interests if it comes to view it that way. Otherwise, it will continue, particularly as the Chinese Communist Party sees the criticism of Japan as a way to strengthen its nationalist credentials and keep its hold on power.

In any event, I do not expect these issues artificially created in Japan to last more than a generation from now. If that is the case, I wonder what future Japanese generations, which will have no clue about these issues, as they do not need to have, will think of a history book gripped by these issues. Unable to understand why an author spends so much space for such incidents as the Nanjing Massacre and the comfort women issue that are not particularly related to the larger flow of history, they may end up suspecting the impartiality of the book itself. They may even suspect that the author is driven by a bizarre motivation, having abnormal interest in sexual conduct and atrocities. In fact, there have been a number of this kind of bizarre history book.

I am of the view that it is not necessary to go to the trouble of taking up atrocities during the war and the comfort women issue in discussions of the history of the early Shōwa period. While it might be necessary to touch on the Nanjing Massacre because it had provoked some international repercussions, other events and incidents really do not warrant attention by an author who is trying not to lose sight of the major flow of the political and diplomatic history of the time. As far as their historical significance is concerned, these issues should actually be taken up as a part of Japan's post–World War II history. It might prove worthwhile to analyze them as a phenomenon generated by peculiar psychological and political situations in the postwar Japanese society.

Anyone who writes, and particularly those who write about history, must be prepared and resolved to see that their work will be read by future generations. Naturally, they should not indulge in things that would be worthless for readers one generation later, even though they may be urged to write about them by their contemporaries.

Most of books and documents that I rely on in writing this book are either products of the pre–World War II emperor-centered historiography or those of the postwar biased leftist historical views. While I learn a lot from their inquiries into historical evidence, oftentimes I encounter historical views that are so absurdly biased that I am discouraged from reading them further—views that nobody today would dare to write. For instance, in the pre–World War II emperor-centered historiography, Toyotomi Hideyoshi (豊富秀吉) was highly regarded for his deep reverence for the Emperor, which he had demonstrated by financially assisting the Imperial Family in a time of domestic wars and destitution. Hideyoshi, as he is commonly known deserves a place in history, but not for this reason. This kind of historical view is utterly worthless today. On the other hand, some writings about the history of the introduction of the parliamentary democracy in 1889, written in the 1970s at the apex of the anti-U.S.-Japan Security pact/anti-establishment movements, describe some who had negative views on this achievement as good men and those who had cooperated with the authorities as traitors. And nowadays these writings written in the 1970s, only a generation earlier, are completely forgotten. I do not wish to bring the same shame to my book.

What, then, should I do?

In the end, one should return to the basics of history writing and trace only the historical truth. One must particularly refrain from being gripped by values peculiar to the time one lives in, which have become a political tool. One should earnestly pursue objective truth alone.

As I have written elsewhere, while nobody today disputes the evilness of imperialism, to criticize people of the era of imperialism as imperialists would be the same as calling medieval people medieval or pre-modern. Or calling people who lived during wars, warriors. It may not be inaccurate, but it would only obstruct the understanding of the medieval era. One should avoid to the extent possible judging history based solely on contemporary values and criteria.

While it might be possible to carefully avoid a biased historical view, the most challenging accomplishment would be to maintain a proper balance among various truths. Although each fact may be a truth in and of itself, the book would lack a healthy balance if the author only collects facts that are suited to his personal conviction. In fact, there already are a number of history books that fail to represent, or even misinterpret, the flow of events by deliberately exaggerating selective facts.

This maintenance of a proper balance is the most challenging task. While it can be academically verified whether an event is a historical fact or not, there exists no objective criterion or rule to decide the relative weight of each historical fact. Only common sense is there to guide you. In earlier times, it would have been the task of an eminent historian who was highly regarded by all for his academic accomplishments to write an overview of history. It appears, however, that historians in recent years tend to be specialized in specific areas and/or eras, and an eminent authority on complete history is hard to come by. While this false egalitarianism, or narrow-mindedness, that blocks the development of a historian who can write an overview of history itself is a problem, an alternative must be found to fill the place of the missing eminent authority on complete history.

Turning to my self, I have no intention to claim that I am endowed with better common sense and knowledge than others, which I am not. My only advantage might be that I have had practical experience both in diplomacy and military affairs, and that I was born in the prewar era, experienced wartime, and have lived most of my life in the postwar. Therefore, as I have written earlier, I decided to resort to a "symposium" method, i.e., asking quite a few learned and insightful historians to read and comment on my draft so that I could rewrite it repeatedly until it was accepted by all the participating experts.

By constantly seeking the counsel of learned experts, I did my best to eliminate all the prejudices, fixations, and subjective elements that may be issues of some political significance now but are trivial in the broad flow of history. If I had an emotional motivation or obsession as some may call it, it is my wish, as someone who had spent his boyhood in the early Shōwa period, to leave behind for future generations as accurate a description as possible of how leaders in those days, our fathers and grandfathers, had acted sincerely and lived for the people and the country in the midst of the irreversible trend of history.

No one can deny that each leader of early Shōwa Japan, without exception, wished the best for the country no matter how he had inadvertently ended up committing errors. It is highly unlikely that they were driven purely, or even at all, by self-interest or greed. To be sure, Matsuoka Yōsuke, for instance, failed to see the larger picture because he was too obsessed with his personal pride and vanity. While, in this sense, it might be said that his judgment was clouded by his internal demons, Matsuoka, nevertheless, did not have any intention or wish to enrich his personal fortune. This absence of desire to enrich oneself was commonly observed among all the leaders of the time, including Tōjō Hideki (東条英機) and Itagaki Seishirō (板垣征四郎), about whom nobody even dreamed of their building private fortunes, absolutely not a secret bank account in Switzerland. As far as integrity is concerned, at least, they were much more noble-minded and purer than politicians and bureaucrats around us in the post–World War II days or today.

Objectively speaking, members of the generation of our fathers and grandfathers were without exception people of tragedy. Trained and educated to maintain their self-respect and principles as Japanese, they first grew up at the apex of the Empire of Japan, fully enjoying the freedom of the Taishō Democracy. In the latter half of their lives, however, they had to go through many hardships during the war and, after the defeat, witness the collapse of social environments and traditional values that they had been familiar with since childhood. And yet, even though they had been totally deprived of their pride, they still had to fight to protect their families. This was the generation they belonged to.

In particular, the misery and hardship military personnel and their families had to endure was tragic. According to Horiba Kazuo, "surviving children of deceased soldiers suffered from starvation, while soldiers who had survived the war were immediately looked down upon afterwards." The history of Shōwa is, therefore, a history of these people, and it will be a task of writing an epitaph for each and every member of this generation.

It would not be possible to write the history of this area with a biography of a single individual because no one in particular stood out as a national hero.

CHAPTER

1

Recognition of Manchukuo

—Speedy Seizure of Manchuria—

Ishihara Kanji's Calculation

With only 10,000 men, the Kanto Army swiftly conquered the central part of Manchuria in the time between the Liutiaohu Incident (柳条湖事件) on September 18, 1931, and the forenoon of September 20. In just a day and a half, the entire region along the South Manchurian Railway from Yingkou to Mukden and Changchun came under the control of the Imperial Japanese Army. The surprise tactics that Ishihara Kanji (石原莞爾) had carefully schemed with Itagaki Seishirō were the driving force behind this speedy seizure of Manchuria.

From the beginning, the Chinese troops had been ordered not to resist a Japanese offensive. Expelling the Japanese through anti-Japan movements or by slighting Japan was believed to be a better tactic. The Chinese strategy was not to provoke the Japanese troops, lest any provocation be used as an excuse for further military interference.

The Chinese troops were at their wit's end with the complete surprise attack. Chiang Kai-shek (蒋介石) later reminisced, "In the course of one night, before we knew what was going on, major regions of Manchuria came under the armed control of the Kanto Army." Believing their non-resistance would prevent the worsening of the situation, Zhang Xueliang (張

学良) maintained the tactic, thus aiding the Kanto Army to act promptly.

The Kanto Army succeeded in conquering Jilin on September 21 and Dunhua on September 22. With the help of the Japanese Korean Army, which had crossed the border to guard its rear, the Kanto Army was able to capture almost all of eastern and southern Manchuria.

Only the western and northern regions of Manchuria were left to be conquered.

Having met the surprise attack, leaders of the Zhang Xueliang government fled to Jinzhou near the Great Wall. Zhang decided to attempt the recovery of lost territory through guerilla warfare, using Jinzhou as his last foothold in Manchuria. Among the warlords who had been competing with each other for control of northern Manchuria, Ma Zhanshan, a former bandit based in Qiqihar, was an influential figure known for his magnetic personality and quick actions.

On October 31, the Kanto Army sent a wire to the Imperial Japanese Army General Staff Office to ask for freedom of movement. "We request your understanding that conquering Jinzhou and Qiqihar would be a short cut to settling the issue in Manchuria," the wire read. The General Staff Office, however, made it clear that it would maintain its policy to refrain from expanding the battle. The Staff Office prohibited operations beyond the Nen River running in front of Qiqihar from east to west in northern Manchuria.

When things are moving, however, troops in the actual battlefield can have tremendous freedom of action, especially with the help of a little ingenuity. By that time, Ma Zhanshan's army had destroyed a bridge over the Nen River in an attempt to arrest the northward advance of the rival Zhang Haipeng's troops, who had sided with the Japanese. Taking advantage of the incident, the Japanese side claimed that termination of traffic over the bridge would be a matter of life and death for the South Manchurian Railway and thus issued an ultimatum to the Chinese side that it should rebuild the bridge—practically an impossible demand in such a short period of time.

Ma's true intention—that is, whether he intended to put up a full-fledged resistance to the demand—remains unknown, and the Japanese government took the stance that the bridge issue ought to be settled with negotiations. In order to break this stalemate, Ishihara proposed to the Kanto Army leadership, "We should lose the fight by deploying our troops piecemeal and loudly proclaim our defeat. This will, at the same time, encourage the Chinese side to take a firm stand against the Japanese, who, in turn, have a tendency to react strongly against a defeat." Itagaki expressed his concern, saying, "Who in the world wants to command troops in a battle that is sure to end in defeat?" In response, Ishihara said, "None other than me," and led a small army unit to the battle himself despite his ill health.

This small Japanese army unit was surrounded by Ma's troops and, as expected from the beginning, suffered defeat. Humiliated by the defeat, the unit commander proposed to burn the military flag and commence a last *banzai* charge to save the unit's honor. Ishihara successfully dissuaded him from pursuing this suicide attack.

As Ishihara had correctly predicted, Ma's "grand victory" was reported with great fanfare in China, which praised Ma as "a hero who salvaged the country" and an "Oriental Napoleon." This was followed by an endless flow of telegrams of praise as well as donations as tokens of people's appreciation.

In Japan, too, the bureau chief of the *Asahi Shimbun* in Manchuria, to whom Ishihara had made his intention known beforehand, gave this defeat extensive coverage, stimulating other newspapers to follow suit. In this way, a media frenzy was created. The Kanto Army was inundated with donations and gifts from all over Japan.

Ishihara's uncanny gift for strategy allowed him to use the mass media to his advantage, which was simply unthinkable in those days. His bold manipulation of the mass media to advertize the defeat, when an ordinary leader would have tried to conceal it, was truly comparable to the legendary great Oriental strategists like Kusunoki Masashige (楠正成) and Zhuge Liang (諸葛孔明).

At this stage, as Ishihara had calculated beforehand, neither Ma nor the Kanto Army could withdraw their troops even if they so wished. While instructing the Kanto Army to retreat as soon as the operation was completed, the Imperial Japanese Army General Staff Office also instructed commanders of the Kanto Army to deliver a decisive blow to Ma's army. With this long-awaited instruction, 6,000 troops of the Second Division immediately defeated Ma's 20,000-man army in a frontal attack and triumphantly entered Qiqihar on November 19.

Subsequently, various regions of northern Manchuria declared independence from China one after another, encouraged by the military might of the Japanese Army maneuvered by Itagaki and Ishihara. The declarations of independence created a fait accompli that the independence of Manchukuo was the wish of the Manchurian people. Later, Ma Zhanshan himself was persuaded by Itagaki to participate in the independence of Manchukuo as Governor of Heilongjiang Province and led the three cheers for Emperor Pu Yi (愛新覚羅 溥儀) of Manchukuo at his inaugural ceremony in March 1932.

The next target was Jinzhou.

The Kanto Army plotted to cause a disturbance in Tianjin, which would give it an excuse to deploy its forces to protect the Japanese residents and the troops stationed in northern China. During this deployment, the Japanese Army was expected to defeat Zhang Xueliang's troops in Jinzhou and advance to the Great Wall. The disturbance in Tianjin had a second purpose—the evacuation of dethroned emperor Pu Yi by Major General Doihara Kenji, head of the Houten Special Agency. As I wrote in *Shidehara Kijūrō and His Age*, this plot failed because the Imperial Japanese Army General Staff Office deemed it a violation of orders having been warned by Foreign Minister Shidehara.

But by the time Shidehara stepped down with the Wakatsuki cabinet on December 11, the atmosphere within Japan had changed drastically. The Japanese government and the military no longer attempted to restrain the Kanto Army against the patriotic surge of public opinion.

Taking advantage of the right to "subjugate bandits" that the Japanese delegation had secured at the Council of the League of Nations on December 10, the Kanto Army ordered the suppression of Liáoxī—that is to say, an attack on Jinzhou. The Kanto Army troops captured Jinzhou on January 3, 1932, and used the momentum to gain control over the territory north of the Great Wall.

Ishihara Kanji

The whole of Manchuria was conquered in only four months. Tokyo was filled with cheers, and no voice opposing this conduct was heard.

Even Saionji Kinmochi would not restrict the military. He was heard to confide to Ugaki Kazushige, who visited him on November 1: "Although until today I have supported Shidehara's diplomacy as an orthodox and rightful foreign policy, now that all public opinion finds fault with it, I must reconsider it as a means of pursuing truly effective diplomacy— even though its rightfulness may remain." In the memories of the generations that still remembered those days, the name Shidehara had always been associated with weak-kneed diplomacy, despised by the public while praised by the experts.

Of utmost importance to Saionji was the safety of the Imperial Family. With public opinion having turned so decidedly against Shidehara diplomacy, Saionji must have judged that it would be harmful for the Emperor to issue instructions that would interfere with the course of events. Saionji, therefore, left the Manchurian affair to take its own course.

The imperial edict that was issued on January 8 confirmed the fait accompli:

> When the incident erupted in Manchuria, officers and soldiers of the Kanto Army swiftly suppressed the massive opponent with a small force in an act of self-defense. . . . Our troops fought bravely along the Nen River, in the Qiqihar region, Liáoxī, and Jinzhou. Ice and snow were not obstacles . . . We deeply appreciate their loyalty and valor. It is our hope that our warriors shall respond to our confidence by remaining patient and prudent and, thus, consolidating the foundation of peace in the Orient.

This imperial edict might have been drafted by the Imperial Japanese Army General Staff Office. In any event, even if the government had wished to restrict the military, the situation was already beyond its control.

On November 30, the eve of the Kanto Army's advance to Jinzhou, the Japanese consul in China, Morishima Morito, sent the following confidential telegram to the home ministry to explain the inevitability of the occupation of Jinzhou:

> As a matter of fact, not a small number of influential officers openly

spoke of the necessity to build a new state and to destroy the Jinzhou government. When the central government [in Japan] tried to restrict their conduct, some even spoke of abandoning their military careers and giving up Japanese citizenship to build the new state. . . . They insist that all Japanese residents in Manchuria should renounce their Japanese citizenship and participate in the republic of "the harmony among five races," i.e. Japanese, Manchurian, Korean, Mongolian, and Russian.

The Japanese residents had previously declared autonomy from the home government, distrusting Shidehara's diplomacy. The military stationed in Manchuria and the Japanese residents together contemplated the establishment of a Manchurian state. These people would no longer listen to Tokyo's instructions.

Although it was obvious to everyone that the Kanto Army was behind the birth of Manchukuo, the establishment of Manchukuo was, on the surface, an act of separation and independence decided by local leaders in Manchuria. Thus, a fait accompli was created that defied interference from the Japanese government.

Shanghai—A Wrong War in the Wrong Place

Meanwhile, China's diplomatic strategy had remained consistent since the eruption of the Manchurian Incident. China was determined to resist Japan's aggression with the help of international public opinion by appealing to the League of Nations so that it would not be pressured into agreeing to the Japanese terms in a bilateral negotiation.

International public opinion was the only thing China could rely on. Although the United States failed to join the League of Nations due to the opposition of its Senate, it was nevertheless an architecture based on President Woodrow Wilson's proposal. When the League was criticized that it could not function as a mechanism to protect peace and stability in the world, the only counterargument that Wilson could present was that it could mobilize international public opinion. The League of Nations' resolution at the time of the Manchurian Incident might have been the only example of diplomacy based on international public opinion that had a substantive effect.

In fact, as Shidehara had feared, the session on the Manchurian Incident at the League of Nations became something akin to a speech contest among minor countries in Europe and Latin America, which were ignorant of the situation in East Asia.

In the 1960s, delegates from the newly independent countries in Asia and Africa relished their newly acquired sense of independence by taking the United Nations' podium one after another. Their euphoric expressions of naïve idealism bored the Western industrialized countries to death, and this became one of the causes of the U.S. disenchantment with the United Nations. What took place in the League of Nations in 1933 might have been a precursor of the United Nations in the 1960s. When every delegate was fervently raising their voice in an international forum captivated by the new atmosphere, it would have been difficult to counter-argue.

To be sure, Japan had the option of ignoring international public opinion, as the Soviet Union would later do in the course of the Hungarian Revolution, and having the Kanto Army remain in Manchuria. Without any precedent to emulate in a situation that no other country in the world had ever encountered and given the temperament of the Japanese, Japan ended up withdrawing from the League of Nations, failing to display the perseverance of the Soviet Union in the face of criticism.

This did not necessarily mean, however, that public opinion at the League of Nations had been unfavorable toward Japan from the beginning. At least until the December 1933 League of Nations' resolution that decided the dispatch of the Lytton Commission to Manchuria, the atmosphere was so favorable toward Japan that a June 1932 Ministry of Foreign Affairs record noted, "On many occasions, discussions at the League of Nations were inclined to accept our arguments and suppress the Chinese side."

The respect of the international community for Japan, an unarguable world power with resourceful diplomats who were conversant in international laws, was naturally different from that for China, which had yet to be unified and responsible for the conduct of its people. Furthermore, Japan and Britain shared a common interest in arguing against China's demand for prompt abolition of unequal treaties.

It does not bring any practical benefit to readers to bore them with the details on the discussions at the League of Nations during this session.

While leading diplomats of the world racked their brains to propose a variety of compromise ideas, their common purpose was, simply put, to achieve a prompt truce and make the Japanese troops withdraw to the area inside the property of the South Manchurian Railway. Because the Kanto Army was unwilling to compromise and constantly acted one step ahead of any proposals, all of the ideas were easily nullified by them.

In this sense, the resolution on the dispatch of the Lytton Commission was a "victory of Japan's diplomacy." Because it was a decision to send a fact-finding mission first, thus temporarily shelving truce and troop withdrawal issues, this resolution would provide an opportunity for the Kanto Army to create a fait accompli.

The formation of a fact-finding mission is a well-worn measure that is employed when an international conference comes to a dead end. As a matter of fact, delegates of all the participating countries welcomed the resolution because it would give them a Christmas break.

This "victory for Japan's diplomacy" notwithstanding, the Japanese military did one thing that was totally unnecessary—the January 28 Incident.

It started with an assault on a Japanese Buddhist monk in Shanghai by a Chinese thug on January 18, 1932, a plot devised by Itagaki to start an incident in Shanghai to draw the world's attention away from Manchuria, according to postwar testimonies of those who had been involved.

Considering that the League of Nations, which was tired of the speech extravaganza, had already been in recess, what Itagaki did was totally uncalled for. It was a useless cheap trick played by the military in Manchuria that had no knowledge of the subtle change of air that had taken place at the League of Nations.

Once kindled, however, there was enough fuel for the fire to burn.

Japanese residents in mainland China, whose life and properties had been threatened daily by the anti-Japanese movements, were envious of their counterparts in Manchuria who had come under the protection of the Japanese army. They were also infuriated by reports in Chinese newspapers that called the Sakuradamon Incident (桜田門事件) in Japan on January 8 an "unfortunate failure." The incident was an attempt by a Korean to assassinate the Emperor by explosion.

These developments spurred the Japanese residents in Shanghai to adopt a resolution to request the Japanese government to "dispatch the Imperial Army and Navy immediately to eradicate anti-Japanese movements as an exercise of the right of self-defense."

Thereafter, the Japanese government continued to be manipulated by Japanese residents in China. On January 28, the Chinese side compromised by accepting Japanese demands for the settlement of the aftermath. According to Japanese minister Shigemitsu Mamoru, however, the Japanese residents hysterically opposed the settlement, lamenting the loss of a golden opportunity. This prompted the Japanese consulate general in Shanghai, which had initially intended to suppress the Japanese residents, to change his plan and, instead, impose hard-line demands on the Chinese side. The situation was, according to Shigemitsu's report, such that "the consulate general was at a loss to suppress extremely agitated residents and his consulate staff, who sympathized with the general atmosphere in Japan and advocated hard-line arguments."

Looking back, what were the Manchurian Incident and the January 28 Incident in Shanghai all about? They could be summarized as cases of the use of force by the Japanese military in response to artificial crises facing the Japanese residents in China. These artificial crises were plotted by the Japanese military so that it could be seen as acting to protect the lives and properties of the compatriots from Chinese agitation to expel the Japanese. The artificial crises were necessary because the Chinese anti-Japanese movements were carefully calculated not to give the Japanese side an excuse to resort to the use of force.

On guard in Shanghai were fewer than 1,000 troops of the Imperial Japanese Navy Land Forces. They had to face the 31,000 elite troops of the Chinese 19th Route Army. This was actually an extremely dangerous situation. Behind the riotous psychology of the Japanese residents might have been what had appeared to them an easy victory in the Manchurian Incident; perhaps this made them overconfident. The sweet experience of Ishihara's plot, which had worked so perfectly in the Manchurian Incident, misguided the subsequent conduct of the Japanese residents in China.

The Japanese troops guarding Shanghai almost immediately got into a predicament, forcing the government to dispatch an Imperial Army division. This dispatch of army troops was a dream-come-true for the Japanese residents in Shanghai. The February 14 issue of the *Asahi Shimbun* carried the caption, "Dispatch of Long-Awaited Imperial Army Revives the Entire Japanese Community in Shanghai."

The Chinese 19th Route Army bravely put up resistance for a month, and it was only after the Japanese side incurred some 3,000 casualties that it finally succeeded in overwhelming the Chinese side. A truce was agreed on March 3.

Internationally, the January 28 Incident was a wrong war in the wrong place. This was particularly so when one realizes that it was artificially caused by Itagaki's blatant trick, a plot which was far from being inevitable.

Strong resistance by the Chinese troops during the incident inspired nationalism among the Chinese people. The valor of their troops later fueled Chinese confidence in fighting the Japanese military.

Military action in Shanghai, where the economic interests of world powers were concentrated, became the target of international criticism. The incident also changed the atmosphere at the League of Nations overnight. As Japanese delegate Satō Naotake reported to the home office, "At the Council meeting in which the visitors' gallery was filled with newspaper reporters, Japan found itself completely friendless and isolated vis-à-vis international public opinion."

The Lytton Commission was the first League of Nations' mission that not only studied the situation but also made a recommendation. Taking advantage of the January 28 Incident, China requested the application of Article 15 of the Covenant of the League of Nations (an article that stipulates that the Council of the League would endeavor to effect a settlement to a dispute between members, a precursor to Article 16 on economic sanctions in the event that the Council's recommendation should be ignored) to the conflict between China and Japan. This request was accepted. When the Commission submitted its report to the Council, Japan refused to comply with its recommendations, and it withdrew from the League of Nations.

Assassination of Prime Minister Inukai Tsuyoshi

Since joining Ōkuma Shigenobu's *Rikken Kaishintō* in 1882 (15th Year of Meiji), Inukai Tsuyoshi had consistently remained a party politician. He played an active role in the first and second constitution protection movements. But because he occasionally resorted to tricks and was known for having a sharp tongue, he made too many enemies unnecessarily. As a result, Inukai became both a much-praised and much-maligned person in political circles in the Meiji and Taishō eras. Because he was not endowed with an aptitude for fundraising, he remained affiliated with minor parties throughout his career, far removed from the center of power.

When the second constitution protection movement proved successful, Inukai joined Katō Takaaki's *Goken Sanpa Naikaku* (Cabinet based on the three pro-constitution factions) as president of the *Kakushin Kurabu*. Before long, however, he successfully engineered the merger of his *Kakushin Kurabu* with the *Seiyūkai*, upon which he retired from politics. Inukai could no longer support the *Kakushin Kurabu* financially. On his frame of mind at that time, Inukai reminisced, "It would be more effective for me to use my remaining time . . . to advise young people as a genuinely free man without any encumbrance, both in name and reality, or worldly desire."

With the general election for the House of Representatives approaching, Inukai's constituents did not heed his declaration of retirement from politics. The result was another election win for Inukai, who was forced to remain in politics as supreme advisor to the *Seiyūkai*.

Here we have a selfless statesman whose only concern was the state and society and who knew when to retire coupled with a constituency that never turned its back on its representative. This episode testifies to the fact that, despite abundant power struggles and corruption in the 40 years since the establishment of parliamentary democracy, the samurai democracy exhibited in the first general election in 1890 remained faithful to its roots.

It was Mori Kaku who persuaded the half-retired Inukai to run in the election. When Tanaka Giichi, president of the *Seiyūkai*, passed away in 1929, there was nobody who could maintain the unity of the party, which faced other concerns about a breakup. To cope with the situation, Mori persuaded factions in the *Seiyūkai* to support Inukai's candidacy. When Inukai was recommended by Saionji to form a cabinet to succeed the second Wakatsuki cabinet, Mori became the chief cabinet secretary of the Inukai cabinet. It was toward the end of Inukai's 77th year. As it turned out, his cabinet was a short-lived one of half a year. The cabinet dissolved with his assassination in May of the subsequent year.

During Inukai's short tenure, a general election was held in which the *Seiyūkai* won a landslide victory of 301 seats. This was attributable to the

Inukai cabinet's positive fiscal policy and business-stimulating measures, which were supported by voters tired of the recession caused by the *Minseitō* government's resumption of the gold standard and tight fiscal policy. The Japanese people's resentment of Shidehara diplomacy also played a role.

What distinguished Inukai as a statesman from others was his Pan-Asianism. Inukai had a long, close association with revolutionary movements in China. He was once schoolmaster of a school for Chinese students in Kobe that Kang Youwei had established after his abortive reforms in China (Hundred Day's Reform) and modeled after the Meiji Restoration. Inukai also became a close friend to Sun Yat-sen, who had temporarily sought refuge in Japan. Sun's pseudonym Zhongshan (中山 pronounced as Nakayama in Japanese) derived from the Japanese family name on the doorplate of the house in Ushigome, Tokyo, that Inukai rented for Sun.

Aside from Sun, Inukai also protected such Asian revolutionaries as Kim Ok-gyun of Korea, Phan Boi Chau of Vietnam, and members of the Filipino and Indian independence movements. It may not be an exaggeration to say that there were no Asian expatriates in Japan who had not been protected by Inukai at some point.

The most urgent task for the Inukai cabinet was the settlement of the Manchurian Incident, which was still ongoing.

As soon as Inukai formed his cabinet, he dispatched a special envoy to Shanghai in order to convey his proposal for the settlement. He did not tell this to his chief cabinet secretary Mori or the Imperial Army. Inukai proposed that Japan should recognize China's suzerainty over Manchuria, upon which Japan and China should jointly establish a new government in Manchuria. Although the Chinese side was initially hesitant, anticipating strong opposition from within China, it agreed to sit down at the negotiating table in the end. However, because Mori found out about this secret mission and intercepted the Chinese reply before it reached Inukai, the negotiations did not materialize.

Inukai also wrote a letter to Field Marshal Uehara Yūsaku, one of the most influential figures in the Imperial Army in those days, to secure the military's support for his policy. While lamenting the trend of defiant junior officers in the Army, Inukai proposed that he should make his own efforts to settle the Manchurian Incident because "I have a long-standing friendship with leaders of both regimes in China, which puts me in a better position to negotiate with the Chinese side than ordinary officials." He concluded his letter by saying, "Establishment of an independent state in Manchuria would inevitably clash head-on with the Nine-Power Treaty of 1922. I have therefore been racking my brain about how to accomplish our goals in reality while maintaining the form of an autonomous branch of the Chinese government in appearance."

In other words, Inukai proposed that defiant junior officers in the Army should be restrained; Japan should grant China suzerainty over Manchuria; and a realistic compromise had to be struck.

But Inukai was assassinated by a young navy officer on May 15, 1932, at the prime minister's residence.

Although a policeman rushed into Inukai's room to inform him of an intruder and urged Inukai to flee immediately, Inukai said, "I certainly will not." Hearing this, Takeshi, Inukai's eldest son, thought to himself with a deep sigh that a man's nature was truly unchangeable.

After the intruder shot Inukai at the head and left the room, Inukai shouted as he fell, "Call back that young man. I will talk some sense into him." But Inukai took his last breath.

Fearless and indomitable, his spirit was truly one of a samurai, paying no heed to life or death.

At this moment, the possibility of striking a compromise between Japan and China based on mutual trust perished forever.

The Lytton Commission's Proposal

Giving China nominal suzerainty while putting Manchuria under de facto control of Japan was a realistic compromise that anyone sensible enough in those days contemplated. There was a good possibility that, had Inukai escaped death by the hand of an assassin and carried out the policy that he had believed in, he would have drafted and proposed a workable compromise based on the Lytton Commission's report.

The Lytton Commission's report was made public on October 2, 1932, four months after Inukai's death. While the report was a voluminous compilation, its main point was chapter 9, "Principles and Conditions of Settlement," and chapter 10, "Proposals."

Chapter 9 assessed the origins of the situation. Given that Manchuria was an exceptional region incomparable to any other region in the world, says the report, the Manchurian Incident was not a simple armed conflict between two countries or a forceful invasion of a country's territory by another country. Under this complicated situation, the report continued, mere restoration of the pre-incident conditions would not suffice because similar incidents would recur. To recognize the regime that was established in Manchuria, however, would not provide the foundation for peace because it came into existence in violation of international agreements and is totally unacceptable to China. The chapter concluded that, instead of "restoring conditions to those before September 1931, the new civil regime must be so constituted and conducted as to satisfy its essential requirements of good government."

Chapter 10 proposed that the territorial and administrative rights of China should be recognized and that "a vast array of autonomy" should be granted. At the same time, the report recommended that amnesty be granted to all who had participated in the founding of Manchukuo since the Manchurian Incident. The chapter also stipulated that the Japanese should account for a substantial percentage of the foreign advisers that the autonomous government in Manchuria would appoint. Moreover, it proposed that the public order of Manchuria should be maintained by the "special military police," which would be aided by "foreign advisors."

The report also suggested that, after the settlement, the Chinese side should restrict anti-Japanese demonstrations by its citizens.

These recommendations appeared to be close enough to what Inukai had proposed. Had he survived, he would have been able to negotiate a compromise settlement. As a matter of fact, when the Lytton Commission visited Beijing in June of that year, some Chinese leaders expressed their intention to grant Manchuria a vast array of autonomy if China were allowed to retain its nominal sovereignty over the territory. The Commission was favorably disposed to this. It is conjectured that behind this constructive attitude on the Chinese side was prior engineering by Inukai.

Even if Inukai had not been killed, however, the Japanese government might not have been able to resist public demands for the recognition of Manchukuo under the pressure of the unanimous resolution of the House of Representatives.

It appears that the Lytton Commission had anticipated this kind of complication due to domestic resistance in Japan. As a matter of fact, its report stated that should Japan recognize Manchukuo before the report was submitted, that "would not nullify the Commission's efforts, even though it is a serious matter that cannot be overlooked."

Recognition of Manchukuo

Inukai led the *Seiyūkai* to a landslide victory in the general election in February 1932, winning 301 seats in the House of Representatives. In the general election of 1920, the *Seiyūkai* under Hara Takashi had won 278 seats, thus raising the curtain on the beginning of a golden age of parliamentary democracy in Japan. The Inukai cabinet, however, was destined to bring down that curtain.

Perhaps it was not a matter of the number of seats, the quality of the policies, or differences in the personal scale between Hara and Inukai. The decisive factor must have been the flow of time, and with that the changes in the perception of the Japanese people.

Soon after the landslide victory, inter-factional strife within the *Seiyūkai* surfaced, and it was widely covered by newspapers. When the Japanese people were feeling insecure due to the ongoing Manchurian Incident and fervently hoping to come out of the economic recession of the time, the reporting made them lament, "Party politics again?" People also suspected the *Seiyūkai* of hunting for a concession about the proposed nationalization of railways in Japan by floating ¥30 million in public bonds. The military was particularly indignant at this proposal, saying, "They have the nerve to propose such nonsense at this critical juncture." Having long suffered from the arms reduction efforts, the Japanese military was hoping that the Manchurian Incident would give it a chance to reinforce its armaments.

Any party cabinet, including that of Hara Takashi, would have behaved in a similar way. But the important thing here is that the Japanese people had already become fed up with party politics by this time. Every time the *Seiyūkai*, the majority party, tried to relive the past dream of Hara Takashi's era, people became more disillusioned with party politics.

By February 1920, soon after the *Seiyūkai*'s landslide victory, public opinion appeared to have given up on party cabinets and become increasingly hopeful for the rise of a government of national unity. It was, however, not a coalition of political parties, such as that between the *Minseitō* and *Seiyūkai* toward the end of the *Minseitō* government, that the Japanese were after. What the public wanted was a supra-party government that transcended party politics.

Such right-wing individuals as Hiranuma Kiichirō (平沼騏一郎) and War Minister Araki Sadao (荒木貞夫) were slated for appointment as the next prime minister. Hiranuma, a former Ministry of Justice official, was Vice President of the Privy Council. As president of the *Kokuhonsha*, a nationalist political society that Hiranuma himself had founded, he had a wide range of supporters in the military, officialdom, business, and academia.

Engineering by Mori Kaku of the *Seiyūkai* was said to be behind the rise of expectations for a supra-party or bipartisan government. There were also constant rumors about a military coup. Konoe Fumimaro, who had been in close contact with Saionji in those days, was also heard to say that only Hiranuma or Araki could get the situation under control. It appears that by that time people were talking everywhere about the hopelessness of the incumbent government and their hope for a supra-party cabinet. By April, the name of Admiral Saitō Makoto (斎藤実) began to be murmured as a possible head of the next government in meetings attended by Konoe and Kido Kōichi.

Then the May 15 Incident occurred, during which Inukai was assassinated. Although the *Seiyūkai* with 300 seats in the House of Representatives elected Suzuki Kisaburō as the new president, expecting him to be appointed to prime minister as a matter of course, the request for Suzuki to form a cabinet never materialized.

At this point, Emperor Shōwa conveyed his thought on the new government to Saionji through Grand Chamberlain Suzuki Kantarō, expressing both his aversion to anything that was fascistic and his request for a foreign policy that pursued international peace and friendly international relations. This precluded the appointment of Hiranuma and Araki.

Hearing the Emperor's wish, Saionji listened to what senior leaders had to say for two days. During these two days, leaders of the military conveyed their opposition to another party cabinet overtly and covertly. Thus, Saionji realized that it would be highly difficult to have the army and navy recommend war and navy ministers, respectively, if another party cabinet were formed.

Thus, Saionji decided to recommend Saitō Makoto to the Emperor.

Moderate and stable, Saitō was Navy Minister in both the first and second Saionji cabinets. When he was Governor-General of Korea, he successfully shifted the administrative style from a militaristic government to a civilian government, proving his administrative ability. Saito also participated in the Geneva Naval Conference in 1927 as Japan's plenipotentiary delegate.

While Saitō might have been on the borderline in terms of fulfilling the Emperor's wishes, he had little political clout vis-à-vis domestic politics and, most particularly, the military.

Uchida Kōsai served the Saito cabinet as foreign minister from July 1920 until September 1921, when he was succeeded by Hirota Kōki.

While Uchida had always occupied key diplomatic positions in the history of the Empire of Japan from the Russo-Japanese War through the Manchurian Incident, serving as foreign minister longer than anyone else, it is difficult to learn about his personal thinking and convictions from the record on him. Perhaps, Uchida was simply a competent bureaucrat devoid of his own philosophy. Therefore, his words and deeds fluctuated, following the trend of the times.

After the Manchurian Incident, Uchida announced, "Now that the armed conflict has erupted, we have no other choice than to help the military to thoroughly settle the issue. In short, we need to establish Manchukuo." A person without his own philosophy changes words and deeds according to his environment and the atmosphere surrounding it. In that sense, it may be said that Uchida Kōsai's view reflected changes in the perceptions of people in Japan.

Immediately before Uchida took office as foreign minister, the House of Representatives plenary session unanimously passed a resolution requesting that the Japanese government promptly recognize Manchukuo. Upon the passing of this resolution, Foreign Minister Uchida on July 12 explicitly told members of the Lytton Commission, who were visiting Tokyo at that time, that, now that Manchukuo had already been founded, the only solution to the issue would be the recognition of Manchukuo. A French member of the Commission encouraged the Japanese side to explore a compromise—that is, to set some kind of relations between Manchukuo and China on the basis of the recognition of Manchukuo. Uchida rejected this suggestion, saying, "Because retention of some relations between China and Manchukuo could become a source of complications in the future, the only viable solution would be for both Japan and China to recognize Manchukuo as a friendly neighbor."

During this exchange, Lytton made a comment that touched the core of the Manchukuo recognition issue. He said, "In my judgment, recognition of Manchukuo calls for two prerequisites: (1) that there really was an act of aggression on the part of China and (2) that it was the Manchu people's own decision to found Manchukuo."

According to international law, what Japan had done would have been an appropriate act if Japan had acquired the territory as the result of a war that had been triggered by Chinese provocation. In that sense, it was regretted that the Japanese side had to use as an excuse for its military action the slovenly blasting of a railroad, which could hardly constitute a cause of war, because Ishihara decided to move up the date of operation. Ishihara, therefore, did indeed have reason to deplore the failure to take military actions in response to the Nakamura Incident in 1931.

In later days, at the International Military Tribunal for the Far East, the Japanese side insisted that the Manchurian Incident was an act of self-defense, that Japan was protecting the lives of the Japanese residents as well as the legally justifiable rights and interests of Japan in Manchuria that had been threatened by the anti-Japanese movements. This claim reflects the genuine perception of the situation among the Japanese in those days. Among definitions of self-defense, the most irrefutable is the case of resistance to direct armed attacks, particularly when the opponent initiates the battle. It would not be difficult to convince others that it is an act of self-defense when one is cornered into starting a battle. The same can be said about the later attack on Pearl Harbor.

The Cabinet meeting on August 17, 1932, adopted the draft of the Japan-Manchukuo Protocol (日満議定書). It was a simple affair composed of two items: (1) that Manchukuo should recognize Japan's rights and interests in Manchuria; and (2) that threat to Manchukuo be regarded as a common threat to Japan and Manchukuo, and there should be a defensive military agreement between the two governments. The official signing of this protocol was automatically the formal recognition of Manchukuo.

At the Diet session on August 25, Foreign Minister Uchida raised the issue of the recognition of Manchukuo. In response to Mori Kaku's question on the government's preparation for the possible worsening of relations with foreign powers, Uchida replied, "Uniting the whole nation, we shall not give in even an inch until we are all reduced to ashes." It is believed that this reply of Uchida's was an emotional outburst aimed at Mori, who had always advocated radical policies ahead of others and accused anyone else of being weak-kneed. If that was indeed the case, the exchange was a mere low-level ego battle. In any event, this so-called "until we are all reduced to ashes" speech by Uchida evoked a massive response both domestically and internationally.

Subsequently, the Japan-Manchukuo Protocol was signed on September 15.

In his letter addressed to the commanding officer of the Kanto Army, an appendix to the protocol, Head of State Puyi promises that Manchukuo would rely on Japan for its defense and public order and that its entire cost would be born by Manchukuo. Here one can depict an eagerness to build a new nation under the initiative of the Kanto Army without financial and other interferences from the Japanese home government.

The Lytton Commission's report was delivered to the diplomatic authorities of China and Japan fifteen days later on September 30. Thus, a fait accompli of Japan's recognition of Manchukuo had already been created before the report was deliberated at the League of Nations.

CHAPTER
2

Withdrawal from the League of Nations and Establishment of Manchukuo

—State Socialism and Harmony of Five Races in Manchuria—

Unreliable Matsuoka Yōsuke

It was at this timing that a man named Matsuoka Yōsuke came on the stage of Japanese history.

Born to an ill-fated shipping family in Muromitsunoura, Yamaguchi Prefecture, Matsuoka was a child prodigy. While his father and older brothers continued to fail in one business after another, Matsuoka grew up shouldering the expectation that he would be the one to restore the family's fortunes.

In 1893 (26th Year of Meiji) at the age of thirteen, Matsuoka migrated to Portland, Oregon, on board an immigrant ship. He was taken into an American family, where he helped with household chores in return for the right to attend school during the day. Paying his way by various odd jobs, Matsuoka enrolled at the University of Oregon night school. He graduated second in his class in 1900. Upon his return to Japan, Matsuoka set his mind to become a diplomat, and passed the Foreign Service Examination in 1904.

Matsuoka maintained a spirit of self-reliance and independence throughout his life. Behind his conduct (aside from his natural disposition) was his personal experience of completing his education while working to support himself in his youth.

Two anecdotes are useful for understanding Matsuoka's nature. One comes from his reflections on his days in the United States. When he returned to Japan, Matsuoka commented:

> The important thing is not to let Americans slight you. Americans will become scornful of anyone who, for example, gives way to a passing person on a narrow path. They will only regard as their equal a person who is aggressive enough to strike the other party to have his own way. This is something Japanese diplomats must keep in mind when dealing with Americans.

While, normally, it is the sophisticated manners and behavior of the American East Coast establishment that is called for in a diplomat, the foundation of Matsuoka's conduct was the street wisdom that he had cultivated from his own experiences on the West Coast, where in those days the atmosphere was quite different from the East Coast. This remained unchanged throughout his life. Indeed, it was this aggressive disposition that was behind the later signing of the Tripartite Pact, which proved to be a fatal step toward the Pacific War.

The other anecdote is about his conduct during the oral examination for the Foreign Service Examination.

Matsuoka ended up having a heated argument on the interpretation of the letter of the law with the examiner Ichiki Kitokurō, who later became president of the Privy Council. After consulting with the Compendium of Laws, Matsuoka was found to be correct. When Ichiki asked Matsuoka, "It so happened that your interpretation was correct this time, but what would you have done if you were found to be wrong," Matsuoka answered that he would have reversed the logic to come up with a new argument.

Matsuoka had had a way with words since his early childhood. Even in his elementary school days, he picked an argument with teachers and never gave even an inch, resorting to all kinds of quibbles. It was this oratorical talent of Matsuoka that made his speeches at the time of Japan's withdrawal from the League of Nations so moving to the Japanese people, who praised him for speaking the Japanese mind so freely in an international arena.

One cannot help but find something dangerous about Matsuoka's disposition in these episodes. His tale of two persons on a narrow path demonstrated a lack of the kind of broadmindedness that would have allowed him to give way for the sake of a peaceful settlement, even if doing so might have earned contempt. It also appears that he was not endowed with the magnanimity to respect an opponent in a debate when the latter was found to be correct.

The more fundamental problem, however, was that, as demonstrated in the above episodes, Matsuoka depended on his tactical skills in interpersonal relations rather than on following his own philosophy or personal convictions. Reviewing Matsuoka's life, in fact, one can hardly find a trace of conviction or philosophy in Matsuoka. If anything, his conduct was based on a vague nationalism and expansionism that was in vogue in Japan in those days. While his actions occasionally received support from radicals with the tide of the time, it only showed that Matsuoka did not have a philosophy of his own. Judging from his method of reversing logic to win a debate, one cannot expect consistency in this person's thinking.

Such a person, blessed only with technical abilities, has a strong tendency to be ambitious and seek a post that allows him to fully utilize his abilities. Should he be deprived of such a post, he becomes a broken man, having no other self to assert. And this is how Matsuoka appeared in his late years, having been deprived of the responsibilities to carry out the war. When he was indicted for war crimes, therefore, he appeared in court in high spirits, declaring, "Now I have become a man again."

Matsuoka's death poem reads:

> Free from resentment or a grudge
> I am travelling on the road to Hades.

Judging from Matsuoka's disposition, this must be the peaceful state of mind that he had attained after having been haunted by numerous personal resentments and grudges. This would have been fine if it had occurred to an ordinary person. Coming from a political leader who had professed that "Entering into the Tripartite Pact was the mistake of my life," however, this swan song must be criticized for the writer's being preoccupied with concern over his personal honor, with no consideration for the state whatsoever.

While Matsuoka might have been extremely competent as a low-ranking military officer, this type of person should never be promoted to become a commanding general. In fact, he only deserved to be a mere division chief in a bureaucracy. It would be extremely dangerous to assign him to a higher post because he is liable to confuse the grand strategy of a state with squabbling tactics, and the fundamental goals of a nation with personal vanity.

Withdrawal from the League of Nations, Driven by the Current of the Times

In July 1932, Foreign Minister Uchida Kōsai of the Saitō Makoto government appointed Matsuoka to head Japan's delegation to the League of Nations.

Neither Uchida nor Matsuoka hoped for or insisted on Japan's withdrawal from the League of Nations at the beginning.

To be sure, in the "Guideline for Actions in the Current State of Affairs" that Foreign Minister Uchida had compiled in a month after assuming office, Uchida hinted at Japan's withdrawal from the League of Nations if and when "the League should decide to overturn the foundation of Japan's management of Manchuria and threaten the future of Japan's fortunes." Nevertheless, as it happened, nobody, including Uchida and Matsuoka, decided their stances on this issue until the very last minute.

League Secretary-General Sir James Eric Drummond and Under-Secretary-General Sugimura Yōtarō struggled to work out a compromise right up to the end. While it might have been an orthodox approach to work out reconciliation in the case of a traditional negotiation between two major powers, Japan had become isolated within the League, where the majority was occupied by small countries, to the extent that even Britain became unable to resist the pressure from the majority, forcing it to give up on the compromise attempt.

At this point, Japan had only two options left to choose from. It could either remain

Matsuoka Yōsuke

in the League and single-handedly endure a storm of criticism, just like the Soviet Union after the Hungarian Revolution of 1956 and the Prague Spring in 1968 during the Cold War, being targeted with a sanctions resolution, even though the resolution would not be expected to produce anything tangible. Alternatively, Japan could announce its withdrawal from the League.

When the Tokyo government did not seem to have a definitive view on which option Japan should take, one possible determinant was the recommendation submitted by the delegation.

Three plenipotentiaries, including Matsuoka, sent a telegram on February 15 informing the urgency of the matter, followed by another one the next day that said, "At this point, Japan would only attract ridicule if it did not withdraw from the League without delay." Receiving these telegrams, the Prime Minister consulted with Saionji Kinmochi, an elder statesman who had hitherto opposed withdrawal from the League because he believed that "Japan had better remain in a commanding position together with Britain and the United States." Upon reading the recommendation of the delegation, however, he said, if that was the recommendation of the plenipotentiaries of the Japanese government, "We have no other choice than to follow their recommendation." The subsequent cabinet meeting decided on withdrawal from the League of Nations.

Matsuoka was found responsible for Japan's withdrawal from the League because it was the plenipotentiaries including Matsuoka who had sent the telegrams. It was indeed Matsuoka who made the farewell speech at the League, which made him an instant hero in the eyes of the Japanese people and media. Because the welcome that he enjoyed when he returned home remained Matsuoka's asset throughout Japan's period of militarism, he had no reason to deny responsibility. All he had to do, instead, was to take the credit proudly.

However, it should be recalled that Matsuoka made the following radio speech after his return to Japan:

> I have made at least one complete mistake. . . . While I might have succeeded in presenting Japan's point of view, I failed in the other mandate of keeping Japan's membership in the League. . . . I am solely to blame for the latter and I really do not know how to apologize to my fellow countrymen. . . .

In the days before World War II, this speech became totally forgotten.

It appears, therefore, that even though Matsuoka had at first regretted Japan's withdrawal from the League of Nations, he must have had a change of heart after receiving such an unexpected and fervent welcome when he returned home.

If that was indeed the case, one can't help wondering what that recommendation in the telegram was all about.

It should probably be interpreted as the only kind of telegram that, given the situation, a plenipotentiary could send to the home government. All it said was that the Japanese delegation was at the end of its tether and there was nothing more that it could do. Having explained that to remain in the League would mean that Japan would certainly become the target of humiliating censure throughout the general assembly, the plenipotentiaries left the decision to the home government. A cynic might say it was a bureaucratic telegram that would allow the senders to evade responsibility. In fact, it was not in the psychology of any one of those in a responsible position in Japan to insist that Japan should remain in the League and endure ridicule from other members.

Uchida and Matsuoka, two people without firm convictions, may be blamed for being in key positions in Tokyo and Geneva, respectively, at a critical juncture. Since these two were also driven by the current of the times, however, it was, in the end, the public opinion in Japan or, more generally, the current of the times itself that made Japan withdraw from the League of Nations.

Unparalleled, Strange Existence Called Manchuria

As stated in the Lytton Commission's report, Manchuria was "an area with numerous peculiar conditions . . . an area, strictly speaking, unparalleled by any other region in the world." Therefore, the Manchurian Incident was not "a simple incident of invasion of one country by another." And the Manchukuo that was built in the aftermath of the incident was an equally strange, unparalleled entity.

The Japanese arguments on the separation of Manchuria from China proper can be summarized as follows.

First, Japan contended that Manchuria was different from China proper from the start. Immediately before assuming the post of foreign minister, Uchida Kōsai said,

> Manchuria is not an integral part of China proper. Since ancient times, dynasties in China proper had consistently treated Manchuria as a foreign land. When this foreign land conquered China proper, China distinguished Manchuria from China as a special district.

In fact, Uchida recalled that the Chinese side had expressed its willingness to give Japan a free hand in Manchuria when "China wished to accomplish something else, such as the return of Shangdong."

The Japanese side refuted the counterargument that the overwhelming majority of the population in Manchuria was Chinese by claiming that the presence of the Japanese military since the Russo-Japanese War, which controlled the areas along the South Manchurian Railway, maintained such good law and order that mainland Chinese relocated to Manchuria en masse at the demise of the Qing Dynasty.

Nobody would argue against the notion that, had Japan not have fought the Russo-Japanese War, Manchuria would have been a Russian territory. However, the assertion that Manchuria was the land for which the Japanese had shed their blood—or, worse yet, that Japan could not let it go because acquisition of Manchuria had been the death wish of Emperor Meiji—was a sentimental argument appreciated only within Japan.

It had been argued by several Japanese leaders, including Shidehara Kijūrō and Matsuoka Yōsuke, that if Japan had known that Russia had advanced into Manchuria on the basis of the Li-Lobanov Treaty of the Sino-Russian alliance, it could have insisted on stronger sovereignty over Manchuria as the result of victory in the Russo-Japanese War.

Aside from the argument that Manchuria was not an integral part of China, it was also pointed out that China itself was not a unified nation at that time; it controlled only four of the 18 provinces at the time of Japan's withdrawal from the League of Nations, as portrayed in Matsuoka's farewell speech. Readers might be interested to know that the Chinese side argued back cynically that it was Japan that was unable to control the arbitrary conduct of its military and lacked governability. It was also frequently pointed out from the Japanese side that the Zhang Zuolin regime, which had become prominent under Japanese protection, did not pay heed to protecting the welfare of its people and, instead, extorted heavy taxes from local residents in order to finance its military expenditures in preparation for advancement to China proper.

As a matter of fact, many of those who participated in the building of Manchukuo were local politicians who demanded that the Zhang government pay more attention to defending the territorial integrity of Manchuria and the welfare of its people than to making military advances into China proper.

And it remained the consistent position of Japan throughout the International Military Tribunal for the Far East (1946-48) to defend its position on the Manchurian Incident as an act of self-defense against the anti-Japanese movement that was, according to the Japanese explanation, Zhang Xueliang's deliberate strategy to deprive Japan of its vested interests in Manchuria.

The Chinese side, in return, maintained a highly formalistic argument—that China was a unified nation and a member of the League of Nations and Manchuria was an integral part of China, and that the Nine-Power Treaty internationally guaranteed China's territorial integrity.

At the League of Nations, Japan persisted with its position that Manchukuo was a state that had already been built on the wishes of local people. In this one can hear the echo of the U.S. argument in defense of its support of Panamanian independence. When asked if Japan would promptly recognize Manchukuo, a Japanese dignitary replied that Japan had no reason to hasten the recognition because there was no canal in Manchuria (in contrast to the U.S. hasty recognition of the Panamanian puppet government), annoying the United States. This position might well have been accepted in a negotiation among major powers alone instead of the League of Nations. After all, among major powers, it was power relations that determined the outcome of an argument as long as it stood to reason.

Paper Thin Difference between Leftism and Rightism

It was not only the history and the international position of Manchuria that was unique in the world. The philosophical background behind the building of Manchukuo, most conspicuously manifested by the Kanto Army, was also peculiar. To paraphrase Shigemitsu Mamoru in *Shōwa no Dōran*

(昭和の動乱, Upheavals in Showa), it was a mixed bag of left-wing and right-wing thinking.

In later days, around the time of World War II, a sharp distinction was drawn between socialism (led by the Soviet Union and Comintern) and state socialism (fascism), even though both were different manifestations of the same totalitarianism. The principal reason behind this distinction was the need for the United States and Britain to take an official position that, unlike fascism, socialism was righteous because the Soviet Union was their ally during World War II.

Even in those days, realists like Harry Truman took a pragmatic position saying, "From our viewpoint, since it is fortunate that two totalitarian nations, Germany and the Soviet Union, fight one another in a war, all we need to do is to support the underdog." It was, however, positions of the likes of Franklin Roosevelt with a more optimistic view of Communism that were adopted in U.S. policy.

During the Cold War, the Japanese leftists worshiped socialism in the Soviet Union and China while loathing and criticizing Japan's militaristic regime in Japan during World War II. And this view had more or less permeated all historical views in post–World War II Japan for half a century.

In his 1928 treatise in defense of democracy, Japanese political scientist Yoshino Sakuzō argued that among the "most conspicuous movements against democracy" in recent years was "the restoration of governments under autocratic rule, most remarkably pursued in Italy and Russia." Yoshino followed up by saying, "Although Italy embraces dictatorship by Mussolini while Russia is under oligarchic rule of the Communists in the name of the proletariat, they are the same in terms of their autocratic roots."

Today, over 80 years later, this analysis by Yoshino still rings true.

In studying the labor movements in Japan around the time of the Manchurian Incident, a commonality between the left and the right is obvious. There was a nationalistic tendency in the proletariat political parties that brought about convergence between socialistic thinking and fascistic movements.

Behind the ideological conversion of Sano Manabu and Nabeyama Sadachika was their personal belief in "Tennoism," or the emperor system of Japan, rather than any fundamental doubts about such socialistic theory as the value of labor. Because Japan had enjoyed solidarity as a nation and as a state unbroken by foreign conquest, these two argued, "the political principle of the Comintern to provoke class antagonism among people" would not work in Japan. According to them, therefore, it was wrong to initiate a struggle against the emperor system of Japan by equating it with Russia's czarism.

While the post–World War II historic view usually attributes these ideological conversions to suppression by authority or to the weak will and self-interest of the converts, the truth must lie somewhere else. All of those converts had been faithful to their own convictions in their own right. Their conversion was the result of recognizing the reality—that is, that the Japanese people would not obey instructions from a remote Comintern. Their conversion, therefore, should be interpreted as the product of their own judgments and convictions.

Proletarian parties, which had a much wider support base among the Japanese people than the Communist Party did, also underwent changes. *Shakai Minshūtō* (Social Democratic Party), for instance, approved of the Manchurian Incident as a means "to secure the right of survival for the ordinary Japanese people." Its spinoff party, *Nippon Kokka Shakaitō* (National Socialist Party), set out the platform for constructing a new Japan under the emperor system, free of social exploitation.

As one can see from the above cases, none of the parties compromised the fundamental principle of socialism. Because the most basic view of Marxism is that value is created by labor, they aimed to create an equal society where capitalists stopped exploiting workers.

Planned economy is a means to prevent exploitation of workers by capitalists, and it is one of the most fundamental instruments of socialism. It was only after the Soviet Union's perestroika in the 1980s and Deng Xiaoping's "reforms and openness" policy since 1978 that planned economy started crumbling, at least partially. Before this, economic planning remained the foundation of socialism.

Originally, dictatorship by the proletariat was a means of preventing capitalists' exploitation of workers. What resulted in actuality, however, was dictatorship by party and government bureaucrats; in the sense that it was a totalitarian political system, this was no different from fascism, as Yoshino had pointed out.

The international socialism movement was rooted in the notion that classes are more important than the state. The international solidarity of the proletariat was based on this notion, and became a mere instrument to serve the national interest of the Soviet Union as it became a nationalistic state of "Socialism in One Country" under Stalin's rule. While the international socialism movement still survives as an abstract view, it has lost all of its political power. Moreover, proletariat internationalism has long since perished in present-day China, which has become a bastion of nationalism.

In retrospect, therefore, Japanese radicals who in those days criticized proletariat internationalism and prioritized the nation-state over classes followed the same path as the socialistic states themselves, just as the Soviet Union and China did in later years. If Stalin's Soviet Union and Communist China could claim that they were orthodox socialist countries, so could those converts in Japan claim their authenticity as they did.

Dictatorial Centralization Devoid of Exploitation

Rightists also claimed to be socialists. It was Kita Ikki's (北一輝) proposal on national reform that became the bible for the young military officers who led the reform movement that culminated in the February 26 Incident (2.26事件). Kita argued for establishing "genuine socialism" through "a second (Meiji) restoration."

More specifically, Kita's proposals were centered around egalitarian policies such as abolishment of the peerage and the House of Peers and prohibition of private property in excess of one million yen. As for the means to accomplish these policies, Kita envisaged dictatorship through suspension of the constitution by the supreme authority of the emperor and declaration of martial law.

When one removes the notion of proletariat internationalism, which already existed only in name in the Soviet Union under Stalin, from Marx-Leninism and removes the word "proletariat" from the "dictatorship of the proletariat," what is left would be egalitarianism. Egalitarianism is the grand principle of Marxism, in opposition to exploitation of workers by capitalists, together with planned economy based on a concentration of dictatorial power. In this formula, there is no difference between the left and the right.

The Japanese in early Shōwa found, rightly, only a paper-thin difference between the left and the right.

The concentration of dictatorial power was also applied to Manchukuo, which originally had been a part of the reform movement pursued by the military. The *Outlines for Economic Construction in Manchukuo* (満州国経済建設綱要), published on March 1, 1933, on the occasion of the country's one-year anniversary, declares at the outset that "[construction of the Manchukuo economy would] put priority on benefits for the entire nation and would not allow monopoly of benefits by the privileged class" and that "important economic sectors would be under state control."

When Koiso Kuniaki, Chief of Staff of the Kanto Army, declared that he had no intention to allow capitalists to enter Manchukuo, he was under the influence of residual Marxism. As it subsequently became obvious that economic development would be unattainable without corporate capital, however, this policy was amended. One can see a parallel with this development in the post-perestroika Soviet Union and post–Deng Xiaoping China.

As for the administrative mechanism in Manchukuo, the Kanto Army envisaged the "dictatorial centralization of power" as early as January 1932. In order to ensure Japan's primacy in the newly built empire, a governing mechanism was invented that was unique among governments worldwide. The prime minister was the only state minister in Manchukuo, while the heads of all the ministries were mere administrative officials. Underneath the prime minister was a management and coordination agency through which all administrative decisions had to be made without exception. Monopolizing the posts of the agency's head as well as all the bureau chiefs, this system allowed the Japanese to dictate the government. This was the substance of the Japanese-dominated power in Manchukuo.

As seen above, the Kanto Army was driven by the ideal of Shōwa reformation—that is, accomplishing a dictatorial concentration of power by its own hand and eliminating exploitation by capitalists. In order to pursue this ideal in an area other than Japan, however, the Kanto Army had to invent a new ideology to justify it. Hence, the "Harmony among Five

Races" and the "Ideal Kingdom" ideologies came into being.

The origin of Ishihara Kanji's management plan for Manchuria was a military strategy. In preparation for future war with the United States, Japan had to put Manchuria under its control in order to block a Soviet attack from the rear and mobilize all the resources in Japan, Korea, and Manchuria vis-à-vis the United States. Ishihara, therefore, was not interested in what kind of a country Japan should build in Manchuria. In fact, in the beginning, he had considered the direct occupation of Manchuria because it would be most useful for Japan's military strategy.

In actuality, however, in order to create a fait accompli in Manchuria, forestalling the League of Nations' recommendation and the intention of the home government in Tokyo, the Kanto Army had to win over local leaders to secure their support. Because the Japanese government had signed the Nine-Party Treaty by which it was committed to the territorial integrity of China, it was utterly impossible even for the army to think about annexing Manchuria. The Kanto Army, therefore, had no other recourse than to make a pretense of helping the Manchu people's spontaneous effort in building their own country.

As he reminisced ten years later in his 1943 memoirs, Ishihara "completely abandoned the idea of occupying Manchuria and Mongolia that I had unbendingly insisted on toward the end of 1932" and decided to base the building of Manchukuo on "harmony among five races, i.e., Japanese, Manchu, Chinese, Mongolian, and Korean, but particularly on the trust of the Chinese people."

It takes a man to have consistency in his thought to be called a thinker. Once he set his mind, Ishihara remained consistent all the way, proving his quality as a thinker.

In his August 1933 essay, "Private View," Ishihara said:

> If Japan failed to obtain the Manchurian and Mongolian people's support, Japan-Manchurian harmony or Japan-China friendship would be hard to come by. It also shows that Japan is not qualified to be the leader of East Asia. In that case, Japan has only two options: either to withdraw from Manchuria and Mongolia or to venture into the European-style colonial policies, forcefully exploiting the Chinese people in order to satisfy its thirst for material gains.

At the time of the annexation of Korea (1910), Itō Hirobumi had initially envisioned a protectorate that would give Korean people autonomy, believing Japan could gain the trust of the local people. However, witnessing the tyrannical conduct of the Japanese in Korea, which proved that "Japan is not qualified to be the leader," Itō had to agree with the position of annexing Korea.

Nevertheless, Ishihara chose to gamble his policy on the option that seemed to be most desirable. Thus, he wrote in his "Private View":

> We will have to realize the ideal for mankind on Manchurian and Mongolian soils by promoting fair competition and open-minded harmony among peoples, which will be the first step toward the Japan-China friendship and, eventually, unification of the world.

Subsequently, Ishihara became an advocate of Pan-Asianism, launching a Pan-Asianistic organization called the East Asia Federation (東亜連盟). Ishihara held on to his conviction to the end.

Ishihara also remained faithful to the logical outcomes of his policy arguments. When Japan advocated harmony among the five races, it also had to accommodate the Korean people's nationalistic aspirations. While advocating liberation of Asian peoples from Western colonial rule during the Great East Asia War, the Japanese government continued to impose the "Tennoization" (皇民化政策 or Japanization) policy on the Korean people. Against this, Ishihara recognized the Korean people as a component member of the nation based on harmony of the five races. Ishihara also opposed the aggrandizement of the war with China (支那事変) consistently. In the *Outline of the War Plan* (戦争計画要綱) that he compiled in 1938, one year into the Second Sino-Japanese War, he said,

> [The current war with China] would only drive two great nations in the Orient to endless animosity and conflict, making attainment of peace utterly hopeless.

Those Who Lived Earnestly

It was indeed the Second Sino-Japanese War that delivered the fatal blow to the ideal of harmony among the five races.

In order to finance the war, a massive amount of the government funds set aside for the construction of Manchukuo had to be diverted to military spending. A much graver outcome, however, was that possibilities for building mutual trust with the Chinese, who were by far the largest ethnic group in Manchuria, were lost forever.

Itō Musojirō, who had actively promoted the building of Manchukuo, particularly deplored the procession celebrating the fall of Nanjing in which local Chinese people were forced to participate. To Itō, it was like "forcing the children of Japanese residents in Manchuria to join a procession to celebrate the fall of Tokyo." As a result, Itō observed, "Manchukuo rapidly lost popular support among the Han People."

Economic development and improvement in people's livelihood since the birth of Manchukuo had been quite remarkable. While the entire Eurasian continent was suffering from battles and starvation during World War II, Manchukuo alone remained a peaceful paradise. When their national pride had been so brutally offended, however, this was, to the Chinese people, nothing but the "peace of a slave," as the Chinese like to say even today. After all, man does not live by bread alone.

Indeed, the management of the Manchukuo economy had been steadily moving toward the ideals of Ishihara and his associates until the eruption of the Sino-Japanese War. Among the Chinese and Japanese individuals who participated in the building of Manchukuo, not a small number of them made sincere efforts to really achieve harmony among the five races. It is undeniable that, at least in the beginning, Japan's presence in Manchukuo was a much more idealistic endeavor than its rule in the Korean Peninsula, which was nothing but a rule of force without a philosophy.

The last emperor of the Qing Dynasty, Xuantong Emperor Puyi, was declared the Emperor of Manchukuo. Although he later testified at the International Military Tribunal for the Far East that, including his ascent to the throne, that everything he did had been forced on him by the Japanese military, an abundance of evidence proved otherwise.

In *Twilight in the Forbidden City*, which was ruled inadmissible during the Tribunal, Reginald Johnston stated that Puyi could have fled on board a British ship from Shanghai if he so wished and that "Emperor Puyi decided to depart Tianjin for Manchuria by his free will."

It was only natural for the dethroned Qing Emperor Puyi to have a desire to become emperor of Manchuria, his ancestral homeland. And given conditions in those days, it must have been impossible for him to side with Chinese nationalism and resist the Japanese military, even though some historians today unrealistically argue that he could have done so. Because he had been detained in the Soviet Union before the Tribunal and was to be transferred to Chinese custody as a war criminal suspect after the Tribunal, it is easy to believe that he testified only as he had been instructed to by the Communist government.

On Puyi's attitude, Ben Bruce Blakeney, an American lawyer who served as a defense counsel at the Tokyo War Crimes Tribunal, said, "As long as a man has conscience, it is painful to tell a lie and to be investigated about it thoroughly. . . . However, I have come across a person whose egoism can easily suppress his conscience." Blakeney deplored how low a man can fall. Joseph Keenan, the chief prosecutor in the Tribunal, left a memo saying, "[Puyi had] no dignity of an emperor, and he had no light of self-respect in his eyes." Shigemitsu wrote the following observation in his journal on the same day:

> It was pitiful to see the former emperor, now at the mercy of the Soviet Union as its captive, try all kinds of rhetoric to avoid execution by the Chinese authorities. . . . I failed to detect any shade of dignity or appearance as the former emperor of Manchukuo. . . .

While there is no written document on this issue left in Japan, which was under strict censorship by the occupation forces in those days, derogatory remarks against Puyi were rampant in Japan wherever people got together, including public baths and family living rooms.

Puyi was accompanied by his loyal vassal, Zheng Xiaoxu, when he entered Manchukuo. Although Zheng was an unparalleled talent at the twilight of the Qing Dynasty, obtaining degrees of "licentiate" (秀才), "recommended man" (挙人), and "presented scholar" (進士) through the imperial examinations, he declined a government post offered by Yuan Shikai and Duan Qirui after the fall of the Qing Dynasty. Instead, he chose to remain as teacher of kingcraft to Puyi.

When Zheng was appointed as the first prime minister of Manchukuo, he was believed to harbor a dream of realizing the righteous government of legendary King Wen of Zhou (1099 BC–1050 BC). Magnanimous to anyone whom he came into contact with, Zheng was a man of such great virtue that, when the properness of promoting Japanese nationals to high-ranking governmental officials became an issue, he did not pay attention, saying, "It is like the Jin Dynasty, a great dynasty in the Chinese history, using the resources of Chu, southern barbarians." Whether his was an act of self-effacement so as to wait for the chance to restore the Qing Dynasty or a philosophical belief in the rule of right, quite transcendent of all worldly considerations, we don't know. Zheng was a man of unfathomable depth to whom no modern measures, such as Chinese nationalism or anti-imperialism, should be applied. Doing so would only lose sight of the truth of history.

In May 1934, Zhang Jinghui succeeded Zheng as prime minister. While he was a man of such moral courage that he had adamantly resisted the Japanese residents' violation of Han Chinese residents in Manchuria, he was also a typical pro-Japanese member of the Russo-Japanese War generation.

Having witnessed atrocities by Russia, Zhang raised his voice of admiration when Japan defeated Russia in the Russo-Japanese War. He had nothing but praise for the iron discipline of the Japanese military in those days, saying all the people in Manchuria, young and old, male and female, prayed from the bottom of their hearts for Japan's victory.

When Japan was defeated, Zhang lamented:

> We have lost the world's strongest military. Japanese military leaders did not have a full understanding of the meaning of war, which was only meant to facilitate negotiations. . . . I just cannot regret enough the loss of a great army.

It is a well-known fact that, during his detention in Siberia, Zhang gave comforting words to his fellow Japanese detainees.

The difference in dignity and grace between Puyi and his prime ministers, Zheng and Zhang, was stark. Zheng and Zhang are paragons of manhood. Their episodes show that there must have been not a small number of individuals, both Chinese and Japanese, who tried to live earnestly, faithful to their own convictions, through those days of turmoil. Sadly, episodes of these and other sincere people have been buried in a corner of history, forgotten in the midst of Japan's defeat and collapse of Manchukuo. There must be more who were not even given a corner of history to be buried. I dedicate the above few paragraphs describing the Manchukuo Prime Ministers Zheng and Zhang as an epitaph for all of those decent persons.

CHAPTER
3

Last Days of Peace

*—After the Manchurian Incident, an Opportunity
to Improve Sino-Japanese Relations—*

Tanggu Truce

Since the time of the Qing Dynasty, China's Three Northeast Provinces of Lioaning, Jilin, and Heilongjiang had been referred to collectively as Manchuria. While the Kanto Army had already conquered almost the entire Three Northeast Provinces by 1932 (7th Year of Shōwa), the province of Rehe, which was controlled by warlord Tang Yulin, remained unconquered.

Given the momentum, it was only natural for the Kanto Army to demarcate the border of Manchukuo by conquering Rehe Province. Having already made up its mind to build Manchukuo, the Japanese government had no intention to restrict this operation of the Kanto Army. The operation began in January 1933 (8th Year of Shōwa), and the original aim had been more or less accomplished by March.

But this operation coincided with the last stretch of the League of Nations' deliberation on the Manchurian Incident, which in the end led to Japan's withdrawal from the League. The Kanto Army's action became the target of harsh criticism by League member countries, isolating Japan completely. Because the Rehe operation was a new operation that covered areas beyond those under Zhang Xueliang's control, it was liable to

Okamura Yasuji (center-left) and Hsiung Ping (center-right),
right after counter-signing on the contract of Tanggu Truce.

become subject to League sanctions. This became an additional reason for
Japan to withdraw from the League of Nations.

Meanwhile, since the top priority for Chiang Kai-shek and the Kuomintang was to wipe out communists from China, Chiang was prepared to
minimize confrontation with the Japanese army. The British minister to
China offered to mediate a truce between China and Japan. On May 19,
U.S. President Franklin Roosevelt announced that he wished to see peace
restored in the Far East.

It was under these circumstances that the Tanggu Truce (塘沽停戦協定)
was signed on May 31 by Okamura Yasuji, Deputy Chief of Staff of the
Kanto Army, and Hsiung Ping representing the Kuomintang's National
Military Council in Beijing.

The truce called for the establishment of a demilitarized zone as a buffer zone in the south of the Great Wall, extending from Beijing to Tianjin.
The armies of the two sides were to be withdrawn from this zone.

Later, after the end of World War II, Okamura reminisced as follows:

> I believe the Tanggu Truce was the most important watershed in
> the long history of Japan's war from the Manchurian Incident to
> the Greater East Asia War. Perhaps, we could have reviewed our
> aggressive external policies at that point. No, we definitely should
> have done so.

To be sure, a certain kind of equilibrium had been accomplished by this point, in the sense that neither side wished for a further military clash. As a result of this truce, Manchukuo became a fait accompli and a possibility of future Sino-Japanese military clash on the Manchurian border was eliminated.

Okamura was not the only person to mull over what would have happened if Japan had stopped the aggression there, at the line of the Great Wall. This scenario is at least worth some attention.

The Tanggu Truce notwithstanding, China did not recognize Manchukuo. Chiang Kai-shek at that time believed in the strategy of "domestic pacification first before expelling foreign evils," which was, so to speak, cut from the same cloth as Yoshida Shōin's advocacy of "opening the door of Japan first [to expand the country's power and military might] before expelling foreign evils" at the height of the "Jōi-Ron" (a slogan meaning "Expel foreign barbarians!") movement at the twilight of the shogunate.

Obviously, then, China would sooner or later attempt to recover Manchuria and Mongolia once it attained national unification. How much sooner or later would it have been?

It is a historical fact that a unified China was achieved by the Communist Party of China (CPC) in 1949. Had Japan not advanced to North China, however, there was no knowing whether the United Fronts (or a Kuomintang-CPC Alliance) and a subsequent weakening of Kuomintang would have been achieved as the CPC had expected. Furthermore, the earlier unification of all the warlords by Kuomintang under the banner of Chinese nationalism might not have taken place.

If a degree of Japan's military strength had been preserved when the unification was accomplished in 1949, the Chinese side would not have confronted the Japanese forces militarily until much later. It would be almost unthinkable for the United States and Soviet Union to side with China and participate in a war that would topple the fait accompli in Manchuria.

Algerian-style guerilla warfare by Han Chinese residents, who were by far the largest ethnic group in Manchuria, could have been possible. This would have led to a tug of war over local people's support between Chinese nationalism and the Japanese policy that aimed at building a peaceful "Ideal Kingdom." Nobody could have predicted the winner of that game. Considering that the people in China Proper had to await the leadership of Deng Xiaoping after 1978—a full generation after the achievement of national unification—before they started to enjoy their lives genuinely, it seems unlikely that the Chinese side could have won hearts of the Manchurian people easily in this tug of war. It may not be utterly unrealistic to imagine that Japan would have returned its entire concessions in Manchuria, including the Liaodong Peninsula, to China in 1997 along with the British return of Hong Kong.

This means that if the Kanto Army had refrained from advancing beyond the Great Wall after the Tanggu Truce, the Manchurian border might have remained intact for about two generations—although Manchuria would have been returned to China anyway in 1997, regardless of what the Kanto Army did or did not do. While this might have meant another half century of frustrated nationalism and humiliation for the Chinese people, it could also have meant that local people were spared from the ravages of war. It is, however, meaningless to discuss the rights and wrongs of this possibility. History shows that this did not happen.

In any event, after the Tanggu Truce, the Far East enjoyed relatively peaceful days for about four years until the Sino-Japanese War.

The Golden Decade

To quote Chiang Kai-shek, the Tanggu Truce "was a humiliating arrangement, but it provided us with an opportunity to concentrate on internal unification first so that we could subsequently protect ourselves from external indignity."

Taking advantage of the truce, Chiang achieved complete success in the Fifth Encirclement Campaign against the Communists (October 1933–October 1934). To face the 150,000 Communist forces stationed in Jiangxi Soviet, the 65 Kuomintang divisions with 800,000-strong forces adopted the battle plan of "strategic offense, tactical defense." In other words, they tightly encircled the enemy forces, constructing plum blossom-shaped pillboxes along with the line of the encirclement. Fully protecting themselves from the Communists' offensives, they gradually narrowed the encirclement's perimeter except when the enemy used heavy weapons. Mao Zedong's People's War guerilla tactics were totally ineffective against this battle plan. Thus, the Fifth Encirclement Campaign forced the Communists to abandon soviets they had laboriously built in various places and embark on what later came to be called the Long March (or the "25,000-ri Chase" from the Kuomintang's perspective), leaving the heartland of China under the Kuomintang's control.

The subsequent four years until the Sino-Japanese War were the good old days for Kuomintang China. Quoting Albert Wedemeyer, an American Chief of Staff to Chiang Kai-shek during World War II, who called the ten years between the end of the Northern Expedition in 1928 and the start of the Sino-Japanese War in 1937 a "golden decade," the *Shō Kaiseki Hiroku* (「蒋介石秘録」, Secret Memoirs of Chiang Kai-Shek) refers to this decade with admiration as a period when the Republic of China achieved dramatic progress as a modern nation-state.

Looking at statistics on China in those days for infrastructure development such as railways, roads, and postal services as well as for industrial and educational developments, one realizes that there was indeed a dash for the modernization that had been frustrated since the fall of the Qing Dynasty. This resulted in a great leap forward in terms of societal modernization and people's standard of living. The prosperity of lilac-scented Shanghai, which still induces nostalgia in survivors of the era, symbolized this decade.

Chiang Kai-shek cannot be the only one to wish that this Golden Decade had continued indefinitely. This alone would bring home to us the misery that Chinese and Japanese people had to suffer from the folly of the Sino-Japanese War.

Shanghai was at the apex of its prosperity. Recently, I heard a Chinese citizen say, "China has been a capitalist country since Deng Xiaoping. It is actually a revival of what was happening before World War II but was temporarily interrupted by the war with Japan." There is some truth in this observation.

Hirota Kōki's Peace and Harmony Diplomacy

In September 1933, Foreign Minister Uchida Kōsai stepped down, citing his advanced age, and recommended Hirota Kōki as his successor. Hirota's diplomacy soon came to be called "peace and harmony diplomacy" in contrast to Uchida's "until we are all reduced to ashes" diplomacy.

Hirota accepted the nomination only after he had obtained the following two assurances from Prime Minister Saitō Makoto. One was an assurance that the diplomacy of Saitō's cabinet would be foreign ministry-led. The other was that diplomacy would be pursued in the spirit of the imperial edict issued at Japan's withdrawal from the League of Nations—that is, that "Japan must further enhance its trustworthiness and promote its grand cause to the world." In other words, Hirota's wish was to pursue diplomacy based on international trust and to control unauthorized arbitrary conduct of the military.

Hirota's proposition was also a timely one. Tension in the Far East had been significantly reduced by that time due to the Tanggu Truce in May 1933. The intra-ministry schism within the foreign ministry caused by the emergence of the so-called reformist group had just been settled. Since the Manchurian Incident, the "reformist faction," including information department director Shiratori Toshio, who had a tacit understanding with the military and *Seiyūkai*'s Mori Kaku, had been rebellious toward the leadership including vice minister Arita Hachirō. This intra-ministry feud was finally settled by Shiratori's assignment to an overseas post and Arita's resignation. Exhaustion from this internal feud was one of the causes of Uchida's resignation. Thus, the conditions for peace and harmony diplomacy were set.

What kind of a man was Hirota Kōki?

Hirota became the only civilian who was executed by hanging as the result of the International Military Tribunal for the Far East. He was found guilty of waging wars and of negligence of the laws of war in his key governmental roles. He served as foreign minister for the Saitō and Okada Keisuke cabinets (1933–36), as prime minister (1936–37), and as foreign minister of the first Konoe Fumimaro cabinet (1937–39)—all at a critical juncture of Japan's entry into World War II.

He was condemned for being party to a "conspiracy." It was presumed that there had been a group of conspirators who had made and implemented a plan for Japan to invade Asian territories. In light of the reality that not only the foreign ministry but even the military itself had been unable to control the arbitrary conduct of the Kanto Army and the historical fact that Japan had gotten deeply involved in the war with China without any strategy or long-term perspective, it is obvious that this accusation was complete nonsense.

The judges were divided over the death sentence for Hirota. Not a small number of them found him not guilty. In the end, allegedly, it was by only one vote that his death sentence was decided. Outside the courtroom, too, there were many who felt compassion for Hirota.

It is a proven fact that Hirota remained gallant throughout the tribunal, taking full responsibility and making no attempt on the witness stand to vindicate himself. In the end, Hirota heard his death sentence calmly. To make no excuse for one's actions and to refrain from plotting anything for one's own benefit—these are the basic principles of a samurai.

To a friend who advised Hirota that he should defend himself on the witness stand, he replied as follows:

> Never in my life have I plotted something for my own benefit. I became foreign minister and prime minister because I could not decline the nomination. For most of my life so far, I have done nothing to benefit myself. Why, then, should I defend myself for my own benefit at this point?

Born to a stonemason family in Fukuoka, Kyūshū, Hirota had worked to help the family since his grade school days. Although it had been determined that after elementary school he would become an apprentice in his father's business, his academic achievements were so remarkable that he was sent to a junior high school instead. There he far excelled over the other students. With the help of a philanthropist who offered to assist him financially, Hirota proceeded to *Daiichi Kōtō Gakko* (First High School) and Tokyo Imperial University. Hirota passed the Foreign Service Examination in 1906.

Hirota's life was a typical success story of a local prodigy in the Meiji and Taishō eras. Japan's social mechanism in those days promoted youths with promising futures regardless of their social status or breeding, even from the remotest corner of the country.

One peculiar part of Hirota's background was his association with *Genyōsha* (玄洋社) since his junior high school days. *Genyōsha* was the most influential Pan-Asianism/ultranationalist group in pre–World War II

Japan. It was founded in 1881 at the apex of the Freedom and People's Rights Movement by Tōyama Mitsuru (頭山満). He had been imprisoned for his participation in such anti-government movements as the Shinpūren Rebellion (1876) and the Hagi Rebellion (1876), which took place prior to the Satsuma Rebellion. The association's slogan was to revere the Imperial Family, love the country, and protect the people's rights.

It was from a member of this *Genyōsha* that young Hirota earnestly learned Chinese classics and poetry. It is believed that Hirota was particularly and deeply influenced by reading the philosophy of Wang Yangming (王陽明).

Nevertheless, Hirota did not become a member of this association. Judging from his later words and deeds, Hirota was more of a practitioner of Oriental philosophy than a rightwing ultranationalist. Although *Genyōsha* is categorized as having been a nationalist or ultra-nationalist group, it contained a wide variety of people. Among those whose memories are still fresh in our minds is Yasuoka Masahiro. While discussing high affairs of state, Yasuoka stayed away from being involved with current policy debates because his ultimate goal was to perfect his character as an individual. It seems appropriate to understand that Hirota also belonged to this category of thinker.

"While I remain foreign minister, Japan will never fight a war" is Hirota's most well-known pro-peace and harmony diplomacy remark, one that hemade in a 1935 Diet session. This remark was often contrasted with Uchida Kōsai's "until we are all reduced to ashes" diplomacy.

Hirota's comment was made in response to Ashida Hitoshi of the *Seiyūkai*, who criticized Hirota's previous foreign policy speech as being too naïve and optimistic in assessing Japan's circumstances. In this foreign policy speech, Hirota had revealed his conviction about diplomacy based on a sense of justice, saying, "As long as its words are sincere and its deeds are discreet, even a barbarian country shall be the subject of Japan's peace and harmony diplomacy."

At the House of Peers, Hirota responded to a question from Yoshizawa Kenkichi as follows:

> I think the most important thing is to enhance the world's trust in Japan. When a person wishes to strengthen his credibility, he must have a conscience that he himself can trust. I believe the same thing

can be said about a state. Thus, it is imperative, above all, for the Japanese people to maintain attitudes for which they have no reason to be ashamed of in the presence of all the people in the world, including themselves.

The words indeed reflected the spirit of Wang Yangming's philosophy that applied the Confucian teachings of "To put the world in order, first train one's own moral, then put one's own family in order, then put the nation in order, and, finally, bring peace into the world" to real politics, with the principle of inseparability of knowledge and practice.

Traditional Oriental Character?

One critical pitfall for practitioners of Wang Yangming's philosophy is self-complacency. It teaches that as long as one has nothing to be ashamed of about one's belief, one does not need to explain. One only need trust the heavens. The focus of the teachings on doing/saying nothing that is shameful easily leads to do-nothingism. Because it was Hirota's personal life or death that was at stake at the International Military Tribunal for the Far East, it was fine for Hirota to practice say-nothingism and calmly accept the death sentence.

But the same thing cannot be said about the fate of a state. Domestically, there were forces that were all too eager to devise schemes leading Japan in a totally opposite direction from Hirota's intentions. And internationally, China was prepared to resort to all manner of diplomatic techniques to separate Japan from Britain and the United States in its pursuit of restoring its own sovereignty. At the same time, the Communist Party of China was plotting to make the Kuomintang army confront the Kanto Army by undermining the former's "domestic pacification first before expelling foreign evils" strategy. Against this background, it would certainly imperil Japan not to prepare countermeasures, believing that sincerity would solve all the problems.

Hirota Kōki

This might be one reason we find something wanting in Hirota's achievements as foreign minister and, subsequently, as prime minister.

It was the Hirota cabinet that reinstated the system by which only active-duty army or navy officers could serve in the cabinet posts of war and navy ministers. This had been the critical point of contention between the military and the party government since the Meiji era. It was also Prime Minister Hirota who catered to the military by adopting without any modification the *Kokusaku Taikō* (Outline of National Defense Policies), the most frequently quoted document during the International Military Tribunal for the Far East. At the time of the Marco Polo Bridge Incident, too, it was Hirota who, despite full readiness to turn it down, allowed the Imperial Army's proposition to mobilize three army divisions pass the Diet. In each of the above cases, Hirota did not exercise any leadership.

It was not that Hirota had been a rightist or a pro-military from the beginning, adhering to the tradition of *Genyōsha*. After all, he was an advocate of peace and harmony diplomacy, which would be totally incompatible with *Genyōsha*'s ideological inclinations.

It was not Hirota's principle to be antagonistic toward a policy that everyone else had decided on. Instead, as he showed, he would actually accept the policy, saying, "If you all say so." Put in the context of a period of militarism and a strong inclination toward nationalism, this attitude in effect mirrored the attitude of an opportunist who shows no resistance to pressure from the military.

Perhaps taking full responsibility for having agreed with a certain policy was more important for Hirota than the actual substance of the policy he had agreed with. To keep one's promise was of the utmost importance to Hirota.

In this attitude of Hirota's, one can find an echo of the words and deeds of Saigō Takamori after retiring from national politics. Disheartened to hear of his men's uprising, all Saigō said was, "Oh, no, I shouldn't have let them!" After that, he never said a word of criticism. Leaving the military command to his deputies, Saigō just calmly followed the fate bestowed on him by his followers. He was able to die unashamed of himself even after causing a totally meaningless war that led to hundreds of wasteful deaths on both sides, because he was firmly convinced that he did nothing that ran counter to the ways of heaven.

Under normal circumstances, this type of traditional Oriental person may be regarded as a sincere statesman who is prepared to take full responsibility for his own conduct as he does not resist the trend of the times. When things are not normal, however, he becomes a mere opportunist who lacks leadership.

When pursuing his peace and harmony diplomacy, Hirota was fortunate to be assisted by highly competent diplomats.

Hirota had Shigemitsu Mamoru and Tōgō Shigenori as his vice-minister for foreign affairs and director of the Europe and America department, respectively. He also appointed Saitō Hiroshi (斉藤博) as ambassador to the United States. Saitō became so well trusted in his post that, when he passed away from illness, the U.S. government sent his remains onboard the USS *Astoria* ship back to Japan, which was highly unusual. Shigemitsu and Tōgō were two of the most outstanding diplomats in Japan during World War II, both in terms of their insights as well as their convictions. Shigemitsu's *Shōwa no Dōran* (Upheavals in Showa) and Tōgō's *Jidai no Ichimen* (An Aspect of an Era) were memoirs of masterpiece quality on Japan's diplomacy during the war.

Incidentally, these two memoirs do not even refer to Foreign Minister Hirota's role in pursuit of peace and harmony diplomacy. Shigemitsu's memoir simply narrates, the "Ministry of Foreign Affairs, foreign policy authorities of Japan . . . attempted to move forward toward the settlement," which may reveal something negative about Hirota's diplomacy or leadership.

Soon after Hirota joined the cabinet, a conference was convened among the prime minister and the ministers of foreign affairs, war, navy, and finance. Henceforth, this five-minister conference became the inner cabinet and remained the nucleus of decision-making.

Tōgō was assigned to the secretariat of this conference. He left the following memos on this conference:

> Against the background of the rapid rise of a hardliner foreign policy after the Manchurian Incident, which began to adversely affect compiling the budget, this conference was convened to coordinate government policies. In the main, moderate arguments by the finance and foreign ministers were dominant and the hardliner arguments of the military were never adopted.

And:

> Although many believed and even preached that, since the First
> Sino-Japanese and Russo-Japanese Wars, particularly since the
> Manchurian Incident, Japan had single-mindedly pursued a path
> toward militaristic invasions, the situation inside the Japanese gov-
> ernment was never that simple. As exemplified by the five-minis-
> ter conference, a great number of attempts were made to normalize
> Japan's national policies.

And history shows that Japan's diplomacy in those days was indeed fair
and unbiased, as envisioned by Tōgō.

An April 1934 announcement by a Japanese diplomat, however, which
later became known as the Amau Statement, caused a little stir. It was a
remark made by Amau Eiji, then the director of the information department of the Ministry of Foreign Affairs, at a press conference. The remark
was reported internationally as the declaration of Japan's Monroe Doctrine, sending shock waves both within and outside Japan.

Afterwards, Amau explained that he had simply repeated what the
Japanese government had announced earlier. In effect, Amau's remark
declared that Japan would not sit idly by and watch Western powers
form a consortium to expand their influences in China. Because neither
the Western powers nor China were enthusiastic about this endeavor,
however, what Amau did was totally uncalled for. His remark might be
attributed to the demand for hardliner foreign policy which had already
permeated the foreign ministry by that time.

The Japanese government received a complaint from China that this
statement put Wang Jingwei, its foreign minister who had been trying to
promote collaboration with Japan within the Kuomintang government, in
a difficult position. Even within the Japanese foreign ministry, this remark
was criticized as being utterly unnecessary, and Amau was reprimanded
by Hirota.

Subsequently, Foreign Minister Hirota explained Japan's intentions
to Britain, the United States, and China, all of which, for the time being,
accepted the explanation. That settled the issue.

Settlement of the Manchurian Incident

Tōgō, who had been the director of the European and American department before Hirota's appointment as foreign minister, formulated a lengthy recommendation on Japan's diplomacy vis-à-vis the United States, Britain, and the Soviet Union in April 1934, immediately after Japan's withdrawal from the League of Nations. In this document, Tōgō deplored the fact that U.S.-Japan relations had never been so bad. He referred to the possibility of even a war between the two countries and proposed to maintain equal economic opportunities and the open-door policy in Manchukuo and declare a "no territorial ambition" policy on the part of Japan. Subsequent U.S.-Japan relations were adjusted along the lines of Tōgō's proposal.

The largest and most urgent challenge for the entire world at that time was the recovery of the world economy from the Great Depression. To this end, the United States proposed that a preliminary conference be convened in Washington, D.C., in preparation for a full-fledged world economic conference. Japan was invited to this conference even though it had just withdrawn from the League of Nations two weeks earlier. After all, Japan was a major power and a stabilizer in the Far East that could not be neglected.

Taking advantage of this invitation, the Japanese government attempted to resume communication with the United States by dispatching Ishii Kikujirō, a co-signee of the U.S.-Japan Lansing-Ishii Agreement in 1917, as its plenipotentiary representative.

In his conversation with Ishii, newly elected U.S. President Franklin D. Roosevelt said, "As for the settlement of the Manchurian Incident, we have no other recourse but to wait. Time will permit a settlement." In the context of his proposal on the achievement of order in the world economy and peace through arms reduction, Roosevelt said, "The Manchurian Incident does not pose any obstacle as long as it does not go beyond a certain just limit."

Roosevelt's "wait for time" implied that the United States could not change its stance immediately. But, at the same time, it also meant that the United States recognized that what had already been done could not be undone instantly. Thus, the Manchurian Incident had been de facto settled as far as the United States and Japan were concerned.

This conversation coincided with the signing of the Tanggu Truce. Even U.S. Ambassador to Japan Joseph Grew, who had been furious about Japan's conduct in Manchuria, reported to the home government that lately Japan's attitude had improved remarkably.

Soon after assuming his post, Foreign Minister Hirota entrusted the newly appointed Japanese Ambassador to the United States Saitō Hiroshi with his personal message to U.S. Secretary of State Cordell Hull. Hull responded immediately. In this exchange, the two sides reached an agreement that there were no issue that would fundamentally defy an amicable settlement between the two countries.

It is said that this exchange between Hirota and Hull subsequently affected the power relations between pro-Western and pro-Japanese factions within the Kuomintang government. As the pro-Western faction members had expected that the United States would never let Japan do as it pleased in Manchuria, it is not hard to imagine how disappointed they were.

Later, when Ambassador Saitō met U.S. Senator Key Pittman over the London Naval Treaty issue, the latter said, "As long as Japan keeps China's door open and refrains from advancing south of the Great Wall, the U.S. government would be satisfied and it would not interfere in other issues."

This was as far as the improvement of relations with the United States could come. But that was enough for Japan.

While the United States hardly gives in an inch once it raises a principle high, it often happens that the country fails to form a consensus on measures to put that principle into practice, and so ends up doing nothing. One can only recall the U.S. inaction against Russia's occupation of Manchuria on the eve of the Russo-Japanese War. Although U.S. President Theodore Roosevelt did not approve of Russia's action, the United States did nothing because a principle is only a principle but reality is a totally different thing. The Stimson Doctrine enunciated in January 1932 hardly affected U.S. action in substance.

What Japan should have done to improve its relations with the United States was to keep the doors of Manchuria open for economic activities and refrain from advancing south of the Great Wall, as Tōgō had proposed. Japan should also have given the time for mutual communication to ripen, as President Franklin Roosevelt had suggested. In later days, the

Soviet Union was expelled from the League of Nations after invading Poland, Finland, and three Baltic countries in 1939. But during the Cold War, it stayed in the United Nations even though it was denounced by that body for suppressing Hungary and Czechoslovakia. When the United States ended up recognizing the existing borders surrounding the Soviet Union by signing the Helsinki Accords in 1975, it even surrendered its principle.

In contrast, by starting the war with China, Japan lost the opportunity to let time settle the issue by its own hand.

Withdrawal from the London Naval Treaty

The "Fleet Faction," which had been restrained by the "Treaty Faction" due to the Washington and London Naval Treaties, became the mainstream in the Imperial Japanese Navy by this point. Admiral Katō Hiroharu, the leadership figure of the Fleet Faction, succeeded in appointing Prince Fushimi Hiroyasu as chief of the Imperial Japanese Navy General Staff. Furthermore, with the support of Admiral Tōgō Heihachirō all the way down to junior naval officers, Katō put pressure on Navy Minister Ōsumi Mineo to expel such Treaty Faction officers as Hori Teikichi, Yamanashi Katsunoshin, and Sakonji Seizō from active duty.

The Saitō cabinet was forced to step down in July 1934 because it was involved in the Teijin Incident, which was later proven to be an absurd scandal without criminality. Okada Keisuke became the new prime minister, succeeding Saitō Makoto. Although there was some pressure to appoint Katō Hiroharu as prime minister, elder statesman Saionji Kinmochi chose Okada instead. Saionji valued Okada's contribution in past naval conferences toward Japan's moderate stance.

By early 1934, however, withdrawal from the London Naval Treaty had already become something close to a consensus within the IJN. While Foreign Minister Hirota and Navy Minister Ōsumi remained in the newly formed Okada cabinet, Ōsumi was tacitly allowed to retain his cabinet post in exchange for his support for withdrawal from the treaty. Although unexposed, this was another example of the independence of the military command restricting a cabinet's policy and personnel decisions.

Shortly thereafter, the Japanese government announced in 1934 that it would withdraw from the Washington Naval Treaty in 1936, when the London Naval Treaty would expire automatically. Thus, as far as armaments were concerned, Japan had just entered an era of no restricting international treaty.

Determined to enhance its security by concluding neutrality pacts and mutual non-aggression treaties with neighboring countries, the Soviet Union had started sounding out Japan about the possibility of concluding a neutrality pact with it by as early as 1926, only a few years after the Russian Revolution.

From the Soviet perspective, the significance of the Manchurian Incident was that the Japanese military had closed in on the Soviet-Manchurian border. The Soviet Union in those days had not yet completed its first five-year plan and it could not afford to deploy heavy defenses along the Soviet-Manchurian border. Thus, it assumed a humble attitude toward Japan, proposing a mutual or even a Japan-Manchukuo-Soviet tripartite non-aggression treaty. This was tantamount to Soviet recognition of Manchukuo, revealing the Soviet Union's cool-headedness in discarding everything else for the sake of its own safety.

Hirota had been Japanese ambassador to Moscow for nearly three years before he was appointed as foreign minister. While he himself was not against the non-aggression treaty with the Soviet Union, it seemed highly unlikely for bilateral relations to develop beyond the normalization of diplomatic relations that Shidehara Kijūrō had accomplished, given Japanese wariness of Communist Russia as well as the argument for Japanese control of Siberia advocated by some in the military.

Since his ambassador days, Hirota had consistently advocated acquisition of the Chinese Eastern Railway, and this would become a major accomplishment of Hirota's diplomacy in less than two years' time. The Chinese Eastern Railway ran through northern Manchuria and linked Chita near Lake Baikal with Vladivostok. Sergei Witte, Chairman of the Council of Ministers (Prime Minister) of the Russian Empire, had obtained the railway from Li Hongzhang with cajolery and bribery, together with the right to station the Russian army in areas along the railway.

It took 56 negotiations over 22 months before the agreement was reached between the Japanese and Russian governments that the Chinese Eastern Railway would be acquired by Manchukuo with the Japanese government's certification of payment. Thus, everything that Imperial Russia had obtained from China in the days preceding the Russo-Japanese War was now put under Japan's control.

In the very same month that the agreement was signed (March 1935), the Soviet Union allowed Manchukuo to open legations in Vladivostok and Khabarovsk, effectively entering diplomatic relations with the latter.

As Tōgō had also pointed out in the proposal mentioned earlier, Britain and Japan had had a common interest in protecting their respective interests in China from the beginning. Britain at that time was wary of the conduct of the Soviet Union, and valued Japan's role in restricting Russian movements in China.

Britain was particularly pleased with the appointment of Hirota as foreign minister. British Foreign Minister John Simon sent Hirota a secret letter in December 1933 to emphasize the crucial importance of British-Japanese cooperation.

In the fall of 1934, a mission of the Federation of British Industries led by Lord Bamby visited Manchuria and requested an open-door policy there. On this visit, journalist Ozaki Hotsumi said, "It must be obvious to the eyes of economically pragmatic Britons that Manchukuo is an undeniable presence."

At this juncture, Britain decided to send Frederick Leith-Ross, chief economic advisor to the government, to China. The intention behind this decision was for Britain and Japan to take advantage of the peace restored by the Tanggu Truce and to jointly support China in reforming its monetary system, which had been in a shambles due to the war. Although Britain had long recognized the need to support China in this regard, its leaders thought Britain should not go over Japan's head to approach China.

In Japan, Leith-Ross met Foreign Minister Hirota and Vice-Minister Shigemitsu in September 1935. Leith-Ross started the conversation with the British assessment that it was desirable to make China recognize Manchukuo in order to stabilize Sino-Japanese relations, which was the prerequisite for stabilization of the Chinese economy. For this purpose, he suggested, Japan should shoulder 30 percent of China's external debt as that of Manchuria and have Manchukuo pay the debt to China so that Japan could use it to fund its monetary reform. Even though the money would go through a complicated mechanism, it would be Japanese money that would go to China. Thus, it was a plot to make China effectively recognize Manchukuo by offering China Japanese financial assistance.

The entire Ministry of Foreign Affairs, including diplomats stationed in China, reacted favorably to this proposition. When they consulted with the Ministry of Finance, however, they were told that it would be extremely difficult for the Japanese government to finance a substantial amount for at least a year or two due to a worsening balance of payments, investments in Manchuria, and acquisition of the Chinese Eastern Railway.

Unwilling to give up on this British proposal, Suma Yakichirō, Consul-General at Nanjing and representing Japanese residents in China, negotiated directly with Finance Minister Takahashi Korekiyo, saying, "We have at last come within one step of genuinely improving relations with China." Nevertheless, Takahashi turned down the plea, declaring, "While I wholeheartedly agree with the spirit of the plan, the fact is that you can't get blood out of a stone."

After all, Japan still was a poor country and it could not afford to assist China for the sake of the long-term stability of Asia on top of expanding its military capabilities and investments in Manchuria. Of course, it would have been a golden opportunity and a small investment compared to the tremendous amount of military expenditures that would later become necessary. But there is a limit to what mortals can imagine.

Leith-Ross expressed his disappointment with the Japanese attitude before entering China. It so happened, at that time, that the financial crisis in China further worsened, calling for emergency measures. The loan of £10 million that Britain provided had an immediate effect, stabilizing the financial market and, in time, leading to successful monetary reform. Had Japan participated in this endeavor, subsequent Sino-Japanese relations and the situation in Asia would have been completely different.

Given the principle laid out by the Amau Statement, the Japanese government found it necessary to lodge a protest against the British government for pursuing monetary reform in China over Japan's head. This forced Japan to forgo a golden opportunity for Japan-Britain-China cooperation.

On the bright side, as Shigemitsu writes in his *Shōwa no Dōran*, Leith-Ross's case was, "an indication that the British government still highly values relations with Japan. It attempted to mediate the improvement of Sino-Japanese relations."

Shigemitsu, however, laments as follows:

China was . . . struck with wonder at Japan. Contrary to predictions by world powers that Japan's adventure would immediately lead the country to bankruptcy, Japan instead demonstrated the vigor to become increasingly powerful. Revolutionary China became convinced that it had to study Japan closely so that it could emulate its eastern neighbor, which is an echo of the psychology of Chinese intellectuals immediately after the First Sino-Japanese War. With this conviction, a large number of Chinese students and observers began to visit Japan. Visits by Chinese politicians and diplomats visits to Japan also increased rapidly.

It was felt at that time that, if Japan had grabbed this opportunity, it might have been able to turn misfortune into a blessing in terms of Sino-Japanese relations. But, in order to accomplish this, the Japanese side needed patience, tolerance, and discipline. Most of all, the wisdom to judge things from a broad perspective was called for. Little of this existed at the time.

Good Old Days

Meanwhile, the dust of the Manchurian Incident subsided and Japan's relations with the United States, the Soviet Union, and Britain stabilized, allowing Japan to enjoy the last "good old days" until the war with China erupted.

The Japanese economy, which had bottomed out in 1931, started to pick up, with production recovering to the pre–Great Depression level in 1933–34. And it continued to grow further.

The post–World War II leftist-revisionist historical view characterizes this period as one of decadence with anticipation of an imminent fate, calling it the "Era of Erotic and Grotesque Nonsense." This was a term originally invented during the era of militarism to criticize the days of liberal democracy. Postwar leftists borrowed it to describe early to mid-1930s Japan. If the days of that minor level of decadence were to be called an "Era of Erotic and Grotesque Nonsense," what stronger language can we use to describe the degeneration of television and magazines in Japan today? Some historians see an analogy between the Tokyo Ondo *bonodori* dance tune that became extremely popular in those days and the *Ee ja nai ka* (ええじゃないか or "Isn't It Great?") cult toward the end of the Edo period, and describe these six years as nihilistic years foreshadowing a societal upheaval. Judging from the origins and form of these two fads, however, it is unlikely that there is any relation between them.

These observations are "wisdom after the event," and they are not historical facts at all. It would be more accurate to describe those six years as an era in which the common people became self-confident with the rise of the Empire of Japan and enjoyed economic recovery during a brief period of peace and stability.

Vivid still in peoples' memories about the era are the Keiō-Waseda college baseball tournaments, which were arguably more popular than present-day professional baseball games, as well as the introduction of talking movies and jazz music. It was also this period that witnessed educational, cultural, and technological levels reach an apex because of the maturation of the generations that had grown up during the rise of nationalism around the Russo-Japanese War. Had peace persisted longer, these levels would have risen much higher.

When those Japanese born in Taishō or in the first ten years of Shōwa look back on the "prewar days" with nostalgia or bitterness for what was lost, they usually think of this period. This time was also the remainder of the Golden Decade for Continental China and the last days of peace for East Asia.

CHAPTER
4

The February 26 Incident

—Drastic Change of Current in Japan in 1935–36—

Public Opinion Swings Right

Between the Tanggu Truce in 1933 and the eruption of the Sino-Japanese War in 1937, the Japanese people enjoyed a last period of peace. Nevertheless, it was a totally different era from that of the Taishō Democracy.

Parliamentary democracy had already lost people's support. In the 1932 general election, the *Seiyūkai* won 301 seats in the House of Representatives, the largest win for the party since the days of Hara Takashi. While the *Seiyūkai* members rejoiced in anticipation of the comeback of the era of their party, the public in Japan had already given up on party politics due to scandals, corruption, unpopular domestic and foreign policies, and short-lived governments. There would be no more party government in Japan until after the end of World War II.

The February 26 Incident erupted in 1936 as if to mark the end of the era of party government.

In an opinion poll taken of Japanese citizens who had lived both before and after World War II, the vast majority singled out the February 26 Incident as the most shocking event in their lives. It should be recalled that this period contains so many poignant, unforgettable occurrences including several wars, heavy air-raids on major cities, the atomic bombs dropped on Hiroshima and Nagasaki, and famine following the defeat. Neverthe-less, the majority of the respondents chose the February 26 Incident.

The Japanese people believe in the society they live in. While wars and the defeat in World War II undoubtedly posed tremendous difficulties for them, the entire nation faced the hardship squarely, as one, trusting in the government. A revolution or an attempted coup d'état, however, was a totally different thing, because it would shake up the consensus among people and make them wary of the collapse of the society they had believed in. As a matter of fact, history shows that the society on which the Empire of Japan had been based was destined to collapse in less than ten years. The Japanese had never felt this kind of anxiety since Commo-dore Perry's fleet arrived in Uraga and Ii Naosuke, a high-ranking official (similar to a prime minister) in the Tokugawa government, was assassi-nated on a cold, snowy morning.

Until the February 26 Incident, people in Japan had been enjoying eco-nomic recovery and peace, unaffected by political change. Starting in around 1935 (10th Year of Shōwa), however, the political atmosphere in Japan undoubtedly began to shift.

At the dawn of 1935, the theory of the Emperor as an organ of gov-ernment (天皇機関説) was debated hotly in the Imperial Diet. This clearly marked a change in the current of Japanese politics.

The theory of the Emperor as an organ of government had been almost officially recognized as the correct interpretation of the constitution since it had been advanced by Minobe Tatsukichi (美濃部達吉) in the first year of the Taishō era. This theory was a natural outcome of the interpretation of the Meiji Constitution that was presumed to be able to restrict even the supreme authority of the emperor. But in 1935, nationalist elements both inside and outside the Imperial Diet who had been displeased with the liberalistic tendency in Japan since the Taishō Democracy took a political stand that the theory was wrong. This led to the banning of Minobe's works and even to interrogation of Minobe himself for suspected lese-majesty. Those who rejected this interpretation argued that the Emperor was a supreme ruler and, therefore, he was no organ of government under the constitution. Pursuing this interpretation to the extreme, these people held that the emperor would not be restricted either by the Imperial Diet or the Meiji Constitution, contrary to the intention of the drafters of the constitution. And, as a corollary, so their thinking went, the military, being under the supreme command of the Emperor, was an independent organization outside the constitutional framework.

Prior to this shift in the political current, nationalistic elements had gradually attempted to overturn the liberal democratic tendency through such incidents as the dismissals of Kyoto University Professor Takigawa Yukitoki and Minister of Commerce and Industry Nakajima Kumakichi. Takigawa had been suspected of leftist inclinations, and Nakajima had praised Ashikaga Takauji, the 14-century traitor against the Emperor. The special significance of the argument against the theory of the Emperor as an organ of government lies in the fact that all of Japan—public opinion and the Imperial Diet—took the side of this argument. In the end, the Declaration of Clarification of the National Polity was issued twice by Prime Minister Okada Keisuke, in August and October 1935. This was a victory for right-wing tendencies in the political thinking of Japan.

In March 1936, the Ministry of Education issued the *Kokutai no Hongi* (「国体の本義」, Cardinal Principles of the National Polity), declaring that the essence of the Japanese people was totally different from Western peoples. Henceforth, "that all of our national policy originates from the Emperor" became the foundation of education in Japan.

Although *Kokutai no Hongi* was merely an abstract document, it was inevitable that it led to the unconditional worship of the Emperor. Among the policies and measures taken by Japan's colonial administration and occupational rule during the Greater East Asia War, the coercive imposition of emperor worship on other peoples is often singled out as Japan's greatest mistake. One may find the origin of this mistake in this document. Although the content of the document had originally been intended to apply only to the Japanese, it was essentially impossible for anyone in Japan to protest when some began to coerce other peoples into emperor worship.

Remarkable Recovery of the Japanese Economy

Why, then, did Japanese society take such a sharp right swing? Before exploring the source of rightist thinking in Japan, it seems necessary to momentarily depart from politics and diplomacy and take a look at the economic and social conditions in those days.

Throughout the pre–World War II and postwar days, it has been frequently argued—and generally accepted—that resource-poor prewar Japan had no choice but to follow expansionistic external policies in the era of the Great Depression and the bloc economy. Domestically, radicalization of the military was often attributed to young officers' aspirations for social reform, or even for a revolution. It was their sympathy with the destitution of rural areas, which had provided conscript soldiers, that drove the young officers' conduct.

The first of the two arguments—that is, that Japan's expansionistic policies were justified because Japan had no other choice—seems unwarranted in light of the actual state of the economy.

The impact of the Great Depression on the Japanese economy was certainly atrocious. In 1931 (6th Year of Shōwa), Japan's national income and stock market both declined by 30 percent compared with 1926, while consumer prices also dropped by 35 percent. But actually it was the anxiety of the Japanese residents in Manchuria over Zhang Xueliang's anti-Japanese policy that triggered the Manchurian Incident. It is unjustifiable to attribute the incident to the Great Depression.

As a matter of fact, Japan's economic recovery was notably faster than that of the Western powers. Both national product and national income started to pick up as early as 1932 to regain pre-Depression levels in 1933–34. And growth continued. This was in stark contrast to the United States, which suffered a second, deep depression in 1937 before showing any noticeable recovery.

What made the difference was Takahashi Korekiyo's fiscal policy. Takahashi reintroduced the gold embargo to depreciate the yen's exchange rate and, simultaneously, followed an expansionary fiscal policy by issuing deficit bonds. These were very orthodox, Keynesian remedies for recession. Because John Maynard Keynes' *The General Theory of Employment, Interest and Money* was to be published only in 1936, Takahashi today is deservingly appreciated as a precursor in this field, quite ahead of Keynes.

As Keynes himself once admitted, his was a theorization of what everybody in those days knew would work in coping with economic recession. In this sense, when things got as bad as they did in Japan in the 1930s, remedies must have been self-evident to just about anyone, but particularly to such a seasoned expert of fiscal policy as Takahashi.

Nevertheless, to understand what is required theoretically is one thing; to promptly and dauntlessly put that into practice is another. It must have been difficult to do what Takahashi actually did regardless of the time or location. In this conjunction, Japan benefitted from a past mistake. Compared to the Western economies, particularly the U.S. economy, which had fallen from a bubble economy, the impact of the Great Depression on the Japanese economy had been smaller because it had not fully recovered from the post–World War I recession in the first place. Since this impact was magnified by the lifting of the gold embargo without depreciating the yen, a mere reintroduction of the gold embargo was enough to mitigate the economic devastation.

It was still the pre-Keynes days, and no country paid too much attention to economic remedies through fiscal and monetary policies. An outflow of gold was regarded in those days as a flight of national wealth and, therefore, a national crisis. Since the tight fiscal policy taken to facilitate the lifting of the gold embargo by the preceding *Minseitō* government had been a point of contention between the *Seiyūkai* and *Minseitō* political parties, it was only natural for that policy to be reversed now that the *Seiyūkai* was in power.

Under these circumstances, while the rest of the world remained undecided on what to do, the Saitō cabinet promptly took domestic economic stimulus measures, as well as export offensives that took advantage of the weakened yen externally.

It was in 1930 that the Smoot-Hawley Tariff Act imposed high tariffs on imports in the United States and in 1932 that the British Commonwealth became an economic bloc as the result of the Ottawa Conference. Despite these developments, Japan's exports, which had been expected to suffer, actually grew steadily. In fact, only Japan enjoyed an expansion of exports, eating up the shares of other countries whose exports shrank dramatically. From the viewpoint of the British Commonwealth, the bloc economy was a consequence of the global recession, rather than its cause, launched as a countermeasure to Japan's export offensive.

Incidentally, it was around this time that Japan began to be criticized for social dumping—that is, conducting an export drive by taking advantage of cheap labor. Japan continued to be nagged about this until its living standards became on a par with those of Western countries.

Leith-Ross's visit to Japan and China was also a product of British pragmatism. The United Kingdom found it in its interest to expand Japan's exports to China by improving the bilateral relations between the two. Otherwise, Britons feared, inexpensive Japanese products that were boycotted by the China market might gush into the Commonwealth market.

Given the above, it is a little unwarranted to justify Japan's expansionistic conduct as a means of survival in the world bloc economy. It would be more accurate to attribute Japan's conduct to its resentment of the Western powers' monopoly of colonies while Japan had kept its doors closed for over two centuries. And this resentment in turn led to Japan's argument for the liberation of Asia and, subsequently, its rationalization of the challenge of "have-nots" to "haves" in partnership with Germany and Italy.

The destitution in Japan's rural areas, on the other hand, was a reality. One unique feature of Japan's economic comeback in those days was the delay in the recovery of commodity prices, particularly those of agricultural products, compared to the rebound of national product and national income.

Among the primary products whose prices declined across the board during the economic recession, the price drop for rice and silkworm cocoons, two of Japan's top products in those days, was particularly sharp. The price of rice was affected by the massive importation of cheap rice from Taiwan and Korea, where Japan's colonial management had begun to bear fruit at last. The demand for silkworm cocoons declined drastically due to the prolonged recession in the United States and the development of synthetic fabrics.

Even toward the end of the first decade of Shōwa (1935), prices of Japan's agricultural products remained 20 to 30 percent lower than before the Great Depression. Years of low prices for agricultural products naturally took a toll on Japan's rural areas. Average debt per agricultural household reached the level of ¥2,000 (about ¥6 million in today's value). In rural Japan, an endless chain of family suicides, selling of daughters into brothels, and increase of undernourished children resulted.

Young military officers, as platoon and company commanders, had to listen daily to the pitiful stories of the families of their soldiers who had been conscripted from agricultural and fishing villages. It was only natural and human for them to be indignant at social injustices and, in time, to become indoctrinated with thinking that demanded societal reform.

It would be proper to label the thinking of those young officers as "reformist thinking," as it was actually called in those days. During the Cold War days, only leftist, pro-socialist thinking was regarded as reformist and, therefore, any rightist thinking was strictly eliminated from the reformist camp. In today's world, however, now that Soviet Communism has already collapsed, this distinction is almost pointless. It seems more appropriate today to group the left and right together as reformist thinking as long as that thinking is dissatisfied with the existing order and is not afraid to use violence in order to overturn it. In those pre–World War II days, too, the truth was that the demarcation between the left and the right was only paper thin.

Reformist thinking in pre–World War II Japan can be sorted into four categories, according to the target of its antipathy: (1) the Pan-Asianism against the Western colonialism; (2) the Japan-German-Italy Axis Powers' resistance to the status quo orientation among the "haves" countries; (3) egalitarianism, heavily influenced by socialism, against exploitation by capitalists under the liberal economy; and (4) dictatorship by the reformist military as an antithesis to parliamentary democracy.

Genesis of Shōwa Reformist Thinking

Japan's Pan-Asianism had had a long history since the Meiji period. Its advocates included, for instance, Konoe Atsumaro's *Tōa Dōbunkai* (東亜同文会, East Asia Common Literary Culture Society) and many other groups. Ōkawa Shūmei (大川周明) was Pan-Asianism's chief ideologue in the first years of Shōwa. Many in Japan remember him as one of the accused who lost sanity during the International Military Tribunal for the Far East, slapping the head of Tōjō Hideki who was seated in front of him. This visual image is so strong that it has made people believe, even today, that everything about Ōkawa, including his thinking and personality, was destroyed by the defeat in the war.

In reality, by the time Ōkawa was admitted to Matsuzawa Mental Hospital for about six months since the episode with Tōjō, he had fully recovered. He completely regained his usual self as if "coming cleanly out of a hangover" and had begun preparations to return to the courtroom, though his charges were dropped. During this period and thereafter,

Ōkawa produced numerous written works, all of which were worthy products as a leading intellectual of the time and in which no irregularity in logic or written expression was detected.

Ōkawa was still a high school student at Kumamoto's Fifth High School when he set his sights on religion and entered Tokyo Imperial University to major in Indian philosophy. It was through a book on colonial administration in India that he happened to come across that he learned that there was no land in Asia that had not been ravaged nor a people that had not been enslaved by white men. Ōkawa writes in his autobiography that this realization transformed him from "a mere truth seeker, who almost became a hermit only ten years ago" into "a lecturer on the history of colonialism at Takushoku University and a chivalrous warrior who devotes his life to the restoration of Asia."

In 1915, a large-scale rebellion plot was disclosed in India, resulting in massive arrests and executions. Some of the plot's masterminds, including Rash Behari Bose, fled to Japan under false names. Ōkawa and his associates sheltered them. *Indo ni Okeru Kokumin Undō no Genjō oyobi Sono Yurai* (Status and Origin of Nationalism Movements in India), a book Ōkawa wrote around that time, still remains a masterpiece on the history of the colonization of India. His works were well respected in India. During his visit to Japan in 1957 (32nd Year of Shōwa), Jawaharlal Nehru, India's first prime minister, wanted to invite the author to India only to find Ōkawa on his death bed. Ōkawa passed away later that year.

In 1919 (8th Year of Taishō), Ōkawa co-founded *Yūzonsha* (猶存社), a nationalist organization, with his comrades in the Asian restoration movement. Their aim was to present a new ideal to the Japanese, whose morale had deteriorated since the victory in the Russo-Japanese War had left them temporarily without a national goal. The group's name represented its members' mettle, i.e. even if all the other grasses wither away, there still remain (猶存す) pine trees and chrysanthemum flowers in Japan.

Members of *Yūzonsha* who deeply resonated with the arguments of Kita Ikki suggested that they invite Kita to become a member. With a small amount of money in pocket that members had laboriously made by selling their books, Ōkawa departed for Shanghai to meet Kita.

It so happened that Kita had just completed drafting the seventh volume of *Nippon Kaizō Hōan Taikō* (「日本改造法案大綱」, An Outline Plan for the Reorganization of Japan). When Ōkawa visited him in Shanghai, Kita was struggling with the eighth and concluding volume on "The Powers of the State" to lay out concrete measures for the reorganization of Japan.

It was when Kita was taking a break from his writing, having finished the following sentence, that he met with Ōkawa:

> Independence movements in India might lead to the Second World War, just as those in Bosnia triggered the First World War. It is the mission that Japan is entrusted with by Heaven to assist these movements in India with the use of force.

Ōkawa and Kita found that they shared an identical ideology. Hitting it off immediately, the two talked deep into the night. Convinced that Ōkawa's visit was the will of Heaven, Kita returned to Japan with Ōkawa and started living on *Yūzonsha*'s property. In Volume 8 of *Nippon Kaizō Hōan Taikō*, Kita writes:

> Unarguably, the present situation is not just. Just like the situation in which England used India as a beast of burden for its interest is not just, in the same manner the condition in which Australia is blockaded from the 700 million people of neighbouring Japan and Asia is also not a just one. Just as the self-interest of the Tsar in trying to annex China and colonize Korea was unjust, so the present policy of the "Lenin" government is unjust if it is seeking to monopolize the wide and barren spaces of Siberia and ignoring the interests of other countries. . . . Within the country the proletariat is organizing itself institutionally and preparing to seek power. If they seek to emphasize that they will change this unjust condition with violence, then Japan, which internationally is a proletariat, should be allowed to strengthen its army and navy, which are the institutions within which power is concentrated, and then start a war to change the unjust line of division...[1]

---

1   Excerpts from Kita Ikki's "An Outline Plan for the Reorganization of Japan" translated by Brij Tanaka (http://www.personal.ashland.edu/~jmoser1/japan/kita.htm) with slight modification by current author.

Thus, Kita declares, "The Western socialists have a fundamental contradiction in their thinking when they criticize Japan's war as an aggression and militarism."[2]

Here, Kita's theory of domestic revolution to reorganize Japan based on "pure socialism" was merged with the Pan-Asianistic ideal of correcting international injustices imposed by the status quo powers even if doing so called for the use of force. A prototype of the reformist thinking of the Shōwa era was thus created. Although this prototype could be labeled "fascism," "militarism," "totalitarianism," or "advocacy of aggression," depending on where one stands, it provided young military officers of the time with the guiding principle for the Shōwa Restoration (昭和維新).

At *Yūzonsha* Ōkawa formed a close friendship with Kita but, due to some temporary conflict of opinions, Ōkawa left the group to found *Kōchisha*. Nevertheless, it is obvious that the two continued to revere and trust one another as exemplified in the letters quoted in *Kita Ikki-kun wo Omou* (Remembering My Friend Kita Ikki) that Ōkawa wrote in 1953.

Ōkawa's new group's name, *Kōchisha*, came from his peom *Sokuten Kōchi-ka* (To Act on Earth in Accordance with Heaven). This poem was heavily quoted in *Shōwa Ishin no Uta* (Song of Shōwa Restoration), a poem composed by Mikami Taku, the man who later assassinated Prime Minister Inukai Tsuyoshi. The underlined portions of Ōkawa's poem below were borrowed by Mikami:

1. Standing in the chaotic world, with eternal ideal in my mind, I become so indignant that my blood runs hot. Ah, what fills my heart is a high aim to carry out the rule of right in accordance with Heaven.

2. Although powerful families show off their privileges, they have no sincerity to be concerned about their country. Even such prominent omens as a major earthquake[3] or the white rainbow penetrating the sun would not wake them up and they simply continue to indulge themselves, never fearing Heaven.

---

2   Ibid.

3   The Great Kanto Earthquake struck Tokyo in 1923, one year before the founding of *Kōchisha*.

3. Zaibatsu boast of their wealth but they have no compassion for underprivileged people. Even though their starving brethren curse the country and wish for upheaval in vain, zaibatsu clans do not pay heed and indulge in sharpening their claws of greed.
4. The mission for the warriors who have united for justice is heavy. If we do not stand up with double-edged swords in our hand to save our country and people, what will become of the Country of the Rising Sun?

To see how these underlined portions were integrated in Mikami's *Shōwa Ishin no Uta*,

1. Waves are high on the Miluo River, while clouds scatter over the Wushan mountains. Standing in the chaotic world, I become so indignant that my blood runs hot.
2. Although powerful families show off their privileges, they have no sincerity to be concerned about their country. Financial combines boast of their wealth but they have no compassion for the country.
3. Alas, people may prosper but their country falls into ruin. Blinded people dance through their life. Peace and upheaval, rise and fall are like dreams and the world resembles one game of *Go*.
   . . . .
10. Stop citing the elegy of *Li Sao* because the days for singing and deploring the depraved state of our own country are over. Now is the time to wet our swords with the blood to cleanse and purify our country.

While Ōkawa's poem still contains a remnant of socialistic thinking as symbolized by his reference to "underprivileged people," Mikami's *Shōwa Ishin no Uta* shows no sign of the trait, perhaps reflecting the generational difference between the two.

Mikami was endowed with so much literary talent as to start his poem with "Waves are high on the Miluo River, while clouds scatter over the Wushan mountains," quoting *Li Sao*, arguably the most important work of poet Qu Yuan (屈原), of China's Warring States Period, who had committed ritual suicide as a form of protest against corruption of the era. It is perhaps this literary talent that made Mikami's poem a little more emotional than Ōkawa's. Another marked difference is Mikami's last verse, i.e. "Stop citing the elegy of *Li Sao* . . . Now is the time to wet our swords with the blood to cleanse and purify our country," which clearly reveals the writer's terroristic intention. Other than these differences, one may say that the two works were cut from the same cloth in spirit.

Genealogy of the Reformist Faction in the Military and the Shōwa Military Clique

Since Meiji days, the leading positions of the Imperial Japanese Navy had been monopolized by the Satsuma *han*-clique. The Imperial Japanese Army, on the other hand, had been mainly under the influence of the Satsuma- Chōshū *han*-clique. Taking advantage of Ōyama Iwao and Kawakami Sōroku, who believed in assigning the right person to the right job irrelevant to their origins despite their own Satsuma background, the Chōshū clan that centered around Yamagata Aritomo showed its competitive edge in the power struggle and, in time, dominated the army.

The origin of the Shōwa Military Clique can be sought in the resistance to the Chōshū clan. A group of young military officers, all graduates of the sixteenth class of the Imperial Japanese Army Academy stationed in Europe including Nagata Tetsuzan and Okamura Yasuji, concluded a Baden-Baden pact with the aim of overthrowing the Chōshū clan. This pact is considered as one of the origins of the Shōwa Military Clique.

After the death of Yamagata Aritomo, Tanaka Giichi rose to leadership of the Chōshū clan. Tanaka was later assisted by Ugaki Kazushige. Although Ugaki was originally from Okayama Prefecture, he became heir apparent of the main stream of the Imperial Japanese Army.

Although the anti-Chōshū clan faction, which centered around Uehara Yūsaku from Satsuma, had frequently challenged the Chōshū clan in the race for the top leadership positions in the army, it had been effectively restricted by Tanaka and Ugaki. Some members of this anti-Chōshū clan faction later formed the *Kōdōha* (Imperial Way Faction).

In this sense, the reformist Shōwa Military Clique was generally an anti-Ugaki group. What distinguished this rivalry from a mere factional feud was the ideological makeup of the contending factions in accordance with the current of the times. In terms of ideology, too, those who belonged to the radical segment of the Shōwa Military Clique were anti-Ugaki.

Ugaki was a military man of the era of the Taishō Democracy.

According to Itō Masanori's *Gunbatsu Kōbō-shi* (Rise and Fall of the Military Clique in Japan), Ugaki wished to settle the Manchurian/Mongolian issue within the framework of parliamentary democracy. Although Ugaki saw the necessity to reform political parties, he had no intention to deny the existence of political parties themselves. That was why army officers of the Imperial Way Faction, who rejected political parties, reviled Ugaki, saying he conspired with political parties to corrupt the Imperial Army. To them, to be "party-man (i.e., politician) like" was a derogatory thing, the party cabinet was their enemy, and, therefore, Ugaki was a villain who clandestinely consorted with the enemy. Some even called Ugaki a traitor.

Meanwhile, young officers of the reformist faction formed various private groups within the military, including the *Isseki-kai* which was formed by Ishihara Kanji in the same year and others in 1928, the *Ōshikai* by Navy Lieutenant Fujii Hitoshi, and the *Sakura-kai* formed by Hashimoto Kingorō and his associates in 1930. These groups kept contact with Ōkawa Shūmei and Kita Ikki, who occasionally joined the groups as comrades. Nishida Mitsugu, a graduate of the Imperial Japanese Army Academy, attempted to expand the influence of the reformist faction that had initially been under Ōkawa's influence but which later came to be led by Kita.

When Inukai Tsuyoshi formed his cabinet in 1931 (6th Year of Shōwa), Governor-General of Korea Ugaki, a long-time acquaintance of Inukai's, sent a letter to Inukai to offer some advice on the selection of minister of war. It was the gravest blunder of Ugaki's life that he did not specifically advise Inukai not to choose Araki Sadao or Masaki Jinzaburō, both of whom had been leading figures in the Imperial Way Faction.

Because Inukai had no idea about the seriousness of the intra-military feud, he appointed Araki to war minister, thinking that it would be within a normal personnel change and, besides, he had heard that Araki was well respected by young officers. This appointment was tantamount to letting the leader of the faction that had called Ugaki a traitor grab the power of the Ministry of War.

As soon as Araki assumed the post, he demoted members of the Ugaki faction to sinecure jobs and appointed members of the Imperial Way Faction to all the key positions in the ministry. Nevertheless, nobody found fault with Araki's appointments and, in fact, his reformist ideas, when delivered with his eloquence, were met with applause. Apparently, the season for party politics had already passed and the times called for domination by the reformists. It was also this trend of the times that ended the party politics in Japan with the passing of Inukai or even earlier, in spite of the *Seiyūkai* winning 300 seats in the general election.

In one of his admonitory lectures, Araki said,

> Young officers' conduct these days has created controversy, but, in my judgment, they were like revolutionaries at the time of the Meiji Restoration. While their ranks may be low, their integrity is high and they are full of burning patriotism. In contrast, senior officers nowadays are quite like chief retainers of a feudal lord in olden days who were concerned only about their *han*'s welfare. We must urgently address this problem and solidify the unity of our entire forces.

This was like encouraging young officers to defy senior officers and ignore the military rule of unconditionally obeying orders. As a result of Araki's encouragement, young captains and first lieutenants frequently began to visit the office of the war minister brazenly. At New Year, a young officer visited Araki's residence. When this junior officer held out his sake cup to Araki, saying, "Hey, Arai, how about a drink?" the war minister accepted the offer, saying, "All right, all right," instead of reprimanding the young officer for disrespect. It was such an unpleasant sight that some people left the gathering early out of disgust.

It was only natural, however, that Araki was not able to maintain the favor of young officers indefinitely only with this kind of blandishment. In no time, young officers began to demand that Araki boldly carry out reforms. When it came to an armed revolt, however, Araki had no other choice than to restrain its advocates. Seeing the change of his attitude, young officers also changed their attitudes toward Araki, saying, "Araki is no good. He's only talk." This disillusionment with Araki led those young military officers to take radical and insubordinate actions.

Control Faction vs. Imperial Way Faction

The *Tōseiha* (Control Faction) was not the name its members gave themselves. It was the members of the *Kōdōha* who started to refer categorically to those who antagonized them as *Tōseiha*. Although the two factions shared a goal of accomplishing reforms, the Control Faction, which centered around Nagata Tetsuzan (永野鉄山) and Tōjō Hideki, envisioned reform through cabinet meetings with the war minister playing the central role, backed up by perfectly controlled military forces. The Imperial Way Faction, on the other hand, advocated a coup d'état by a few young officers.

While the original action plan of the Control Faction had also been for an armed revolution, reflecting the aspirations of young officers, Nagata and Tōjō fully utilized their bureaucratic regulatory capabilities to remake the plan into a "measure to carry out innovation of the country while preserving the current constitutional regime" through a planning meeting that lasted dozens of days.

Because the reform of a country encompasses all policy areas, it cannot be done by professional warriors alone. Thus, the Control Faction members collaborated with reformist bureaucrats of various government ministries to formulate their own policies. These reformist bureaucrats included, among others, Kishi Nobusuke (岸信介), who later became Japan's 56th prime minister, and Wada Hiroo, the 4th Minister for Agriculture after World War II.

In contrast to the young officers of the Imperial Way Faction who had not formulated a concrete post–coup d'état plan, the Control Faction was able to work out a concrete vision for an innovative centralized regime that would enable Japan to depart from party politics, thanks to contributions from civilian bureaucrats, paving the way for the formation of Tōjō Hideki's wartime cabinet.

Although Araki remained in the cabinet even after the assassination of Inukai, backed up by the Imperial Way Faction, he had to resign due to illness in January 1934. Araki was succeeded by Hayashi Senjūrō, who had been perceived as a hardliner due to his nickname as the "cross-border general." Hayashi had obtained the nickname when, as commander in chief of the Japanese Korean Army at the time of the Manchurian Incident, he had ordered his troops to cross the Yalu River without authorization of the central government. It was natural for the Imperial Way Faction officers to expect him to be sympathetic to their cause.

Having been secretly displeased with the *Kōdōha*'s faction-based moves, however, Hayashi took two steps. As his first act as war minister, he appointed Nagata as director-general of the Bureau of Military Affairs. Then, in July 1935, Hayashi requested General Masaki Jin'ichirō to step down as Inspector General of Military Education as a step toward a cleanout of *Kōdōha* personnel. Believing his resignation would ruin the Imperial Way Faction, Masaki attempted a frontal resistance to Hayashi's request—only to be dismissed. Details of how Hayashi accomplished this were unknown, but some believed he used an imperial edict. Hayashi appointed Watanabe Jōtarō as Masaki's successor. Watanabe was an orthodox military man critical of the attack on the theory of the Emperor as an organ of government and the Declaration of Clarification of the National Polity. At his inaugural press conference, Watanabe declared that it was sufficient for the military to concentrate on military affairs. This made him a target of the Imperial Way Faction's blazing hatred. At the February 26 Incident, Watanabe became the first victim to be gunned down by rebel forces.

No sooner had Masaki been dismissed than an incendiary leaflet denouncing Hayashi and Nagata was circulated in various places. The leaflet read:

> Hayashi is a puppet of Nagata. Ah, those with eyes must see, while those with ears should listen. Hayashi and Nagata are plotting to throw the Imperial Army into confusion, expose the state to humiliation from foreign powers, and, thereby, satisfy their brutal hearts by benefitting their own faction.

Reading this leaflet, which was rumored to have been authored by Nishida Mitsugu, Lieutenant Colonel Aizawa Saburō departed Fukuyama City for the war ministry in Tokyo. There he slaughtered Nagata in his office of the Bureau of Military Affairs around noon on August 12.

Many lamented Nagata's untimely death. He was senior to Tōjō and, thus, it can be said that it was the death of Nagata that enabled Tōjō to become war minister and, subsequently, prime minister. Nagata was often said to be a considerably larger scale person than Tōjō. Had Nagata survived and taken leadership of the military, it is not hard to imagine that Japan's fate would have been quite different.

Tōjō himself lamented Nagata's death more than anyone else. It was a known fact that Tōjō never failed to donate a part of the Imperial grant that he received each yearend as a state minister to the bereaved family of Nagata.

Spring Snow—February 26 Incident

Spring snow always evokes special memories within the Japanese.

It was on a morning of heavy snow on March 3, 1860, on the lunar calendar that *Tairō* Ii Naosuke was assassinated by *rōnin* samurai of the Mito *han* outside the Sakuradamon gate of Edo Castle. It was also snowing heavily on the morning of the February 26 Incident in 1936. Just as the shogunate had collapsed within eight years of the Sakuradamon Incident, so did the Empire of Japan collapse within nine years of the February 26 Incident. The chill of a snowy breeze sends a shudder as an omen of collapse of a regime.

On the morning of February 26, 1936, officers and some 1,500 soldiers, mostly from the First and Third Infantry Regiments of the First Division, trudged through the heavy snow that had started the previous night to raid the residences of selected senior statesmen. During this raid, Home Minister Saitō Makoto, Finance Minister Takahashi Korekiyo, and Inspector General of Military Education Watanabe Jōtarō were shot to death; Grand Chamberlain Suzuki Kantarō was seriously injured; and the brother-in-law of Prime Minister Okada Keisuke, who was mistaken for Okada, was shot to death. The rebel force, however, failed to carry out its mission as far as Makino Nobuaki and Saionji Kinmochi were concerned.

All the senior statesmen who were targeted for assassination were regarded as moderates and advocates of international cooperation. These actions reveal careful calculations behind the rebel's plans.

After the raids, the rebel forces seized the prime minister's official residence and the National Police Headquarters. From these locations they announced statements of purpose and issued a variety of demands. Included in their demands were the immediate arrest of Ugaki and Saionji, the appointment of Araki Sadao as commander in chief of the Kanto Army, and the accomplishment of the Shōwa Restoration by the hand of the war minister (presumed to mean Masaki Jin'ichirō). It was obvious to anyone's eyes that this coup d'état was carried out by affiliates of the Imperial Way Faction.

While Ishihara Kanji, then the director of operations at the Imperial Japanese Army General Staff Office, insisted on taking strong action against the rebels, the war ministry decided to make them return quietly to their original duties.

In the afternoon of February 26, a notice was announced in the name of the war minister. This appeasing statement included such assurances as:

1. The purpose of your actions is on its way to be reported to His Majesty.
2. We recognize that your motives are based on a sincere desire to clarify the national polity.

With this announcement, Masaki attempted to persuade the rebels to abort the coup. While some among the rebels were impressed enough by this announcement that they started talking about returning to their own units, the encouragement from Kita and Nishida, who had been guiding the rebels from the outside by assuring them that they could accomplish their goals if they stayed put, was more convincing. Thus officers and soldiers decided to reject Masaki's persuasion.

The advertising balloon showing the statement of "Imperial command was surrendered"

At last Masaki gave up on swaying the rebels. Believing that issuing an Imperial edict would be the only way to dissolve the rebel forces, War Minister Kawashima Yoshiyuki proceeded to the Imperial Palace.

It was during Kawashima's visit to the Imperial Palace that Emperor Shōwa, as he was authorizing the Imperial Edict, stated, "We ourselves may lead the Imperial Guard to suppress the rebels."[4] In this way the emperor showed his impatience with the half-hearted measures.

Throughout the previous six centuries since the Kemmu Restoration (1333–36),

---

4   Emperor refers to himself in the first person plural form.

it had been extremely rare for the emperor to show such strong initiative. One may wonder how young Emperor Shōwa, who was only in his mid-thirties at that time, could have such unshakable insight and conviction. Perhaps it was partially due to his deep understanding and sympathy with British politics and culture nurtured during his formative years (1901–28, the latter being when his enthronement took place on his 27th birthday) under the influence of the Anglo-Japanese Alliance (1902-1922) as well as his tour, as Crown Prince, of Europe in 1921. It could have been the common sense that Emperor Shōwa had attained through these experiences that convinced him firmly that what the rebels were doing was an unforgiveable challenge to him and to the State.

When it came to that, there was nothing more that the rebels or the army generals who were sympathetic with them could do. After making the soldiers return to their own units, the rebel officers reported to the war minister's residence to surrender. It was two o'clock in the afternoon of March 29.

At the Imperial Army Court Martial convened at three o'clock, seventeen junior officers who played central roles in the coup, as well as Kita Ikki and Nishida Mitsugu, were sentenced to death. Masaki and other sympathizers were acquitted.

An Important Turning Point in the History of Shōwa

The Okada cabinet stepped down on March 9, a few days after the February 26 Incident. Many elder statesmen and senior government officials recommended Konoe Fumimaro (近衛文麿), president of the House of Peers and the prime-minister hopeful among the peers, to succeed Okada. When Konoe firmly declined the nomination, however, consensus was reached that the next prime minister should be Foreign Minister Hirota Kōki.

Hirota initially declared his intention to respect parliamentary government. But Hirota's position met an immediate setback due to the military's resistance.

In return for the appointment of Terauchi Hisaichi as war minister, the military made several demands concerning Hirota cabinet's policies as well as other appointments. In terms of policies, the military demanded implementation of the Declaration of Clarification of the National Polity—that is, the abolishment of liberal democratic thinking and the absolutization of the supreme authority of the emperor. In terms of personnel, the military aimed to eliminate all those who showed liberal democratic inclinations.

The military's interference was blatant and specific. For instance, the military opposed the appointments of Yoshida Shigeru as foreign minister and Shimomura Hiroshi as colonial affairs minister on the grounds that the former was the son-in-law of Makino Nobuaki, who had been a target for assassination during the February 26 Incident, and the latter had been a reporter of the daily *Asahi Shimbun*, another target of the rebels. In other words, the military claimed that these appointments constituted gross neglect of the intention of the military.

There was, therefore, no sign of repentance for the February 26 Incident on the part of the military. It was as if the military was saying that while the rebels have failed to accomplish what they had set out to do, their ideals were righteous and reflected the collective will of the military. To be sure, the only difference between the *Tōseiha* and the opposing *Kōdōha* was the methodology. And now, in the wake of the *Kōdōha*'s abortive coup attempt, the *Tōseiha* came to the fore with the full intention of getting its way, true to its declaration, via the war minister in all state affairs.

Hirota, at this point, had the option to bow out of the imperial appointment, citing interference from the military as the reason. But Hirota did not have a particular political conviction that he would stand behind at any cost. He was, instead, a man of compromise who ended up following what others around him decided. He negotiated with the military to strike a compromise and, when forming his cabinet, accepted all the demands of the military except that for a reduction in the number of cabinet members representing political parties.

Given that the Hirota cabinet assumed office immediately after the February 26 Incident, the purging of disloyal elements from the military was naturally one of the cabinet's major tasks. The purge, however, took the form of a complete victory of the *Tōseiha* over the *Kōdōha* in the intra-military feud, instead of an investigation into the military's involvement in politics. Moreover, the military took advantage of this opportunity to make a big gain in the name of the military purge: reinstatement of the system by which only active-duty army or navy officers could serve in the cabinet posts of war minister or navy minister. When War Minister Terauchi stressed that only the reinstatement of the said system would allow the military to pursue the purge without fear of the imminent comeback of retired generals, other members of the cabinet granted his request without much debate.

Restriction of the autonomy of military command had been a fruit of laborious efforts on the part of party government in Japan. Those efforts had started with the abolishment of the system by which only active-duty army or navy officers could serve in the cabinet posts of war minister or navy minister during the early-Taishō constitutional protection movement and culminated in Prime Minister Hara Takashi, a civilian, who concurrently served as navy minister in 1921, albeit provisionary. What Hirota did was to nullify all of those efforts.

The decision by Hirota had an immediate and decisive effect in the ensuing year when Ugaki received an Imperial mandate to form a new cabinet to succeed the Hirota cabinet.

Although Ugaki had been determined to form his cabinet at any cost, fully aware of the unwillingness of the Imperial Japanese Army to cooperate, he was eventually unable to appoint a war minister. Had it not been for reinstatement of the controversial system only a few months earlier, Ugaki himself could have served concurrently as war minister.

Had Ugaki been prime minister, the Marco Polo Bridge Incident in the summer of 1937 would probably not have developed automatically into a major war with China. The history of Shōwa Japan underwent a number of decisive turning points, and the Hirota cabinet's decision to reinstate the system by which only active-duty army or navy officers could serve in the cabinet posts of war minister or navy minister was definitely one of them.

CHAPTER
5

The Looming Shadow of War

—Drastic Changes in Asia and Europe, 1935 and 1936—

Did a Fascist Regime Really Exist In Japan?

The origin of the term "fascism" is *Fasci italiani di combattimento* (Italian League of Combat) founded by Benito Mussolini in 1919 and renamed *Partito Nazionale Fascista* in 1921.

Fascism is a form of dictatorship. While human history has been full of dictatorship, fascism in the 20th century was different from other previous forms of dictatorship. Fascism derived from people's desire for a powerful, centralized government born out of their disillusionment with parliamentary democracy. It is, therefore, regarded as a totally opposite polity to democracy.

Since the Russian Revolution in 1917, the desire for dictatorship followed two channels: (1) the international communist movement under the banner of proletarian dictatorship and (2) state socialism movements based on individual ethnic groups and individual states as an antithesis to the first channel. It was the latter of the two that came to be called fascism.

Middle-class people in many countries were terrified by communism, which advocated an armed revolution based on class hatred. Their fear was proven by the atrocious tragedies that the middle class had to experience in post-revolution Soviet Union and China and, more recently, in Pol Pot–controlled Cambodia.

It is often said that "the masses are wise but unwise, unwise but wise." This means that while people may appear to know nothing, they actually do have a grasp of the big picture of politics and the true nature of man. People's fear of communism, thus, proves that the masses saw through into something terribly inhumane contained in this ideology.

Sure enough, it was only in Russia, which had been in a state of utmost confusion after the defeat in World War I, that communists succeeded in taking over the government thanks to the military genius of Leon Trotsky. In all the other European countries where people were able to express their views, communists failed to accomplish similar success.

Fascism, in contrast, captured the hearts of people who had been experiencing post–World War I social instabilities. Fascist governments were born not only in Italy but also in Hungary, Bulgaria, and Spain.

It is, however, highly doubtful whether Japan's political system in the 1930s and 1940s could be defined as a fascist regime.

Certainly, it is beyond doubt that the general inclination of the government as well as the people was in favor of anti-party politics, nationalism, statism, and anti-communism. In that sense, it can be said that all of Japanese society was fascist.

The "unity of the whole nation" regime, or statism, is not a uniquely Japanese phenomenon; it can arise more or less in any country on a war footing. What was unique in Japan's case was that this so-called national emergency regime lasted more than a decade after the Manchurian Incident, and left a strong impression in people's minds as if it had been an institutionalized, permanent system.

In terms of a political institution, however, Japan's national emergency regime was totally different from fascist regimes in Europe. Even during the war, the Diet continued to operate and criticism of the government was formally heard. The national emergency regime was not at all a form of one-party rule by a fascist party or a militaristic party. Even the National Mobilization Law (国家総動員法) of 1934 was a provisional measure in a time of national emergency, and the government explicitly explained that the law was completely different from Nazi Germany's Enabling Act of 1933.

While Prime Minister Tōjō Hideki may appear to have enjoyed a monopoly of power when he served concurrently as ministers of foreign affairs, home, war, education, and munitions as well as Chief of the Imperial Japanese Army General Staff in the 1940s, he was easily dismissed in 1944 by the decision of elder statesmen.

To be sure, the power of the military in Japan in those days was abnormally greater than in other democratic countries because of the system by which only active-duty army or navy officers could serve in the cabinet posts of war minister or navy minister. But it should be recalled that it was under exactly the same system that Japan had earlier enjoyed the Taishō Democracy and the cooperative diplomacy of Shidehara Kijūrō. During those years, Japan was no different in substance from other democratic countries.

The autonomy of the military command was buried during the Taishō Democracy. Ironically, it was dug out by parliamentary democracy and used as a tool for inter-party feuds.

Dazzling Rise of Nazi Germany

Compared to the complicated history behind the rise of militarism in Japan, the background of the rise of Nazism in Germany was simple and straightforward.

First, the Treaty of Versailles at the end of World War I was unreasonably harsh on Germany, even though the war had been fought between countries with respective imperialistic motives in which there was no right or wrong. In this sense, it was unjust for the victorious Allied Powers to demand territories and reparations from Germany simply because they had won the war. Thus it was only natural for a movement to emerge in Germany that opposed the international regime created by the treaty and demanded the return of territories that were separated from mainland Germany.

Second, the full effect of the Great Depression kicked in. In spite of the overwhelming burden of reparation payment, the German economy finally managed to attain stable growth around 1923. The six years from this point until the Great Depression in 1929 were the good old days of the Weimar Republic for Germany. During this period, parliamentary democracy was protected by the moderate centralists, despite strong pressures from both the rightists and the leftists.

It was only due to the infusion of American capital that Germany was somehow able to manage its economy in spite of the loss of its capital reserves during the war and then under the heavy burden of reparation. But the Great Depression of 1929 forced American capital to withdraw from Germany.

To be sure, the atrocious nature of the Nazi leaders, including Hitler, was beyond the comprehension of West European intellectuals. The Treaty of Versailles and the Great Depression alone, however, would inevitably have made Germany swing far right toward military dictatorship had it not been for the Nazis.

The Nazi Party became the leading party in 1932, in the midst of the Manchurian Incident in East Asia. As soon as Adolf Hitler was appointed as chancellor in January 1933, he transformed the Weimar Republic into the Third Reich, a single-party dictatorship. This was possible only under the crisis during the Great Depression.

The Japanese military admired the Nazis to the extent that the Japanese Ambassador to Germany Obata Yūkichi (1931–32) remarked as follows:

> The Japanese military officers blindly believe in whatever Nazis say. Even without this recent tendency, the Japanese military tends to be partial to anything German. Further increase of Germanophiles would be harmful for Japan. . . . I wish to see more military officers of the non-German club appointed as military attachés and aides here at the Japanese embassy.

Since the Meiji Restoration, Germany had been one of the two leading civilizations, along with the United Kingdom, that Japan had wished to emulate. Although the Meiji government at first looked to France for its army system, the German Empire's power began to eclipse France after the Franco-Prussian War in 1870, two years after the Meiji Restoration. After Major Jakob Meckel arrived in Japan as an advisor to the Japanese government in 1885 under the direct recommendation of Kaiser Wilhelm II, the Imperial Japanese Army began to take on a German army style completely.

In subsequent years, it became a fast track to success in the Imperial

Army for the elite graduates of the Army War College to be sent to Germany to study or to serve as military attachés in the Japanese embassy. The Imperial Japanese Army was, on all accounts, pro-Germany.

Japan's admiration of German culture was not confined to the military. In fact, the whole range of German cultural heritages, including its law, philosophy, literature, medicine, science and technology, was deeply admired in Japan. And, moreover, it was not only in Japan but also throughout pre-World War I Europe that Germany was viewed as a paragon of culture. This was in contrast to Britain, which was thought to be representing civilization.

Konoe Fumimaro, who later became prime minister of Japan, toured around Europe in the wake of World War I. When he was told of the German military's atrocities during the war, he lamented, "I cannot help but wonder how Germany, home of such tremendous culture and the fatherland of Immanuel Kant and Johann Wolfgang von Goethe, could have committed such acts of barbarity."

Incidentally, it is a customary propaganda practice for warring parties to mutually denounce their adversary's atrocities during a war. When a war ends, though, only the conduct of the defeated remain unforgotten and are criticized.

Barbaric acts by soldiers during a war have nothing to do with the culture of their homeland. During and immediately after a war, however, the contrast between the two often tends to be emphasized. In her book, *The Chrysanthemum and the Sword*, American sociologist Ruth Benedict, for instance, contrasted the artistic sensitivity of the Japanese in the horticulture of exquisite chrysanthemums with their brutality as represented by the sword. This tendency to compare culture and wartime barbarism is to be interpreted as an aftereffect of a modern, all-out war that calls for total denial of the enemy as evil.

To the Japanese, who had long admired German culture, the rise of the Nazis, which coincided with the Great Depression and disillusionment with party politics in Japan, was all the more dazzling.

Indeed, the German economy under the Nazis was showing a remarkable recovery. Under the strong leadership of the Nazis' single-party dictatorship, national-level megaprojects were implemented, including construction of roads and airfields, one after another. The practice of mandatory labor at these projects as well as the restoration of conscription helped decrease the number of the unemployed drastically from over 6 million in early 1933 to almost zero on the eve of World War II.

Private associations among military officers, who had lamented economic impoverishment in rural areas and corrupted party politics, were all pro-Nazi.

Foundation of the German-Japan Alliance: Nothing but Psychological

The Japanese admiration of anything German notwithstanding, an alliance between Japan and Germany had no logic or real benefit because the two countries were geographically too far apart from one another. What triggered the alliance was the emergence of a communist Soviet Union in between the two countries. And the Comintern, which guided communist movements worldwide, adopted an anti-fascism strategy, targeting, among others, Japan and Germany during the seventh convention in Moscow in the summer of 1935 (10th Year of Shōwa).

It was soon after this Comintern convention that Joachim von Ribbentrop, who later became foreign minister of Nazi Germany, approached Major General Ōshima Hiroshi, military attaché to the Japanese embassy in Berlin, with a proposal for German-Japanese partnership to counter the threat of international communism.

On the German-Japanese relations between the time of the German-Japanese Anti-Communist Pact (1936) and the Tripartite Pact (1940), one can learn a lot from German journalist Theo Sommer's monumental work, *Deutschland und Japan zwischen den Machten 1935–1940* (Germany and Japan between the Powers, 1935–1940)[5].

According to Sommer, Ribbentrop, foreign policy advisor to Hitler in those days, had his own private office from which he carried out diplomacy over the head of the German foreign ministry. Sommer believed

---

5   Theo Sommer. *Deutschland und Japan zwischen den Machten 1935–1940* (Tubingen: Mohr, 1962).

that Ribbentrop's hunger for personal fame was very much behind his approach to Ōshima.

It was with this proposal that the Imperial Japanese Army General Staff Office began to act arbitrarily not only in the realm of military command but also in diplomacy.

Stationed in Germany for the second time, Ōshima was fluent in German and one of the most prominent pro-German officers in the Imperial Army. He was later appointed as Japanese ambassador to Germany, and he actively promoted the Tripartite Pact among Japan, Germany, and Italy.

This negotiation between Ribbentrop and Ōshima was conducted via the Imperial Japanese Army General Staff Office without knowledge of the foreign ministries of the two countries.

And when this negotiation finally came to the attention of the Japanese government, the signing of this partnership treaty was inevitable. This was so partly because it was strongly requested by the Imperial Army. But more importantly, the threat of Soviet communism had already become imminent because the seventh Comintern's anti-fascist resolution in the summer of 1935 was followed by the announcement of the Soviet-Outer Mongolia Mutual Assistance Treaty the following April.

Arita Hachirō, who became the new foreign minister in the Hirota Kōki cabinet, believed that "an agreement that is not too conspicuous" would be permissible if it would "mitigate the Japanese people's sense of isolation." No other member of the cabinet voiced a protest to this opinion.

Within the foreign ministry, Tōgō Shigenori, then Director-General of European and American Affairs, staunchly opposed the partnership in consideration of adverse effects on Japan's relations with Britain and the United States. It was only on the condition that the Imperial Army would agree to a parallel political agreement with Britain that the foreign ministry finally approved the German-Japan partnership.

In fact, that was exactly what Hitler wished for at that time. When Ribbentrop was departing for London in August 1936 as the newly appointed ambassador to Britain, Hitler was reported to have said, "I beg you to make Britain participate in the Anti-Communist Pact. This is my greatest wish." Revealed here was the true structure of international relations in the period before the eruption of World War II.

From the viewpoint of the international politics at that time, the benefit for Germany from an alliance with Japan was negligible. It was an alliance with Britain that Germany really sought. What was most important for Japan too was an alliance with Britain, the most influential power in the Far East; compared with this, an alliance with Germany was almost meaningless. It would be absurd beyond a doubt for both countries to form an alliance with the other so as to antagonize the powerful Britain. Yet this is what happened. While Hitler allowed his apprentice Ribbentrop to have his way, Hitler was fully aware of the importance of Britain. And so was Tōgō, it appears.

If there was any meaning at all to the German-Japan pact for Japan, it would have been what Arita characterized as "mitigation of the Japanese sense of isolation." Even after the signing of the Tripartite Pact, the most important issue for Hitler was still to avoid a war with the United States. When he declared war on the United States after Japan's attack on Pearl Harbor, it was believed that he aimed to inspire German morale in the midst of the predicament on the Eastern Front. The true reason behind Hitler's declaration of war against the United States is a mystery of history, and there have been a number of interpretations. If this "inspiration effect" was indeed a major reason, it must be said that it was superficial psychological factors that were at the foundation of the German-Japan alliance and, as such, the alliance lacked any real substance or strategic need.

The pact was the result of arbitrary actions on the part of Ribbentrop and the Imperial Japanese Army General Staff Office not properly thought-out or vetted until too late. The pact's initial fault—that is, lack of a realistic calculation of international politics—remained with it until the very end.

Tōgō, for his part, writes in his *Jidai no Ichimen* that during the International Military Tribunal for the Far East, he complained that there was nothing wrong to be anti-communist in itself because that stance shared the same ideology with Harry Truman, U.S. president at the time the trials were being held, vis-à-vis the Soviet threat. Had Britain joined the Japan-Germany anti-communist pact, as Tōgō had strongly hoped for, it could have become a purely anti-Comintern agreement. Subsequent developments, however, made the German-Japan pact a more anti-West European alliance instead.

The German-Japan anti-communist pact had an immediate adverse effect on Japan's relations with the Soviet Union. The signing of the bilateral fishery pact that had already been agreed to by the two governments was postponed indefinitely. While Tōgō attempted to reason with the Soviets that the anti-Comintern pact must not affect Japan–Soviet Union relations because the Soviet Union itself had declared that it had nothing to do with the Comintern, it was obvious to anyone that this pact was in substance anti–Soviet Union. As a matter of fact, an auxiliary secret agreement was explicitly targeted at the Soviet Union.

Thus, ever since this pre–World War II time, Japan and the Soviet Union entered a long period of cold relations that lasted throughout the postwar Cold War days.

As if to respond to the Comintern's call for an anti-fascist popular front in 1935, the Popular Front government was established in Spain in February 1936. General Francisco Franco, who had been stationed in Morocco, a Spanish colony in those days, advanced his troops to mainland Spain against the Popular Front government in July. Germany and Italy immediately recognized Franco's regime and offered him military assistance. Thus emerged a partnership among the fascist regimes in Europe.

It was in November in the same year that Japan signed the anti-communist pact with Germany. Italy joined in 1937.

Following Japan, Germany withdrew from the League of Nations and the London Naval Treaty in 1933. Italy, whose annexation of Ethiopia had been criticized internationally, also withdrew from the League of Nations after signing the anti-communist pact in 1937. In this way, a Japan-Germany-Italy fascist alliance emerged step-by-step internationally.

At that time the Japanese people were still enjoying the last peace in the pre–World War II days. The Hirota cabinet had no intention of doing anything that would jeopardize relations with Britain and the United States. And Foreign Minister Arita had already approved the pact with Germany as long as it remained inconspicuous. It was under these circumstances that Japan strayed away from the mainstream of the world and became a member of a group of outsiders.

Pursuit of the Same Glory as Manchukuo

The Tanggu Truce, which effectively demarcated the Manchurian border, brought momentary peace to East Asia.

This truce, however, also created an area along the southern border of Manchukuo that was beyond the control of the Chinese military. In China where the country was divided among rivaling warlords, only military power was able to maintain public order in those days. A vacuum of military power, therefore, automatically meant an administrative and political vacuum.

Japanese diplomat Uemura Shin'ichi wrote about the situation in China in those days:

> The Beiping-Tianjing region was crowded with disappointed political aspirants and petty warlords, who continued their respective maneuvers in hopes of a chance. These people were crafty with hands fully equipped with traditional Chinese scheming skills. It is no wonder that simple and naïve Japanese military officers became captivated by these people's dubious enticement. Besides, the Japanese military officers in those days were hungry for fame. Particularly those who failed to make a name for themselves during the Manchurian Incident were anxious to boost their stature in the region.

Allow me to quote a story from Itō Masanori's *Gunbatsu Kōbōshi* again in order to capture the spirit of a Japanese military man in those days.

In the fall of 1937, Ishihara Kanji, the then director of the warfare guidance division of the Ministry of War, repeatedly issued orders to contain the spread of the war. Ishihara issued these orders in an attempt to restrict the army's advance toward Inner Mongolia and North China even after the founding of Manchukuo. But Ishihara's orders fell on deaf ears. After several abortive attempts at stopping the spread of the war, Ishihara went to Changchun (Hsinking, the capital of Manchukuo) himself, where he gave instructions directly to his former subordinates. When Ishihara finished talking, Mutō Akira, one of the army officers present, asked Ishihara if he really meant what he said. Appalled, Ishihara reprimanded Mutō, explaining the policy of the central command and his view on the grand strategy. In response, Mutō said, "We have emulated what you did at the time of the Manchurian Incident. We naturally deserve to be commended, and we never imagined that we would be reprimanded by you." To this, Ishihara was at a loss for words.

Mutō was an outstanding officer on whom Ishihara had pinned great hopes. At the time of the February 26 Incident, Mutō, along with Ishihara, insisted on the firm suppression of the rebels, which earned him a reputation as an army officer worth noting. At the time of the negotiation with the United States in 1941, Mutō, as director of the Military Affairs Bureau of the Ministry of War, devoted everything he had to achieve a compromise between the two countries.

In the process that ended in the Second Sino-Japanese War in 1937, however, Mutō remained consistently aggressive and expansionist against Ishihara's wishes. The very fact that even a person of Mutō's caliber was anxious to spread the war showed that the general trend within the military had already become uncontrollable.

On this situation, Itō lamented, saying,

> When someone who had once made a name for himself by breaking regulations and then tried to impose regulations on others, people would not listen. The bad habit of junior officers being defiant to seniors cannot be eliminated unless the offenders are punished severely as a warning. One cannot even dream of correcting the habit when the offenders are promoted to higher ranks.

The above two testimonies are sufficient to explain the atmosphere and background of those times.

June of 1935 witnessed the signings of the He-Umezu Agreement and the Chin-Doihara Agreement. In accordance with these agreements, the areas under control of the Japanese military expanded substantially in the direction of North China and Chahar.

The Imperial Army continued to make relentless tough demands on local authorities to suppress the anti-Japan movement by eliminating the influence of the Kuomintang government in Nanjing, but local authorities would not respond to these demands to the satisfaction of the Japanese side out of consideration of the Nanjing government's intention as well as the nationalism of the Chinese people. Faced with this situation, Major General Doihara Kenji established an East Hebei Autonomous Council in November 1935. The council was an attempt to convert the demilitarized zone that had been established by the Tanggu Truce in eastern Hebei into an autonomous region independent of the Kuomintang government. At this point, the Kuomintang government also made a political compromise, launching a Hebei-Chahar Political Council in an attempt to establish a buffer regime in these two provinces that were somewhat distanced from the Nanjing government.

The Dream of Pro-Japan Wang Jinwei

Chiang Kai-shek remained faithful to his policy of "domestic pacification first before expelling foreign evils" by focusing on eliminating the communist forces, and repeatedly making compromises, enduring patiently and prudently. Meanwhile, foreign policy toward Japan was entrusted to Wang Jinwei, premier of the Nanjing government.

Wang belonged to the generation of Asians who were deeply impressed by the passion of the Japanese nation during the days of the Russo-Japanese War. These people were pro-Japanese.

Despite his trading family background, Wang's father was a town scholar, a devout believer of Yangmingism, a devotee of Lu You's poems, and a follower of Tao Yuanming's life. He also composed poems himself. When Wang Jinwei came home from calligraphy class in the evening, his father made him repeat the practice and recite the introductory work of Yangmingism. This ritual was repeated every day without fail until the death of Wang's father from cholera when Wang was fourteen years old.

Behind Wang's daring attempt to assassinate dignitaries in Beijing in later days, which could have cost him his own life, must have been Yangmingism's teaching of the inseparability of knowledge and practice. After becoming a top leader of the Kuomintang, Wang often resigned his post nonchalantly and went overseas whenever he became weary of internal feuding. This too could have been the influence of Tao Yuanming.

Wang also left a number of splendid poems of his own. His knowledge of the Chinese classics was so profound that it would be difficult for the Japanese to comprehend his highly refined poems.

Wang Jingwei

One example is a poem that Wang composed in a Beijing prison after an abortive attempt to assassinate the then prince regent Chun. As the Chinese poem's fixed form calls for, the first half of this poem is extravagant and ornate. Although this first half is probably where the literary value of the poem lies, it is also the portion that is extremely difficult to understand. The latter half of the poem showed Wang's resolve to fight and die for his country:

> Singing patriotism in Beijing, I calmly accepted imprisonment
> When a boy draws his sword and accomplishes a mission, he is ready to be beheaded
> While his spirit and heart will not perish, his remains can be cremated
> The blue phosphorescent glow of his spirit will never die away but will remain lit in Beijing throughout the night

Wang arrived in Japan in 1904 as a government scholar sponsored by the Qing Dynasty. He attended Hosei University's intensive training course and graduated in 1906 as the second best student among 300 classmates. This was in the very midst of the Russo-Japanese War when patriotism was already high.

Thirty-eight years later, Wang returned to Tokyo to deliver a lecture at the University of Tokyo. He reminisced:

> Even though it was only ten years after the First Sino-Japanese War, all of the Chinese people wished for Japan's victory. . . . In those days, there were more than 10,000 Chinese residents in Tokyo, and all of them, without exception, supported Japan from the bottom of their heart. Whenever I hear people today say that, considering the current state of Sino-Japanese relations, it would be utterly impossible for the two peoples to be true friends, I recall those Russo-Japanese War days that I spent in Tokyo.

Elsewhere, Wang also said, "It would not be an exaggeration to say that it was Japan's assistance, given out of a chivalrous spirit, that helped the Chinese Revolution succeed." In fact, as far as Wang could count, thirty Japanese activists contributed to the success of the Xinhai Revolution. It is also reported that Wang had idolized Saigō Takamori and Katsu Kai-shū. Contrary to the moderates' argument, including Kang Youwei, who believed that "a revolution would disintegrate China," Wang was convinced that, as Saigō and Katsu had exemplified earlier in Japan, they did not have to worry about the breakup of China.

One can say that Wang Jinwei was a staunch believer, right to the last minute, of the Oriental philosophy that taught that no difficulty was insurmountable when outstanding individuals on contending sides understood and trusted each other. But the Oriental world of mutual understanding that Wang dreamed of had no chance in the face of the surging waves of Chinese nationalism, which showed nothing but enmity toward Japan's imperialism; communist ideology, which would do anything for the cause; and the arbitrary conduct of the Japanese military officers stationed in China who, in their single-minded pursuit of expansionism, would not listen to their senior officers. And that was the tragedy for Wang.

Although Chiang Kai-shek successfully accomplished the Northern Expedition in 1928, senior leaders of the revolution from the Sun Yat-sen days were not eager to serve under Chiang, who was still a junior member of the Kuomintang at that time. Among those senior leaders, Wang Jinwei, in particular, was a person whom Sun had trusted most deeply. It is believed that it was Wang who either took dictation of Sun's last political will on his death bed or drafted it with others for Sun's approval.

Thus, even after Chiang entered Beijing triumphantly, the Guangdong government under the leadership of Wang remained in Guangdong to rival Chiang. After the Manchurian Incident, it was agreed that a unity based on broad common interests should be formed and, accordingly, the governments in Nanjing and Guangdong merged into one. Wang was appointed to premier and Eugene Ch'en of the Guangdong side became foreign minister. While Chiang put the entire Kuomintang forces under his control, he remained a mere chairman of the military committee in terms of his party rank.

Not only Wang but also Chiang was convinced of the crucial importance of developing partnership with Japan. Uemura Shin'ichi himself once heard Chiang say that he would aim to "turn major events into minor incidents and minor incidents into nothing." Apparently, Chiang hoped that both China and Japan would refrain from stirring things up so that their relations would be problem-free.

Indeed, that must have been the only solution to the situation. If one considers Manchuria to be "a major occurrence," then Chiang's plan to break the deadlock in Sino-Japanese relations was a plausible solution. Subsequent history shows, however, that whenever Japan faced a critical choice in its China policy, the hardliner argument of the military stationed in China always prevailed, turning minor incidents into major disasters.

Nevertheless, the Sino-Japanese partnership was not yet entirely hopeless.

In Japan, a foreign policy speech by Foreign Minister Hirota Kōki at a Diet Session in early 1935 led to the agreement on the Hirota Three Principles with the War and Navy Ministries in the fall. In a nutshell, the Three Principles called for (1) suppression by China of all anti-Japanese movements; (2) establishment of economic cooperation between China, Japan, and Manchukuo (when China's recognition of Manchukuo could not be obtained immediately); and (3) joint defense by China and Japan against communism.[6] These demands were undoubtedly severe for China, but for Chiang and Wang they were not entirely out of question, either.

Even if top leaders of the two governments agree on a policy, however, the policy would fail if a country could not control the arbitrary conduct of its military stationed in the other country. As a matter of fact, before the agreement was reached on the Three Principles, the Japanese military in China had already started working steadily toward the separation of North China from China proper.

Wang's agony during this period truly deserves deep sympathy. In June 1935, Wang issued an ordinance in an attempt to coordinate official bilateral relations. The ordinance, which included a clause mandating severe punishment for those who provoked Japan, became the target of harsh criticism and intense resistance both within and outside the Chinese government. Later Wang himself even came to be called a *Hanjian* (a traitor to the Han Chinese race and nation) and was criticized for his accommodating attitude toward the Japanese. Judging from Wang's words and deeds in those days, however, it is beyond doubt that what he did was not for his own benefit or well-being. Wang followed his convictions in the midst of the flaring anti-Japanese movement, paying no heed to his own safety.

It was during the Kuomintang's 6th Plenary Session on November 1, 1935, that an assassin shot Wang. Having long anticipated this ordeal,

---

6   http://www.marxists.org/reference/archive/mao/selected-works/volume-1/mswv1_11.htm

Wang calmly stood there to receive three shots. Wang was always ready to accept his death calmly, just as he would expect the arrival of night after daytime, which was what Wang Yangming's teaching dictated. He Yingqin was standing next to Wang Jinwei when the shooting occurred and, seeing Wang taking bullets, He pushed Wang away, unable to remain a mere spectator. Fortunately, all of the shots missed the vital organs and Wang survived his wounds. However, even before Wang recovered from his injuries, Tan Youren, Wang's right-hand man in engineering bilateral relations with Japan, was assassinated in December. After this tragedy, Wang wrote, "It made me realize how gloomy the outlook was. It was, to me, the end of the effort to coordinate official relations with Japan."

Mao Tse-tung—A Lone Revolutionary

Meanwhile, chased after by Chiang Kai-shek, Mao Tse-tung (毛沢東) fled to the northern city of Yan'an, where he recouped his strength for a renewed attack on the Kuomintang. It was around this time, in early 1936, that Mao composed *SNOW*, a poetic masterpiece that was later adopted as a postal stamp. It was due to this poem that Mao, who had been slighted as a mere rusty communist, came to be acknowledged as a respectable man of letters even by traditional Chinese intellectuals.

SNOW

Mao Tse-tung

North country scene:
A hundred leagues locked in ice,
A thousand leagues of whirling snow.
Both sides of the Great Wall
One single white immensity.
The Yellow River's swift current
Is stilled from end to end.
The mountains dance like silver snakes
And the highlands charge like wax-hued elephants,
Vying with heaven in stature.
On a fine day, the land,
Clad in white, adorned in red,

Grows more enchanting.

This land so rich in beauty
Has made countless heroes bow in homage.
But alas! Chin Shih-huang and Han Wu-ti
Were lacking in literary grace,
And Tang Tai-tsung and Sung Tai-tsu
Had little poetry in their souls;
And Genghis Khan,
Proud Son of Heaven for a day,
Knew only shooting eagles, bow outstretched
All are past and gone!
For truly great men
Look to this age alone.[7]

Starting with the words "North country scene," this poem praises the beauty of a snowfield on a fine day—which must have enchanted numerous heroes in the past. But in terms of great literary talent, it says, "For truly great men / Look to this age alone," claiming that none in the past is superior to the poet. The grand scale of the poem is particularly represented by the words "And Genghis Khan / Proud Son of Heaven for a day / Knew only shooting eagles, bow outstretched," which look down even on the historic hero who had founded an empire of unprecedented scale.

The Communist Party of China and left-wing intellectuals of post–World War II Japan (e.g., Takeda Taijun and Takeuchi Minoru who wrote *Mō Takutō—Sono Shi to Jinsei* [Mao Tse-tung—His Poetry and Life]) interpreted "this age" and "truly great men" to be the "revolutionary masses" and "those with the spirit to create a new society," respectively. To me, this is nothing but a leftist-biased interpretation. In light of Mao's past learning, it seems more appropriate to understand that Mao regarded himself a hero and discussed other heroes in the past, in a manner reminiscent of Cao Cao's discussion on heroes with Liu Bei in a plum garden.

American journalist Agnes Smedley, who visited Yan'an around that

---

7   http://history.cultural-china.com/en/60History10484.html. Also http://www.marxists.org/reference/archive/mao/selected-works/poems/poems18.htm

time, left the following impression of Mao:

> Whatever else he might be, it was beyond doubt that Mao was an aesthete. Honestly speaking, I found the feminine quality in him and the darkness of his background repulsive, and an instinctive hostility surged within me. . . . Mao Tse-tung had a cynical and terrifying sense of humor that seemed to gush out of a deep cave of loneliness. His presence had a door that would perhaps never be opened to anyone.

I believe this is still the most accurate description of Mao's true nature. While he was a revolutionary genius and a highly talented thinker and poet, he must also have been a solitary person with narcissistic, aesthetic, and epicurean inclinations hidden deeply inside.

A biased historical view of post–World War II Japan argues that it is only after one looks into the depth of solitude can one come to embrace genuine love for people. This is a sophistry, and the truth must have been totally the opposite. To be "cynical" entails an attitude that rejects love, goodwill, or ethics, and it must contain some element of being cold, too.

Charismatic and revered though Mao might have been, he was a lonely man who could not love or be loved. And this must have been behind both his marriage to Jiang Qing and the miserable failures in the Great Leap Forward campaign and the Cultural Revolution.

All being said, Mao was still a super-class revolutionary leader. American journalist Edgar Snow once described Mao as a "teacher, statesman, strategist, philosopher poet laureate, national hero, head of the family, and greatest liberator in history." This also must have been an accurate portrayal of Mao.

Mao's strategy centered around the people's war.

Underlying the argument of the time for developing partnership with Japan, supported by those including Wang Jingwei, was an assessment of the reality that China could never rival Japanese military power. It would make innocent Chinese people suffer more, it was argued, to insist on resistance against the Japanese forces for no purpose. Mao criticized these arguments, calling them "those who believe in 'weapon only theory'."

In 1938, Mao said, "While Japan may be dreaming of becoming the second Yuan Dynasty, which took over the Song Dynasty, or the second Qing Dynasty, which overthrew the Ming Dynasty, new elements are being born in China today that did not exist in the past." Included in these new elements were the awakening of Chinese nationalism and guerrilla warfare—i.e., people's war, which was underpinned by nationalism.

Yet Chiang Kai-shek was also a great strategist. In 1934, he wrote the following editorial for the internal organ of the Kuomintang military:

> Japanese military might is so strong that Japan's military could conquer China's coastal cities within three days. Our forces have not yet fulfilled any condition of a modern army. It would be suicidal, therefore, for the Chinese forces to go up against the Japanese forces at this stage. Because the Japanese Army targets the Soviet Union and the Imperial Navy targets Britain and the United States, I am convinced that some day Japan will start a grand war in which it will certainly be defeated. That will be the best opportunity for us to restore China.

And Chiang went on to assure his readers that, even if and when China found itself confronting Japan single-handedly, "because Japan is not equipped with those factors more important than weapons, including economy, governance, and military command, it can never gain the last victory in a war of international scale."

It was against these great strategists that Japan fought a war. It is generally recognized that, historically, the Chinese are better strategists than are the Japanese. On top of that, it was circumstances threatening the survival of the state and nation that forced those great strategists—Mao and Chiang—to think so thoroughly about their future. It should be recalled that Japan had been like that at the time of the First Sino-Japanese War and the Russo-Japanese War.

In contrast, the strategies of Shōwa Japan were basically based on two different types of approaches: the "outline" or "guideline" drafted on the desks of bureaucrats in the ministries of foreign affairs, war, and navy, and the arbitrary acts of the military stationed in China in pursuit of fame and distinguished service, unrelated to what the central ministries in Tokyo had decided. In terms of strategy, therefore, Japan was no match for China from the beginning.

Verifying the strategies of Mao and Chiang by comparing them with actual history, we find that it was Chiang who predicted Japan's defeat and its reasons more accurately than Mao. To be sure, Mao's people's war strategy succeeded in getting the North China fronts deadlocked, but this success was more attributable to Japan's shift toward a defensive posture, unrelated to the overall situation of the state of the war. In retrospect, the Empire of Japan fell exactly as Chiang had predicted.

Rather, the victory of the Communist Party of China was more due to its persistent pursuit of a united front with the Kuomintang, in which the Communist Party successfully directed the Kuomintang to attack the Japanese forces instead of the communist forces. This was more in line with the tactic that Lenin and Stalin had adopted—i.e., "to delay the inevitable war between the communist and the capitalist world until after the war between capitalist countries," than with Mao Tse-tung's strategy. In this sense, credit for the successful communist revolution in China belongs more to Zhou Enlai (周恩来) than Mao. Zhou engineered the united front in the aftermath of the Xi'an Incident in 1936, contributing to the eventual eruption of the Sino-Japanese War.

Chiang Kai-shek was recognized both by himself and by others as an expert on the Soviet Union; he was well aware of the Lenin-Stalin tactic mentioned above. In a speech delivered in June 1934, Chiang said, "Foreign invasions can be repelled at any time when China becomes powerful enough. Once communism permeates a nation, however, it turns to an incurable disease from which the nation can never recover." In the treatise he wrote the next year, Chiang developed an argument that was deeply insightful even from today's vantage point. He wrote, "Who do you think is waiting for the clash between China and Japan in which both should fall? Sensible persons on both sides now must swallow their pride and do everything to break the current impasse."

It was the Xi'an Incident that damaged Chiang's strategy.

When the communist forces, which had earlier fled to Yan'an, Shaanxi Province, to escape Chiang's army, attempted to advance east to Shanxi Province, Chiang not only drove them away but also decided to wipe them out. To that end, Chiang appointed Zhang Xueliang, who had lost Manchuria to the Japanese, as deputy commander in chief and stationed him at the warfront in Shaanxi. Despite Chiang's expectation, however, Zhang Xueliang's soldiers longed for their homeland Manchuria and showed little eagerness to fight against the communist forces. With low morale, they naturally tended to be susceptible to communist propaganda proposing that they fight the Japanese together.

When, after a while, a rumor began to spread that a mutual nonaggression agreement had been signed between Zhang Xueliang's troops and the communist forces, Chiang, wary of the situation and its implications, rushed to Yan'an to talk directly with Zhang. This was toward the end of 1936 (11th Year of Shōwa). Early one morning, Zhang raided Chiang's quarters, placed Chiang under house arrest, and demanded an immediate cease-fire in the civil war so as to establish a national unity government.

But the majority of the Kuomintang leaders denounced Zhang's action. Regional commanders of the Kuomintang forces demanded that Zhang release Chiang immediately, while the Nanjing government mobilized 20 divisions of its army to subjugate his rebellion. It was believed that even Stalin instructed Mao to work toward the release of Chiang, which made perfect sense in the context of the communist strategy introduced earlier in this chapter.

Soong May-ling, wife of Chiang, and K'ung Hsiang-hsi, acting premier in the absence of Chiang, flew to Yan'an from Nanjing. The Chinese Communist Party dispatched Zhou Enlai to persuade Chiang into the united front with the communists. It was this outstanding contribution to the united front that was praised and eternally memorialized when he died in 1976.

The content of the negotiations that took place between Chiang and Zhou until the release of the former has remained a mystery of history. Remarks by Chiang after his release or in his memoir did not refer to any terms of exchange for his release. Zhang Xueliang was court-martialed and sentenced to 10 years of imprisonment by the Kuomintang. Although Zhang was subsequently granted a special pardon, thanks to Chiang's petition, he was placed under house arrest, losing all the political clout he used to enjoy.

After this incident, however, a marked change in behavior occurred within the Kuomintang government. In as early as January 1937 (12th Year of Shōwa), its pro-Japanese foreign minister Chang Ch'un resigned. Chang was succeeded by Wang Chunghui, who had become anti-Japanese during his studies in Europe and the United States.

While the Chinese Communist Party started acting as if Chiang Kai-shek's agreement with the united front was a fait accompli, it appeared that the Nanjing government had no further intention to suppress the communist forces. On March 1, an agreement was signed between the Communist Party represented by Zhou Enlai and the Kuomintang on the termination of the civil war and collaboration for the cause to resist Japan.

The situation within China had changed this much. It was in July, only four months later, that the Marco Polo Bridge Incident erupted.

In closing this chapter, allow me to quote the last paragraph of the 19th volume of *Nippon Gaikō-shi* (Diplomatic History of Japan), written by Uemura Shin'ichi:

> After the Xi'an Incident, Chiang Kai-shek lost his usual flexibility, becoming entangled with a dubious spider's thread. The anti-Japan mood was rising to a fever pitch. The situation in North China appeared to have reached a flash point. Once North China flared up, it would inevitably spread all over China overnight. Although Sino-Japanese relations at that time had come to a lull, it was more like the calm before a storm.

Having written ex post facto, this observation is written in fatalistic tone. Yet the overall atmosphere at that time must have been just like this.

CHAPTER

6

Marco Polo Bridge Incident

—China Getting Ready to Fight Back Against Japan—

Dwindling Light of Parliamentary Democracy

The year 1937 began with the resignation of the Hirota cabinet, followed by the abortive attempt to form the Ugaki Kazushige (宇垣一成) government, and then by the resignation of the succeeding Hayashi Senjūrō (林銑十郎) cabinet owing to defeat in the general election. The Konoe Fumimaro government was formed in June and, finally, the Marco Polo Bridge Incident took place in July.

It should be recalled, however, that these events did not by any means lead Japan straight to militarism or, eventually, war. Along the way, the country still had to deal with the remaining influence of the Meiji era's Freedom and People's Rights Movement as well as the strong tradition of parliamentary democracy dating back to the Taishō era.

In fact, the fall of the Hirota cabinet was triggered by the so-called *harakiri* argument between the *Seiyūkai*'s Hamada Kunimatsu and War Minister Terauchi Hisaichi in the Diet.

As soon as the Hirota cabinet was formed in the aftermath of the February 26 Incident in 1936, the *Seiyūkai* and other political parties started developing a sense of crisis over the military's conduct. At the Diet session, Saitō Takao of the *Seiyūkai* tenaciously questioned whether there

129

had been someone in the military leadership who had given spiritual incentives to the young officers to trigger the February 26 Incident. During the same session, Saitō also criticized the military intervention at the time of the formation of the Hirota cabinet, saying, "It is truly regrettable that a one-sided view of some in the military appeared to have crushed the wishes of the people."

These were both striking the heart of the problem. What Saitō said at the Imperial Diet, which was the most legitimate forum of speech, was a gallant expression of things that everyone in those days had known but was too afraid to say aloud.

In a January 1937 Diet session, *Seiyūkai*'s Hamada Kunimatsu criticized the military, saying, "Political ideology that approves the promotion of autocracy is a strong undercurrent in the military."

When at a subsequent Diet session War Minister Terauchi attempted to refute Hamada's statement by saying, "Your words insult the military," Hamada retorted, "I have never said anything to insult the military. Go back and read the proceeding. If you find any such remark, I will commit *harakiri*. But if you don't find any, I expect you to disembowel yourself." It was obvious to anyone who was present that Terauchi had no edge on the issue.

At the emergency cabinet meeting that was hastily convened after the above Diet session, War Minister Terauchi insisted on the dissolution of the House of Representatives. While the dissolution and the resultant general election was no big deal for the military and the bureaucrats, it was extremely taxing for party politicians in terms of campaign funds and energy. It was a strategy on the part of the military to punish party politicians who had sullied the prestige of the war minister, by forcing them to go through grueling election processes over and over.

Other non-military members of the cabinet naturally opposed the dissolution, which, they felt, was without any moral justification. Prime Minister Hirota encouraged both sides to strike a compromise. His effort did not bear fruit, forcing his cabinet to resign.

Both Saitō and Hamada beautifully showed their mettle as party politicians who grew up in the era of the Taishō Democracy. The popularity of these political leaders among the Japanese people was not necessarily high, however, because people in those days were already disillusioned with party politics. To them, a political party represented corrupted and degraded politicians who indulged in inter-party feuds, paying no heed to state affairs. No matter how righteous the arguments of Saitō and Hamada might have been, therefore, people took them as mere empty propaganda in the party's interest by men who were good only in words.

Certainly, the conduct of these parliamentarians underwent reevaluation in Japan after World War II. It was, however, a small number of leftists—who, to be sure, had been oppressed before and during the war—that have become heroes in the postwar history books. In contrast, orthodox and unbiased liberal democrats were not given due historical recognition.

The days of the Anglo-Japanese Alliance and the Taishō Democracy, when moderation and common sense were highly valued, had long been gone. In fact, it appears that these values have not been restored in Japan even today.

The Ugaki Kazushige Cabinet Miscarriage

When the Hirota cabinet resigned, Saionji Kinmochi appointed General Ugaki Kazushige as Hirota's successor. Believing Ugaki to be the best choice at that time, both the *Seiyūkai* and *Minseitō* parties welcomed the appointment. Saionji was unable to play his strongest card until this time because there had long been resistance to Ugaki within the military; the young officers who plotted the February 26 Incident were openly anti-Ugaki. When Home Minister Yuasa Kurahei sounded out General Terauchi privately about the appointment of Ugaki, however, Terauchi replied, "Although opposition to Ugaki in the military had been strong earlier, I think it is high time for him to be made prime minister." This remark indicated that the time was ripe for putting Ugaki at the helm of government.

Nevertheless, a few mid-level officers, including Ishihara Kanji, who was at that time acting director of operations at the Imperial Japanese Army General Staff Office, opposed the appointment. In order to promote his own grand scheme of economically integrating Japan, Manchukuo, and China to prepare for a war with the Soviet Union, Ishihara had hoped for a cabinet to be formed by his puppet Hayashi Senjūrō instead. In reality, forming a puppet cabinet of his own was nothing but a dream, which Ishihara himself later had to admit.

Having a bold disposition, Ugaki did not pay the slightest heed to what such insignificant subordinates as Ishihara and his mid-level colleagues had to say. When top leaders of the military tried to persuade Ugaki to decline the nomination as a wiser move, they were scolded and whisked away.

Facing Ugaki's resistance, the military had no other option than to fall back on its final resort, which was to refuse to recommend a war minister to the new cabinet. The system by which only active duty army or navy officers could serve in the cabinet posts of war minister or navy minister that the Hirota cabinet had reinstated was already in effect. Had it not been for that system, Ugaki could have formed his cabinet by serving concurrently as its war minister.

Ugaki requested Koiso Kuniaki, commander of the Japanese Korean Army, and, subsequently, Sugiyama Hajime, Inspector General of Military Training, to join his cabinet as war minister, but neither one of them had the courage to resist defiance of his subordinates.

When World War II ended in Japan's defeat, Sugiyama killed himself in his office. His wife immediately did the same after hearing of her husband's suicide over the phone.

Hearing this, Ugaki wrote a letter to Sugiyama's aide-de-camp reminiscing about his earlier interaction with Sugiyama over Ugaki's appointment. When Sugiyama said, "The Imperial Army opposes your appointment. Some are loudly voicing their dissatisfaction, apparently for no particular reason. In order to pacify them, I would like you to decline the appointment," Ugaki replied, "It is the responsibility of you and the war minister to put the army's house in order. It is wrong of you to come and ask me to do something about it." Based on this exchange, Ugaki reminisced,

> Since that exchange, my perception of Field Marshal Sugiyama changed and I had come to regard him as a man without a proper sense of responsibility. Hearing of his admirable death, however, I have revised my opinion of Field Marshal Sugiyama again. He must indeed have been a man with a strong sense of responsibility.

This episode alone reflects the atmosphere in those days. It was utterly nonsensical to request Ugaki to decline the Imperial appointment only because "Some [in the military] are loudly voicing their dissatisfaction, apparently for no particular reason." But this clearly indicated that by this time nobody, not even the top army leadership, could resist the defiance of its young subordinates.

According to an old Japanese notion, all of one's sins on earth are forgiven as long as one admirably terminates one's life. An admirable suicide proves that one holds some value that is more important than one's own life and that one has a sense of honor.

The problem was that, even though Sugiyama appeared to hold a value that is more important than his own life, he did not try to persuade his subordinates by risking his own life.

Later, Hirota also met his fate admirably. And, like Sugiyama, Hirota was also guilty for misleading the nation by going with the times. By calmly meeting one's death, a person may be satisfied with himself, but the people around him may have to suffer from his aesthetics. When national leaders are not equipped with insights on national strategy, the nation will be misguided.

What would have happened if Ugaki had actually become prime minister?

There might have been a coup d'etat or two at the outset, but it would have been difficult to actually carry them out in light of the failure of the February 26 Incident. Meanwhile, Ugaki would have strengthened his control over the military by means of personnel appointments, among other actions, to suppress junior officers' defiance. In terms of policy, judging from Ugaki's earlier record of eliminating four infantry divisions in 1925, he does not appear to be a man who would have been easily swayed by the pressure of junior officers.

As a military man himself, Ugaki was naturally critical of the corruption in party politics. And it is also hard to imagine that he would have pursued the same cooperative diplomacy as Shidehara Kijūrō's. Nevertheless, it seems quite plausible that, in carrying out policies, he would have maintained firm control based on a realistic assessment of the situation instead of endorsing ex post facto the arbitrary conduct of the military stationed in China.

Taking into consideration the Marco Polo Bridge Incident in the same year, which later escalated into the Second Sino-Japanese War and, eventually, the Greater East Asia War, it seems quite plausible that, had Ugaki actually formed a cabinet, he would have dealt with the situation quite differently. In this sense, the miscarriage of the Ugaki government was a matter of great regret in the history of the Shōwa era.

Ugaki himself must have known that only he could change the course of events. In fact, he would not give up on forming his cabinet until the last minute. His last resort was to request a gracious imperial message directly from the emperor.

Believing it would be a violation of imperial authority to obstruct an imperial appointment just because a few in the military made a fuss about it, Ugaki requested Minister of the Imperial Household Yuasa Kurahei to petition the emperor to issue an imperial command ordering the Imperial Army to appoint a war minister. While this might have enabled Ugaki to form his cabinet, Yuasa refused Ugaki's request, saying it would be too much to bother the emperor. Yuasa believed that the utmost prudence was called for in considering an action that might "put the emperor on board a boat that sails against the current of the time." For Yuasa, the major concern at that time was also the security of the sovereign.

Saionji also once contemplated a forced breakthrough, but he allegedly changed his mind, "taking into consideration the advice of a close confidant (presumably Yuasa)."

Saionji's deteriorating health was also a factor here. When he was in prime health, he would immediately rush to Tokyo whenever a political turmoil occurred to listen to key persons involved. After that, he would make a decision. This way of handling things was a process he took at prior incidents. But this time, Saionji was immobilized due to advanced age as well as sickness. Thus, it was Minister for Imperial Household Yuasa who had visited Saionji in Shimizu, Shizuoka, to hear what Saionji had to say. Therefore, when his view was overruled due to the military's opposition, Saionji was unable to be on the spot.

Short-Lived Hayashi Cabinet

When the Ugaki cabinet did not materialize, it was decided that Hirota would be succeeded by Hayashi Senjūrō as prime minister, just as Ishihara Kanji had calculated. Saionji, who had been recuperating in Shimizu, agreed to make Hiranuma Kiichirō the first candidate and Hayashi Senjūrō the second, following the advice of visiting Imperial Household Minister

Yuasa. Saionji had long held a strong aversion to the rightist Hiranuma, who had been popular among the military. When selecting Hiranuma as the first candidate, Saionji said, "Although I am not fully convinced about Hiranuma, I shall follow the advice of the Imperial Household Minister," thus revealing his reluctance. Seeing that it was obvious that the military was strongly supporting the appointment of Hayashi, Saionji attempted subtle resistance by making Hiranuma his first choice.

Fully aware of the military's wish, however, Hiranuma declined the appointment. This led to the birth of the Hayashi cabinet, as Ishihara had long schemed.

But that was as far as Ishihara's scheme succeeded. Despite Ishihara's high hopes, Hayashi did not turn out to be a robot whom Ishihara could freely maneuver, nor was he magnanimous enough to allow Ishihara to pursue his grand strategy. In other words, Hayashi turned out to be a mere military bureaucrat with a strong lust for power.

Ishihara also attempted to make Itagaki Seishirō war minister. Although Hayashi once accepted Ishihara's recommendation, he eventually changed his mind, persuaded by people around him, and appointed a person who was more universally acceptable instead. He realized that it would not be generally acceptable to appoint Itagaki, a 16th-year graduate of the Imperial Japanese Army Academy, to succeed Terauchi, an 11th-year graduate, when there were Sugiyama, a 12th-year graduate, and Umezu Yoshijirō, a 15th-year graduate, before Itagaki. In the end, Hayashi appointed Nakamura Kōtarō, a 13th-year graduate, as war minister. Later Nakamura was succeeded by Sugiyama, who was Nakamura's senior by one year, when the subsequent Konoe cabinet was formed.

This was the extent of what the genius Ishihara could accomplish. In retrospect, he was instrumental in conquering Manchuria, founding Manchukuo, blocking the Ugaki cabinet, and realizing the Hayashi cabinet.

But there was also a limit to what Ishihara could accomplish alone. He was aided in the conquest of Manchuria by Itagaki as well as by the trend of the times. It only takes one rebel to block a cabinet. But to promote his grand strategy, Ishihara either had to seize power himself via a coup d'état or secure the full cooperation of those who completely understood his strategy and would carry it out. Had Ugaki teamed up with Ishihara, Shōwa history might have been totally different. The fact that such collaboration did not materialize might point to Ishihara's limits. Despite his enormous talent, Ishihara had a strong inclination for isolation and self-righteousness.

Although a collective will of the military existed—and which Hayashi represented—it was a simplistic, incoherent notion and a far cry from Ishihara's strategic insight. The military wished to punish political parties by dissolving the House of Representatives on behalf of Terauchi by doing the same thing he had wanted to do.

But the military still had to act within the boundary of the Meiji Constitution, which remained valid even under the militarist rule. The budget had to be passed by the Diet. Thus, as soon as the Diet passed the budget, Hayashi dissolved it without any justifiable reason. This was what was popularly known as "*kuinige kaisan*" ("eat and run" dissolution), and it had the opposite effect on the public contrary to what Hayashi had expected.

In the subsequent general election, the *Minseitō* and *Seiyūkai* won 179 and 175 seats respectively, proving the continued prominence of existing political parties, which had maintained their own constituencies since the Freedom and People's Rights movement days. Moreover, even the moderate leftist *Shakai Taishūtō* (Socialist Masses Party) won as many as 37 seats.

At this point, the Imperial Army gave up on Hayashi, whose cabinet had to resign within three months of its formation.

Konoe Fumimaro: Blessed by Both Political Parties and the Military

When Hayashi stepped down, the Imperial Army recommended Itagaki as his successor, and senior statesmen appeared to be resigned to accept this recommendation. This might have been the last maneuvering of Ishihara.

Only Saionji was indignant, saying, "I would not advise the Emperor to sanction this appointment." He recommended Konoe Fumimaro instead. In retrospect, this was one of the last occasions for Saionji to exercise his leadership as an elder statesman.

Actually, Saionji had once recommended Konoe immediately after the February 26 Incident in 1936. Although Konoe had firmly declined the appointment at that time, he did not find it possible to evade the appointment this time.

Formation of the Konoe cabinet was welcomed by all corners, including the right and the left, political parties and the military alike. Japanese people were excited to see a young, tall, and handsome prime minister who was the direct descendent of the princely Konoe family, the noblest among the peerage, and an intellectual educated at Ikkō (First High School), Tokyo Imperial University, and Kyoto University. Newspapers called him the "unbeknown charm." The Japanese people, who had been weary of both political parties and the military clique, felt as if the world had become a brighter place.

People in those days might have enjoyed a similar freshness in Prime Minister Konoe as they did in Hosokawa Morihiro, a grandson of Konoe, who became prime minister in 1993 after people had gotten tired of the long one-party rule by the Liberal Democratic Party.

Judging from the results, however, it must be said that Konoe led Japan to disaster. He mishandled the aftermath of the Marco Polo Bridge Incident, which was only the beginning of a chain of failures. Konoe hardly showed any effective leadership at critical junctures in the quagmire of the war with China, followed by his appointment of Matsuoka Yōsuke as foreign minister, which led Japan to an inextricable confrontation with Britain and the United States. It was also under the Konoe cabinet that *Taisei Yokusankai* (大政翼賛会, Imperial Rule Assistance Association), Japan's para-fascist organization, was organized, finishing off Japan's pre–World War II democratic politics.

One may wonder if these phenomena are to be attributed to the trend of the times, which no one could resist, or to shortcomings of Konoe as a statesman. While many have written about Konoe, *Konoe Fumimaro* written by Shōwa-era political scientist Yabe Teiji is by far the most detailed. I myself relied mostly on this book.

In terms of his health, Konoe had had a weak constitution since his early childhood. Many of his retirements from political posts were attributed to health problems. Rather than being haunted by a specific chronic illness, he was constantly laid up with common colds or stomach aches. In early Shōwa days, people often referred to weak intellectuals as "pale-faced intellectuals." Much earlier, there were such popular phrases as "Too wise to live long," and "Beauties die young." Konoe was a typical example of a well-bred prewar man who took to his bed even with a common cold, under the devoted care of his family.

It might have been at least partially due to his ill health that Konoe was described as having a gloomy disposition rather than being merry and cheerful. It was said that he was never seen laughing heartily.

While Konoe liked to mingle with a wide range of dignitaries, from politicians to military officers, bureaucrats, businessmen, scholars, and men of letters, whose ideological inclinations also varied widely from left to right, Yabe observed that there were only a few people whom Konoe regarded as close friends.

Flighty and dilettantish, Konoe liked to be surrounded by a wide range of followers. But he could not make decisions on his own. Instead, he ended up going with the flow of the times, overwhelmed by the powerful and forcible.

These attributes alone are enough to explain Konoe's misrule by inaction or nonfeasance at critical junctures before and during the war.

These characteristic shortcomings of Konoe seemed to have become visible to people around him almost as soon as he took the helm of the government. Even Saionji became disillusioned with Konoe when it became obvious that the first Konoe cabinet was not capable of exercising any leadership toward the settlement of the Second Sino-Japanese War.

Saionji was so disillusioned that he started describing the prime minister as a "cock-and-bull story" man who had no definite opinion of his own. Saionji moaned, presumably about Konoe, to people around him: "If I could regain my health and perseverance a little more, I wish to request an audience with the Emperor and discuss various matters. Now that I am too old and tired, however, I have no other choice than to quietly watch what he is going to do." This was Saionji's expression of deep disappointment with Konoe, whom the last elder statesman had placed high hopes on as his possible successor.

From the beginning, Saionji had looked forward to seeing Konoe some day succeed him and grow into the role of guardian of the Imperial Family. In anticipation of the day when Konoe would become prime minister, Saionji had made several preparations, including the appointment of Konoe as president of the House of Peers.

For Konoe, who had lost his father early, Saionji wanted to play the role of father. Although both men were from the noblest of the noble families that had long been the guardians of the Imperial Family, in terms of political philosophy, Konoe was closer to his own father, Konoe Atsumaro, who was a pan-Asianist, than to Saionji's Western liberalism.

Konoe left a lot of writings on his own thinking, which makes it easy for us to trace his philosophy.

His often-quoted *Genrō Jūshin to Yo* ("Elder Statesmen, Senior Statesmen, and Me" which is presumed to have been published on the eve of Japan's defeat in World War II) starts with the following confession: "Around the time of the eruption of the Manchurian Incident in the 6th year of Shōwa, I came to realize that there was quite a distance in views on the state of affairs between Prince Saionji and other senior statesmen and me."

In the same book, Konoe also referred to his participation in the Paris Peace Conference in 1919 as a member of the Japanese delegation led by Saionji.

It should be pointed out here that, having graduated from Kyoto University in 1917, Konoe had already written a treatise under the title of *Eibei Hon'i no Heiwa Shugi wo Haisu* (Rejection of Britain/United States Centered Pacifism) in 1918, one year before his visit to Europe. In this treatise, Konoe summarizes World War I as a feud between countries for the status quo and countries against it, rather than as a struggle between pacifism and militarism. According to Konoe, the real issue was what the status really was. If the status in Europe at that time was a rightful one, those who attempted to overthrow it were certainly enemies of justice. But the reality was that Britain and France had already monopolized all the colonies in the world, leaving no obtainable land for not only Germany but for all latecomers. Konoe argued that the demand for the overthrow of this inequality was fully justified and, therefore, Japan had to sympathize with Germany. Summarizing his arguments, Konoe denounced British and American pacifism as "nothing but a policy advocated by those who find the status quo to be convenient" and that had nothing to do with justice or humanity.

At the Paris Conference, Konoe found it impossible to "rejoice in the British/American-centered League of Nations." Instead, he

Konoe Fumimaro

predicted an early collapse of the League. In *Genrō Jūshin to Yo,* Konoe reminisced:

> Therefore, I was quite unhappy with our government's tendency to follow in the footsteps of Britain, as shown by elder and senior statesmen in those days. When I conveyed my dissatisfaction to Prince Saionji as the occasion arose, he retorted by quoting an old proverb, "Don't kick against the pricks."

What we see here is a conflict between realism and the aspiration for autonomy and independence. This conflict is, actually, still ongoing even in the post-World War II Japan. Young Konoe must have found in Saionji's realism—that is, that Japan's security and prosperity would be guaranteed as long as it followed in the footsteps of the world's hegemon of the time—the Japanese government's "follow-Britain-no-matter-what" attitude, which he did not find too valiant. Konoe also said:

> With the Manchurian Incident as the turning point, the leadership position of elder and senior statesmen quickly weakened, to be taken over eventually by the military. . . . The force of reaction is formidable. The military's resentment at and frustration with the government's pacifism and emphasis on international cooperation as well as the Japanese people's blind belief in the omnipotence of parliament and political parties flared up at once, so that elder and senior statesmen were denounced as the Emperor's evil vassals and party parliamentarians were denounced as destroyers of the national polity. The May 15 and February 26 Incidents were the results of this denunciation.

This goes to show that Konoe, too, had been frustrated during the days of Shidehara diplomacy and Taishō Democracy. It appears to be true that Konoe was close to military officers of the Imperial Way Faction (皇道派). While Konoe claimed that, "Just as elder and senior statesmen have had doubts about me, I have never expressed my unconditional approval of them," he continued to say, "Although there is a lot in the remarks of junior officers of which I do not approve, the direction in which they have guided Japan since the Manchurian Incident is the direction that Japan is destined to take."

Konoe also said:

> Prince Saionji used to say, "Junior officers today are overly excited. It is best to wait for the fever to cool down, trying not to stimulate them while the fever is still high. As soon as calm is restored, Japan's diplomacy will get back on track and return to pursuing international cooperation as in the days of the Shidehara Diplomacy." In return, I would say, "It is the world's state of affairs that determines the direction for Japan to take. While your excellency suggests that we should wait for the fever among military officers to go down, I would say it will never go down as long as politicians today show no recognition of Japan's fate. It is extremely dangerous for a nation to be led by the military. The only way to take politics back from the hand of the military as soon as possible is for politicians to recognize Japan's fate and implement a variety of reforms, thus forestalling the military." Because I repeated "forestalling the military" over and over, Prince Saionji laughed and said, "You and your forestalling the military again?"

Konoe continues to reminisces:

> Prince Saionji petitioned the Emperor to sanction the appointment of Viscount Saitō as prime minister, hoping it would cool down the head of the military. This was followed by the appointment of General Okada two years later with the same hope.

Perhaps the back-to-back appointments of these two military generals who were nevertheless moderate and harmless as prime ministers were indeed made out of Saionji's wish to buy time by parrying the military's anger. However, even these military men became the targets of radical officers. Konoe wrote:

> Prince Saionji's wish was completely shattered by the February 26 Incident. Upon this mishap, Prince Saionji recommended me to the Emperor as the succeeding prime minister. . . . I respectfully declined the nomination, not only because I had health and other problems but, more importantly, because I found a significant

difference in opinion between Prince Saionji and myself.

When he was appointed again in 1937, however, Konoe recalled:

> I had to accept the nomination this time because it was not the way
> of the Emperor's loyal subject [to refuse a second time]. . . . It was
> a month after the formation of the first Konoe cabinet that the Sec-
> ond Sino-Japanese War erupted. . . . When a war begins, it becomes
> highly difficult for a prime minister to carry out his policies, because
> he is not in the position to violate the autonomy of military com-
> mand. . . .
>
> Nevertheless, I still cannot say that elder and senior statesmen
> had wisdom and foresight. On the contrary, I believe Japan could
> have taken more sound steps and avoided the difficulties it now
> faces had those elder and senior statesmen been more deeply aware
> of the world's trends and Japan's fate and constantly forestalled the
> military instead of indulging in the desultory dream of international
> cooperation.

Was this notion of Konoe's possible at all? Certainly, when Foreign
Minister Eugene Ch'en of the Guangdong Government proposed that
Manchuria should be placed under a high commissioner appointed
by Japan, Shidehara Kijūrō could have chosen to accept the proposal.
Because the proposal was made a month before the Manchurian Incident,
by accepting it Shidehara could have forestalled Ishihara. But Shide-
hara decided to strictly comply with the Nine-Power Treaty and rejected
Ch'en's proposal.

By the time Konoe became prime minister, there was little room left for
his government to forestall the military. This fact notwithstanding, Konoe
still intended to announce policies that would forestall the military's plans.

Konoe left a few memos on remarks he had intended to make at the first
cabinet meeting and press conference immediately following the formation of the cabinet. In those memos, Konoe defined the mission of his government as being to "mitigate both the international conflict between the
haves and the have-nots and the domestic struggle between the haves and
the have-nots" through international justice to enhance equity in the inter-

national distribution of wealth and through social justice for more equal domestic distribution of wealth. He went on to say:

> International justice cannot be fully accomplished unless the world's entire territories are divided equally among states. While the next best measure would be free immigration and trade among nations, today's world situation that does not allow even this second best measure would be a good justification for Japan's continental policy as one of the have-nots.

Konoe's notion here is essentially the same as that of junior military officers represented by such ideologues as Ōkawa Shūmei and Kita Ikki. At this point, Konoe had already been following the military, not forestalling it. In any event, neither public opinion in those days nor the military found it uncomfortable to have Konoe as head of the government.

Thus, because Konoe enjoyed general popularity, the formation of his cabinet also proceeded smoothly. In the end, both War Minister Sugiyama and Navy Minister Yonai remained in their posts, while Hirota Kōki was appointed as foreign minister and Kazami Akira, an ex-journalist who in those days was pro-military but who became a leftist member of the Japan Socialist Party after World War II, was appointed as chief cabinet secretary.

It was only one month after the Konoe cabinet's formation, however, that the Marco Polo Bridge Incident erupted.

Origin of the Marco Polo Bridge Incident

Who fired the first shot on the night of July 7, 1937, still remains a mystery.

There is little historical significance in identifying of who fired the first shot, though. Generally speaking, who fires the first shot has little, if any, meaning as the cause of a war. Much more important is the strategic environment—that is, which side wants a war more.

At the Battle of Pungdo (1894), which was the first battle of the First Sino-Japanese War, both sides claimed that it was the opponent that had fired the first shot. History as taught in Japan, winner of that war, still claims that it was the Qing side that fired first.

But at that time the aim of the Qing side was to transport its soldiers safely to Korea before a war started. Therefore, it was their strategy to avoid any fighting. In contrast, the Japanese side had already been determined to start a war and, in fact, its fleet had been instructed to open fire if need be. The Japanese side had been mentally prepared to start a full-fledged battle should such a thing happen, while the Qing side was not prepared. Thus, common sense tells us that it should have been the Japanese side that fired the first shot.

The origin of the Marco Polo Bridge Incident is still being debated even today, but it is obvious that the first shot could not have been fired by the Japanese side. This means that it must have been fired by the Chinese side, whether it was the nationalist or the communist elements.

The fact that who fired the first shot still remains a mystery is itself a key to solving this mystery. Considering that all the historical documents from Japan, the defeated country, were exposed to the public eye after the war, the fact that the side which fired first is still unclear can only mean that there is no evidence on the shot from the Japanese side.

Although it had been the official interpretation in Japan before the end of World War II that the assassination of Zhang Zuolin, the Manchurian Incident, the January 28 Incident, and the incident that led to a subsequent series of maneuvers in North China had been triggered by provocations from the Chinese side, it became clear one by one after the war that almost all of the incidents had been engineered by the Japanese side. Nevertheless, no evidence has been found that hints at secret engineering on the part of Japan as far as the Marco Polo Bridge Incident is concerned. Even at the International Military Tribunal for the Far East, this incident was not attributed to Japan.

Perhaps, as in the case of the Battle of Pungdo, it might be easier to reach a more accurate conclusion if one uses common sense to assess the strategic environment surrounding the incident.

In previous cases whenever the Japanese Imperial Army wanted to make an excuse for certain actions, it worked out some kind of plot, albeit rather crudely designed, to cover up the truth. At times a plot included diversionary tactics to make it look as though conduct by the Japanese army had actually been carried out by the Chinese; at other times it included buying off the Chinese to launch an attack on the Japanese.

The Japan side has never done such a tactless thing as simply firing at the opponent and insisting that the other side did it.

Because blank shots were used during drills, accidental discharges were quite unthinkable. If an accidental discharge had indeed occurred, it could have been verified after the war by reviewing the record.

The more fundamental issue was changes in the strategic environments.

From the Liutiaohu Incident in 1931 through the attempt in 1935 to separate five North China provinces from China to put them under its control, it had always been the Japanese Imperial Army stationed in China that caused problems and mobilized its troops using those problems as pretexts for obtaining something new. Because the Chinese side was fully aware that armed conflict would do no good for it, it resorted, instead, to non-violent measures such as the anti-Japanese/slight-Japanese movements to oppress the Japanese residents.

But the atmosphere in China began to change.

Journalist Matsumoto Shigeharu, who was counted as one of the sharpest observers on the Chinese situation in those days, happened to be in Shanghai. He reminisces:

> In those days, diplomatic negotiation between Japan and China was utterly unthinkable. Neither side trusted the other and, in contrast to the Japanese side, which remained quite relaxed about it, the Chinese side was anxious to look for an occasion to launch a full-scale counterattack. A Korean friend of mine, whom I met in Beijing on the eve of the Marco Polo Bridge Incident, went as far as to say that there would be an all-out confrontation within a week.

Self-confidence on the Chinese side derived from the formation of a common front against Japan since the days of the Xi'an Incident (1936).

Another source of the Chinese self-confidence was the Suiyuan Campaign toward the end of 1936 (11th Year of Shōwa), which saw the advance of the Inner Mongolian/Grand Han Righteous Armies into Suiyuan Province (presently the Inner Mongolia Autonomous Region) with the aim of expanding the territory. It so happened that, by that time, the National Revolution Army under Chiang Kai-shek had completed its war readiness to annihilate the communist forces in Yan'an and, therefore, it could easily defeat the invaders. Although the Kanto Army did not participate in the campaign, Tōjō Hideki, chief of staff of the Kanto Army, was believed to have plotted the invasion and, in fact, Tanaka Ryūkichi, the Kanto Army's strategy staff officer, was in command of the invasion forces. This victory brought enormous self-confidence to the Chinese side, which came to believe that the Kanto Army was not much of an opponent.

In the first days of the Second Sino-Japanese War, Japanese troops sensed the heightened morale in their Chinese opponents. It was as if the Chinese troops belonged to the army of a different country from the one the Japanese had confronted during the Manchurian Incident.

In terms of a grand strategy, the strategy of the Communist Party of China was unmistakable. It would be best if Chiang Kai-shek's forces fought the Japanese instead of the communist forces; the more extensive the battle between the Kuomintang and the Japanese became, the easier it got for the communists, who could use this time to expand their sphere of influence and, some day, overwhelm the Kuomintang army. The Communist Party may have resorted to clandestine schemes, including provoking altercations over who fired first, in the hope of expanding friction and confrontations between the Kuomintang and the Japanese troops.

Chiang Kai-shek, for his part, was well aware of this strategy of the Communist Party. It is conjectured that, at that point, he had not personally made up his mind to have an all-out confrontation with Japan.

Among the rank and file as well as ordinary citizens, however, the mood that they could no longer tolerate Japan's arrogance and insolence became pervasive.

As a matter of fact, the mood inside China had already begun to change even before the Xi'an Incident. The year 1936 witnessed a series of killings of Japanese sailors, consulate-policemen, and civilian residents, followed by the Chengdu Incident in which two *Mainichi Shimbun* reporters were beaten to death by a Chinese mob while two employees of the South Manchuria Railway were seriously injured. At the time of the Manchurian Incident, Ishihara Kanji intended to use the murder of Captain Nakamura Shintarō as a pretext for war. Restrained by his superiors, though, Ishihara ended up resorting to the clumsy strategy of deliberately causing self-inflicted damage to the railroad line so as to start the Manchurian Incident. From the Japanese perspective, there were frequent occurrences of incidents comparable to the killing of Captain Nakamura in those days that Japan could have used as an excuse to start a war.

It was during the conference that Chiang Kai-shek organized in Lushan, a summer resort in southeastern China, from July 1, inviting some 150 representatives of politics, academia, business, and journalism that word came that the Marco Polo Bridge Incident had erupted. With the majority of the participants blaring vehement hardliner arguments, even Chiang could not control the tone of this conference. Zhou Fohai, a member of the Kuomintang who later broke off to become a cabinet member of the collaborationist Nanjing Nationalist Government, reminisced that, "Had there not been this conference in Lushan, Sino-Japanese relations would have been quite different." Zhou's remark indicates that the anti-Japan consensus was formed during this conference among intellectuals in China.

Of course, at the base of this consensus must have been the assessment of the situation that it was again the doing of Japanese troops, which was a commonsense view in China in those days. It would have caused quite a different reaction among the participants had they known that the cause of the incident had been a provocation from the Chinese side.

And the same thing could be said about the Japanese side. The immediate reaction of Prime Minister Konoe, upon hearing the news, was to ask Chief Cabinet Secretary Kazami Akira, "This cannot be a premeditated act of the Imperial Army, can it?"

Frequent Occurrences of Chinese Provocations

Against this background, Chiang Kai-shek made an extremely hardline announcement on July 17, inspiring nationalism all over China. In this announcement, Chiang said,

> If we tolerate Japan's military occupation of the Marco Polo Bridge, Beijing would become the second Mukden and North China the second Manchuria. . . . The survival of the entire nation hinges on the territorial integrity of the Marco Polo Bridge and we must at any cost resist Japan's attempt at occupying the bridge.

When one considers that this announcement was based on a misjudgment of facts around the Marco Polo Bridge Incident, it was tragic that this incident became the origin of the Second Sino-Japanese War.

After this announcement, all the incidents that took place within a month or two of the Marco Polo Bridge Incident were without exception initiated by rank and file organizations in China, with or without directives from the center. In retrospect, these were the critical two months that determined the fate to come. This was a major departure from past patterns, and the Chinese side did not even bother to conceal who took the initiative.

Although the Imperial Japanese Army's policy was not to escalate the confrontation, it nevertheless maintained a highly haughty posture of tolerating nothing that would damage the military's prestige. No other army in the world has ever been more prone to provocation.

Immediately after the eruption of the Marco Polo Bridge Incident, commanders of both forces in the field agreed to a truce on July 11. Although the Japanese government had already issued an order mobilizing reinforcements, subsequent developments made Japan defer the mobilization. Despite the unfortunate accident of Chiang's hardliner speech delivered around that time, local settlement was in the making in the field. Soon after, however, the Langfang Incident (July 25) and Guanganmen Incident (July 26) erupted, in which the Japanese troops were attacked by the Chinese army.

In the Guanganmen Incident, the Chinese troops opened fire on Japanese troops bound for the Japanese barracks within the walls of Beijing in order to protect Japanese residents. The Chinese side had given prior approval of this movement to the Japanese troops. The Chinese garrison, however, closed the gate suddenly after two-thirds of the Japanese unit got through and started firing mercilessly at the remaining troops. With this and other similar incidents, it was actually only natural for the confrontation to escalate. A Japanese cabinet meeting on July 27 decided to mobilize the army divisions stationed in China. Accordingly, the Imperial Japanese Army in China initiated military action in Beijing and Tianjin on July 28 and completed its mission on July 30, suppressing the enemy forces in the Beijing-Tianjin region.

Among the numerous incidents around this time, it was the Tungchow Mutiny of 1937 that had the greatest impact on the Japanese side.

Tungchow was the capital of the East Hopei Government, a Japanese puppet state established inside the demilitarized zone. A large number of Japanese resided in this city, which was under Japan's stable control. On

July 29, taking advantage of the temporary absence of the Japanese garrison, the 3,000-man-strong East Hopei Army attached to the Japanese army mutinied and killed many of the Japanese residents. What happened was an explosion of frustration among members of the Chinese garrison that had long accumulated over their humiliating position and by being bossed by the Japanese, causing them to ride the pervasive mood for anti-Japanese resistance. In all, 200 Japanese residents were brutally slaughtered, with evidence on the female corpses of dreadful sexual assault.

Failing to acknowledge the Chinese change of heart, the Japanese side had taken things easy, as the journalist Matsumoto had accurately observed, until this point. Shocked by the Tungchow Mutiny, a consensus was formed among the Japanese that the "atrocious Chinese must be punished" so that they could no longer take advantage of Japan's oversight.

While the confrontation between the two sides temporarily subsided in North China, it escalated to central China. It is undeniable that the Battle of Shanghai, which triggered the transformation of what used to be battles in north China into the Second Sino-Japanese War, was initiated by provocations from the Chinese side. Like the Tungchow Mutiny, the Battle of Shanghai was also the mutiny of a Chinese garrison attached to the Japanese army. Now that the garrison that was supposed to protect the Japanese residents had actually assaulted the Japanese, short of evacuating all Japanese residents from China, Japan had no other option than to make war. After the summer of 1937, thus, the objective situation was such that a war was inevitable no matter how much the Japanese side exercised self-restraint.

When asked who I think started the Second Sino-Japanese War, I have to conclude that both the direct cause of the war as well as the failure of all attempts to achieve local settlement and contain the confrontation were mostly attributable to the Chinese side.

I have no intention here to present a unique view of mine on the issue.

In fact, what I find strange is that what I have concluded above has not yet become a commonsense historical view among the Japanese, even though it has been a matter of common knowledge within a small circle of experts, including Hata Ikuhiko, and despite an abundance of situational evidence and concrete facts that all point to my conclusion.

From the viewpoint of propaganda, it was only natural that the

Chinese side explained that it had to fight back because it believed that the Marco Polo Bridge Incident was the beginning of Japan's new invasion. Perhaps the failure of the Japanese side to refute this allegation could be attributed to a dearth of inquiring minds. Since the Manchurian Incident, it had already become common to believe that whatever happened was a clandestine scheme of the Japanese military. Even when an attempt was made to inquire into the true cause, people in Japan knew that the military would most certainly cover up the truth. Thus, until Japan's defeat in the Second World War even the Japanese people vaguely believed that it was Japan which had started the Marco Polo Bridge Incident.

In other words, the biased historical view of post–World War II Japan actually dates back to the prewar days when the Japanese people tacitly accepted the Chinese historical view.

Having established this historical fact, however, I have no intention here to argue which side was more responsible for the Second Sino-Japanese War, China or Japan.

Obviously, it is a historical fact that the Manchurian Incident and the Japanese attempt to separate northern Chinese provinces from China were definitely remote causes of the Marco Polo Bridge Incident and that Chinese resentment had accumulated throughout the entire period. Applying the same logic that China was forced to attack Japan, by the way, it can also be then a historical fact that Japan was cornered into launching the attack on Pearl Harbor by the oil embargo by the United States and the Hull note. One could continue to apply this logic endlessly with no constructive outcome.

When one seeks to assign responsibility for starting a war, it boils down to who fires the first shot. But it hardly has any historical meaning.

Since the International Military Tribunal for the Far East, it appears to have become a custom to argue who is right and who is wrong when discussing history. Spending too much energy and time on this train of thought may make one lose sight of the truth of history.

History is a flow, and both peace and war take place within this flow. What is expected of us is to investigate the truth of history. And we should leave it to the people of the time to argue the rights and wrongs, and what lessons to draw from history.

Were I to be requested to write a history textbook for junior and senior high school students, it would read something like the following:

Behind the Chinese resentment of the Japanese was a long historical background starting with the Twenty-One Demands in 1915 through the Shandong Problem (1919), the Manchurian Incident (1931–32), and the Japanese attempt at separating northern Chinese provinces from China (1935). Because it was impossible for China in those days to stop Japan militarily, its resistance was for a long time confined to nonviolent measures such as boycotting Japanese products and the anti-Japanese/Japan-slighting movements.

After the Xi'an Incident (1936), however, the sense that the time had come to oppose Japan militarily became pervasive in China with the successful formation of the Second United Front between the Kuomintang and the Communist forces, coupled with the improvement of Chinese military capabilities. At this point, even the Kuomintang government found it difficult to restrict military actions against Japan. By 1936–37, most of the provocations were initiated by the Chinese side. The Marco Polo Bridge Incident, whose facts still remain unknown, can be considered as one of those provocations under the Chinese initiatives together with subsequent incidents that obstructed early settlement of the confrontation.

For Japan's part, the Japanese Imperial Army stationed in China never revised its tactic of launching immediate counterattacks, and took actions without the approval of the headquarters in Tokyo, whenever the military prestige was at risk. Failing to recognize the great changes in circumstances, the army retained its habitual notion of taking advantage of an opponent's provocation to invade further, which actually made the army unstoppable once provoked. There were also strong calls among the Japanese public demanding punishment for the atrocities committed by the Chinese.

Against this backdrop, despite the Japanese government's intention to confine the confrontation, the Marco Polo Bridge Incident very quickly escalated to Shanghai, transforming itself from a local confrontation in north China to the Second Sino-Japanese War and turning all of China into a battlefield.

CHAPTER
7

Siege of Nanjing

—Diplomatic Efforts to Settle the Issue Continue in Earnest—

An Unusual Diplomat

After the Marco Polo Bridge Incident in 1937, all attempts at an early settlement of the issue failed one after another, thus turning the situation on the Chinese continent into a quagmire.

An abundance of excellent works and testimonies on this process exists. In this chapter, I will rely on these documents, particularly the memoir of Ishii Itarō, to review what actually happened.

Ishii served the Japanese Ministry of Foreign Affairs as Director-General of East Asian Affairs throughout the entire tenure of the first Konoe Fumimaro cabinet. He was an unusual diplomat. Diplomats in those days were almost without exception either graduates of the Tokyo Imperial University, the pride and hope of their hometowns or the sons of distinguished families. In contrast, Ishii was a graduate of *Dōbun Shoin* (同文書院, East Asia Common Cultural College) in Shanghai.

After finishing college, Ishii worked for about three years at the South Manchuria Railway before returning to Japan to assist his father's business. His father's bankruptcy, however, found him unemployed with a family to feed. In order to obtain a credential that would allow him to be employed satisfactorily in Japan, he self-studied to pass the higher civil service examination, which gave him the same credential as a university graduate. Finding no satisfactory job, however, Ishii decided to take the Foreign Service Examination because passing it would ensure employment at the foreign ministry. He passed the exam after two attempts.

On this personal experience, Ishii reminisced as follows: "It was the difficulty of finding a good job that cornered me into taking the Foreign Service Examination. I was fully aware that I had not been endowed with any of the qualities that were generally regarded as requisites for a good diplomat, such as sociability, agility, or presentable appearances."

When people with this background somehow manage to get into the foreign ministry, more often than not they do not have a very successful career. Nevertheless, Ishii assumed the heavy responsibility of Director-General of East Asian Affairs during critical times in Sino-Japanese relations and subsequently served as minister (equivalent to present-day ambassador) to Siam and the Netherlands, and then as ambassador to Brazil and Burma until Japan's defeat in World War II. This career is an indication of Ishii's immense talent, which everybody around him simply could not ignore.

It also happens that people like Ishii often keep a low profile due to self-deprecation and an inferiority complex. Yet some of them are bold enough to utilize their insights and convictions in ways rarely exemplified in a good school student.

While many of his colleagues were stationed in fashionable European and American posts, Ishii was assigned to consulates in various Chinese cities immediately after he joined the ministry. After a while, though, Ishii was stationed in Washington, D.C., where he had a chance to receive guidance from then-Ambassador Shidehara Kijūrō and Saburi Sadao. It was during these days that Ishii's convictions concerning cooperative diplomacy and peace diplomacy were established.

Ishii was consul-general at Jilin when the Manchurian Incident, which he judged to be a mutiny by the Japanese military, erupted. In May of the ensuing year (1932), Ishii submitted a request to the foreign ministry for his return to Japan. His reason, he said explicitly, was that he had "found himself incompatible with the Kanto Army."

In 1937 (12th Year of Shōwa), when he was stationed in Bangkok, Ishii received a telegram from the foreign ministry requesting him to become

Director-General of East Asian Affairs. After pondering the appointment overnight, he sent back a telegram that said, "Please arrange this matter as you think fit, provided you are fully aware of the difference of views between the military and myself on the China issue from the broad perspective." Soon after this telegram, Ishii was appointed to the said post.

Immediately after he reported back to Tokyo, the Konoe Fumimaro cabinet was formed. Ishii found himself working under its foreign minister, Hirota Kōki.

As a man who had gone through hardship in his formative years, Ishii had an eye for men. He was interested in physiognomy and phrenology and developed his own approach to personality psychology. When he saw Pu Yi for the first time when the latter became the head of Manchukuo, Ishii was startled at the ill-fated future that he saw on Pu Yi's face. Ishii got the impression that, under Pu Yi, Manchukuo would meet an unhappy ending.

On Hirota, Ishii wrote,

> I found no originality or strength in him—I was simply disillusioned by his effete attitudes, how he submissively granted requests imposed by the military and reinstated the system by which only active duty army or navy officers could serve in the cabinet posts of war minister or navy minister. . . . While I had no doubt that Mr. Hirota was a pacifist and an advocate of international cooperation, he had, in my opinion, little ability to resist the military and the rightists.

I find this observation of Hirota's personality to be highly accurate.

The first thing that came to Ishii's mind when he heard of the Marco Polo Bridge Incident was, "The military did it again."

As discussed in the previous chapter, however, the truth was the complete opposite. The most horrifying situation for any intelligence analyst is for a familiar situation to undergo a sea change overnight, just when one has taken his or her eyes off it. It often happens that even the assessment of a professional observer with decades of experience but who has not followed the situation for, say, a year is outdated and inferior to that of an upstart who had closely followed the changing situation during that same period.

Prior to his assignment to the Japanese legation to Siam (present day

Thailand), Ishii had been the Japanese Consul General in Shanghai until July 19, 1936. Had he been made to stay one more year in Shanghai, the year of the turn of the tide in China, professional analyzer of situations such as he was, Ishii would not have failed to detect the profound change in the situation. However, what remained in Ishii's memory, instead, was the image of a peaceful Shanghai, which had indulged in the last, short-lived prosperity before the Second Sino-Japanese War, despite constant threats from provocations by the Japanese military.

Contrary to Ishii's image, the atmosphere in Shanghai made a 180-degree turn in one year. It was the Chinese side that had been impatiently waiting for the eruption of a war—a resistance war against the Japanese military. But this went unknown to the Japanese, except for a very few who had been on the spot, including Matsumoto Shigeharu.

Behind the escalation of the Marco Polo Bridge Incident into the quagmire of the Second Sino-Japanese War was definitely a lack of understanding on the Japanese side about the rise of Chinese nationalism. It was understandable, however, that the Japanese general public failed to notice this sea change in China when even such a professional as Ishii had also overlooked it.

"Like Throwing Raw Meat to a Beast"

The morning after the eruption of the Marco Polo Bridge Incident, Ishii met Ushiroku Jun and Toyoda Soemu, directors-general of the military affairs bureaus of the Imperial Japanese Army and Navy, respectively, at the foreign ministry. The three decided on the policy of non-escalation of the incident. This decision was subsequently endorsed at the cabinet meeting convened in the afternoon.

An emergency cabinet meeting was convened on July 11, even though it was on a Sunday. In the wee hours of the morning, a young foreign ministry official rushed to Ishii, highly agitated. He told Ishii that he had received a request from the army's military affairs bureau, asking the foreign minister to "kill the proposal on the mobilization of three army divisions to China when the war minister submits it." This young official told Ishii that he had argued back that it was cowardly for the war ministry officials not to bloc their minister's proposal themselves.

When Ishii went to Tokyo Station to meet Hirota, who was returning from Kugenuma, Kanagawa, Ishii told Hirota of this episode and emphasized that, "Further provocation toward the Chinese must be avoided at any cost."

When Hirota returned from the cabinet meeting, however, he told Ishii that the "[war minister's proposal] passed the cabinet meeting." He said the dispatch would be carried out only when it became absolutely necessary for the safety of the local Japanese residents and the self-defense of the Japanese army stationed in China. Hirota told Ishii that he had approved the war minister's proposal at the cabinet meeting for military preparation.

On this explanation, Ishii wrote, "The staff of the First East Asian Affairs Department and myself were extremely disappointed by our foreign minister."

To be sure, Hirota did oppose the mobilization during the cabinet meeting. But he should not have been fooled by a play of words and compromised at the most critical moment. When the Japanese Imperial Army showed its intention to remain stationed in Manchuria in 1905 immediately after the Russo-Japanese War, inviting criticism from the international community, an apprehensive Itō Hirobumi convened a meeting among elder statesmen and key cabinet members. In this meeting, Itō circulated a paper he had written to stimulate discussions on the policies that Japan should take in the days to come. During the meeting, War Minister Terauchi Masatake (father of War Minister Terauchi Hisaichi of the Hirota cabinet) responded by saying, "While it is difficult to go into the details here, I agree with the spirit of Prince Itō's paper." Hearing this, Itō retorted, saying, "It is not good enough to say that you have no objection. If you have no objection to my argument, you should tell me how it can be implemented."

Hirota should have been equally tenacious at the cabinet meeting on July 11, 1937. Certainly, Hirota or Konoe did not have authority comparable to Itō's. Nevertheless, it must have been obvious to a careful observer of the situation that it would be dangerous to refrain from adamantly opposing the war minister's proposal then and there. At least, it was obvious to Ishii. Indeed, Hirota's irresponsibility was grave.

Ishii also recorded his impression of Konoe. He evaluated Konoe no higher than an "intellectual without his own self."

On the same day as the above cabinet meeting, Konoe obtained imperial sanction of the decision and then announced it as a government decision. The announcement concluded that, "there is no room for doubt that the current incident was a premeditated anti-Japanese action by the Chinese side" and declared, "The Japanese government made an important decision today at the cabinet meeting. It was determined that the government would take necessary measures to dispatch the Imperial Japanese Army to north China."

It was also decided that the incident that had prompted the decision would be officially called *Hokushi Jihen* (the North China Incident). On the evening of the announcement, Konoe hosted a gathering of political and business leaders and the press to reveal the government's decision and request their support.

Konoe, it seemed, was convinced that moving first and catching the military off balance would contribute more to settling the incident than having the government pushed around by the military as usual. This was a natural outcome of Konoe's belief in "forestalling the military" that I introduced in the previous chapter.

But Ishii succinctly criticized Konoe's action, saying, "Absolutely ridiculous. It was like throwing a piece of raw meat to a beast."

It was this decision of the Konoe government that provoked the Kuomintang Government and prompted Chiang Kai-shek to make the so-called Lushan Speech on July 17, in which he declared, "Today, China faces the last turning point in its relations with Japan."

Ishihara Kanji's Consistency

Disappointed with Konoe and Hirota, Ishii pinned his faint hope on Ishihara Kanji, Director of the Operations Bureau of the Imperial Japanese Army General Staff Office at that time. Ishii had been deeply impressed with Ishihara's remark in a conference at the foreign ministry convened a month before the eruption of the incident. In this conference, Ishihara had insisted that the central concern of Japan must be defense against the Soviet Union. Ishihara had said, "As long as I am alive, I will not allow the dispatch of even a single soldier to China."

Ishii secretly met Ishihara to confirm whether the latter's conviction remained unchanged. Ishii admitted that it was "very reassuring" to find that Ishihara had not changed his mind,

Ishihara was a thinker, a rare breed among the Japanese, and, as such, he would not easily change the system of thought that he had laboriously constructed. Although he had originally been an advocate of the colonization of Manchuria, once he decided on the construction of Manchukuo based on the ideology of "harmony of the five races," Ishihara consistently pursued this policy.

In January 1937, Ishihara wrote *Teikoku Gaikō Hōshin Kaisei Iken* (A Proposal on Reforming the Diplomacy of the Empire of Japan), in which he outlined his basic philosophy as follows:

> Sino-Japanese friendship is at the core of the management of East Asia. For this purpose, the Empire of Japan should endure earnestly . . . recognize the tremendous hardship the Chinese people have been under, and help China overcome the present situation and explore future directions . . . and assist China's effort to build and unify the nation . . .
>
> The above should be the foundation of our diplomacy. With this diplomacy, the Empire of Japan can become a pillar of support for the survival of China. This diplomacy would also give the Empire the foundation of becoming a genuine leader in East Asia...

In his *Taishi Jikkō-saku Kaisei Iken* (Proposal on Reform of China Policy) that Ishihara wrote at the same time, he enumerated specific actions to take:

> (1) The Empire should ameliorate its coercive and condescending attitudes toward China and seek genuinely friendly relations on equal footing; (2) The Empire should abandon the notion that North China is a special region, rectify its policy to stimulate the wish for independence among the people in North China's five provinces, and announce clearly that the region currently under the control of the Hebei-Charhar Political Council is without doubt the territory of the Republic of China and that its sovereignty belongs to its central government . . . ; (5) The anti-Japanese people's front is an expression of the Chinese people's agony. It needs to be converted to a

legitimate popular movement for the unification and construction of a new China.

It is amazing how accurately Ishihara had grasped the situation. This could not be merely a logical conclusion from his thought. Probably, his theory was also supplemented with the aspirations of the Chinese, Manchurian, and Korean youths with whom Ishihara had frequently interacted toward the ultimate goal of forming an East Asian union.

Immediately before Ishihara was relieved of his post as Director of the Operations Bureau and transferred to Manchuria in September 1937, he completed guidelines for steering a war. According to *Ishihara Kanji Shiryō—Kokubō Ronsaku*[8], Ishihara wrote three such "guidelines" by June of 1938, but their contents are mostly identical. One can see here again the consistency of Ishihara's thinking.

In these guidelines, Ishihara stated:

> 1. [Japan's leaders should] promptly decide on specific conditions for peace and thereby clarify the purpose of the war . . . 2. [Japan] should try to minimize the size of the war in order to prevent the exhaustion of national resources . . . and conclude a peace agreement as soon as possible. . . . The military force should be used in a concentrated manner only when it has a good chance of destroying the enemy force quickly and decisively so that a peace agreement can be reached.

In other words, before the eruption of the Second Sino-Japanese War, Ishihara had opposed the use of the military, but after the eruption of the war, he started to advocate an early peace agreement and urged the use of military force only when it would have a decisive effect.

The so-called piecemeal deployment of forces—that is, deploying small forces one after another into situations with no prospects—is a strategic taboo. As it turned out, the war turned into a quagmire due to this "piecemeal deployment of forces" by the Japanese side.

---

8   Tsunoda Jun, ed., *Ishihara Kanji Shiryō—Kokubō Ronsaku* (Ishihara Kanji References—Volume on National Defense) (Tokyo: Hara-Shobō, 1967).

Horiba Kazuo was a chief staff officer of the war leadership section of the Imperial Japanese Army General Staff Office under Ishihara when the war erupted. He wrote reviews on the war leadership during the war, which were compiled and published as *Shina Jihen Sensō Shido-shi* (History of War Leadership during the Second Sino-Japanese War) in 1962. In this masterpiece, Horiba wrote, "[On July 10,] the war leadership decided that the use of armed forces was absolutely inacceptable and it would not send even a single additional soldier to China." If the situation called for settlement by force, however, the war leadership held the view that the military should be ready to mobilize 15 army divisions simultaneously and invest \5.5 billion in war expenditures to settle the situation in one fell swoop. Horiba wrote that the authority had decided that it "should choose one of these two options because any halfway stop-gap measure would misguide the country."

Even though there were as many as 26 army divisions and 36 brigades under the command of General Okamura Yasuji pinned down in China at the time of Japan's defeat in 1945, Ishihara's proposal to dispatch 15 divisions was found so absurd when it was first presented that the departments of operations, military affairs, and China affairs of the Imperial Japanese Army General Staff Office did not even bother to consider it seriously. This was a pattern typical of policy decisions that led to a piecemeal deployment of forces. The United States faced similar problems decades later in Vietnam, Afghanistan, and Iraq.

An All-out War without Declaration

Because a truce was reached in the battlefield in China after the cabinet's decision on July 11, the dispatch of Imperial Army divisions to China was put on hold. Despite the truce, the rank and file on the Chinese side was beyond the control of the central government, leading to sporadic skirmishes which the Japanese side immediately retaliated. Friction was rampant in north China, re-stimulating the argument for dispatch of the Imperial Army in Japan. With the strong backing of public opinion, the Imperial Army submitted a proposal for the dispatch of three divisions to the cabinet meeting again on July 20. When Ishii consulted with Directors-General Ushiroku and Toyoda, the latter expressed his opposition.

Ushiroku, on the other hand, viewed the dispatch as inevitable, given the situation within the Army, even though he personally opposed the proposal. By the "situation within the Army," Ushiroku was referring to fierce pressure from the hardliners.

Despite Ishii's petition to Hirota that he do his "best at the cabinet meeting for the long-term future of Sino-Japanese relations," Hirota told Ishii that the cabinet had decided to mobilize three army divisions. The next morning when Ishii tendered a letter of resignation co-signed by Uemura Shin'ichi, a division director under Ishii, Ishii claimed that Hirota's behavior during the cabinet meeting was tantamount to distrust of his subordinates, because he disregarded their advice. Hirota justified his action, saying, "The war minister promised that those mobilized divisions would not be dispatched unless the situation in north China became urgent." On this exchange, Ishii wrote that he was "conciliated by Hirota."

Around that time, however, the predominant mood among senior leaders of the government was for an early settlement of the issue. While the Japanese government did not wish to see the issue escalate, repeated provocations from the Chinese side occurred in north China toward the end of July, including the Langfang Incident, the Guanganmen Incident, and the Tungchow Mutiny.

By this time, it had already become the general mood among the rank and file of the Chinese forces that the time was ripe to start a war of resistance against Japan. For this purpose, they would not hesitate to provoke the Japanese side. Each provocation was confronted by the Imperial Japanese Army, perhaps the easiest organization to be provoked because of its zero tolerance of anything that would damage the military's prestige. Thus, provocations from the Chinese side immediately invited Japan's use of armed forces.

Despite all the skirmishes and the belligerent mood on the Chinese side, efforts to settle the issue diplomatically continued. For one thing, Prime Minister Konoe received an imperial "suggestion" on July 30 that said, "Is it not the time to solve the problem through diplomatic negotiation?" The Emperor's words naturally carried significant weight in the government. According to Uemura Shin'ichi's *Nikka Jihen,*[9] however, the military's cooperative attitude in these diplomatic negotiations owed a lot to "extraordinary efforts demonstrated by Ishihara Kanji, Director of the Operations Bureau." I am in full agreement with this assessment. When a chain of provocations occurred, each one of which could easily have become a reason to start a war, nobody but Ishihara could have controlled the military.

The Ministries of Foreign Affairs, War, and Navy agreed on a negotiation proposal with the Chinese side that for the most part followed the lines of Ishii's argument. In a nutshell, the Japanese side proposed that (1) all agreements that gave special status to the five provinces in north China would be abolished, including the Tanggu Truce, the He-Umezu Agreement, and the Chin-Doihara Agreement, if the Chinese side would secretly promise that it would no longer make Manchukuo an issue; and (2) Japan would recognize the administrative authority of the Nanjing government in return for its suppression of anti-Japanese movements. Objectively speaking, it was a reasonable and realistic proposal.

Ishii wrote, however, "Even if we had had successful communications with the Chinese side, the negotiation would not have born fruit." This was because the Battle of Shanghai erupted just at that timing.

On August 9, Lieutenant Isao Ōyama of the Imperial Japanese Navy Land Forces was shot dead by Chinese Peace Preservation Corps troops while he was traveling down a road under the control of the Shanghai Settlement in a car chauffeured by First-Class Seaman Saitō Yōzō. Like the Tungchow Mutiny, this incident was also instigated by a defiant Chinese garrison attached to the Japanese army. On this incident, Uemura observed, "The anti-Japanese sentiment among the Chinese soldiers on the front line has already grown beyond the control of the central government."

Although the Imperial Navy requested the dispatch of Imperial Army troops to Shanghai, the army leadership was hesitant to carry out the request in the hope that the incident could be settled promptly through

---

9   Uemura Shin'ichi. *Nikka Jihen* (Second Sino-Japanese War). Tokyo: Kajima Kenkyu-sho Shuppankai. 1971.

negotiations. Even Navy Minister Yonai Mitsumasa, who had consistently and adamantly opposed the dispatch of army troops to north China, had to submit the navy's request this time. However, as Ogata Taketora reminisced, when he visited Yonai at his official residence on August 23, Yonai expressed his deep concern over the adverse effects of the dispatch of Imperial Army troops.

One may wonder why Yonai did not persist with his initial opposition as he had been so clear about the negative impact of dispatching the troops to China. There would not have been a dispatch without a request from the navy. Did Yonai also decide to go with the current of the times?

While I have no intention to defend Yonai, it should be noted that, given how far the situation had gone, he had no other alternative.

The anti-Japanese tide in China was no longer stoppable, and the danger to the safety of the Japanese residents was imminent, given the gap in military strength between the two sides in Shanghai. While the dispatch of Japanese troops would most certainly nip in the bud any possibility of a local settlement of the incident, it was utterly unthinkable to abandon the Japanese residents in Shanghai. As Ishii had pointed out earlier, once the fire spread to Shanghai, there was no longer a chance for an early peace settlement.

With things having gotten this far, Japan really had no other choice than to go all the way. Perhaps Yonai requested the dispatch of the army troops dolefully and in full acknowledgment of the situation, despite his remarks in Ogata's memoir.

Because there had been a prior agreement between the Imperial Army and Navy on the dispatch of two army divisions in case of an emergency in Shanghai, Ishihara had to agree with the dispatch.

But, of course, a mere two army divisions would by no means be sufficient. The Japanese side had a hard time suppressing the rebels even with three and a half divisions at the time of the January 28 Incident (also known as the Shanghai War of 1932). Besides, the Chinese forces this time were far superior to those of the earlier incident in terms of their size, equipment, and morale—particularly their *esprit de résistance*. In no time, therefore, the Japanese Army was forced to escalate its engagement in China, dispatching three additional divisions.

Since the Langfang Incident in 1937, the Imperial Japanese Army, particularly its Tianjin Garrison, had succeeded in occupying and pacifying Beijing and Tianjin regions in north China. Once the Japanese side resorted to dispatching reinforcements, however, friction and battles erupted inevitably in various places throughout north China. The Japanese army stationed in China, which received reinforcement of three divisions, began to pursue its own operations aggressively, totally ignoring the non-escalation policy of the Japanese government.

Prince Demchugdongrub of Mongolia, who had been looking for an opportunity to make a comeback since the failure of the Suiyuan Campaign, was ecstatic to see the advance of the Imperial Japanese Army to north China. He offered his full cooperation to the Japanese forces and, as a result, his Mongolian cavalry always spearheaded all the operations of the Japanese Army, helping it occupy Suiyuan. In October 1937, Prince Demchugdongrub declared the formation of the Mongol United Autonomous Government.

Thus, the war spread to the entire Chinese continent in no time. Accordingly, on September 2, the name of the incident was changed from the original *Hokushi Jihen* (North China Incident) to *Shina Jihen* (literally meaning China Incident, but more commonly known as the Second Sino-Japanese War).

At this point, it was effectively an all-out war and there were enough provocations from the Chinese side for Japan to formally declare war. But the Japanese government was dissuaded by the Imperial Army and Navy from declaring war because doing so would have made the United States and other countries restrict their export of war supplies to Japan as neutral parties, which would have been detrimental to Japan's war effort.

It is not hard to imagine that the Chinese side faced a similar problem.

Japan had to rely on the United States for the supply of war materials in order to wage a war with China. This fact alone is enough to make us realize that it really was utterly impossible for Japan to win the war that it later fought with the United States.

As the war escalated, making peace negotiations increasingly infeasible, hardliner elements within the military began to maneuver to oust Ishihara. Mutō Akira, Director of the Operations Division directly under Ishihara, was, from the beginning, a central figure in the hardliners in the military.

It is written in Konoe's memorandum that, in later days, he had once asked Ishihara, "Why was the war escalated even when you, Director of the Operations Bureau, insisted on non-escalation and the government supported your argument?" In return, Ishihara replied that he was "betrayed through the false obedience of my subordinates, who had agreed with me on the surface but engineered the escalation behind my back."

It is said that whenever the Imperial Japanese Army General Staff Office ordered commanders in the field in China to exercise self-restraint, the order was immediately followed by phone calls from Ishihara's subordinates telling them to "disregard the order and go ahead with what you have to do." It must already have been impossible for anyone, including Ishihara, to stop this.

At this point, Ishihara had to recognize his defeat. On September 27, he was transferred to the Kanto Army. Shimomura Sadamu assumed the post of Director of the Operations Bureau.

U.S. President Roosevelt's Quarantine Speech

Meanwhile, the United States was in the depths of isolationism. In three years between 1935 and 1937, the U.S. Congress passed three neutrality acts. Because Europe had already been confronted with Hitler's threat, Britain at least wished to settle the turmoil in the Far East in cooperation with the United States—a wish that the United States found impossible to respond to. Even within the United States, its massive export of scrap iron to Japan became controversial, but the government could not ban the exports because of the neutrality acts.

At last, President Franklin Roosevelt delivered what came to be known as the Quarantine Speech on October 5, 1937, in Chicago. In this speech, Roosevelt warned of the threat from elements that were destroying international law and order. He said:

> It seems to be unfortunately true that the epidemic of world lawlessness is spreading.
>
> When an epidemic of physical disease starts to spread, the community approves and joins in a quarantine of the patients in order to protect the health of the community against the spread of the disease.

Henry Kissinger observed that, "Roosevelt had achieved his goals patiently and inexorably, educating his people one step at a time about the necessities before them."[10]

During the off-the-record question and answer period after the Quarantine Speech, Roosevelt did not deny that his speech "advocated a new approach" and "contained actions beyond a mere moral condemnation." Roosevelt stressed that "there are a number of untried measures in the world."

If it is perceived that an epidemic of world lawlessness is spreading, then some form of sanction is naturally called for. Yet, American isolationism would not allow the United States to meddle with other country's affairs. That was why Roosevelt used the term "quarantine," which is not in the terminology of international law. Using that term prevented him from being criticized for doing something that was in violation of the U. S. isolation policy.

This trick of Roosevelt was passed on to President Kennedy. When the Soviet Union attempted to bring missiles into Cuba in 1962, the Kennedy administration used the term "quarantine" to describe what was de facto a blockade and inspection as defined in international laws in order to avoid legal disputes.

The true origin of the war between Japan and the United States was not John Hays' Open Door Policy or the Stimson Doctrine of non-recognition of the fait accompli in Manchuria. Both of them were nullified, at least temporarily, due to changes in circumstances after they were announced. What eventually led to the confrontation between the two countries, instead, were actions by Roosevelt, starting with this very speech.

Henry Kissinger writes, "America's entry into the war marked the culmination of a great and daring leader's extraordinary diplomatic enterprise."[11] He continues to observe, ". . . there can be little doubt that, in the end, [Roosevelt] would have somehow managed to enlist America in the struggle he considered so decisive to both the future of freedom and to American security,"[12] had it not been for the attack on Pearl Harbor. It has been repeatedly argued by historians that the attack on Pearl Harbor

---

10   Henry Kissinger, *Diplomacy* (New York: Simon & Schuster, Inc. 1994), p.392.
11   Ibid.
12   Ibid, p.393.

was caused by American provocations. Whether this argument can be substantiated with solid evidence or not, it is beyond doubt, thinking strategically, that it was exactly what Roosevelt had longed for. And it must be Kissinger's intention to praise Roosevelt for having protected the world's freedom by provoking Japan to start a war.

The Quarantine Speech was the visible beginning of Roosevelt's effort. In the ensuing year (1938), both the U.S. Congress and American public opinion began to support compulsory measures vis-à-vis Japan via economic sanctions. In 1939, under the pretext of the pressures from Congress and the public opinion, Roosevelt banned the export of aircrafts and other products to Japan in January and went as far as announcing the abrogation of the Treaty of Commerce and Navigation between Japan and the United States in July. It began to be pointed out around that time that Japan would not be able to continue its war with China if the United States imposed an embargo on oil. And as it turned out, the oil embargo made the Greater East Asia War unavoidable in 1941. It was obvious to anyone in the United States with enough foresight that an oil embargo by the United States would corner Japan into either total submission or war with the United States.

Mediation Attempt by German Ambassador to China Oscar Trautmann

In September 1937, China appealed to the League of Nations for help in resolving the Second Sino-Japanese War. The League forwarded the appeal to the Nine-Party Treaty conference.

Although the Japanese government naturally abstained from participating in this conference, Foreign Minister Hirota met the British, American, French, German, and Italian ambassadors to Japan individually on October 27, with prior approvals from pertinent cabinet members, to explain why Japan did not participate in the conference. In these meetings, Hirota told Western ambassadors that, while Japan would not accept interferences that put Japan in the position of a defendant, it would welcome friendly mediation by a third country.

Although the first to offer mediation was Britain, the Imperial Japanese Army rejected the offer due to strong anti-British sentiment within Japan over the issue of British aid to China. The army from the beginning had wished Germany to play the role of the mediator, and it secretly requested such through the military attaché to the Japanese embassy in Germany. In the end, it was decided that Japan would accept mediation by German Ambassador to China Oscar Trautmann, with Ambassador to Japan Herbert von Dirksen functioning as liaison.

The Japanese proposal submitted to Ambassador Dirksen on November 2 made no reference to Manchuria. It maintained the basic position in terms of entrusting the administration of north China to the Nanjing government after a peaceful settlement. Besides that, the proposal only made a few provisos, including establishment of an autonomous government in Inner Mongolia and expansion of the demilitarized zone in Shanghai.

When Trautmann conveyed this proposal to Chiang Kai-shek, Bai Chongxi, Chiang's Deputy Chief of the General Staff, said, "If these are the conditions, why do we have to continue the war?" This opinion was seconded by Chiang's other aides.

While agreeing to adopt this proposal as a basis for negotiation, Chiang said to Trautmann, "Mediation is highly unlikely to be successful when we are in the midst of such a fierce war. I'd like the German government to advise the Japanese government to consider a truce."

Scheme of Holding back Troops without Moving

In order to induce the Chinese side to sit at the peace negotiation table without making them lose face, the scheme of "holding back the Japanese troops" was proposed at the Imperial Japanese Army General Staff Office. Short of a truce, the proposal called for the Japanese troops to halt their advance unilaterally outside Nanjing and enter negotiations with the Chinese side. According to Horiba Kazuo of the War Leadership Division and the architect of the plan, however,

> While we had a fierce argument about this idea with officers of the operations department, I found their enthusiasm about it to be very low. They just kept on stressing how opportune the tide of the war was for the Japanese troops and, obviously, they were at a loss as to what to do to stop the galloping horse.

Thus, despite the plan discussed at the general headquarters in Tokyo, the Imperial Army stationed in China conquered Nanjing. Troops even competed with one another to be the first unit in the charge.

In the same memoir, Horiba also left the following observation:

> Perhaps due to the reaction to the bitter fights in Shanghai, the presence of undertrained conscripts, and other factors, a few cases of undisciplined conduct were observed. The misconduct by the occupying troops in Nanjing, which was magnified by the rampage carried out by remnants of defeated Chinese troops and rowdies, incurred Chinese ill will that would last ten years and damaged the prestige of the Imperial Japanese Army.

As it turned out, "ten years" was a gross underestimation of the Chinese resentment, which is still very much alive today more than half a century after the incident.

Receiving reports on the misconduct of Japanese soldiers in Nanjing from various legations in China, Ishii entered the following reflections in his journal:

> Telegram arrived from consulate in Shanghai with details on unruly conduct by our military. It says their acts of plunder and rape were too horrible to look at. Were these acts really done by our Imperial Japanese Army? They must be the result of moral decay of the Japanese people.

Ishii also wrote that one of the most conspicuous ringleaders of the atrocity was an enlisted first lieutenant, a former lawyer, who ordered his men to abduct local women and rape them in the barracks like demons.

This incident in Nanjing was widely reported overseas, tarnishing Japan's image and strengthening Chinese determination to fight the Japanese.

Nothing is better propaganda during wartime than atrocities conducted by adversaries. Japan, too, propagated atrocities by the U.S. troops during World War II, calling them *Kichiku Bei-Ei* (brutal Americans and Britons). British military affairs commentator Basil Liddell-Hart once said, "Chivalry in war can be a most effective weapon in weakening the opponent's will to resist." What the Japanese military did in Nanjing was the complete opposite of this.

The problem is, while the wartime propaganda of the defeated ends with the conclusion of a war, those of the winners remain. Because of its purpose, wartime propaganda is allowed to be exaggerated limitlessly. Thus, in the case of Nanjing, because the highly exaggerated propaganda lingered after the war, such an absurd view as the massacre of more than 200,000 citizens took on a life of its own. This piece of propaganda was indeed so exaggerated that it became a target of criticism.

After more than half a century since the Nanjing Incident, there is no way today to confirm the number of genuinely noncombatant victims. Nevertheless, it seems undeniable that aberrant conduct on the part of the Japanese military occurred on a large scale. It is true that the Japanese military was faced with the need to mop up plain-clothes Chinese soldiers and that mobs taking advantage of the vacuum in public order engaged in riotous conduct and plunder. Even so, it is hardly deniable that the magnitude of the aberrant conduct by the Japanese military in Nanjing was incomparable to anything that had happened in Shanghai, Guangdong, Wuhan, or any other cities all through the war. The extent of the carnage was such that General Matsui Iwane, Commander-in-Chief of the Japanese Central China Area Army, was compelled to deplore it with the words, "My god, what have you done?" and Horiba and Ishii were so shocked that they left the above reflections.

Why and how did such a thing happen?

Ishii attributed the situation to moral decay of the Japanese people. It may be true that the Japanese by that time had left behind the original zeal of a young empire to be recognized as a civilized nation by the world. This was the zeal Japan had demonstrated during the Boxer Rebellion and the Russo-Japanese War. If the discipline of the entire military had degenerated as such, however, similar atrocities must also have occurred in other cities such as later occupied Wuhan and Guangdong, just like the Mongol Empire's army, which conducted repeated massacres wherever they advanced, including in Samarkand and Baghdad, and the Soviet army, which ravaged civilians in Manchuria and Germany. But incidences of repeated massacres did not happen. While there certainly were civilian casualties by bombardments and air raids during the battle, no other case of aberrant conduct by the occupation forces was reported. The military discipline of the Japanese army that occupied Beijing, the very first target of the Japanese occupation, was particularly stringent and strictly enforced to the extent that some Beijing citizens, whose memories of rampage and plunder by Caucasian soldiers during the Boxer Rebellion were still fresh after 26 years, later proposed the erection of a bronze statue of Ikeda Sumihisa, a staff officer of the occupation army.

Simply put, the Nanjing Incident should be attributed to the circumstances and atmosphere of a war that were bound to provoke this kind of atrocity from time to time.

The histories of Europe, Middle East, Africa, North America, and China are filled with incidents of capturing enemy cities. Some were done in a highly orderly fashion, while others ended up in horrible rampages and plunders, including the sacking of Antwerp by Spanish troops in 1576 called the "Spanish Fury."

A newer example is the occupation of Berlin by the Soviet Army during World War II. While Russian soldiers were rampant all over Eastern Europe, those at the time of the Battle of Berlin were of an unprecedented scale in history. Two elements were common in the Berlin incident and the Nanjing Incident. One was the total anarchy in the two occupied cities, where administrative structures to deal with the occupation troops ceased to function. The second was the sense of freedom among soldiers derived from the knowledge that their long battle was finally over (this was not true in case of the Japanese military in Nanjing, but the soldiers believed it to be true), which led to the spread of imprudence and a lack of restraint. In the case of Soviet soldiers, an additional psychological push was driven by the resentment at the Nazis' invasion of their homeland. For the Japanese soldiers, their grudge against the Chinese for the years of anti-Japanese/slight-Japanese movements as well as the Tungchow Mutiny was the added psychological push.

Also in the background must have been the historical climate of China, which had invited countless cases of atrocities and massacres in the past, as well as the atmosphere of China in those days. Perhaps it should be pointed out that Nanjing had witnessed gruesome massacres during the Boxer Rebellion and the Nanjing Incident of 1927 at the time of the Kuomintang's Northern Expedition.

Slaughter was an everyday event during in the civil war between the Kuomintang and the Communists. The *Shō Kaiseki Hiroku* (Secret Memoir of Chiang Kai-Shek) includes the following description of the Guangzhou Uprising (the so-called Guangzhou Commune) led by Ye Jianying and others in December 1927:

> Anyone who showed the slightest hint of resistance was killed. Even an old woman who was just bringing water to extinguish fire was shot to death then and there by the Communist elements . . . [They] tied a college professor, who was accused of being an anti-communist, and his wife to a utility pole and brutally vivisected them . . . Total lawlessness lasted for three days, during which 15,000 Guangzhou citizens were victimized.

A prominent member of the Communist Party wrote about the Guangzhou Commune and its predecessor, Haifeng-Lufeng Soviet in November of the same year, as follows:

> According to the most recent and reliable statistics, 1,822 landlords, local clans, and lesser gentry were killed in the past few months in Haifeng County alone. This is almost an embarrassingly small figure compared to 5,700 laborer and peasant citizens slaughtered in a matter of a couple of days at the time of the Guangzhou Uprising. *The North China Daily News* carried a lengthy article on details of how the communists had killed people in Haifeng and Lufeng, including a case of a woman in childbed, which "defied any further description because of its unspeakable brutality." It also reported that it was the Communist Party's official policy to slaughter one-third of a local population in order to improve the relative living standard of the surviving two-thirds. Is it not absolutely absurd to even speak of killing one-third of the 800,000 citizens of the Haifeng-Lufeng regions?

One can glean from this memoir the conditions within China on the eve of the Second Sino-Japanese War as well as the Chinese propensity to exaggerate opponents' atrocities. This peculiar propensity notwithstanding, it is highly interesting to read that a Chinese himself found the killing of over 200,000 citizens (one-third of the Haifeng-Lufeng population) absurd in light of the Chinese propaganda that highlighted the Japanese massacre of 300,000 Nanjing citizens. It should also be pointed out that the case of the Guangzhou Commune was the result of a mutual, intentional purge of enemy elements. As such, the number of victims exceeding a few thousand was not entirely unrealistic. Taking into consideration that the incident in Nanjing in 1937 was the result of self-indulgent and lawless conduct by some soldiers drunk on victory rather than a premeditated campaign of genocide, it would be more sensible to estimate the number of genuinely civilian victims, excluding those who had been suspected to be combatants, in the vicinity of 1,000.

The Nanjing Incident Did Occur

The dispute over the incident in Nanjing has not yet been settled even though more than half a century has elapsed since the end of the war. One reason for this is the fact that the International Military Tribunal for the Far East, whose legitimacy and procedural validity were highly questionable, was the first official arena (other than the media) where the incident was taken up. Another reason is that proponents of the leftist historical view in the post–World War II Japan that is determined to see all Japan's past deeds in a negative light have been behind the emphasis on this incident. The view that all of Japan's actions were bad has engendered among the Japanese an attitude of uncritical acceptance of such an absurd factual error as putting the number of citizens massacred at 300,000. This attitude has naturally drawn the strong resentment that it deserves.

There has even been an attempt to treat the Nanjing Incident as the same as the Holocaust. In contrast to the Holocaust, which was the premeditated annihilation of an ethnic group, the Nanjing Incident was essentially a problem of civilian casualties during a state of war. Legally speaking, the Nanjing Incident should rather be categorized together with the atomic bombs on Hiroshima and Nagasaki, the carpet-bombing raids on Dresden and Tokyo, and the lawless conduct of Soviet soldiers in Manchuria and Sakhalin. To categorize the Nanjing Incident with the Holocaust naturally invites more incredulity and resentment.

Nevertheless, in any event, it is an undeniable fact that aberrant conduct took place on a significant scale when the Imperial Japanese Army occupied Nanjing. To deny this fact would make us lose sight of the truth of history.

The Nanjing Incident did happen. There is no doubt about it. In fact, it can be proven by the subsequent conduct of the Japanese military.

In recognition of the gravity of what its soldiers had done in Nanjing, the Japanese military doubled its efforts to enforce stringent military discipline. According to Shimomura Kainan's *Shūsen Hishi* (Secret History of the End of the War), General Okamura Yasuji, commander-in-chief of the China Expeditionary Army, saw to it that the spirit of benevolence was strictly enforced throughout the troops under the slogan of "Don't burn, don't rape, don't kill." Because rape was an offense indictable only on complaint, making it difficult to punish rapists, Okamura advised the deputy minister of war on the reform of the army's criminal law at the time of his temporary return to Tokyo and succeeded in making rape a punishable offense regardless of a complaint.

And history shows that after the Nanjing Incident in 1937, the first year of the Second Sino-Japanese War, until Japan's surrender in 1945, there were no more incidents of large-scale civilian massacre or acts of violence, although there were collateral battle casualties.

Evacuations of the Japanese military and the Japanese residents after the end of the war were carried out more or less peacefully. It was reported that, in some cases, their departure was even regretted by the local people. There is no knowing how prevalent this sentiment was, but undoubtedly such cases did exist. There are even examples of Chinese cities concluding sister city relationships with the Japanese hometowns of the occupation troops after the war. This is a phenomenon that is totally unthinkable in the case of Russian, Polish, and French cities occupied by the Germans, or German cities occupied by American, British, and French armies.

As detailed in Chinese documents, warlords and local rebels who had dominated various localities in China since the 1910s perpetrated all manner of atrocities. It is quite imaginable that living under occupation by the Japanese troops after the Nanjing Incident might well have been easier for ordinary Chinese people than living under the rule of warlords.

Undoubtedly, Chiang Kai-shek's policy to "repay a grudge with kindness" played a role here. But if the Japanese military had continued elsewhere the same aberrant conduct it had shown in Nanjing, it is quite possible that the resentment built up among the local people would have exploded at Japan's defeat. Yet it is a fact that evacuations of the Japanese troops and civilians were carried out orderly and peacefully.

Because the wars that the Japanese had experienced until the time Japan opened its doors to the outside world had been mainly civil wars, killing was confined between fighting warriors. Unlike in other countries, Japan had never seen a massacre of ordinary citizens. With the proud memory of the Imperial Army's conduct during the Boxer Rebellion still fresh in people's minds, the Japanese had believed that no other nation was freer from abominable cruelty than the Japanese. The Nanjing Incident, however, made the Japanese realize that, after all, they were no exception—they too possessed the weakness to be influenced by local historical/cultural climates and the peculiar atmosphere of war. This realization will help the Japanese people to have a fair perception of other peoples and to be tolerant of others in the future.

It should be pointed out that after the Imperial Japanese Army woke up from this single incident of madness, a restorative force kicked in to bring them back to traditional Japanese decency until the end of the war.

The End of Trautmann's Mediation

Prior to the Siege of Nanjing on December 13, German Ambassador Dirksen informed the Japanese government on December 7 that the Chinese side was prepared to enter negotiation based on the conditions presented by the Japanese side earlier. Dirksen requested the Japanese government's confirmation. Japan's Ministers of Foreign Affairs, War, and Navy committed to agree on the terms with minor modifications to the previous conditions.

Early the next morning, however, War Minister Sugiyama Hajime visited Foreign Minister Hirota and said, "We'd prefer to decline the mediation by Germany. We have already obtained the prime minister's consent." What this meant was that war minister had retracted his earlier commitment under pressure from his subordinates.

"What appalling fools those ministers are," wrote Ishii in his journal.

Ishii soon found that views within the Imperial Army were still divided. Taking advantage of the schism, the Ministries of Foreign Affairs and

Navy jointly attempted to persuade the War Ministry, which resulted in the confirmation of peace conditions at the government–Imperial General Headquarters liaison conference.

Ishii reminisced over the exchanges that took place in this conference. It was only Navy Minister Yonai and Koga Mineichi, Deputy Chief of the Imperial Japanese Navy General Staff, who faithfully supported the original package. Others present kept insisting on additional conditions one after another.

In the course of discussion, the original proposal to restore the Nanjing Government's administrative authority was replaced by a demand to convert north China into a special district. The condition that all previous agreements, including the Tanggu Truce, be abolished was retracted. Even a demand for reparation of war expenses was newly added.

This was not a mere modification of conditions. The revised package was tantamount to a 180-degree shift in Japan's strategy toward China— that is, a full reversal from the strategy to foster Sino-Japanese friendship by forgetting and forgiving everything if the Chinese side gave its tacit approval of Manchukuo, to a scheme to build a second Manchukuo in north China and subjugate China as the defeated.

This is a point that demarcates those who can think strategically from those who cannot. It is immediately obvious to those who apply strategic thinking to a country's future that this is a boundary that should not be crossed.

Shifting from tacit approval of Manchukuo to its formal recognition would still have been a minor tactical change, albeit a significant one. But conversion of north China to a special district could become a turning point for Japan's future policy toward China. And yet, both Prime Minister Konoe and Foreign Minister Hirota remained silent throughout the conference and left the matter to take its own course.

Unable to restrain himself any longer, Ishii spoke up, saying, "If you keep on adding demands like this, the package will be totally unacceptable to the Chinese side and they will not agree on a peace settlement." In speaking up, Ishii had forgotten that, as a bureaucrat, he was not entitled to state his opinion in the conference. Naturally, his remark was ignored.

At this point, the mediation attempt by Trautmann was effectively crippled. When Ambassador Dirksen received the revised proposal from Hirota on December 22, he promised to convey it to the Chinese side, deploring the futility of his doing so.

Ishii wrote on December 22:

> The German ambassador was invited to the foreign minister's official residence, where he received the Japanese reply. Reading the reply, the German ambassador said that Chiang Kai-shek would not accept it. Of course not. Chiang would be a fool to agree to peace negotiations under these new conditions.

Coming out of the prime minister's official residence at dusk after the conference, the crestfallen Ishii encountered a lantern parade filled with crowds of people celebrating the fall of Nanjing.

CHAPTER
8

Into the Quagmire

—Strong Support for Government's Hardliner Policy—

The Japanese Government Would Not Deal with the Kuomintang Government

As reviewed in the previous chapter, toward the end of 1937 (12th Year of Shōwa), the voice of hardliners became predominant within the Japanese government. Japan's conditions for a peace agreement were too demanding for Chiang Kai-shek to accept, thus nullifying all the effort. Moreover, the Japanese government set the deadline for a response from the Chinese side at January 15.

The situation did not require any ultimatum. There was no reason for the Japanese government to set a specific deadline for the reply. The situation facing Japan at that time was totally different from that on the eve of the Russo-Japanese War in 1904, when a day's delay meant Russia becoming stronger in the Far East day by day through the Siberian railroad. Most likely, the setting of a deadline was the tactic of the hardliner elements within the military that wished to derail the process toward peace negotiations as soon as possible.

Simply put, at the root of the thinking of the War Ministry, including War Minister Sugiyama Hajime, was the idea of constructing a second Manchukuo through the establishment of puppet governments in northern

China. As a matter of fact, the Japanese military had occupied Chinese cities one after another by that time, but it had to entrust their administration to local officials, leading to the birth of numerous Chinese local governments with the backing of the Imperial Japanese Army.

These hardliner elements within the war ministry also wished to announce that the Japanese government would not deal with Chiang Kaishek and to establish this position as a fait accompli.

In contrast, the most central concern for the Army General Staff Office since the time of Ishihara Kanji had been the steady expansion of the Soviet Union's military power in the Far East. Its wish was to settle the battles in China so that it could concentrate on the defense of Japan against the Soviet Union.

Although the Imperial Japanese Army General Staff Office also had its own share of hardliner elements vis-à-vis China, its mainstream successfully contained them and promoted continuation of the peace negotiations. As far as this issue was concerned, it can be said that Prime Minister Konoe and Foreign Minister Hirota sided with the war ministry and suppressed the argument of the General Staffs of the Imperial Japanese Army and Navy, which had the prerogative of military command.

It has been a stereotypical assessment of the post–World War II leftist historical view that arbitrary conduct of the General Staff Offices throughout the early part of Shōwa led Japan to its ruin, because they abused its prerogative of military command. Actually, it could have been the patriotic fanaticism of public opinion and the mass media that was the true force that moved Japan. After all, it is only natural for people to be inspired by the rise of their country's national prestige and to support it. This general trend in public opinion was so strong that even those with the prerogative of military command could not resist it.

Even Ishii gave up and said to Hirota,

> A peace agreement will be hopeless for the time being if we demand these conditions. There will be no way to salvage the state of affairs until Japan wakes up, finding the war with China unmanageable. Until then, the position of the Japanese government not to deal with the Kuomintang government would be good enough. I would not dispute it.

For those who were in charge of the actual negotiation with the Chinese side, including Ishii, the conditions that the Japanese side demanded appeared to erase any possibility for continuing the negotiations.

Although the Chinese side responded via Ambassador Dirksen on January 14 that it wished to have more details on the conditions, Hirota decided that the response was a mere time-gaining tactics on the part of the Chinese. On January 16, the Japanese government announced that, "From now on the Empire of Japan will not regard the Kuomintang Government as its negotiation partner."

Many historians view this announcement as a decisive event in turning the Second Sino-Japanese War into a quagmire. In actuality, however, the possibility for a peace agreement had already been nipped in the bud when the Japanese side had set conditions unacceptable to the Chinese side. Actually, only half a year later the Japanese government itself repented this announcement and virtually shelved it.

Spontaneous National Frenzy

Once the Second Sino-Japanese War erupted, the mass media and public opinion in Japan came to unanimously support the government's hardline position and admire the military.

Postwar leftist historical view often attributes this phenomenon to the government's restrictions on freedom of speech. To be sure, it was no longer permissible to openly criticize the military. Even though censorship might have been able to ban undesirable articles, however, it was not possible for the military to coerce newspapers into singing the militarists' tune and inciting readers. Thus, it seems undeniable that in those days nationalism or national frenzy for expansionism grew spontaneously among the Japanese people, more specifically among the mass media.

Besides, Prime Minister Konoe was overwhelmingly popular among the Japanese people. By that time, it had become the worldwide trend for political leaders to use speeches to appeal directly to the public, partially thanks to the widespread use of radio. This trend was well exemplified by Adolf Hitler's impassioned grand speeches, which had a tremendous impact both within and outside Germany. Being a philosophy lover by nature, Konoe was a master of rhetoric. Coupled with his tall figure and noble appearance, his speeches mesmerized the entire nation.

On September 10, 1937 (12th Year of Shōwa), two months after the eruption of the Second Sino-Japanese War, a national convention of the National Spiritual Mobilization Movement was held at the Tokyo Metropolitan Hibiya Public Hall. At this convention, Konoe declared, "For the sake of justice and humanity, and for the sake of a long-term grand design for Asia, it is imperative that we deal a heavy blow to China." This "deal a heavy blow" met with universal applause among the Japanese people and came to be used over and over until deep into the war.

The origin of Konoe's idea was his famous notion of "forestalling the military"—that is, to seize the policy initiative by proposing something bold which even the military hesitated to propose.

It should be easy to imagine that this speech by Konoe appealed to the Japanese people's nationalism, which had already been inflamed. At the same time, the danger of arousing public opinion should also be obvious. Backed by zealous public opinion, hardliner arguments became single-handedly predominant in all forums, including cabinet meetings.

Opposing voices were rarely heard. Kiyosawa Kiyoshi, a representative liberal of the time, started a one-year tour around Europe and the United States immediately after the eruption of the Second Sino-Japanese War. During the trip, he was showered with criticism of Japan wherever he went, to which he responded by actively defending Japan's position to the extent that he entered in his journal, "I myself was playing the role of mini-Matsuoka [Yosuke]." As this episode shows, patriotism was a value equally shared by liberals, too.

It was to his credit that Ishibashi Tanzan (石橋湛山), the Taishō-Shōwa journalist who later became prime minister, wrote in the October 1936 issue of *Tōyō Keizai Shimpō*,

> Unfortunately, newspapers in Japan today appear to be anxious to destroy Japan's diplomatic relations each day, totally devoid of any aspiration to contribute to international peace. . . . Maybe this is the outcome of newspapers becoming too nationalistic. Nay, it must have been the result of newspapers becoming too much like an organ of bureaucracy, [because they misguidedly believed that such would genuinely assist Japan's diplomacy].

While asserting that the direct cause of the war was attributable to the Chinese side, Ishibashi did not fail to point out that the remote cause of the war rested on Japan, as follows:

> Of course, China itself is much to be blamed for its current deterioration and the peril of war it faces. It is the result of China's aimless indulgence in anti-Japanese/slight-Japanese movements without calm assessment of its own power or of what Japan had requested. But we in Japan also have a lot to reflect on concerning our conduct, which might have made the Chinese people turn to such anti-Japanese/slight-Japanese movements.

There are reasons to believe that the Chinese side in the beginning had a certain self-confidence in its capabilities. In an editorial on July 24, 1937, Ishibashi made the following warning:

> Anti-Japanese hardliners in China might think it would be possible to beat the Japanese forces and drive them out of north China and Manchukuo. The tremendous improvement in Chinese war-readiness in recent years coupled with the nationwide anti-Japanese frenzy might have been enough to make the Chinese side become hopeful. But as a number of impartial foreign observers, particularly those who are sympathetic with China, deeply deplore, this is nothing but overconfidence that is most dangerous for the Chinese side.

This came from Ishibashi, who knew China well and cared about its future.

As Ishibashi had feared, the Chinese side proved to be no match for the Japanese once the battle erupted. In fact, a Japanese battalion was more than a good match for a Chinese division.

The bravery of Japanese soldiers at the front was really remarkable.

Although Mizuno Hironori, a former navy officer who turned pacifist military commentator, had already retired from public writing by that time, he left the following reflection in a personal letter he wrote in November after the eruption of the war. He started his reflection with, "I am appalled by how spineless the Chinese troops have been," revealing that he had hoped that the Chinese troops would somehow put up a better fight to stun or rein in the Japanese military to some extent.

> Having said that, I must say I have been impressed by the bravery of
> the Japanese military. . . . The world has come to an era of military
> dominance. Maybe it is time for both of us to shatter our fountain
> pens and sharpen our daggers.

Around the time when U.S.-Japan joint military cooperation became necessary at the height of the Cold War, I had a chance to ask a Korean army
general, who had made a name for his bravery during the Korean War and
become well respected in the United States, what it would take to become
respected after fighting together with the Americans. The general, who
was known for his sharp tongue, said, "Respect? No respect for Korean
soldiers who shoot poorly and run away from enemies. Though, come to
think of it, American soldiers were no different." Then after a pause, he
added, "There will never be soldiers like the Japanese before the defeat."

It was not only in terms of equipment that a Japanese battalion (1,500
troops in wartime) was a good match for a Chinese army division (more
than 10,000 troops in wartime). In terms of discipline, training, and, particularly, morale, the Japanese military far excelled its Chinese opponent.

Breaking through a fortress in the morning and conquering a city at
night, the Japanese military's swift and irresistible advance led to numerous tales of bravery. While there might naturally have been a certain level
of exaggeration and glorification in those tales, they are judged to be true
stories rather than mere propaganda. A battalion on a par with an army
division could have been possible only with the exceptional morale of the
Japanese military, which was unparalleled in the world because each and
every soldier was prepared to sacrifice himself for the country.

The Japanese people were thrilled by victory after victory. They were
convinced that all of China would come under Japan's control in no time.

Ishii reminisced that when foreign ministry officials toured local
regions in Japan, they were warned by residents who said, "If the foreign
ministry should make a peace agreement which makes us lose territories
Japanese soldiers have laboriously captured through this holy war, we
will rise and storm the ministry building." A self-styled China expert visited Ishii and insisted that Japan should take at least Shandong or Hebei

province, while a religious worker pleaded that Japan should snatch an area around Shanghai in order to ensure peace. These anecdotes vividly describe the atmosphere in those days.

National Mobilization Law Enacted

The most central issue at the Imperial Diet session which started in February 1938 was, without doubt, the National Mobilization Law (国家総動員法).

As the war escalated, it began to take the shape of an all-out war involving the entire nation, which is a characteristic feature of modern warfare.

Particularly for Japan, which had been poorly endowed with resources and funds, it was imperative to mobilize everything it had to wage war. While the National Mobilization Law aimed to mobilize all available material and human resources for national defense, it was designed to be implemented by imperial edict. The law was controversial as it could deprive the Imperial Diet of its function to enact a law.

Strong opposition was heard among members of the Diet on the grounds that this law violated the spirit of the Meiji Constitution, making the parliamentary deliberations meaningless.

It so happened that the National Foundation Day on February 11 was to be the fiftieth anniversary of promulgation of the Meiji Constitution. On this occasion, Ishibashi wrote an editorial in praise of the Meiji Constitution. Quoting Itō Hirobumi's *Kenpō Gige* (Commentaries on the Constitution of the Empire of Japan), Ishibashi praised the constitution's guarantee of individual freedom, allowing the Japanese people to enjoy freedom and decent lives to the extent permitted by law. Arguing that the Japanese citizens benefitted from the special privilege of a constitution that was no longer found in Germany or Italy, Ishibashi strongly defended the Meiji Constitution.

During the Diet deliberations, Lieutenant Colonel Satō Kenryō yelled at Diet members to shut up, for which the war minister was forced to formally apologize later. There was also an incident that members of a right-wing organization occupied party headquarters of both the *Seiyūkai* and the *Minseitō*. The deliberations on this law, thus, became very tense both inside and outside the Imperial Diet.

In the end, the Diet passed the law with an amendment: deletion of a provision that regulated political assemblies and newspapers. Prime Minister Konoe was sick in bed from a common cold as usual when the law was passed, but he returned to the Diet chamber after his fever fell and made the following explanation: "This law is by no means permeated with fascist ideology. In contrast to Nazi Germany's enabling statute, which is applied even in peace time, the National Mobilization Law is applied only during wartime."

This was indeed a clarification of the fundamental difference between fascism and Japan's National Mobilization Law. A system to grant the leader with autocratic power in wartime dates back to the ancient Roman Republic. In wartime, even a democratic polity will inevitably have to adopt the system of centralized power, regulated economy, and preservation of confidentiality. As long as the principle that application of this kind of system is kept only temporary, it is not entirely incompatible with democracy.

In the case of Japan, too, had peace been restored somehow, it seems highly unlikely that the military would have continued to monopolize power. Even after the grand victory in the Russo-Japanese War, military servicemen had to hesitate to get on a train in uniform during the Taishō Democracy. It is not hard to imagine that, in the case of the Shōwa period, the return to normalcy must have been quicker since parliamentary democracy had already been firmly established. It seems to be more accurate to equate the so-called militarism in Japan with wartime regimes found in many other countries in the world.

Peace Efforts by Foreign Minister Ugaki

Toward the end of May 1938 (13th Year of Shōwa), Prime Minister Konoe reshuffled his cabinet.

Despite his immense popularity among the people, Konoe in those days often hinted at his resignation. With his disposition as a dilettante and with a weak sense of responsibility, Konoe had always talked about resignation. Added to this natural inclination of his was his dissatisfaction with the conduct of the Imperial Army, particularly War Minister Sugiyama Gen, with whom Konoe had become totally fed up by that time.

Konoe expressed his intention to resign again after the spring session of the Diet was closed. Strongly advised to reconsider by people around him, however, Konoe decided to reshuffle his cabinet instead.

Although dismissal of a war minister was next to impossible under normal conditions in those days, Konoe succeeded in recalling Itagaki Seishirō from the battlefield to replace Sugiyama. He was able to accomplish this partly because of the Imperial wish to dissuade Konoe from resigning.

As it turned out, this change of the war minister amounted to next to nothing. While Itagaki cut a brilliant figure at the time of the Manchurian Incident, it was mainly due to the presence of staff officer Ishihara Kanji. As a war minister, his thinking was more parallel to those of ordinary army officers, wishing for the founding of a second Manchukuo in northern China. He was totally devoid of any definite view of his own concerning the settlement of the war with China.

Dissatisfied also with Foreign Minister Hirota Kōki, Konoe replaced him with Ugaki Kazushige. Ugaki accepted the nomination on the condition that Konoe would rescind his position of "not dealing with the Kuomintang government." Konoe himself wrote in his memoirs that "I have to admit that this announcement [not dealing with the Kuomintang government] was a mistake" and "I even had to reshuffle the cabinet in order to correct this mistake."

The appointment of Ugaki for this purpose notwithstanding, Konoe very quickly decided to go with the flow of the times, totally nullifying this personnel change.

As soon as Ugaki took office as foreign minister, he started talking with British Ambassador Robert Craigie with the intent of aligning interests with Britain and the United States. Ugaki's initiative was immediately met by popular outrage demanding the termination of the Ugaki-Craigie talks and "Ugaki's flirting diplomacy toward Britain." There was an incident of several eccentric military officers bursting into the prime minister's official residence in a rage. There also was a case of pro-Axis Powers foreign ministry officials rushing to Ugaki's private residence to protest.

Along with the dialogue with Britain, Ugaki also resumed negotiations with China. Ugaki's appointment was welcomed by the Chinese Japanophiles. The Kuomintang's foreign minister Zhang Qun, a longtime acquaintance of Ugaki's, sent a congratulatory telegram, conveying his wish to talk with Ugaki. In response, Ugaki suggested it would be more appropriate to negotiate with the more neutral K'ung Hsiang-hsi (premier) than Zhang Qun or Wang Jingwei, who were obvious Japanophiles. This suggestion was accepted by the Chinese side.

Elated, Ishii gladly rendered his assistance toward realizing this negotiation with the Chinese side. Thanks to Ugaki's fundamental stance that Japan had no territorial ambition, preparation for the negotiations went as far as to decide whether they should be held in Taiwan or Nagasaki. The Japanese side even offered to dispatch the Imperial Navy's cruiser to meet the Chinese delegation.

But there was strong opposition to this peace negotiation both within the cabinet as well as among the public. And Ugaki was forced to resign even before prospects for the beginning of negotiations became clear, due to the issue of establishing a central organization to deal with the China issue.

It had been proposed after the eruption of the war with China that a centralized organization dedicated to the settlement of the war should be established. The establishment of this organization would inevitably mean a transfer of the foreign ministry's prerogatives on the China issue to this new organization. The resurfacing of this proposal after the reshuffling of the Konoe cabinet must have been engineered by the hardliners who wished to put a stop to Ugaki's diplomacy.

Although the War and Navy Ministries presented Ishii with a preliminary proposal to persuade him of the virtue of the organization, he would not give in even an inch. When they presented the proposal to Ugaki instead, bypassing Ishii, Ugaki opposed the proposal even more staunchly than Ishii. Having no other recourse, the two ministries decided to obtain Prime Minister Konoe's endorsement and force the proposal through the cabinet meeting.

On the morning of September 29, when Ishii told Ugaki that, now that things had come to this phase, it would be up to his best effort to block the proposal at the cabinet meeting, Ugaki said, "Fine" before heading to the cabinet meeting. It was not even an hour after this that Ishii heard the news of Ugaki's resignation.

The following morning, Ishii also tendered his resignation together with Vice Minister for Foreign Affairs Horiuchi Kensuke. To quote Ishii's memoir:

In the latter half of my tenure as Director-General of East Asian Affairs, I felt as if I were like a fish revived by shallow water in a wheel track when Minister Ugaki was appointed. Placing my hope for the settlement of the war with China on Minister Ugaki's determination and his political clout, I worked assiduously. It was also a pleasure to see my advice being adopted time and time again. . . . Now that Minister Ugaki has left the post, what is the post of the Director-General of East Asian Affairs for . . . ?

Minister Ugaki said to me, "I do not find it in my heart to remain in the Konoe cabinet, which had once entrusted the settlement of the war with China to me, only to deprive me of my authority now. I hope you will understand my feeling."

There always was leniency in Mr. Ugaki's words. It was truly regrettable that he had to resign.

There was no knowing whether Ugaki's peace initiative would have worked. Its success would have required strengthening of control over the military, which was tantamount to a reverse coup d'état. While, no doubt, Ugaki had the will power as well as the determination to carry out this tightening of control over the military if necessary, doing so would also call for the iron-hard support of the prime minister. If the prime minister's support could not be expected, then Ugaki's peace initiative would have no chance from the beginning. It is not hard to imagine that Ugaki must have come to this conclusion.

It is said that Prime Minister Konoe had told Vice Minister for Foreign Affairs Horiuchi, "To tell you the truth, it does not matter who becomes foreign minister." If Konoe indeed believed in what he said, one wonders why he bothered to dismiss Hirota and request Ugaki to succeed him. In any event, after Ugaki's resignation, Horiuchi and Ishii left Tokyo, being respectively appointed to the posts of ambassador to the United States and the Netherlands.

Peace Advocate Wang Jingwei

While the Japanese attempts to initiate a peace negotiation met a series of setbacks due to resistance from the military, there remained a strong pro-peace faction within the Kuomintang government.

Aside from Wang Jingwei, Zhou Fohai was also knowledgeable about Japan within the Kuomintang. Looking up to Professor Kawakami Hajime as his model while at Kyoto University, Zhou became one of the founding members of the Chinese Communist Party after he returned home. But he quit the Communist Party and joined the Kuomintang, where he served Chiang Kai-shek as his adviser in charge of Japan-related information.

Other strong pro-peace advocates included Gao Zongwu, Director-General of Asian Affairs in charge of Japan (a graduate of Kyushu University) and Dong Taoning, Director of Japanese Affairs (a graduate of Kyoto University) of the Kuomintang's ministry of foreign affairs.

The fact that all of the leading foreign ministry officials in charge of Japan were peace advocates signified that the Kuomintang government had not yet been united in anti-Japan policy at that time. It also showed that organizations within the Kuomintang government still functioned to contemplate the future of Chinese diplomacy realistically.

Secretly visiting Japan in February 1938 under Gao's instruction, Dong utilized his personal connection to meet with Colonel Kagesa Sadaaki, director of the newly founded intelligence/counter-intelligence division of the Imperial Japanese Army General Staff Office. During this meeting, Kagesa entrusted Dong with letters to Zhang Qun and He Yingqin, Kagesa's friends from his days at the Imperial Japanese Army Academy. These letters found their way to Chiang Kai-shek, who agreed to use the Kagesa–Zhang-He line as a channel for peace negotiations with Japan. The absolutely non-negotiable condition that Chiang attached to the negotiations at that time was the return of the region south of the Great Wall to China. What this condition effectively meant was that possession of regions north of the Great Wall, such as Manchuria and Mongolia, was open to negotiation. This fact alone clearly showed how wrong it was for Japan strategically to have added the demand to make northern China into a special district to the peace conditions at the December 14 conference of the previous year.

It is not an overstatement to say that Sino-Japanese relations after the founding of Manchukuo depended solely on whether Japanese territorial demands extended to the south of the Great Wall.

While this preparation for peace negotiations had started even with the blessing of Chiang Kai-shek in the beginning, it quickly led to a decisive schism between Chiang and Wang Jingwei, and departure of the latter from the Kuomintang. Allow me here to return to Wang's memoir to trace his thinking in those days.

Although one may suspect that the memoirs' contents have been distorted by censorship, as it was translated and published during the Second Sino-Japanese War, I found this to be an unnecessary worry. You do not even have to read between the lines because Wang said everything he had to say and did not write anything that was against his conviction in this publication. I therefore find it a valuable historical document.

Meiji journalist Fukuchi Gen'ichirō (Ōchi) once said, "It is only poor writers who suffer from restrictions on freedom of speech. A good writer can write anything he wishes to say without provoking censorship."

Judging from his prose and poetry, Wang Jingwei was no doubt a fine writer, and he had also repeatedly succeeded in escaping from the jaws of death, being called a *hanjian* (a traitor to the Chinese nation). It is no wonder, therefore, that his intricate literary technique easily cleared censorship by the Japanese authorities.

First of all, let us visit Wang's view on Communism.

At the outset of the Northern Expedition in 1926, Chiang Kai-shek severed ties with the Chinese Communist Party, which marked the end of the First United Front. The leftwing faction of the Kuomintang, however, formed an anti-Chiang government in Wuhan jointly with the Communists. They elected Wang, who had sought asylum in France, as its leader. Chiang, for his part, also encouraged Wang to return home, believing Wang would understand him and coordinate relations with the dissidents.

Although Wang had initially tried to seek cooperation between the Kuomintang and the Chinese Communist Party, despite Chiang's strong request to sever the tie with the communists, he was astonished by a secret directive from the Comintern that he happened to have seen.

Wang reminisced in his memoir as follows:

At first, I did not quite understand why members of the Chinese Communist Party insisted on remaining in the Kuomintang even after they withdrew themselves from the Kuomintang government. This secret telegram [from the Comintern] made me realize that it was because it would be convenient for them to sabotage the Kuomintang from inside.

This secret directive instructed those Communist members to expel leaders of the Kuomintang, replace revolutionary armies in Hunan and Hubei provinces with Communist forces, and, when the Communist revolution was successfully launched, reorganize the Kuomintang in accordance with orders from the Comintern.

Although this is only a common strategy of the Communist Party today, it was at that time a secret technique of the Communists that even Wang Jingwei had never heard of before.

At this point, Wang's Wuhan regime united with Chiang Kai-shek's Nanjing government. It appears to be a universal phenomenon for those who once embraced Communism to become staunchly anti-Communists after becoming disillusioned with its true nature. Thus, Wang as well as Zhou Fohai, who had once been a member of the Communist Party, became thoroughly anti-Communist.

It was the Xi'an Incident of December 1936 that led to an insurmountable chasm between Chiang and Wang, who had been longstanding comrades with mutual trust and respect on the deepest level despite occasional differences in political stances.

The compromise Chiang made in the Xi'an Incident has been and perhaps will remain an eternal mystery in history. In his memoir, Wang conjectured that Chiang must have made the following and possibly more secret promises on (1) waging a war against Japan to realize Sung Yatsen's policy of "tolerating Communism and cooperating with the Soviet Union," (2) including the Communist Party in the Kuomintang government, and (3) cooperating with all foreign powers that are sympathetic with China's war of resistance against Japan.

Wang quoted reminiscences of Soong May-ling, Chiang's wife who was instrumental in rescuing Chiang from captivity, saying, "The Xi'an Incident forcefully destroyed the Chinese state. Xi'an was a death trap." I wonder when Soong said this. Since Wang had passed away before Japan's defeat in the war, this remark must have been made before the Kuomintang was finally defeated by the communist forces and chased down to Taiwan. What it signifies is that Soong had regarded that it was the post–Xi'an Incident United Front that dragged China into the Second Sino-Japanese War.

It is clear that Wang Jingwei shared her interpretation. He said,

The Second Sino-Japanese War was triggered by the Marco Polo Bridge Incident. Because the secret pact had already been agreed on in Xi'an to collaborate with the Communist Party in the war against Japan, it was obvious that he [Chiang] would have willingly attacked the Japanese troops determinedly and fiercely even if Japan hesitated in the escalation of battle. It was after the initial collision that Chiang resorted to an attempt to imperil Japan internationally by proclaiming it to be an invader. The world should see through this vicious scheme of Chiang and realize that it would be extremely absurd to believe that he had no will to fight a war.

One could certainly detect China's offensive intentions from the degree of concentration of the Chinese military after the Marco Polo Bridge Incident.

But all of those things are of the remote past. Today, it has become an orthodox interpretation of history to attribute the Second Sino-Japanese War to Japan's renewed invasion and China's resistance against it. Testimony such as Wang's above has been wiped out from history. Because the Japanese side had also been fighting the war without a clear understanding of why things had turned around that way, it easily accepted the above interpretation.

It is also a historical fact, however, that the moderate segment of the Kuomintang's leadership in those days harbored resentments against the Communists. They believed that China had been engineered to provoke Japan and dragged into an unnecessary war with Japan by the Chinese Communist Party.

It should be pointed out that Wang Jingwei belonged to the generation of Asians who became ecstatic at Japan's victory in the Russo-Japanese War, which was a case of a non-white race beating a Caucasian nation. Wang never gave up hope of improving Sino-Japanese relations based on mutual trust. And he tried to detect Japan's sincerity in each announcement the Japanese side made, including those by Hirota and Konoe.

Chiang Kai-shek

But more central in Wang's strategy for China was the perception that Japan's military power was so overwhelming that China's attempt to resist it would only have a slim chance of winning and would lead to destruction. Wang writes in his memoirs, "The Song Dynasty's national ruin lasted close to one hundred years, while that of the Ming Dynasty lasted almost three hundred years. We no longer wish to suffer from such a long period of national ruin."

And, "Germany and Turkey were once on the verge of national ruin when they were defeated by the Entente Powers. It was the determination of each and every citizen of these countries to save his country from ruin that allowed him to survive and reconstruct."

In other words, Wang emphasized the importance of admitting defeat first and attempting to revive from there.

In response to the argument that, even if China could not beat Japan singlehandedly, "it could expect assistance from other peace-loving countries," Wang denounced such unfounded optimism that placed hopes on "chivalrous aid" when every state and people were fighting for their own survival to the best of their ability. It was beyond his imagination at this point that Japan would eventually initiate a disastrous war with the United States later.

In order to counter "the anti-Japan resistance fever that was at its apex," with the upsurge of nationalism that had exploded since around the time of the Marco Polo Bridge Incident, Wang organized a "Lower Tone Club" among like-minded comrades. The club busied itself to bring about the realization of peace on the conviction that "While China would most certainly sustain a crushing defeat if it fought Japan, peace with Japan would not necessarily lead to total destruction."

Wang's was indeed the courage of a daredevil.

Was there a single Japanese who was courageous enough to organize something like a "club not to exalt national prestige" when everyone in Japan was frenzied with expansionistic nationalism, i.e., the exaltation of national prestige? This episode makes me ponder on the unfathomable depth of the Chinese tradition.

New Regime in Nanjing

In December 1938, Wang Jingwei flew from Chongqing to Kunming, from which he escaped to Shanghai via Hanoi in May of the ensuing year.

The circumstances of the previous half year were politically complex, and Wang's activities were almost melodramatic. Allow me to review briefly what took place.

Efforts to initiate a peace settlement via Colonel Kagesa continued and, in fact, Gao Zongwu had visited Japan for this purpose in July 1938. As it so happened, however, the military was adamantly against Foreign Minister Ugaki's peace initiative at that time, having just decided on two major operations in Hankou and Guangdong. Thus, Gao could not even gain a foothold to enter negotiations on peace conditions with the Japanese side.

At this point, Ugaki and his sympathizers concluded that a peace settlement would only get underway by having Wang Jingwei propose peace negotiations with Japan. Wang had been well known even in Japan for his devotion to the salvation of China through a peace settlement with Japan. In the five-minister conference on July 12, the Japanese side decided on the policy of "mobilization of a first-class person in China." These movements strongly suggested that the Japanese side at this point was more inclined to establish a separate regime independent of the Chongqing government with Wang as its head than to seek peace with Chiang through Wang.

Elder statesman Saionji Kinmochi's grandson Kinkazu was engaged in this peace initiative. The elder Saionji said the following to his grandson:

> The military is a firm believer in establishing a puppet government. I don't think you can form the kind of regime that you have wished for. In the end, you will find yourself being used by the military. . . . It would be regrettable to involve such a virtuous man as Wang Jingwei in such a worthless scheme.

While Foreign Minister Ugaki lost his position, the Kagesa-Gao peace exploration still continued. At the same time, the leadership of Japan's China diplomacy completely shifted to the hands of the Imperial Japanese Army General Staff Office. The Imperial Army vigorously pursued peace negotiations in Shanghai, and in November it finally signed the document on mutually agreed conditions. The agreement was centered around the withdrawal of the Japanese military from China proper after the peace settlement. In the end, these were the same peace conditions as those proposed by Ishii and Ugaki and to which the military had objected. This reveals that, no matter who was in charge of the peace negotiations, those were the only conditions that both China and Japan could agree on.

Because the peace negotiations in this case were initiated by the Japanese military, it was easier to secure a consensus within the government. The proposal was endorsed without modification by the cabinet meeting held in the presence of the Emperor on November 30, 1938.

However, this time, Wang's persuasion of Chiang Kai-shek in Chongqing floundered. Taishō- Shōwa military journalist Itō Masanori once wrote,

> Just like Japanese politics were in the hands of the Shōwa military clique, so did Chinese politics tend to be dominated by the Communist Party . . . [so much so that] there could be no politics that did not take the Communist Party into account. . . . The political position of Wang Jingwei, who had rejected the Communist Party, had deteriorated.

It must be true that the power of such peace advocates as Wang Jingwei had been greatly undermined after the formation of the United Front. It was a matter of life or death for the Communist Party, because peace with Japan would automatically mean resumption of the Kuomintang's attempt at annihilating the communists.

Wang tried to persuade Chiang until late night on November 1, five days after the fall of Hankou. Wang felt that Chiang accepted his persuasion. However, on November 13, Chiang made a radio speech, saying, "Because the United Front troops retreated to mountain areas and successfully held the Japanese army in check, our future prospect is extremely bright." This comment was like a carbon copy of the Communist Party's strategy. Hearing this speech, Wang fiercely demanded Chiang's resignation on November 16, saying, "It is the fault of the Kuomintang that China has deteriorated this far. You and I should resign from our posts together and apologize for our wrongdoings to the entire Chinese people."

And, thus, two sworn friends of more than 30 years parted for good.

At this point, Wang decided that he had no other choice than to gather together all the peace advocates in order to salvage the country. But this was a miscalculation on his part, because the atmosphere was such that unanimous unification of the peace advocates was already unthinkable.

Although Long Yun, Governor of Yunnan, had been a sworn friend of Wang's and had assisted Wang's departure for Hanoi, he could not stand up against Chiang. Also, even if Wang wanted to restore the Guangdong government that he used to lead, he could not regain his own foothold there because the city had already been occupied by the Japanese Army.

Seen from a different angle, Wang's day might already have passed. Real power now lay in the hands of Chiang Kai-shek, who controlled all of the military leaders who were graduates of the Whampoa Military Academy, and Mao Tse-tung and Zhou En-lai, who led the Chinese Communist Party and the Red Army with the iron solidarity generated by the Communist revolution philosophy. Common among them was the fact that they were leaders of organizations that they grasped completely. There was no longer a space for such a literary salon intelligentsia cum revolutionary/poet of earlier days of the revolution as Wang Jingwei.

Initially, Wang had no intention of forming a government separate from that of Chongqing. He was contemplating assembling like-minded advocates who sought national salvation through peace with Japan in such a third country location as Hanoi. While Wang found Hanoi no less dangerous, with no safe place to stay, the Japanese side concentrated its effort on inviting Wang to Nanjing.

On December 22, the Japanese government declared, through an announcement by Prime Minister Konoe, that it was "not the trivial territories or war reparations" but the minimum guarantee necessary for Japan to act as a partner in the new order in East Asia that Japan requested of China. The announcement even revealed that Japan was considering the abolishment of the consular jurisdiction and return of the settlement.

At this point, Wang Jingwei suddenly accepted the Konoe announcement on the condition of a prompt withdrawal of the Japanese troops from China, saying reasons to fight a war had mostly disappeared. Wang visited Japan in May 1939 to confirm the thinking of key cabinet ministers. Returning home, Wang preached the importance of peace with Japan in his July 14 speech, saying Chiang's resistance was an act of "striking a stone with an egg" and "We should not revenge ourselves and we should, instead, let go of the resentment."

Subsequently, Wang entered negotiations on the conditions for the formation of a new government in China. Wang was determined to abolish the new government scheme entirely if and when he detected even a hint of aggressive intention in Japan's demand, based on his conviction concerning the partnership between two great East Asian nations.

In the actual negotiations, however, Wang's side was forced to make a lot of compromises on the stationing of Japanese troops. Even so, the agreement on Wang's new government would became valid only after peace was accomplished. Because the agreement would remain ineffective as long as Chiang Kai-shek continued a thorough resistance against Japan in cooperation with the Communist Party, the significance of the Wang government was only to give a few propaganda benefits to Japan. Everything was settled after Japan started a war with the United States and lost it.

In retrospect, how should we evaluate the thinking and conduct of Wang Jingwei?

Subsequent history shows that Chiang Kai-shek, in the end, was pushed out of China exactly following the United Front formula prepared by the Communist Party. The Communist Party, in a sense, would take a mile when Chiang gave an inch. On this point, Wang had been correct. But the Chinese Communist Party proved to be a legitimate government representing Chinese nationalism, instead of a "running dog" of the Comintern that pays no heed to the Chinese nation as Wang had feared. Therefore, as long as the Communist regime survives in China (and controls the narrative), Wang's ideas and conduct are unlikely to be reevaluated positively.

Also, before Chiang Kai-shek's Chinese Nationalist Party was taken over by the Communist Party, Japan launched an attack on Pearl Harbor, which Wang had never even dreamed of, leading to war with the United States. When Japan was defeated in this war, Chiang ended up being a hero of national salvation, while Wang was labeled a traitor to the Chinese nation.

Had there not been a war between Japan and the United States, there was a possibility that Wang's forecast could have been proven correct. If the war did not indeed happen, Wang's determination not to give even an inch in terms of sovereignty over the China proper south of the Great Wall in spite of a series of compromises vis-à-vis the Japanese Army's demands would have proven to be significant. Because Japan had promised to refrain from establishing a second and third Manchukuo, if not anything else, it would have been bound by this promise. Even if Japan had stationed its troops somewhere south of the Great Wall, it still had to recognize residual sovereignty of China there. Post–World War II Japan had to undergo tremendous hardship to restore its sovereignty over Okinawa even though its residual sovereignty over those islands had been recognized by the United States. Japan today is trying to do the same with Russia over the Northern Territories (Kuril Islands). These cases show how important it is for a country that has lost a war to make its opponent recognize its sovereignty, either residual or in actuality.

It had never been the true wish of Wang to become a leader of the Nanjing government or to make a number of concessions vis-à-vis Japan, including that on Japan's right to station its military in China.

It is not entirely certain whether these miscalculations made Wang a disappointed man. In retrospect, it appears that Wang had deliberately prepared a China that could survive regardless of which side won in the end. If Chiang Kai-shek had won, that would be just fine. Even if Japan had won, it would still have allowed the Nationalist government to survive in Nanjing as well as protected residual sovereignty over territories south of the Great Wall, albeit with short-term restrictions.

Nobody knows what the future would bring. Reviewing Wang's past thinking, I do not find it inconceivable for Wang to have decided that he should sacrifice himself in an attempt to hedge against all the possible outcomes in China.

I must say the true depth of the Chinese thinking is unfathomable to the Japanese.

CHAPTER
9

The Tripartite Pact Signed

—*Some Reject It to the End*—

The Bolsheviks' Coolheaded Diplomacy

After the successful launch of the Russian Revolution in 1917, the Soviet Union continued to be obsessively secretive toward the outside world. The country was governed by a highly distinctive ideology found nowhere else in the world and by the Communist Party's one-party rule.

Winston Churchill thus characterized the Soviet Union as "a riddle in a mystery inside an enigma." The Hiranuma Kiichiro cabinet, which had succeeded the Konoe Fumimaro cabinet, found the Soviet's signing of the nonaggression pact with Germany in 1939 "complicated and inscrutable," and resigned.

Hiranuma was not the only one who could not understand the German-Soviet rapprochement. Kissinger writes in his book *Diplomacy,* "If ideology necessarily determined foreign policy, Hitler and Stalin would never have joined hands any more than Richelieu and the Sultan of Turkey would have three centuries earlier."[13] And he continues, "[Stalin's] task was eased because the Western democracies refused to grasp his strat-

---

13   Henry A. Kissinger, *Diplomacy* (New York: Simon & Schuster, 1995), p. 332.

egy—which would have been quite clear to Richelieu, Metternich, Palmerston, or Bismarck."[14]

Later efforts to solve the mystery of the Soviet conduct converged as a major academic discipline called "Kremlinology," the name being a parody of criminology. This discipline produced a number of prominent experts.

In retrospect, however, the conduct of the Soviet Union was all very simple and straightforward, as Kissinger pointed out. I still remember when the late Japanese Ambassador to the United States Ushiba Nobuhiko said, "Although experts on the communist countries assume an air of esoteric authority, it is actually easy to grasp what is going on in these countries. It is the politics of the United States that is hard to understand correctly." Ambassador Ushiba made this comment on the so-called Nixon Shock when Henry Kissinger secretly visited Beijing at the height of the Cold War.

To quote Kissinger once again, "Stalin's ultimate nightmare, of course, was a coalition of all the capitalist countries attacking the Soviet Union simultaneously."[15] And, "[Nothing could fundamentally deflect Stalin from seeking to fulfill . . .] what he considered his Bolshevik duty—pitting the capitalists against each other and keeping the Soviet Union from becoming a victim of their wars."[16]

One can indeed explain all the Soviet conduct leading up to the Second World War with the above two principles. The only additional factor that should be taken into consideration might be Russia's traditional territorial obsessions: (1) the farther away the border the better, and (2) never giving up even an inch of what is considered to be its own territory.

More concretely, the key to understanding the trend in Soviet policy was to learn how the Soviet Union assessed the situations surrounding itself. Soviet policies were all based on cold-blooded calculations totally devoid of sentiment. The communists were convinced that they were superior to other nations in diplomacy because they believed that they understood others far better than others understood them.

---

14   Ibid, p.343.
15   Ibid, p.334.
16   Ibid, p.337.

The Soviet Union always based its actions on a coolheaded assessment of a situation, and it never did what seemed to be beyond its ability or what the situation did not allow. Its policies were naturally confidential, but its assessment of the situation was made public. Therefore, if one studied the Soviet Union's public assessment of a situation, one would automatically understand Soviet policy.

The Soviet Union's assessment of the situation in the Far East after the Manchurian Incident could be deciphered from the 1932 Thesis of the Japanese Communist Party and the anti-war resolution of the 12th Executive Committee of the Communist International around the same time. These documents characterized the Manchurian Incident as an act of plunder initiated by Japanese imperialism and claimed that support of Japan's conduct by France and Britain at the League of Nations indicated that this international organization had become a tool of French and British imperialism. The United States, in spite of its opposition to the Japanese occupation of Manchuria, was seen to harbor a desire to provoke a Soviet-Japanese war in order to weaken the two countries in the Pacific so that it could strengthen its position in the region and demand a fair share of the sphere of influence in the Far East. Thus, these documents claimed that the intention intensified to form a united front among the imperialistic powers to wage a war against the Soviet Union.

In 1932, one year before Hitler seized power in Germany, what the Soviet Union feared most was its besiegement by Britain, France, and Japan. It felt particularly threatened by the expansion of Japan, with which it now shared a vast extension of the border after the latter conquered all of Manchuria. Previously, the border between Japan and Soviet Union had been limited to a short one between Korea and the Soviet Union.

Arms Buildup in the Far East

After Stalin prevailed in the power struggle and expelled Leon Trotsky from the Communist Party in 1928, he launched the five-year plan to construct heavy industry and achieve collectivization of agriculture. He felt that this plan could determine the fate of the Soviet Union.

When the Manchurian Incident erupted, the five-year plan was only in its third year and, given the condition of domestic politics, the Soviet

Union was in no position to respond to this incident. In his *USSR: The Decisive Years*, Alexander Yakovlev made the following observation on the Soviet conditions in those days:

> In the summer of 1931, the first train carrying eradicated *kulak* arrived in the barren land of Karaganda. . . . Abandoned in the uninhabited wilderness, some 500,000 of them initially lived in crude habitats by digging holes in the ground and covering them with straw or rags. During wintertime, they were packed in shacks without any heating at a density of 70 to 80 people per 50 square meters. By the spring of 1932, half of them had lost their lives. Toward the end of 1933, only one out of four had survived.

Stalin himself once told Churchill that the number of *kulak* who met a similar fate reached 10 million.

Given this situation, the Soviet Union was clearly not in a position to deal with Japan's aggression. Naturally, the Soviet Union aimed to build up its war readiness in the Far East, adopting a reconciliatory policy vis-à-vis Japan in order to avoid confrontation with Japan before its arms buildup was accomplished. Meanwhile, the Soviet Union hoped that Japan's southbound advance would result in a clash with the Kuomintang and Britain/United States.

As I have mentioned earlier, the Soviet Union repeatedly proposed to the Japanese side the conclusion of a mutual nonaggression treaty. In November 1932, Soviet Ambassador to China Lev Karakhan said to the Japanese side, "If Japan so wishes, the Soviet Union is willing to conclude a mutual nonaggression treaty and sign a similar pact with Manchukuo."

This was tantamount to a de facto recognition of Manchukuo. It reflected the Bolsheviks' coolheaded diplomacy: finding themselves in the weaker position, the Bolsheviks would not hesitate to make a verbal compromise as long as doing so would not lead to actual concession of its territory.

The aversion to and suspicion against the communist regime was so strong in Japan, however, that the Soviet proposal was deemed utterly unacceptable. The Japanese government issued an official verbal statement in December turning down the Soviet Union's proposal. The statement said that the time was not yet ripe for that kind of negotiation.

The Soviet Union, for its part, hastily began arms buildup efforts in the Far East. By November 1931, the year of the Manchurian Incident, it was confirmed that reinforcement troops had newly arrived in the Far East. The number continued to expand as detailed in the table below.

Moreover, the Soviet sniper divisions were reinforced both quantitatively and qualitatively, meaning that a Japanese division became significantly inferior to the Soviet divisions in terms of the number of tanks and the amount of firepower. The table below shows that the military balance was particularly unfavorable to the Japanese side in 1935–36, during which more than three hundred border incidents erupted. Most of those disputes occurred in areas where the border had not been firmly established—signifying the Soviet Union's determination to take advantage of its military might and not give even an inch on the border issue.

To Delay the War with Japan as Much as Possible

Year	Japanese Korean Army stationed in Manchuria		Soviet Army in the Far East	
	No. Divisions	No. Aircraft	No. Sniper Divisions	No. Aircraft
1931	3		6	
1932	6	100	8	200
1933	5	130	8	350
1934	5	130	11	500
1935	5	220	14	950
1936	5	230	16	1,200
1937	7	250	20	1,560
1938	10	340	24	2,000
1939	11	560	30	2,500

Its military buildup in the Far East notwithstanding, the Soviet Union had absolutely no intention to escalate the battle with Japan. According to Communist theory, a war with Japan was inevitable. But it had been stressed that it was imperative to "delay the inevitable war [with Japan] until after the war among capitalist countries" (Stalin's speech at the Fifteenth Congress in 1927).

The Soviet Union's policy vis-à-vis Japan was to discourage the argument in Japan for northbound advance (toward the Soviet Union) and encourage that for southbound advance (toward the China mainland and Southeast Asia). More concretely, the Soviet Union aimed to induce Japan to fight a war with Chiang Kai-shek and the United States, during which time the Soviet Union would maintain peaceful relations with Japan so that it could deliver a blow when Japan had exhausted its power. And this turned out to be exactly what happened.

In order to accomplish this, the Soviet Union conducted aggressive intelligence activities. Ozaki Hotsumi, one of the brains behind Prime Minister Konoe, was later found to be a Soviet spy and executed. At the time of the eruption of the Second Sino-Japanese War, Ozaki took advantage of his fame as an outstanding expert on China affairs to carry out a media campaign to escalate the war, contributing articles to the *Asahi Shimbun* newspaper and monthly journal *Chūo Kōron*.

Ozaki, for instance, stated, "The control by the Nanjing government is a type of warlord politics." This statement became a foreshadowing to the Konoe cabinet's subsequent announcement that the Japanese Government would not deal with the Kuomintang Government. Ozaki argued that, "Neither a local settlement nor a policy of non-escalation make sense," and "The only way left for Japan is to win the war . . . there is absolutely no other way Japan can take." Quoting the historical examples of the Yuan Dynasty taking 45 years and the Qing Dynasty taking 46 years to overthrow the Song Dynasty and the Ming Dynasty, respectively, Ozaki incited the Japanese government to escalate the war and thus avoid an early settlement.

It is believed that, during the Xi'an Incident, the Soviet Union pressured the Chinese Communist Party to release Chiang Kai-shek from imprisonment. It also promoted the formation of the United Front between the Communist Party and the Kuomintang and began providing China with arms by concluding a mutual nonaggression treaty with China in August of 1938, the year after the Marco Polo Bridge Incident. In five years between 1937 (12th Year of Shōwa) and 1941, the Soviet Union extended massive military assistance to China, including 1,000 aircraft, 1,000 artillery guns, and 10,000 machine guns.

Knowing these Soviet's strategies alone would be enough to understand the Soviet thinking behind the Second Sino-Japanese War, the Battle of Lake Khasan, the Nomonhan Incident, the Soviet-Japanese Neutrality Pact, and, finally, the Soviet Union's violation of the neutrality pact.

Hitler's Strategy

Kissinger, a German by birth who fled with his family because of their being Jewish, writes,

> His [Hitler's] philosophy, as expressed in *Mein Kampf*, ranged from the banal to the fantastic and consisted of a popularized repackaging of rightwing, radical, conventional wisdom. Standing alone, it could never have launched an intellectual current that culminated in revolution, as had Marx's *Das Kapital* or the works of the philosophers of the eighteenth century.[17]

It is true that while Hitler's philosophy contained such a quixotic idea as supremacy of a certain human race, it offered nothing that could become a universal value for mankind. Nevertheless, Hitler's philosophy did contain a national strategy for Germany—that is, to secure *Lebenstaum* (living space) for Germanic peoples by controlling the breadbasket of Europe all the way to Ukraine.

Aside from this strategic thinking, Hitler's philosophy was also mingled with such low-level prejudice as his hatred of Jews as well as personal motivation and preconception. This deprived Hitler of the cool-headed consistency that was found in Bolshevik thinking.

In the process toward the signing of the Tripartite Pact among Japan, Germany, and Italy, it was the relations with Britain that posed the greatest dilemma for both Germany and Japan and later became the cause of their downfall.

If it was the establishment of *Lebenstaum* in the east that Germany was after, it was only natural that it should try to avoid any confrontation in the west. When Hitler appointed Joachim Ribbentrop as ambassador to Britain in August 1936, Hitler said to him, "I beg you to make Britain par-

---

17   Ibid., p.289.

ticipate in the Anti-Communist Pact. This is my greatest wish." In Japan, too, at the time of the conclusion of the Anti-Communist Pact in November 1936, Tōgō Shigenori, Director-General of European and American Affairs of the foreign ministry, insisted on concluding a political agreement with Britain as a prerequisite for the Anti-Communist Pact. This was despite the unanimous support of the cabinet for the pact as well as War Minister Terauchi's nagging at Tōgō for being overly concerned about Britain even at that stage.

These German and Japanese efforts notwithstanding, the Anti-Communist Pact failed to secure the official endorsement of Britain. On the contrary, it even heightened British suspicions about the intentions of Germany and Japan. At the last stretch toward the conclusion of the Tripartite Pact, its target was shifted from the Soviet Union to Britain.

Ribbentrop's Memorandum

It might have been inevitable. As Tōgō pointed out, the Anti-Communist Pact inherently contained an element that would invite British suspicion. For Germany to become a hegemon in Europe collides head-on with the traditional British balance-of-power policy for the European continent.

As long as France remained a factor of the balance of power in the European continent, with the backing of Britain and the United States at the time of crisis, however, Germany's east-bound advance was not something that Britain had to stop at any cost.

According to British military historian B. H. Liddell Hart's *History of the Second World War*, Hitler believed that Britain agreed to give Germany freedom of action in eastern Europe when Edward Wood, 3rd Earl of Halifax, Speaker of the House of Lords, visited Germany in November 1937. While Britain may not have explicitly spelled out its endorsement, it appeared that it showed enough understanding to Germany's east-bound advance.

The 180-degree shift in Britain's attitude within a span of a year between the Munich Agreement (September 29, 1938) and the German invasion of Poland (September 1, 1939) was attributable to the emphasis on moralistic principles in post–World War I British public opinion under the influence of Wilsonianism along with the traditional realistic thinking.

Being an insular nation, Britain was also endowed with the geopolitical leeway to allow such moralistic thinking.

Kissinger said, "Hitler's blunder was not so much to have violated historic principles of equilibrium as to have offended the moral premises of British postwar foreign policy."[18]

The British were aware of the unfairness of the Treaty of Versailles. Thus, they found it unreasonable that Germany was prohibited from annexing Austria, which was of the same race. They also found it hard to deny Germany retrieval of Sudetenland, which had been inhabited by ethnic Germans, from Czechoslovakia. Nevertheless, when Nazi Germany forcibly dissolved Czechoslovakia and made it its own protectorate, Britain found that morally intolerable from the standpoint of the principle of self-determination of nations. Subsequently, however, the rebound to the hitherto reconciliation policy kicked in, a phenomenon peculiar to a democratic nation, leading public opinion toward the totally opposite direction. Thus, when Nazi Germany invaded Poland, Britain went so far as to declare war against Germany.

As shown above, it had never been Hitler's intention to fight Britain, nor was the war an inevitable outcome of power politics. It was Ribbentrop who played a crucial role in making Britain and the United States the chief targets of the Tripartite Pact.

Ribbentrop was a close confidant of Hitler. Managing a special office outside the foreign ministry, he acted on Hitler's special order in such tasks as the signing of the Anglo-German Naval Agreement of 1935. As is often the case with a person of this position, Ribbentrop found his own importance and personal satisfaction in conducting foreign policy over the head of the foreign ministry. This attitude of Ribbentrop shared a common trait with the Imperial Japanese Army, which also found pleasure in bypassing the Japanese foreign ministry, resulting in advancement of German-Japanese cooperation without the knowledge of the foreign ministries of the two countries.

Although Ribbentrop was appointed ambassador to Britain before

---

18   Ibid., p. 317.

formally assuming the post of German foreign minister, he failed to deliver what he had been ordered to accomplish in Britain by Hitler. Arrogant and uncultured, Ribbentrop was largely ignored while in London. According to Italian foreign minister of the time, Gian Galeazzo Ciano, this experience made Ribbentrop seek to avenge himself on Britain, as though driven by the hatred of a "betrayed lover."

In his "Memorandum for the *Führer*" in January 1938, Ribbentrop wrote,

> For the past few years I have worked for friendly relations with Britain. It would have been the greatest pleasure for me if that had been accomplished. However, today I no longer believe in mutual understanding between Germany and Britain. Unless we thoroughly maintain the notion that Britain is the most dangerous archrival, it will only benefit our enemy.

According to contemporary German journalist Theo Zommer, this memorandum in which Ribbentrop insisted on forming an anti-British alliance with Japan and Italy was written in "utterly incoherent, horrendous German language."

It was four weeks after Ribbentrop wrote this memorandum that he was appointed as foreign minister of Germany.

The Battle of Lake Khasan and the Nomonhan Incident

Meanwhile, Japan did not have a national strategy that was comparable to those of the Bolsheviks or Hitler. This was only natural for Japan, a country of parliamentary democracy instead of dictatorship, where prime ministers were replaced one after another, making it impossible for the cabinets to implement or force a constant policy. Although it was accused at the International Military Tribunal for the Far East that there had been a consistent conspiracy among government leaders in Japan, there was no such thing nor could there have been.

As evidence that Japan's policy toward China had consistently been aggressive, the Tribunal presented the Standard of National Policies (「国策の基準」) that the Hirota Kōki cabinet prepared in 1936 (11th Year of Shōwa). But, in actuality, the standard was nothing more than a mere collection of officialese and a product of compromises among government ministries. The best one can obtain from careful reading of this document would be a vague idea of what the Japanese government was thinking at that time. And subsequent governments had never reviewed it when determining policies. That is the treatment that a document of this kind is often destined for.

If there was something that could be called a national strategy, it must have been Ishihara Kanji's strategic theses and the thinking of the Imperial Japanese Army General Staff Office's Department of War Leadership that succeeded Ishihara's philosophy.

Ishihara wrote an outline of an anti-Soviet war plan in August 1936, one year before the eruption of the Second Sino-Japanese War. In the outline he states that "There is an urgent need to make the utmost effort to make the Soviet Union the only adversary to Japan . . . and avoid a war with China in order to make Britain and the United States maintain their neutrality."

After the Marco Polo Bridge Incident, Ishihara tried to restrict the escalation of the battle and, in his third *Outline of the War Plan* written in June 1938, he stressed that Japan should "prevent exhaustion of national resources by minimizing the size of the war" and "promptly conclude a peace agreement."

These were indeed well-structured strategies that could cope squarely with the Soviet strategy which aimed to get Japan involved in a war with Chiang Kai-shek and into confrontation with Britain and the United States.

History shows that Japan was actually drawn into the quagmire of a war in mainland China and subsequently cornered into fighting a war against the United States, exactly as the Soviet Union and the Chinese Communist Party had hoped for. This was a victory for the communist strategy and a defeat for the Japanese "strategy." The cause was the deficiency in Japan's decision-making process, which failed to maintain consistency even in the strategies of the Imperial General Headquarters.

In the midst of the Second Sino-Japanese War, the Battle of Lake Khasan (張鼓峰事件) and the Nomonhan Incident (ノモンハン事件) erupted along the Soviet-Manchukuo border.

In both incidents, Japan suffered total defeat. Setting aside the difference in the number of casualties between the two sides, the Soviet side succeeded in consolidating what it had claimed to be the national border through these battles, while the Japanese side failed to expel the Soviet troops from the disputed area. But the Soviet side had no intention to further escalate the battle. If the battle escalated to a full-fledged Soviet-Japanese war, the Japanese side would have withdrawn all of its troops from China and poured them into the war with the Soviet Union. This could have fundamentally toppled the grand strategy of the Communist Party that had been going quite well. In contrast to the way the Japanese army handled itself in those days, the Soviet army complied with the instructions from the central government with iron discipline during these two battles.

Neither of the above two incidents had much to do with the broad flow of World War II; as such they do not merit detailed discussion here. It should be pointed out, nevertheless, that these battles were the first occasion for the Japanese military, which had been invincible since the First Sino-Japanese and Russo-Japanese Wars, to taste defeat. As such they became targets of various criticisms and reflections in Japan.

But the Japanese side had been destined to be defeated in those battles from the beginning. Or it might be more accurate to say that the Soviet side, which had troop strength, firepower, and mobility far superior to the Japanese troops, was unlikely to be beaten. Although the Japanese army put up a brave fight worthy of its glorious tradition, the imbalance of power was so great that the combat capabilities of individual soldiers could not change the course of the battle.

It was not the battle plan that was at fault. The defeat should be attributed, instead, to the failure to detect the opponent's level of war readiness, the overconfidence of the dispatched units that made them believe they could win the battle only with what they had, and the arbitrary conduct of those units that completely disregarded the intention of the central command. These were not problems that were peculiar to these battles alone. In fact, these were the very errors that the Japanese military had consistently committed throughout World War II. On the Chinese front, however, the gap in combat capabilities between the Japanese side and the opponent was so great in favor of Japan that these problems did not matter.

Yonai Mitsumasa: A Man Who Stuck to What He Believed In

While the later signing of the Tripartite Pact among Germany, Italy, and

Japan may not have been the only factor that pushed Japan toward World War II, it was definitely one of the decisive factors.

And it was Yonai Mitsumasa (米内光政) who refused to walk the path toward World War II. He did not give even an inch until the Imperial Army forced him to resign as prime minister by refusing to appoint a war minister to his cabinet.

Yonai was born in Iwate Prefecture in a destitute family of an ex-samurai retainer of the Nambu-*han*. At the Imperial Japanese Naval Academy, Yonai's academic performance was mediocre, although he stood unrivaled in judo. During the Russo-Japanese War, Yonai fought bravely on board a torpedo boat. It was after he belatedly started preparing for the entrance examination of the Naval War College, encouraged by friends and far behind his classmates, that he began to study intensively. From average academic standing, he became one of the best students at the Naval War College.

While Yonai assumed various naval posts one after another, people with an eye for talent began to realize that he was the man in whom they could entrust the future of the Imperial Japanese Navy. And it was none other than Yamamoto Isoroku (山本五十六) who was convinced of this more than anyone else.

When the recommendation for the post of navy minister to the Hayashi Senjūrō cabinet was being debated within the Navy, Yamamoto, who was Vice-Minister of Navy at that time, nominated Yonai. In response to some who questioned Yonai's political skills, Yamamoto argued, "It is the true courage of a man who can practice what he believes that will protect the navy as well as Japan. It is not the man's half-baked political skills," forcing others into consent. Yamamoto himself remained in the post of vice-minister and supported Minister Yonai through the Hayashi, Konoe, and Hiranuma cabinets.

During Yonai's tenure, the Imperial Japanese Army repeatedly proposed the signing of a German-Japanese alliance. Ribbentrop started to propose the bilateral alliance to Ōshima Hiroshi, military attaché to the Japanese Embassy in Berlin, in early

Yonai Mitsumasa

1938. The Imperial Japanese Army decided to accept the proposal by the summer of the same year. Although the Army attempted to obtain the government's endorsement of the proposal, Yonai would not hear of it.

After debating with War Minister Itagaki Seishirō for more than five hours on this issue, Yonai said,

> I do not agree with the notion to strengthen the anti-Communist agreement per se. Even if something may have to be done to materialize what the Imperial Army has prepared so far, yet, I am of the conviction that the target should be limited to the Soviet Union. If the army intends to include Britain in the target, I shall prevent the attempt at the risk of my position.

Although the Imperial Army continued to put pressure on Yonai in a variety of forms, he would not budge and remained faithful to his conviction, which was truly commendable. At the same time, Yamamoto's ability to unite the entire Imperial Navy perfectly, which restrained the pro-Axis faction, also merits special attention.

Konoe resigned as prime minister in January 1939, as he had long wished, and was succeeded by Hiranuma Kiichirō. But Konoe remained within the cabinet as president of the Privy Council and minister without portfolio. Konoe cabinet's ministers, as well as his cabinet's policies, were adopted by the Hiranuma cabinet. Thus, Yonai also remained the navy minister.

Intra-government debate over the Tripartite Pact continued. When a compromise proposal was made, Ōshima Hiroshi and Shiratori Toshio, pro-Axis Ambassadors to Germany and Italy respectively, went against the directive of the Japanese government and refused to present the proposal to their host governments, claiming that it would be utterly unacceptable to Germany and Italy. Meanwhile, in August 1939, Germany concluded a mutual nonaggression treaty with the Soviet Union—which had hitherto been the common imaginary enemy of Germany and Japan. The Japanese government lodged a protest with the German government, calling the treaty a violation of the anti-Communist pact, and terminated negotiations with the German government. On August 28, the Hiranuma cabinet stepped down, announcing that "a complicated and inscrutable situation has newly emerged in Europe."

This abrupt turn of German policy came about out of necessity.

Although Germany imposed harsh demands on Poland, the latter would not yield, aided as it was by Britain and France. While the Soviet Union was the only country with military might that could be exercised in the region, Germany learned that Britain had been engineering behind-the-scenes coordination with the Soviet Union. These factors prompted Hitler to dispatch Ribbentrop to Moscow in order to strike an agreement on the division of the sphere of interest in East Europe. This resulted in the prompt signing of the bilateral mutual nonaggression treaty.

In response to Japan's protest that Germany had violated the Anti-Communist Pact, the German side cited the indecisiveness of the Japanese side during the negotiations toward the Tripartite Pact as a justification of its conduct. This encouraged the pro-Axis faction within Japan to enhance its argument for earlier signing of the Tripartite Pact and denounce the wishy-washiness of the Japanese government. At this point, however, Hitler actually had no other recourse. The signing of a German-Japanese alliance would be no help in solving the German-Polish problem. Thus, an alliance between two nations geographically so far apart proved meaningless at a critical juncture.

Prime Minister Hiranuma was succeeded by Abe Nobuyuki, who was strongly endorsed by the Imperial Japanese Army. Abe was a competent military bureaucrat whose sole concern was self-protection. He owed his prime ministership to the mid-level leaders of the military who regarded him as harmless.

Yonai recommended Yoshida Zengo (吉田善吾), Yamamoto's former classmate, to succeed him as navy minister. When Yamamoto expressed his intention to remain in the post of vice-minister so as to support Yoshida, Yonai appointed Yamamoto as Commander-in-Chief of the Combined Fleet. Yonai could have appointed Yamamoto as navy minister, which would have been far more appropriate for Yamamoto than vice-minister. Putting Yamamoto in that post, however, would have made him more liable to assassination. Appointing Yamamoto as Commander-in-Chief, therefore, was Yonai's way of protecting Yamamoto, who was an irreplaceable human resource for the Imperial Navy.

Yamamoto was indeed on the list of assassination targets. However, this did not seem to bother him at all, because he would not stop taking a walk nonchalantly on busy streets. Yamamoto stored his saber behind a desk in the vice-minister's office and told everyone with a laugh that he would cut down any assassin with it.

While Yamamoto appreciated Yonai's consideration, he firmly declined the appointment, saying that priority should be placed on the Imperial Navy's position and Japan's future instead of what might be personally advantageous or disadvantageous for him. Yonai, nevertheless, sent Yamamoto to command the Combined Fleet, saying that Yamamoto should refresh himself with the fresh air of the Pacific. From this point until his death on the Solomon Islands four years later, Yamamoto commanded the entire naval operations during the Greater East Asia War as Commander-in-Chief of the Combined Fleet.

Abe had been requested explicitly by the Emperor to act harmoniously with Britain and the United States. Yet being an average, pro-Germany military man, he was at a loss when he received the Imperial mandate to form a new cabinet. Abe failed to win the confidence of political parties, and even the Imperial Army gave up on him. His cabinet was forced to resign in only four and a half months.

It would not be an overstatement to say that it was the solitary initiative of Yuasa Kurahei, Lord Keeper of the Privy Seal of Japan, to appoint Yonai as the successor to Abe. Ever since the Emperor had once murmured, "How about Yonai," Yuasa had been convinced that only Yonai could control the Imperial Army. Having secured the endorsement of the elder statesman Saionji Kinmochi, Yuasa worked intensely to realize the Yonai cabinet. With the help of a highly unusual, gracious Imperial message requesting the cooperation of War Minister Hata Shunroku, the Yonai cabinet was formed in January 1940 (15th Year of Shōwa). Throughout the entire process, Hiranuma and Konoe were left completely in the dark.

On this development, Takamiya Tahei, a prominent Shōwa military journalist, made the following observation:

> Although the likes of Hiranuma, Konoe, and Kido occasionally expressed their dissatisfaction regarding the Imperial Army, they never dared to restrain it head on. On top of their cowardly fear for their own lives, they also harbored an ambition for power and for securing their own governments. This kept them from making bold moves. In contrast, Yuasa confronted the Imperial Army literally,

with his life on the line. All he cared for was the future of the Empire of Japan. He did not pay heed to his own benefit or personal glory.

In Yuasa, we see the last of the loyal subjects and a righteous warrior. This type of person had been disappearing from Japan. Had there been a few more with similar courage among the Japanese leaders, or had Konoe and Hirota been endowed with the courage of Yuasa, the fate of Japan might have been quite different. And this was a matter for deep regret in the history of Shōwa.

War Minister Hata's Last Minute Change of Heart

The Yonai cabinet had been labeled from the outset a "reward for Yonai's opposition to the Tripartite Pact" and a body for conducting "diplomacy which is overly accommodative to Britain and the United States." As such the cabinet quickly became the target of the military and the rightists. But Yonai remained decisively nonchalant. In April, Yonai declared to U.S. Ambassador to Japan Joseph Grew, "Japan's policy has been firmly determined. You no longer need to worry. We have succeeded in containing those elements in Japan that aspire to see the rise of fascism and partnership with Germany and Italy."

Once dispirited, the pro-Axis faction in Japan bounced back when Hitler achieved one success after another in Europe. After turning its advance westward, the German military swept across Scandinavia and West Europe in no time and entered Paris triumphantly in June. Voices praising Germany regained momentum in Japan.

Even in the midst of this frenzy, some continued to observe the situation calmly. Saionji, for instance, took a farsighted view, saying, "No matter how powerful Hitler might be, the question is whether he can last as long as ten years. It was the same for Napoleon, too." Yonai also said,

> Hitler and Mussolini are but passing phenomena. It would be unproductive to ally ourselves with them, because they, as nouveau-riche, would not care to lose everything. It would be outrageous to form a partnership between the Emperor of Japan with a more than 3,000-year history and those passing phenomena.

By this time, however, the Imperial Army's attempt to topple the Yonai cabinet had already become blatant. The Imperial Army's Director-General of Military Affairs Mutō Akira repeatedly met Chief Cabinet Secretary Ishiwata Sōtarō and demanded the resignation en masse of the Yonai cabinet. He claimed this represented the collective will of the Imperial Army.

Although War Minister Hata Shunroku did not join this movement until the last minute, in accordance with the Emperor's wishes, he changed his attitude abruptly. Out of the blue, Hata thrust a letter at Yonai demanding the intensification of relations with the Axis countries and the resignation of the cabinet. Without flinching, Yonai said to Hata, "The opinion of the Imperial Army differs from the view of my cabinet. If that poses a problem for you, I suggest you should resign."

Hata promptly tendered his resignation, after which the Imperial Army refused to recommend Hata's replacement. This was the end of the Yonai cabinet.

Prior to this, Emperor Shōwa mentioned to Kido Kōichi, Lord Keeper of the Privy Seal of Japan at that time, that "We still place confidence in Yonai." Kido, however, did not convey this Imperial message to Yonai at once. In fact, it was when Yonai visited the Imperial Palace to tender his resignation that Kido finally told Yonai of the episode. The journalist Takamiya believes that Kido deliberately withheld the message. Kido, like his sworn friend Konoe, belonged to the group of people that was accommodative to the flow of the times, and it is quite conceivable that he held back the information in order to prompt the formation of a second Konoe cabinet.

It is believed that Hata's last minute change of heart was attributable to the instruction from Prince Kan'in Haruhito, the seniormost elder in the Imperial Army. Hata could by no means resist the wishes of the prince. Hata kept his mouth shut on this matter, even after World War II during the International Military Tribunal for the Far East. It was through the testimony of the Vice Chief of the General Staff at the time that the truth was finally known.

After handing Yonai the letter with the Imperial Army's demands, Hata resigned from his post obediently "like a sheep being led to the slaughter house." Yonai understood the true mind of Hata and feared that the latter might commit suicide.

When called to testify about the letter during the International Military Tribunal, Yonai remarked that he had "no recollection" of the letter—

though of course it must have been unforgettable to him. In response to the chief justice's persistent questioning and brandishing of the compact edition of the newspaper that had reported Hata's demand, Yonai replied, "I can't read such small characters." When the chief justice insulted Yonai, saying, "I have never seen such a stupid person," Yonai remained completely calm, showing no emotion.

Yonai and Hata both came into their own as true Japanese men in the court held in the name of the occupation forces.

Matsuoka Yōsuke on the Stage

As we have seen, Emperor Shōwa was so adamantly against the Tripartite Pact that he once said, "We will never allow it." And Yonai and Yamamoto tried to resist its conclusion at the risk of their own lives. Nevertheless, no sooner had the second Konoe cabinet been formed than the Pact was signed. While the trend of the times definitely played a role here, the signing of the Pact was chiefly attributable to Matsuoka Yōsuke's aggressive way of doing business.

As soon as the second Konoe cabinet was formed in late July in 1940, Foreign Minister Matsuoka sounded out Germany's intentions for the Tripartite Pact. Although Germany at that point had no clear policy on this matter, it decided to dispatch Heinrich Stahmer as its special envoy.

At the four-minister conference (among the prime minister, the ministers of war and navy, and the foreign minister) on September 4, Matsuoka abruptly handed out a mimeographed proposal some 20 pages long on the Tripartite Pact. Although everyone present was surprised by this, Matsuoka eventually succeeded in obtaining the approval of the three other ministers. They commented, "Although the issues of joining the war and extending military assistance call for extra caution, negotiations with Germany and Italy can be started at this point."

The Matsuoka-Stahmer talks commenced on September 9. Draft of the treaty was prepared in no time and its full text was deliberated at the cabinet meeting held in the Imperial presence on September 19. The Tripartite Pact was signed in Berlin on September 27.

What was the Imperial Navy doing during this process? Minister of Navy Yoshida Zengo fell into a pit of friendless isolation, surrounded by the Imperial Army, the foreign ministry, and public opinion. The situation made him so distressed that he became hospitalized and eventually resigned from his post. Oikawa Koshirō succeeded him. Because Yamamoto Isoroku was no longer there to assist Oikawa as Vice-Minister of the Navy, having been replaced by Toyoda Teijirō, the new Navy leadership was powerless against the trend of the times. Oikawa and Toyoda had to be content with modifying a few words and phrases before approving the draft treaty.

Kido deliberately refrained from informing Saionji of the tripartite negotiations, saying, "I do not have the heart to sadden the prince." For Saionji, the signing of the Tripartite Pact was "a bolt from the blue." Hearing of the signing, Saionji told his mistress, "Now perhaps you won't be able to die peacefully at home," predicting accurately what would ensue.

Knowing that the emperor and Saionji would oppose the signing of the Tripartite Pact, Konoe, Kido, and Matsuoka evaded their interference and created a fait accompli.

Hearing of the signing of the Tripartite Pact, Emperor Shōwa said to people around him, "We deeply worry over what will happen if Japan has to fight a war with the United States and loses it. If it should become a reality, we wonder if Prime Minister Konoe intends to share his agony and pain with us."

As Emperor Shōwa had been rightly concerned, this treaty eventually led Japan to devastation. While it may not be meaningful to examine the content of the treaty in detail now that we know the subsequent history, let me introduce its gist so that we can learn the thinking of the people in those days.

In Article I of the Pact, Japan recognized the leadership positions of Germany and Italy in the construction of a new European order. In Article II, Germany and Italy recognized Japan's leadership position in the Greater East Asian Order.

Because the colonial masters of French Indochina (Vietnam, Cambodia, and Laos) and the Dutch East Indies (Indonesia), areas that Japan had been interested in claiming, were both occupied by Germany, Berlin was entitled to claim sovereignty over those areas. The area also included the Marshall Islands, which Germany had lost as the result of its defeat in World War I. Furthermore, the issue of sovereignty over Malay, Burma, India, and Australia would arise with the demise of the British Empire.

In any event, because Japan succeeded in making Germany acknowledge Japan's priority right in what Japan had considered the Greater East Asian Co-prosperity Sphere, Japan would have won a great concession from Germany with the conclusion of this Pact had the Axis countries won the war. In the abstract, the Pact had the potential to have been good for Japan. However, the Axis powers lost.

Behind the Pact was the geopolitical thinking that Matsuoka had cherished in those days—that is, that Germany-Italy, Japan, and the Soviet Union each should develop its own sphere of influence from the north through south of the old continent (in which both Japan and Germany would not mind giving India to the Soviet Union) and that these three spheres of influence should collaborate together to contain the Monroeism of the United States in the Americas. Actually, Matsuoka's plan was too childish and quixotic to be called a geopolitical strategy. But it should be pointed out that Hitler and Ribbentrop held similar ideas during the time of the German-Soviet collaboration, and it was their thinking that influenced Matsuoka.

Article III of the Pact stipulated that the co-signees should mutually assist other signees when and if they were attacked by a third country that was not currently at war in Europe or Asia—in other words, the Soviet Union and the United States. Because the Soviet Union was exempted in Article V, the target of this Pact was clearly the United States.

The target of the Tripartite Pact thus shifted from the Soviet Union in the beginning, then to Britain, and, finally, to the United States. This alone is enough to testify that this trilateral alliance did not derive from the necessity of power politics.

What Matsuoka and the German leaders expected was that the Tripartite Pact would discourage the United States from participating in the war.

After the signing of the Pact, Ribbentrop sent a warning to the United States. He said that if the United States joined the war, "it would have to fight the combined forces of more than 250 million peoples of the three countries." Even such a coolheaded diplomat as State Secretary Ernst von Weizsacker once announced that the United States would not like to face a two-front war. What this means was that Japan's immense naval capability in those days was regarded in Germany as a great military asset that could rival Britain and the United States.

When Matsuoka explained the merit of the Tripartite Pact to the emperor, he also emphasized that it would be the only way to avoid war with the United States.

Hara Yoshimichi, President of the Privy Council, expressed his apprehension about the possibility of the Pact worsening the relations with the United States at the cabinet meeting attended by the Emperor on September 19. Matsuoka, resorting to his pet sophistry, responded by stating, "At this point, the American attitude toward Japan is so bad that it cannot be restored with a few flattering tricks. Only a dauntless attitude on our part could prevent a war with the United States."

As subsequent history shows, however, both Hitler and Matsuoka had misinterpreted the United States. It was not a country that decided whether to start a war on a profit-and-cost account based on the balance of power. It was a country that based the decision on moral principles and the national sentiment.

By the end of the 20th century, it became common sense. This unique American trait was explicitly pointed out in George Kennan's *American Diplomacy, 1900–1950,* which was published in 1951. This book was followed by a detailed theoretical and historical analysis of Henry Kissinger in his *Diplomacy,* which was published toward the end of the 20th century.

But these analyses are only wisdom after the event. Nobody in those days understood it. At least the United States' way of thinking had not yet become common sense among the world's policy makers. Thus, every one of them groped in the dark for America's next move or cherished an illusion about it.

Nevertheless, there were a few, including Emperor Shōwa and Saionji, who used their common sense and realized that the United States might react decisively against the Tripartite Pact. But, more than anyone else, U.S. Ambassador to Japan Joseph Grew, who had been directly in charge of U.S.-Japan relations, knew the danger. In his diary of October 1, 1940, Grew wrote, "It is obvious that the chief target of the alliance is the United States. . . . I was heavy-hearted while keeping my diary in September. What I had to write about was not the same Japan that I have known."

Imagining how desperate a diplomat must have felt to have had to write about his host country that it was not the same country that he had known, my heart goes out to Grew.

CHAPTER

10

Self-Destructive Matsuoka Diplomacy

—Shin Taisei Undo Is Widely Supported—

Taisei Yokusankai Launched

In Japan today, only a few people remember how things were during World War II, not to mention the prewar days.

When asked about those times or what society was like in the era of militarism, those who were born in the first decade of the Shōwa period (1926–35) naturally recall the days of the second Konoe Fumimaro cabinet.

Just after the formation of the second Konoe Cabinet in July 1940 (15th Year of Shōwa), events symbolic of the era occurred one after another. The Tripartite Pact was signed in September, the Taisei Yokusankai (大政翼賛会、Imperial Rule Assistance Association) was launched in October, the Celebration of the Empire's 2,600th anniversary was held in November, and a state funeral for Saionji Kinmochi took place in December. At the level of everyday life, rationing of sugar and matches took effect in the summer of 1940, charcoal did so that winter, and rice did so in the spring of 1941. Posters appeared on every street corner urging people to "Think of Our Soldiers in the Battlefield" and asserting that "Luxury is the Enemy."

This was the era of militarism in Japan as we envision it. Prior to Pearl Harbor, there still remained an atmosphere of freedom that could be characterized as "prewar." Once the attack on Pearl Harbor was launched, however, Japan, just like any other country at war, entered a wartime regime that was far beyond the state of militarism.

The most symbolic incident during this period was the decline of political parties. Political parties had been the pillar of parliamentary democracy for half a century since the promulgation of the Meiji Constitution.

The Shin Taisei Undō (新体制運動, Movement for a New Order) evolved around Konoe Fumimaro.

Upon his return from the Karuizawa summer resort on June 24, 1940, Konoe made the following announcement:

> No one would question the need to establish a strong political regime in order to cope with the unprecedented emergencies both within and outside Japan. In the face of this need, I have made up my mind to resign as president of the Privy Council in order to contribute my humble efforts to the establishment of such a regime.

While there had been prior attempts to shatter conventional politics, it was after 1940 that the so-called Shin Taisei Uudo was launched. In March, nationalistic elements of the *Seiyūkai*, *Minseitō*, and *Shakai Taishūtō* parties formed the League of Diet Members to Carry Through the Holy War (聖戦貫徹議員連盟). The Movement for a New Order expanded steadily around this league, and became solid by the time Konoe made the above announcement. After the announcement, the *Shakai Taishūtō* led others by declaring its dissolution in mid-July, followed by various factions of the *Seiyūkai*, the Nagai Ryūtarō faction of the *Minseitō*, and the *Kokumin Dōmei*. The mainstream faction of the *Minseitō,* which hesitated to join the bandwagon until the last minute, finally dissolved itself in August.

While all these dissolved political parties had hoped to join the new party led by Konoe, Konoe had had no intention to form a new political party from the beginning. Stressing the meaninglessness of any realignment among the existing parties, Konoe declared that he would pursue a new political regime of national unity instead.

Before the second Konoe cabinet was formed, the Imperial Army had ousted the anti-Tripartite Pact Yonai Mitsumasa cabinet. One factor behind this political drama was the mood of public opinion at the time, which placed high hopes on Konoe's Movement for a New Order. Konoe's conduct, as a result, contributed to the fall of the Yonai cabinet. Prior to the collapse of the Yonai cabinet, Kido Kōichi, a long-time friend of Konoe who had succeeded Yuasa Kurahei as Lord Keeper of the Privy Seal of Japan in June, decided not to convey the Imperial wish to Yonai asking the Yonai cabinet to remain in power. Perhaps Kido believed that not conveying the Imperial wish was in line with the trend of the times. After Yonai's resignation, Kido strongly recommended the formation of the second Konoe cabinet to succeed the Yonai cabinet.

Meanwhile, it appeared that elder statesman Saionji Kinmochi had already given up on Konoe. When Saionji was informed that the senior ministers' conference had unanimously supported the appointment of Konoe, he declined to reply to the Imperial message, citing old age and illness. The source of his disappointment may be found in what he once murmured to people around him. "It is no good," Saionji said in reference to Konoe, "to resort to such an old-fashioned notion as to base his politics on his personal popularity."

The expression "old-fashioned" carried a profound meaning. Perhaps what Saionji meant to say was that Konoe should not have imitated what Hitler had done. The remark should be interpreted as Saionji's way of regretting the resignation of Yonai, who had the "true courage to fearlessly practice what he believes in."

Saionji's worry became reality in no time. The Konoe cabinet immediately signed the Tripartite Pact and set out to pursue the Greater East Asian New Order. Domestically, the Konoe cabinet supported the Movement for a New Order.

Although Konoe had stopped consulting with Saionji by that time, the latter remained clear-headed until his last breath. After sharing his concern with his personal staff and accurately predicting that the Empire of Japan had started to veer toward catastrophe, Saionji died suddenly of pyelitis on November 24.

Saionji's death symbolized both the end of Japan's party politics, which Saionji had personally nurtured since the days of the Freedom and People's Rights Movement, and the end of liberalism in Japan that had been evolving since the days of the Taisho Democracy. Most of all, his death could have been a premonition of the fall of the Empire of Japan.

As soon as the second Konoe cabinet was formed, it disclosed its intention to exercise political initiative to promote the Movement for a New Order. Subsequently, the Taisei Yokusankai was launched on October 12, 1940 after careful preparation.

What this "preparation" entailed was, however, nothing more than a rag-bag grouping of prominent individuals from politics, officialdom, the military, intellectuals, rightists, and liberals and making up a slogan based on their greatest common denominator. In this process, concrete policies advocated by each participating element were abandoned. As a result, Konoe had to announce the following at the kick-off ceremony of the Movement: "It is believed that the only goal of this movement is to practice the way of a loyal subject to assist the imperial rule . . . [As such] I can declare that there is no additional code of conduct or declaration of this movement."

While the Movement for a New Order had originally aimed to function as an organ to facilitate both top-down and bottom-up communications in place of the abolished political parties, it eventually became a mere spiritual movement. During the Tōjō wartime cabinet, it was nothing more than an organ that transmitted the wishes of government leaders to their subordinates.

One may wonder why the political parties in Japan collapsed so easily.

There had been no party government in Japan since the assassination of Prime Minister Inukai Tsuyoshi in 1932 (7th Year of Shōwa). Public opinion no longer tolerated a party cabinet after this incident.

Nevertheless, the Imperial Diet continued to enjoy the power to pass the government budget and call a vote of nonconfidence in the cabinet. It was because the House of Representatives passed a vote of nonconfidence that the Abe Nobuyuki cabinet was forced to step down in 1940. Also, freedom of speech was respected within the Diet. It is well-known that on February 2, 1940, Saitō Takao made a historical, so-called anti-military speech at the House of Representatives. Although the House had to expel Saitō under pressure from the Imperial Army, some House members voted against Saito's expulsion and Saitō himself was re-elected to the House at the subsequent by-election.

While it was true that mid-level leaders of the military labeled his speech as anti-military, the content of the speech was actually not necessarily anti-military. All Saitō did was to lament that such an empty slogan as a "holy war" was endangering the fate of the country. In other words, the speech only criticized the spiritualism that was in vogue in those days.

Nevertheless, looking at the broad trend of the time, we should conclude that cool-headed individuals like Saitō had become almost non-existent in Japan in those days: the Movement for a New Order began with the establishment of the League of Diet Members to Carry Through the Holy War, led to a quick dissolution of all the existing political parties and gave birth to the Imperial Rule Assistance Association, and the resolution to expel Saitō was passed by an overwhelming majority. It must have been clear that the overwhelming majority of party politicians were drunk on the abstractive patriotic slogan together with Konoe, the military, and the general public.

The history of Shōwa defies easy judgment, especially during this period.

By far the easiest interpretation is to blame the military for all the misfortunes in this period. It would be convincing to claim that the political parties and politicians had no other choice than to cater to the military's wishes because they had been terrorized or pressured by the military. As for the general public, it can be argued that restrictions on the freedom of speech did not allow people to oppose government policies or that the public had been manipulated by the military's propaganda.

But perhaps the reality was not that simple. It seems undeniable that public opinion itself had been mesmerized with the dream of expansion of the Empire of Japan and exaltation of national prestige, to which political parties had also responded.

What makes it more difficult to interpret the Shōwa history accurately is the fact that most quotable materials were either memoirs written after World War II or testimonies during the International Military Tribunal for the Far East. All of these documents inevitably contain elements of self-vindication.

On the Movement for a New Order, Konoe wrote as follows in his memoir written after the war:

> By that time, it was no longer possible for political parties to restrict the military. Therefore, it was imperative to establish a new national

organization that was embedded in each and every citizen, an organization that was totally different from existing political parties, as well as a government that was based on the political power of such an organization . . .

Yabe Teiji construed Konoe's vindication at face value, saying, "It is obvious from his memoir that what Konoe wished for was to bring together the Japanese people's political power to counter the military."

Nevertheless, concrete Konoe cabinet policies that were announced immediately after the cabinet was formed adopted the military's viewpoints. At the press conference immediately following the announcement, Prime Minister Konoe said that his cabinet would "go hand in hand with the military," which was indeed an accurate description of the announced policies.

In Konoe's case, there was hardly any difference between "restricting the military's self-assertion" and "forestalling the military." From the beginning, Konoe basically believed in the military's argument, but wanted his cabinet to pursue basically the same policies instead of allowing the military to have its own way.

There was an atmosphere in Japan in those days which claimed that "This is no time to indulge in party struggles. It is time for all people in Japan to join in defending hand in hand the prestige and glory of the Empire of Japan." And it seems undeniable that this atmosphere became at least dominant, if not predominant, among public opinion, mass media, parliamentarians, and intellectuals. Therefore, I must say neither Konoe's postwar vindication—i.e., that he only wished to restrain the military—or the postwar leftist historical view that denounces Konoe for having simply gone along with the military accurately conveyed the true state of the national trend of the time.

It should also be pointed out that there was strong support for the Movement for a New Order among the Japanese people. The national sentiment in those days had been gloomy. The elation caused by a chain of victories at the early stage of the Second Sino-Japanese War had already waned as the battle developed into a war of attrition. People's life became heavily pressured by war expenditures, which, coupled with the chronic shortage of commodities, made people feel restless and wonder how long this oppressive state would last. Thus, people were anxious to look for something that could radically change the negative atmosphere.

While the Movement for a New Order had been evidently affected by the pseudo-socialistic ideology of the Shōwa Restoration, it can be categorized as a type of fundamentalist movement that appears in world history every once in a while. The most central feature of a fundamentalist movement is that it demands the people to follow a moralistic discipline that no one can formally oppose, such as respect for labor, admonition of extravagance, encouragement of thrift and diligence, and restriction of liberty and license in one's private life. The fundamentalist movement does not hesitate to sacrifice individuals for the ideal of the whole. These features are the essence of the fundamentalism that has been repeated over and over in the Islamic world up to the recent Khomeini Revolution. The essence can also be found in similar movements elsewhere in the world. Oliver Cromwell's Puritan Revolution (1641), Saigō Takamori's Satsuma Rebellion (1877), and China's Great Cultural Revolution (1966–76) were all variants of fundamentalism.

When a fundamentalist movement lingers for a long period of time, it can be suffocating for the people. But when it is relatively brief, particularly while the earlier elation still lingers, it can brace people's spirits and make their outlook toward the future more positive.

In Japan, too, the Movement for a New Order was enthusiastically supported by naïve people, particularly peasants in rural areas who in those days still occupied a large proportion of the entire population. It was a period of fundamentalism permeated with such samurai ethics as loyalty and patriotism, militaristic spirit, honor, and austerity.

Let me introduce an *Aikoku Kōshinkyoku* (Patriotic March) that became popular all over Japan in those days, partially thanks to the spread of radio:

> Behold the dawn over the seas of Japan
> Morning sun is high and bright in the sky
> And the energy of the earth and universe
> Enlivens and fills the Japanese Archipelago
> Ah, the very presence of Mount Fuji,
> Solitary against morning clouds and blue sky,
> Is pride in our invincible homeland, Japan.

In contrast to military songs at the time of the Russo-Japanese War, which touched people's hearts with lyrics that paid homage to the heroic conduct of warriors, lyrics of this Patriotic March were nothing but enumerations of abstract expressions. One can see in this song the same symbolism as found in the praise of Mao Zedong and Kim Il-sung that compared them to the "bright red sun."

It can be said that the nationwide popularity of this song was a symbol of the times. Mass propaganda became an important means of implementing policies with the widespread use of radio among the Japanese. In fact, the chanting of slogans proved to be more effective in mobilizing the Japanese people than giving logical explanations to issues. The same can be said about speeches by Hitler and Konoe, which were filled with what Saitō Takao called "empty hypocrisy." Even today, this method continues to be applied in countries under Communist dictatorship.

In any event, the Patriotic March was a musical masterpiece. Reinforced by its light-hearted and bouncy rhythm, the highly abstract but patriotic lyrics were effective in raising the national spirit and inspiring solidarity among the Japanese people. Such was the mood of the day.

The Arbitrary Conduct of Foreign Minister Matsuoka Yōsuke

The diplomacy practiced by the second Konoe cabinet was constantly stirred up and handled aggressively by its foreign minister, Matsuoka Yōsuke.

What Matsuoka brought about was so grave that it affected the fate of the Empire of Japan.

Yet I am not sure whether describing the details of Matsuoka's diplomacy is worthwhile. The reason is that Matsuoka's conduct was largely based on his personal motivations or his habits that were not necessarily elements of historical inevitability. And his actions did not derive from deep thinking or philosophy; they were mostly based on highly personal inclinations and an excessive concern about his reputation. Matsuoka was vainly overconfident about himself and demanded that others blindly follow his lead. If ever he had some theory, it could never have been a long-term strategy but a low-level, tactical calculation, such as belief in high-handed manners to force the other party to give in. And his method of having his own way was simply to blaze away at his opponents without giving them a chance to speak.

As I wrote earlier, while this type of person may be competent as long as he remains a lowly clerk, supervisors must monitor his work closely when he becomes a section chief and make up for his deficiencies in order to fully utilize his ability. He is a type of person that should never have been promoted above section chief.

In the end, it was Konoe's inability to judge a man's character that made him appoint such an inappropriate person as Matsuoka as his foreign minister.

Matsuoka had gained an undeserved reputation as the hero who had walked out of the League of Nations in protest at the adoption of a report blaming Japan for the Manchurian Incident. While Matsuoka himself initially regarded Japan's withdrawal from the League as a diplomatic failure, he gradually began to behave like a rightwing hero, having met with unexpected public applause when he returned to Japan.

Konoe was fond of gathering all kinds of celebrities and intellectuals around him. This fondness must have derived from an aristocratic habit of establishing personal connection with notables. The flip side of this inclination was Konoe's aversion to people who criticized his conduct, particularly those in the military and the rightists among whom Konoe believed himself to be popular. One of the reasons Konoe had already lost enthusiasm by the time the Movement for a New Order began to take concrete shape was the criticism from a segment of rightists who found the movement to be a shogunate-like presence.

Given his idiosyncrasies, Konoe must have viewed Matsuoka, who was popular among the rightists and patriots and tolerated by the military, as a perfect choice for his foreign minister.

Matsuoka, however, was way too individualistic to play the role of a popular figure for the Konoe cabinet.

As explained in the previous chapter, as soon as Matsuoka became foreign minister, he signed the Tripartite Pact. At this stage, Matsuoka had already been contemplating visiting the Tripartite ally countries, prompted by German foreign minister Ribbentrop's request that Matsuoka visit Germany.

One direct motivation behind Matsuoka's trip to Europe was the slow progress made hitherto in ameliorating diplomatic relations with the Soviet Union. While the Japanese side pinned high hopes on mediation by German special envoy Heinrich Stahmer, who visited Japan to facilitate the signing of the Tripartite Pact, Stahmer showed no sign of even starting a mediation attempt.

According to Saitō Ryōei, Matsuoka's foreign policy advisor, Matsuoka intended to consult directly with Hitler on the coordination of Japan-Soviet relations. Furthermore, Matsuoka told Saitō that he was prepared for the following worst situation:

> If coordination proves to be unfeasible, restraining the United States' power would become nothing but a transient dream. When it comes to that, the raison d'etre of the Tripartite Pact itself also disappears . . . and we would have no other option than to let go of the alliance with Germany and Italy.

On February 3, 1941, prior to Matsuoka's visit to Europe, the Japanese government decided on the outline of a negotiation plan with Germany and Italy. According to this outline, the world would be divided into four spheres at a peace conference after the war: Greater East Asia, Europe (including Africa), America, and the Soviet Union (including India and Iran). It was also decided that they would allow Britain to retain Australia and New Zealand.

In retrospect, it is simply amazing that the Japanese government seriously adopted such a megalomaniac scheme as its official policy. It must have been due to Matsuoka's forceful argument and the Konoe cabinet's fervor to establish a new world order.

But it should be pointed out that this scheme was exactly what Ribbentrop had proposed to Soviet foreign minister Vyacheslav Molotov in Berlin in November 1940. According to Kissinger: "Molotov had no interest in so bombastic a proposal. Germany did not yet possess what it purported to offer, and the Soviet Union did not need Germany to conquer these territories for itself."[19]

---

19   Henry Kissinger, *Diplomacy* (New York: Simon & Schuster, 1994), p. 360.

The Soviet Bolshevik's diplomacy was far more realistic, and it demanded Germany make a massive concession on what Germany had already possessed—territories in eastern and northern Europe. The Bolsheviks also applied the same approach to Japan. Based on the highly conceptual logic that when each power expanded its respective sphere of influence vertically north and south, the danger of clashes among them would diminish, Japan expressed the hope to purchase northern Sakhalin. In contrast, the Soviet side demanded that Japan dissolve its concessions on northern Sakhalin in return for a Soviet-Japanese neutrality pact that would make Japan's position in China more advantageous. Communists simply did not live in the same childish world of fantasies as that of Hitler or Matsuoka.

Thus, the German attempt to adjust its relations with the Soviet Union did not proceed as Germany had wished. By the time Matsuoka visited Berlin, Germany had already given up on negotiations with the Soviet Union and, instead, decided on launching Operation Barbarossa against the Soviet Union.

Although the German foreign ministry (particularly State Secretary Ernst von Weizsacker) and the navy advised Hitler that Matsuoka should be notified of Operation Barbarossa, Hitler's headquarters ordered that the operation be kept confidential. Nevertheless, both Hitler and Ribbentrop disclosed to Matsuoka that German-Soviet relations had come to a deadlock and hinted at the possibility of a German-Soviet clash.

What the German side tenaciously requested of Matsuoka, instead, was that Japan attack Singapore in order to bottle up the British navy in Asia. Since Matsuoka had been instructed by the Imperial Army and Navy not to give his word about an attack on Singapore, he replied by saying, "I am not in a position to make the decision on that matter. But offensive action toward Singapore by Japan is a matter of time, and I personally believe that the earlier the attack, the better."

Thus, Matsuoka had to leave Germany for Moscow without having been assured of Germany's intention concerning his grand strategy of accomplishing a balance of power vis-à-vis the United States to prevent its participation in the war. In Moscow, Matsuoka negotiated with Molotov on the Soviet-Japanese neutrality treaty that Matsuoka had proposed to

Molotov on his way to Europe. As is always the case in negotiations with the Soviet Union, this negotiation broke down temporarily. At the final minute the Soviet side requested to resume negotiations, enabling the two sides to reach an agreement.

The resultant treaty was a very simple agreement, stipulating mutual nonaggression in the first article, neutrality in the case of a war with a third party in the second article, and, in the third article, the five-year validity of the treaty with an automatic extension in the event annulment was not announced one year before the expiration date. Additionally, Matsuoka agreed to settle the issue of concession on northern Sakhalin within a few months of his visit.

Conclusion of this treaty was a major success for the Soviet Union both from the viewpoint of the Soviet grand strategy in making Japan fight the United States and Britain and from the strains in its relations with Germany. Stalin saw off Foreign Minister Matsuoka at Moscow Station, a highly unusual gesture of goodwill, and actually embraced the latter to say farewell.

Matsuoka's strategy to restrain the United States with Germany and the Soviet Union was crippled once a war broke out between Germany and the Soviet Union. At the time of the conclusion of the mutual nonaggression treaty, however, Matsuoka could have boasted that he had successfully improved diplomatic relations with the Soviet Union singlehandedly, to which Germany had refused to render cooperation. One can only imagine how proud Matsuoka must have been, being totally ignorant of the reality that he had just played into the hands of the Soviet Union.

Although it was not the intention of Matsuoka, the Soviet-Japanese Neutrality Pact itself was not a bad thing to conclude. The pact eliminated the worry about the danger from being attacked from behind for Japan when it entered the Great East Asia War. It also had the effect of making the Soviet Union feel guilty for violating the pact by starting the Soviet-Japanese War toward the end of World War II while the pact was still valid.

Interference in U.S.-Japanese Negotiations

Among Matsuoka's arbitrary and uncontrollable conduct, by far the most damaging to Japan was his interference in negotiations with the United

States. Moreover, Matsuoka's interference had derived from his narrow-mindedness rather than from differences in views on grand policies.

The preamble of the Tripartite Pact left no doubt that its hypothetical enemy was the United States. As soon as the Pact went into effect, therefore, the United States reinforced the embargo on strategic materials, and public opinion in the United States became more inclined toward restraining Japan even at the risk of war.

Since it had been the intention of Matsuoka diplomacy to make the United States back off by confronting it forcefully, Matsuoka had no reason to take measures to soothe the American public. Angered by Matsuoka's attitude, the U.S. government had no intention of appeasing Japan which increasingly worsened the U.S.-Japan relations.

With intergovernmental relations between Japan and the United States deadlocked, the American private sector began to take action.

Central figures in this private attempt were Bishop James Walsh and Father James Drought of the Catholic Foreign Mission (Maryknoll) Society. Being close to Frank Walker, the pro-Japanese Postmaster General of the Roosevelt administration and Roosevelt's election campaign manager, these two priests offered to mediate a reconciliation between Konoe and Roosevelt.

While these two were visiting Japan in November 1940, they met Foreign Minister Matsuoka and officials at the Imperial Army. Matsuoka and others did not place high hopes on this private initiative. Having confidence in Igawa Tadao, former finance ministry official and an expert on the United States, who coordinated the visit of the two clergymen, however, Konoe gave this private initiative the go-ahead without informing Matsuoka or Nomura Kichisaburō, who was on his way to assume the post of Ambassador to the United States.

Subsequently, the trio (Walsh, Drought, and Igawa) continued consultation among themselves, acting in accord with the respective government leaders. Their talks bore fruit in the form of a U.S.-Japan Draft Agreement completed on April 15, 1941. The next day, it was agreed between U.S. Secretary of State Cordell Hull and Japanese Ambassador Nomura to put this Agreement on the agenda for governmental negotiations between the two countries.

This U.S.-Japan Draft Agreement was truly a product of laborious efforts.

While the U.S. side requested the Japanese side to invalidate the Tripartite Pact, Japan insisted that the Pact was a purely defensive arrangement. From the standpoint of international good faith, Japan found it impossible to emasculate a treaty that had just been concluded.

The greatest bottleneck was the settlement of the Second Sino-Japanese War. The Draft Agreement proposed that China recognize Manchukuo, that Chiang Kai-shek's government and the Wang Jingwei regime be united, that the Japanese military withdraw in accordance with the agreement, and that the president of the United States recommend Chiang Kai-shek to conclude a peace agreement on the basis of no annexation and no reparation.

This Draft Agreement was reported to the Japanese government on April 18, when the cabinet happened to be having a meeting. At night a liaison conference was convened between the cabinet and the Imperial Japanese Army General Staff Office, in which everyone present agreed with the draft agreement. In fact, the Imperial Army and Navy jumped on this Draft Agreement. Although some participants urged an immediate reply to convey that the Japanese side had agreed in principle, the reply was postponed for a couple of days until the return of Matsuoka.

Konoe was so worried about Matsuoka getting cranky upon hearing about the draft agreement that Konoe went to the airport to meet Matsuoka in order to persuade Matsuoka during the car ride. When Matsuoka announced that he planned to worship the Imperial Palace from the foot of *Nijūbashi* en route, a trite performance to demonstrate his allegiance to the Emperor, Konoe, an intelligentsia, hesitated to join the performance. Konoe decided not to ride back together with Matsuoka.

As Konoe had feared, Deputy Foreign Minister Ōhashi Chūichi, who rode with Matsuoka in place of Konoe, failed to persuade Matsuoka. In later days, Konoe was often heard muttering regrettably, "If only had I ridden with Matsuoka . . ."

As a matter of fact, before Matsuoka returned to Japan, Konoe had telephoned Matsuoka in Dalian to request his prompt return in order to study an important proposal the Japanese government had received from the United States.

Hearing this, Matsuoka was at first in good humor. He thought his persuasion of the American ambassador to the Soviet Union in Moscow had led the United States to engage in a Sino-Japanese peace settlement. As soon as he learned that the draft agreement had been worked out by two Catholic priests without his knowledge, however, he rapidly became displeased and broke off the conversation with Konoe.

At the conference at the Prime Minister's Official Residence held just after his return to Tokyo, Matsuoka would not stop bragging about his trip to Europe, referring to "Hitler-san" and "[Galeazzo] Ciano-san" as if they were his personal friends. Unable to take it any longer, Konoe introduced the Draft Agreement. Matsuoka became highly indignant and departed for home. He exited the conference with this parting shot: "We must not be deceived by the United States. In any event, I am too exhausted now. Let me take two weeks or a month to organize my thoughts."

The other conference participants, including War Minister Tōjō, were furious about Matsuoka's insolence and agreed to advance the Draft Agreement. It was undeniable, however, that the chance had already been missed.

This episode is so low level that it embarrasses me just to trace the process. Moreover, I am appalled that the country's fate had been trifled with by the stubbornness of such a petty fellow.

As it turned out, Matsuoka submitted an amended Draft Agreement to the U.S. side on May 11. The amendment was nothing short of a denial of all the compromises that both sides had made to attain the Draft Agreement.

On this counterproposal from the Japanese side, Secretary of State Cordell Hull left the following observations in his memoir: "I hardly found any ray of hope in the Japanese counterproposal. The Japanese side insisted unilaterally only on what would be beneficial to Japan, paying almost no consideration at all to others' rights or interests."

One may wonder what would have happened if the U.S.-Japan negotiations had proceeded on the basis of the Draft Agreement.

It is not hard to imagine that negotiations would not have gone smoothly. In his memoir, Hull wrote that a close study of the Japanese counterproposal had deeply disappointed him because it was largely filled with Japan's imperialistic ambitions. While the counterproposal contained several points that were utterly unacceptable from the beginning, there were some points that were readily acceptable or could become acceptable with some modifications. Thus, Hull decided that he should not let the opportunity slip away.

The Draft Agreement was a proposal with the primary goal of attaining peace at any cost, imposed on both governments by moral authority of the clergymen. As such, it was not the kind of proposal that the United States could have wholeheartedly agreed with, nor was it something that Japan could have bargained about as Matsuoka had thought.

As it happened, Hull actually proposed to resume negotiations on the condition that the Japanese side would accept such principles as respect for territory and sovereignty of all countries, non-interference in internal affairs, and change of status through peaceful means only.

While, admittedly, these conditions were all vague in principle, they, with a stricter interpretation, could have denied the changes of current status dating all the way back to the Manchurian Incident.

Even if the United States had agreed to base negotiations with Japan on the Draft Agreement, it would not have been easy to persuade Chiang Kai-shek to agree with the terms.

Of all the potential stumbling blocks, by far the toughest would have been the withdrawal of the Japanese military from China. Given that the Japanese military had long maintained its presence, establishing an anti-Communist zone in north China, and that it had been unwilling to withdraw its troops from other strategic points, it would not have been easy to settle the issue.

Nevertheless, if, for instance, the Chiang Kai-shek side had agreed on the exchange of ambassadors with Manchukuo, or if the Japanese military had made a major compromise on the conditions of troop withdrawal—that is, finally accepting realistic settlements that had been repeatedly proposed in the past—which might have required the Emperor's initiative similar to the Imperial decision on the termination of the war, a compromise could have been reached.

Moreover, the international situation had been in great turmoil. Had Japan negotiated earnestly with the United States, then the outbreak of war between Germany and the Soviet Union—another breach of trust against the spirit of the Tripartite Pact on the part of Germany—would have provided the golden opportunity to fulfill the American wish to turn the Tripartite Pact into a dead letter.

During the initial stage of the Eastern Front, Germany won one battle after another. Taking into consideration the possibility of Germany emerging triumphant in the war, Britain and the United States might have had to consider a compromise with Japan. Together with the enhanced option for Japan to advance northward facilitated by German victories, this British/American compromise might have given incentives to the Japanese side to drastically withdraw its troops from China.

While asking "what if?" in history may not lead to any convincing conclusion, it seems obvious that we had at least some chances to avoid the U.S.-Japanese war. We cannot regret enough how helplessly we had missed the opportunity.

Resignation of the Second Konoe Cabinet

As Nazi Germany had already hinted during Matsuoka's tour in Europe, it launched an attack against the Soviet Union on June 22. In the evening of the same day, Matsuoka was received in audience by the Emperor. Without prior consultation with Prime Minister Konoe, Matsuoka reported to the Emperor that Japan should fight against the Soviet Union in collaboration with Germany. Matsuoka also told the Emperor that while Japan would have to temporarily restrain its activities in Southeast Asia and Oceania, it eventually would have to fight against Britain and the Unites States in these territories, forcing Japan into simultaneous battles against the Soviet Union, Britain, and the United States. Surprised by this sudden visit, the Emperor explicitly expressed his wish to avoid further meetings with Matsuoka.

The original objective of the Tripartite Pact was to prevent U.S. participation in the war. However, the war between Germany and the Soviet Union immediately led to the formation of an alliance between the United States, Britain, and the Soviet Union.

At this stage, Prime Minister Konoe proposed abolishment of the Tripartite Pact in writing to Matsuoka and the War and Navy Ministers. Matsuoka did not take this proposal seriously. The military also found it unacceptable now that German troops were advancing into Soviet territory, cutting through everything in their path. Realizing further attempts to abolish the Tripartite Pact were futile, Konoe decided that he had no other choice than to proceed with the negotiations with the United States so as to turn the Pact into a de facto dead letter.

Germany, for its part, repeatedly prompted Japan to take military action. On June 30, German Ambassador Eugen Ott conveyed German Foreign Minister Ribbentrop's message to Matsuoka. The message stressed that, as important as an attack on Singapore might be, now was the one and only chance for Japan to strike the Soviet Union.

In the end, the cabinet council attended by the Emperor on July 2 adopted the Outline of Imperial Policy in order to hold back Matsuoka's argument for an immediate northbound advance. According to Yabe Teiji, Shōwa political commentator/scholar and one of Konoe's brains, the Outline included the determination to beef up preparations for the southbound advance "as a kind of compensation" for not making the northbound advance. Yabe testifies that the phrase "we will not hesitate to fight against Britain and the United States" was "just an empty promise to which nobody present gave serious thought." As it turned out, however, inclusion of this particular phrase later became one major factor that cornered Japan into starting a war against the United States.

It was Richard Sorge who reported on the content of this cabinet council to the Soviet government with accurate comments of his own.

Along with the aforementioned Ozaki Hotsumi (Chapter 9), Sorge was a spy with perhaps the best track record among all the Soviet spies who worked during World War II. Sorge was posthumously awarded the title of Hero of the Soviet Union in 1964; the award certificate and the medal are still on display at the Central Museum of the Armed Forces in Moscow.

Sorge came to Japan under the guise of a Nazi. In collaboration with Ozaki, Prime Minister Konoe's right-hand man, he collected inside information of the Japanese government, which he frequently passed on to German Ambassador Ott, who appreciated Sorge's contributions. Sorge was, thus, in a position to access the most important affairs of state.

Not only did Sorge affect Japan's highest national strategy so as to cripple negotiations with the United States and lead Japan to a war against the United States, Sorge also informed the Soviet Union that Japan had no intention to fight a war with it. This information encouraged the Soviet Union to transfer its troops stationed in Siberia to the Eastern Front in Europe, thus contributing to the country's victory over Germany.

Both Sorge and Ozaki were detected as Soviet's spies and arrested two months before the attack on Pearl Harbor. To the examining prosecutor, Ozaki said,

Our Bolshevik movement has already accomplished its goal now that Japan's all-out war with the United States is imminent. This war will make the Communist revolution in Japan inevitable. With 90 percent of our mission accomplished, it is truly regrettable that I must die before witnessing the result of our efforts with my own eyes.

While Konoe wished to restrain Japan's northbound advance and immediately promote negotiations with the United States, it appeared that the United States had already given up on negotiating with Japan via Matsuoka by that time. When a message from the U.S. president was communicated directly to Konoe on July 4, Matsuoka became really cranky at having been bypassed. He became overly aggressive toward the United States to the extent that Ambassador Nomura to the United States expressed his wish to resign, saying he could no longer put up with Matsuoka's provocations. At this point, partially backed by the Emperor's expressed wish, the Konoe cabinet resigned. Ousting Matsuoka was the main purpose. Konoe in no time received an Imperial mandate to form a new cabinet, leading to the launch of the third Konoe cabinet without Matsuoka.

Contradictions and inconsistencies became particularly conspicuous in Matsuoka's words and deeds in those days. Persons like Shigemitsu Mamoru and Itō Masanori went as far as using the expression "madness," albeit in a contained way, when referring to Matsuoka. Some rumors about Matsuoka's mental health in those days also coincided with this view. The greatest share of the responsibility, however, should be born by Konoe because he was the one who had promoted such a controversial person.

CHAPTER
11

Prologue to Attack on Pearl Harbor

—Hull Note Precludes Opposition to War—

U.S. Hardens Its Attitude

The process toward the eruption of the Greater East Asia War has been described by numerous authors.

Because the damage that the Second World War brought to Japan and its history were so devastating, each and every Japanese has looked back to try to understand how things happened as they did. The Japanese have ruminated on the process with the deepest remorse and regret ever since Japan's defeat in the war.

There are a number of unanswered questions about the process through which Japan rushed toward a war with the United States. Withdrawal of the Japanese troops stationed in China had always been the greatest bottleneck among the substantial issues in the U.S.-Japan negotiations. But why did the Imperial Army's attitude become increasingly rigid and uncompromising as negotiations reached the final stage? Why did the Imperial Navy, the chief actor in the war with the United States, abstain from opposing the war outright even though it had been aware, from start to finish, that Japan had no chance of winning a prolonged war?

By far the biggest question, however, has to do with the hardening of the U.S. attitude. Compared to the time of the Draft Agreement in spring

1941, the tone of the Outline of Proposed Basis for Agreement between the United States and Japan (known as the Hull note) in November that same year was remarkably tougher. And what hampered the realization of a Konoe-Roosevelt talk, which would have been the only chance to break the impasse? Was Japan's advance to southern French Indochina the sole factor? How influential was the pressure from Chiang Kai-shek, who opposed a U.S.-Japan compromise; or the conspiracy by the international communist movement; or the mistranslation of the coded message?

Before attempting to answer these questions, let me first chronologically summarize the course of events in order to provide a basic overview of history and also to jog the readers' memory. After that, allow me to share my observations on the above questions.

Because we can't retrace history endlessly, let me use as the starting point the cabinet meeting attended by the Emperor on July 2, 1941 (16th Year of Shōwa), toward the end of the second Konoe cabinet.

July 2, 1941

"Outline of Imperial Policy to Cope with Changes in Situations" adopted by the cabinet meeting attended by the Emperor. While "Changes in Situations" in this case referred to the new developments after the eruption of the war between Germany and the Soviet Union on June 22, the main purpose of the meeting was to contain Foreign Minister Matsuoka's argument for attacking the Soviet Union.

As a "compensation" (Konoe's word found in his memoir) for holding off on attacking the Soviet Union for the time being, the cabinet meeting decided to intensify Japan's preparations for a southbound advance and to upgrade its war-readiness against Britain and the United States.

July 18, 1941

The third Konoe Fumimaro cabinet was formed in order to dismiss Foreign Minister Matsuoka, who was replaced by Toyoda Teijirō.

July 24, 1941

The Japanese government notified the French Indochinese administration of its intention to advance its troops to southern French Indochina. The advancement took place on July 28.

A secret talk between Ambassador Nomura Kichisaburō to the United

States and U.S. President Franklin Roosevelt took place. During the talk Roosevelt said, "Although I have so far tried to contain the public opinion demanding an oil embargo, I now have lost the grounds for an argument. If the Japanese government withdraws its troops from French Indochina and assures its neutrality, the U.S. government would render cooperation for Japan to obtain commodities."

July 25, 1941
Japanese assets in the United States were frozen.

August 1, 1941
The U.S. oil embargo against Japan was initiated.

August 5 through 8, 1941
A consultation was convened in Washington, D.C., in order to break the deadlock. While the Japanese side attempted to win U.S. understanding by stressing that it had no intention of advancing anywhere other than French Indochina, the U.S. side demanded withdrawal of Japanese troops from French Indochina. The consultation was, therefore, getting nowhere.

August 12, 1941
U.S. President Roosevelt and British Prime Minister Winston Churchill met on board the *USS Augusta* on the Atlantic Ocean. During this meeting, the Joint Declaration by the President and the Prime Minister (later known as the Atlantic Charter) was signed. Although the content of the declaration was highly abstract, it nevertheless confirmed British-U.S. cooperation in World War II.

August 28, 1941
The proposal for a Roosevelt-Konoe talk was passed on to President Roosevelt by Japanese Ambassador Nomura. Reacting positively to the proposal, Roosevelt suggested a meeting with Konoe in Juneau, Alaska. But Secretary of State Cordell Hull summoned Nomura that same evening to inform him that lower-level preparations had to be made before the summit meeting could occur.

September 3, 1941

The U.S. government conveyed the above view of Hull to the Japanese side as its official stance, thus effectively rejecting the idea of a Konoe-Roosevelt direct talk.

September 6, 1941

The *Teikoku Kokusaku Suikō Yōryō* (Outline for Executing Imperial National Policy) was adopted at the cabinet meeting attended by the Emperor. It was decided that, should negotiations with the United States offer no prospects for settlement by early October, Japan would declare war with the United States.

During the course of deliberations, Emperor Shōwa persisted to the end in his hope for diplomatic negotiations. He quoted the following poem by Emperor Meiji:

> I wonder why the world stirs up,
> Even though all the countries overseas in all directions
> Are considered to be brothers and sisters in this world.

On the same day, Prime Minister Konoe urged U.S. Ambassador Joseph Grew and Counselor Eugene Dooman (who was the most knowledgeable about Japan among the staff of the U.S. embassy in Tokyo) to make every effort toward the realization of a U.S.-Japan summit talk.

September 25, 1941

A liaison conference decided that the cut-off date for the declaration of war against the United States discussed on September 6 would be October 15.

September 27, 1941

The Japanese response to the U.S. proposal presented in June—which the Japanese embassy in the United States had abstained from submitting to the U.S. side in consideration of Foreign Minister Matsuoka's dismissal—was delivered to Secretary of State Hull. For a document at this critical juncture, this response from the Japanese side was too unfocused. It made the United States all the more suspicious of Japan's true intention.

October 2, 1941

The United States responded to Japan, totally ignoring the above Japanese proposal submitted on September 27. In the concluding segment of its memorandum, the U.S. side wrote, "Seeing various conditions and exceptions that the Japanese side attached to implementation of principles, we cannot help but wonder if the Japanese side really thinks it worthwhile to convene a summit-level meeting."

American historian and author of *The Road to Pearl Harbor: The Coming of the War between the United States and Japan*, Harvard Feis later observed that it was this memorandum from the U.S. side, rather than the Hull note, that finished off the negotiation between the two countries.

Yet Prime Minister Konoe wrote the following on this exchange in his memoir:

> Although recently our side has offered our views on all kinds of issues, the American side only criticized and denounced our views, never disclosing its true intention. The distrust in U.S. sincerity has increasingly deepened, and the accusation that the United States is only trying to prolong the negotiations has come to sound more and more plausible as we reach the height of anxiety, suspicion, and impatience.

October 12 through 14, 1941

In the face of the cut-off date of October 15, Prime Minister Konoe and War Minister Tōjō Hideki exchanged a heated argument that only widened the distance between them. On the withdrawal of Japanese troops from China, by far the most important issue in the U.S.-Japan negotiations, Tōjō insisted, "Stationing our troops in China is truly the lifeline of the Imperial Army. I cannot give even an inch on this." When Tōjō said, "Man sometimes has to close his eyes and jump in at the deep end," Konoe retorted by saying, "While, admittedly, that might be true for a private person, I can never do such a thing when I have to think about the fate of a nation with a 2,600-year history and 100 million citizens."

October 14, 1941

The Imperial Army refused to withdraw its troops from China. Demanding termination of negotiations with the United States, the Imperial Army insisted that the Konoe cabinet resign if it could not decide on the start of the war on October 15 as agreed in the September 6 cabinet meeting attended by the Emperor.

October 16, 1941

The third Konoe cabinet resigned.

October 18, 1941

The Tōjō Hideki cabinet was formed with Tōgō Shigenori as its foreign minister. At first both the Imperial Army and Konoe himself had considered forming the cabinet of Prince Higashikuni Naruhiko. Kido Kōichi, Lord Keeper of the Privy Seal of Japan, objected to that idea in fear of implicating the Imperial Family in a possible war. While some members of the subsequent senior statesmen's conference recommended Ugaki Kazushige as succeeding prime minister, Kido nominated Tōjō as a person who could control the Imperial Army.

Issuing an Imperial mandate to form a new cabinet, Emperor Shōwa conveyed a rare directive for Japan-U.S. negotiations to decide on the fundamentals of national policy "uninhibited by the decision of the September 6 cabinet meeting."

November 5, 1941

In response to the directive of the Emperor on Japan-U.S. negotiations, national policy was thoroughly reviewed, leading to the official adoption of the *Teikoku Kokusaku Suikō Yōryō* (Outline for Executing Imperial National Policy) by the Tōjō cabinet.

The outline advanced two proposals concerning the negotiations with the United States (Proposals A and B). It was decided that diplomatic efforts would be terminated at midnight on December 1 and that Japan would open war with the United States in early December.

Proposal A advocated for continuation of the Japanese military presence in north China, Mongolia, and Hainan Island for 25 years after restoration of peace. Other regions would be vacated within two years of peace, except for French Indochina, from which the Japanese troops would withdraw immediately after the peace settlement.

Proposal B was a provisional plan for crisis prevention. It called for the restoration of the conditions that had existed before the freezing of Japanese assets: Japan would withdraw its troops from French Indochina, on the condition that the United States would not obstruct a peace settlement between Japan and China (in other words, that the United States would terminate assistance to Chiang Kai-shek). Although the military had adamantly opposed withdrawal from French Indochina in the beginning, it concurred in the end, convinced that the U.S. side would not accept this Japanese proposal.

To Ambassador Kurusu Saburō, who was to be dispatched to Washington, D.C., to assist in the negotiations with the United States, Tōjō said, "As far as the troop withdrawal issue is concerned, we cannot give even an inch more. If it so happens that we have to make a further compromise, I cannot hold my head up before the Yasukuni Shrine, where the spirits of our heroes rest."

November 18, 1941

Ambassadors Nomura and Kurusu met U.S. Secretary of State Hull.

The Japanese embassy presented its tentative proposal on restoring the status before the Japanese military's advance to French Indochina, without any other conditions. While Hull at first expressed his disapproval, in the end, he agreed to consider the proposal. But the Japanese ambassadors were reprimanded by the Tokyo government for their violation of

official directives. Tokyo leaders instructed them to deliver Proposal B, "even if doing so broke up the negotiations."

November 20, 1941

The Japanese side submitted Proposal B. While finding it worthless, as Hull wrote in his memoir, he nevertheless drafted a provisional U.S. counterproposal and circulated it among American allies, in light of the U.S. military's delay in war preparedness. This behavior of Hull invited a strong rejection from Chiang Kai-

U.S. Secretary of State Hull (center), Nomura Kichisaburō (left), and Kurusu Saburō at meeting

shek and suspicion from Winston Churchill.

November 25, 1941
A meeting at the White House was convened among the President of the United States, the Secretary of State, the Secretaries of War and Navy, the Chief of Staff of the United States Army, and the Chief of Navy Operations to discuss how to maneuver Japan into delivering the first strike. According to the memoir of Henry Stimson, those present at this meeting predicted the possibility of a Japanese surprise attack around December 1.

November 26, 1941
Secretary Hull abandoned his provisional counterproposal and delivered the Outline of Proposed Basis for Agreement between the United States and Japan (the Hull note) to the Japanese side.

In its preamble, the Hull note stated that, because the Japanese proposals did not seem to contribute to peace under law and justice, the United States would propose an extensive as well as simple and clear solution. In the main text, while the note resorted to all kinds of rhetoric, it demanded, in a nutshell, the full and unconditional withdrawal of the Japanese military from all of China and French Indochina; support for the Chiang Kai-shek regime in Chongqing rather than the Wang Jingwei regime; and conclusion of a multilateral nonaggression treaty among Japan, China, the United States, Britain, the Netherlands, the Soviet Union, and Thailand that would take precedence over the Tripartite Pact. The Hull note did not clarify whether Manchuria would be exempted from the above "all of China." The note was, in effect, a demand for Japan to surrender without fighting.

November 27, 1941
In response to Stimson's inquiry on the negotiation of the provisional agreement, Hull said, "It was disbanded. I now have withdrawn from negotiations with Japan. The matter is now in the hands of the army and navy."

On the same day, commanders of military outposts, including in Honolulu, were warned of the imminence of war.

December 1, 1941
A cabinet meeting attended by the Emperor was convened. It was decided

that Japan would start a war with Britain and the United States due to failed negotiations with the United States.

December 6, 1941

The Japanese government sent a coded telegram to its envoys in the United States to abandon negotiations. Reading the decoded telegram, President Roosevelt said to nearby Commerce Secretary Harry Hopkins, "This means war."

December 7, 1941

President Roosevelt sent a personal telegram to the Emperor.

In the telegram, Roosevelt requested withdrawal of the Japanese military from French Indochina without offering any concrete compensation except for peace in Asia. The Japanese side prepared a response, saying, in summary, that the withdrawal of Japanese troops had been an issue in the U.S.-Japan negotiations and that Japan, too, wished for peace. But it was at seven o'clock in the morning of December 8, after the eruption of the war, that this reply was conveyed to Ambassador Grew.

It should be noted that Secretary Hull said to the U.S. ambassador to China, "Perhaps this personal telegram from the president will be useless, but it should make U.S. documents look good in the future."

December 8, 1941

Japanese envoys were instructed to deliver to the U.S. side a memorandum stating, "Thus the hope of the Imperial government to improve diplomatic relations with the United States and, together, maintain peace in the Pacific has been lost for good." Although the instruction from Tokyo was to deliver the memorandum at one o'clock in the afternoon of December 7, Ambassadors Nomura and Kurusu handed the memorandum to Hull at 2:20 p.m. This was after the attack on Pearl Harbor at 1:25 p.m. on the same day.

"A Surgical Operation Might Be Able To Save Japan."

Reviewing the above chronology, it is clear that it was the September 6 cabinet meeting attended by the Emperor that decided the launch of the Greater East Asia War.

What followed subsequently was basically a process of delaying the termination of negotiations with the United States by one and a half months from the initial October 15 until midnight on December 1, by the Directive of the Emperor.

On September 5, one day before the fateful cabinet meeting, Emperor Shōwa solicited the views of Chief of the Army General Staff Sugiyama Hajime and Chief of Naval General Staff Nagano Osami on the prospects of war. It is recorded that the following exchange took place on this occasion:

Emperor Shōwa: How soon is the Imperial Army convinced that it can finish off the war with the United States?

Sugiyama: We are hoping to finish off the battle in Southeast Asia/Oceania region in three months.

Emperor Shōwa: But you said earlier that the Imperial Army could settle the Second Sino-Japanese War in a month. And look what has happened after four years.

Sugiyama: It is because China has a huge hinterland . . .

Emperor Shōwa: We knew from the beginning that China has a huge hinterland, did we not? And isn't the Pacific much wider than China?

At this point, Sugiyama was at a loss for an answer. Nagano came to Sugiyama's rescue, saying, "Japan is a sick man who is going to collapse soon from exhaustion if he doesn't undergo an operation. Japan is, so to speak, in critical condition. A surgical operation might be able to save it."

This was an accurate assessment in its own way.

Nagano's assessment revealed that Japan was going to war not because it judged that it could win it. It was obvious that Japan would have to succumb to the United States on all fronts sooner or later now that the supply of oil had been cut off. Therefore, it was argued, Japan had to fight a war, hoping against hope for a remote chance of winning it.

Earlier, on July 31, one day before the U.S. oil embargo against Japan, Nagano had already replied as follows to inquiries made by the Emperor: "Although the Imperial Navy has oil reserves for two years, they would be exhausted in a year or a year and a half once a war starts. Thus, I believe we have no other choice than to take the offensive at this point."

Why Did the Japanese Military Advance into Southern French Indochina?

Why was an oil embargo imposed on Japan in the first place? Historically speaking, it was because the Japanese military had advanced into southern French Indochina.

Japan had been able to justify its advance into northern French Indochina as a natural extension of the Second Sino-Japanese War. Because this was a war without a formal declaration of war, third-party countries had no obligation to remain neutral. Thus, they were able to sell weapons to both Japan and China. For China, however, after the Japanese military had seized its coastline regions, French Indochina and Burma were the only routes it could use for import. As soon as France lost the Battle of France to Germany in June 1940, therefore, Japan requested the French Indochinese authority to close the routes used to transport materials for Chiang Kai-shek and moved its troops to northern French Indochina.

But an advance into southern French Indochina was a totally different story. Any such advance would be unnecessary unless Japan intended to use French Indochina as a base to invade Thailand and Singapore. At least that was how the United States perceived it.

It was the cabinet–Imperial General Headquarters liaison conference on June 25, 1941, that decided to advance the troops into southern French Indochina. Even when this decision was made, some foresighted people within the Imperial Navy (such as Inoue Shigeyoshi) thought that such a decision was unthinkable without the determination to go to war with the United States. Foreign Minister Matsuoka opposed the advance into southern Indochina until the last minute, saying, "I predict that a southbound advance will bring a major disaster." It should be recalled, however, that Matsuoka had earlier insisted on capturing Singapore. While Matsuoka's intention was to insist, instead, for a northbound advance—that is, a war with the Soviet Union—his judgment about the risk of an advance into southern French Indochina was nevertheless correct. Matsuoka thought that a southbound advance, which could trigger a war with Britain and the United States, should be postponed for the sake of a war with the Soviet Union.

Was it indeed necessary to advance into southern French Indochina, taking such a great risk? Was Japan really resolved to take that risk? When it comes to these questions, clear-cut explanations are hard to come by.

The direct cause of Japan's decision to advance into southern French Indochina was the deadlock in negotiations with the Dutch East Indies in the early half of June. Even after the Dutch homeland was occupied by Nazi Germany, the Dutch East Indies administration maintained its anti-German stance. It was reluctant to supply commodities to Japan after the signing of the Tripartite Pact. Although the Dutch and Japanese governments had continued to negotiate since the beginning of 1941, the Dutch side would not alter its basic position, taking advantage of the support of Britain and the United States. Its reply on June 6 was almost a de facto announcement of terminating the negotiations. According to the telegram sent by Foreign Minister Matsuoka, it was "almost impossible to fundamentally resolve the deadlock in our relations with the Dutch East Indies without doing something about our relations with Britain and the United States."

Still, an advance into southern French Indochina was a measure that could imperil the oil supply from the United States on top of the oil supply from the Dutch East Indies. It would have made sense if Japan had the determination to forcefully obtain oil from the Dutch East Indies, having abandoned reaching an agreement with the United States and the Netherlands. But the fact of the matter was that neither the Imperial Army nor Navy had been resolved or prepared to advance into Southeast Asia by force.

After all, what lay behind the advance into southern French Indochina must have been an inclination in Japan to vaguely approve a hardliner argument and reject a soft-liner attitude. And behind this inclination must have been an almost quixotic expansionism and the argument for the division of the world. Since the conclusion of the Tripartite Pact, the Greater East Asia Co-prosperity Sphere had become a stage of Japan's influence. It was considered in those days to be Japan's manifest destiny to advance into this region. That notion was clearly evident in Matsuoka's foreign policy speech at the Diet session in January.

And the July 2 cabinet meeting attended by the Emperor decided on an advance into southern French Indochina as compensation for rejecting Matsuoka's proposal for a northbound advance. Seeing as Matsuoka himself strongly insisted on postponing the advance to Indochina, the compensation was not intended for Matsuoka. It must have been made in consideration of the atmosphere, as described in the secret journal of the Imperial General Headquarters as follows:

> We will not advance into the north, nor will we conquer China or Southeast Asia. Can there really be such an inconclusive national policy?

Although the Imperial Navy remained indecisive until the very end, it finally gave in and agreed with the policy after modifying the wording from the original "to use armed force against Britain and the United States" to "not to hesitate to risk a war with Britain and the United States." This was a typical example of Shōwa Japan's evil habit of setting up a strategy only in empty words. Such rhetorical modifications would not restrain the military. Constraint would work only when certain actions were banned outright.

Thus, Japan began to move into southern French Indochina.

The Atmosphere to Acknowledge Every Hardliner Argument as Good

By this time, pressure from the military became increasingly anonymous—that is, everyone in the military had become equally hardline. There was no longer a conflict of policy lines within the military such as that between Ishihara Kanji and his successors against the escalation of the Second Sino-Japanese War on the one hand and the hardliners on the other. For everyone in the military from the mid-level all the way down, hardliner arguments were all good. Anyone who opposed them was ostracized as being weak-kneed. Such was the atmosphere in the military.

Things were different, however, among top military leaders. Even though they were military men, they belonged to the generation that had experienced the days of the Anglo-Japanese Alliance and the Taisho Democracy. Having been exposed to the thinking of Emperor Shōwa as well as that of the elder statesman Saionji Kinmochi, they were more or less aware of the intricacies of international relations in the ten years since the Manchurian Incident.

In his memoir, Konoe wrote about the condition of the U.S.-Japan negotiations in mid-September as follows:

> To begin with, these negotiations with the United States had been
> initiated by top leaders of the government, the Imperial Army and
> Navy, and the Imperial General Headquarters. The negotiations had
> been kept secret from lower echelons. Among these leaders, every-
> one except Foreign Minister Matsuoka hoped for a successful con-
> clusion of the negotiations. That was why the negotiations had been
> kept confidential—lest there should be opposition. But information
> began to leak out gradually, particularly after Foreign Minister Mat-
> suoka's secret report to Germany and Italy. As the overall picture of
> the negotiations became known, albeit vaguely, voices denouncing
> the negotiations began to emerge among the lower echelons.
>
> Opposition was particularly strong among junior officers of the
> Imperial Army. It so happened that the eruption of the German-So-
> viet war had a great impact on us at that time. While the govern-
> ment leaders managed to suppress the ultra-hardliner argument for
> an immediate opening of a war against the Soviet Union, the cabinet
> was cornered into deciding on an advance into French Indochina as
> a kind of compensation . . . , giving momentum to full-scale prepara-
> tion for a war with Britain and the United States.

The withdrawal of troops from China became virtually impossible. Having once called the Second Sino-Japanese War a holy war, declaring that
tyrannical China must be punished for peace in the East, spreading countless moving anecdotes about soldiers, and sacrificing hundreds of thousands of lives, not only the military but also the entire nation could not
allow such an abrupt change of policy as withdrawing troops from China
for the sake of harmonious relations with the United States. Japan by that
time was already unable to change its course of action.

Tōjō, who had welcomed the U.S.-Japan Draft Agreement in the spring,
now claimed that he could not hold his head up before the Yasukuni
Shrine, where the spirits of Japan's heroes rest, if he allowed the withdrawal of troops from China in autumn. His change of heart reflected this
tremendous pressure from the military and the general public.

The hardliner argument among Navy officers from the mid-level down
was the main reason the leadership of the Imperial Navy could not oppose

the war outright. From start to finish, the Imperial Navy left the decisions about the war up to the prime minister.

Inoue Shigehisa, who served the Imperial Navy as an admiral and was Vice-Minister of the Navy, left the following observation after the end of World War II:

> Lower-level officials at the Navy Ministry were haunted by the idea that a war with the United States was an inevitable destiny, . . . while the Ministry's leadership was devoid of the courage or wisdom to control those junior officials, thus creating the crisis step by step.

It was already beyond the power of any politician by that time to withdraw the Japanese troops stationed in China. Only a drastic measure comparable to the Imperial Rescript on the Termination of the War in 1945 would have made it possible. Ishikawa Shingo, a division chief class official who was an opinion leader within the Navy Ministry in those days once said, "In order to change the prearranged plan to see the Second Sino-Japanese War through until the end, we had to be prepared for a war between the Imperial Army and Navy." Japan had already passed the point of no return.

Ishikawa deemed that war between Japan and the United States would be inevitable sooner or later. Even if Japan abolished the Tripartite Pact, this would only mean that the United States could now defeat Japan and Germany separately. Ishikawa believed that the United States would first settle the state of the war in Europe and then confront Japan in the Far East.

To be sure, it would be a correct historical interpretation to judge that had Japan not advanced to southern French Indochina, there would have been no oil embargo against Japan and, therefore, Japan would not have been cornered into starting a war with the United States in 1941. Nevertheless, there was no guarantee that the United States would have continued to export oil to Japan indefinitely even if Japan had not advanced into Southeast Asia. As Ishikawa had correctly analyzed, it was highly likely that the United States would launch an oil embargo against Japan sooner or later after

Tōjō Hideki

it became sure of victory over Germany, given that American public opinion as well as Chiang Kai-shek continued to apply pressure for economic sanctions against Japan, that the United States could see no prospect for concluding the negotiations with Japan, and that the Imperial Army would not agree to a withdrawal from China,.

If that was indeed the case, there was really no other way for Japan to survive than to seize all the oil wells in the Dutch East Indies. Japan's annual demand for oil was 6 million tons at the time; therefore, the supply from the Dutch East Indies, which produced 8 million tons per year, would have been enough to make Japan self-sufficient in oil. Ultimately, those in leadership positions in Japan decided that prompt advance into French Indochina and beyond would be the only way for the country to survive.

Ultimatum to End Negotiations

In order to understand the trend within the U.S. government in those days, the quickest and easiest way is to look into the decisive moments on the delivery of the Hull note.

The Hull note (Outline of Proposed Basis for Agreement between the United States and Japan) was the U.S. reply to Proposal B that Japan had made on November 20. Although Secretary of State Hull had initially reacted negatively toward Proposal B he drafted a preliminary American counterproposal and sounded out British and Chinese reactions. He did this partly because he was obliged by the military to buy time and partly because President Roosevelt expressed interest in a settlement based on the preliminary counterproposal.

In the end, this counterproposal from the U.S. side was never submitted to Japan as an official proposal. As none of its contents were officially finalized, there is no knowing the quantity of strategic goods and oil the United States intended to supply to Japan. On November 25, Hull expressed his displeasure with Chiang Kai-shek's rejection of the preliminary counterproposal, saying, "This plan could postpone the threat of Japan's southbound advance for ninety days by only supplying Japan with a limited amount of low-quality oil. . . ." Judging from this remark, this must have been about the amount of oil that the United States had in mind to export to Japan.

President Roosevelt was infuriated when he heard that a Japanese transport convoy was sailing southbound. To him, this was a military action in the midst of negotiations and, as such, a breach of trust. In light of Roosevelt's reaction, Hull abandoned the preliminary counterproposal and decided to deliver the Hull note instead.

The Hull note consisted of ten proposals. It was originally an attached document to the preliminary U.S. counterproposals that Hull had circulated among allies, including Britain. It enumerated the basic positions that the United States would have taken in the formal negotiation with Japan had Japan accepted the preliminary counterproposal. As such, it consisted of the maximum demands from the U.S. side.

Because the Hull note was an attached document separate from the main text, it could never have contained the U.S. replies to the ongoing negotiations. Containing only the maximum unilateral demands from the U.S. side and lacking reference to past negotiations between the two sides, it was a document that could well be interpreted as an ultimatum.

Although the Hull note was by no means a formal declaration of war, its contents warranted the Japanese side to interpret it as the ultimatum to end negotiations. Thus, at the International Military Tribunal for the Far East, Justice Radhabinod Pal from India said, quoting a historian at the time, "...the Principality of Monaco, the Grand Duchy of Liechtenstein, would have taken up arms against the United States on receipt of such a note [Hull note] as the State Department sent the Japanese government on the eve of Pearl Harbor."

The contents of the Hull note were such that even Foreign Minister Tōgō Shigenori had to say, "Although we tried to gulp it down, closing our eyes to avoid the war, it stuck in our throat and would not go down."

Tōgō was an exceptional person among Japanese leaders in those days; he refused to go with the times. He was a diplomat equipped with conviction in his own analysis and strategy as well as a strong mind that refused to make any compromise that went against his convictions.

During his imprisonment after the war as a war criminal, Tōgō composed the following two *tanka* poems:

> For the past ten years or so
> I have sailed through fire and water
> Never taking refuge in a port of compromise

And,

> It was truly regrettable
> That I made only one compromise
> Which became the cause of all the misfortunes that followed

It is interpreted that "compromise" in the second *tanka* meant the opening of the war with the United States and the fact that Tōgō was persuaded to remain as foreign minister at the eruption of the war when he should have resigned.

After the Hull note was delivered, nobody in Japan could oppose the war.

One may wonder who in the world had drafted the ten proposals contained in the Hull note.

The original text of the Hull note was a proposal that had been drafted by Assistant Secretary of Treasury Harry White and presented to Hull by Secretary of Treasury Henry Morgenthau. The State Department adopted and consolidated some of the proposals contained in this White-Morgenthau document.

While this document was a proposal for a comprehensive solution, including such constructive ideas as a large-scale loan for reconstruction of Asia and abolishment of the Immigration Act of 1924, it also contained requests that Japan could not have possibly accepted, such as full withdrawal from China and abandonment of the Wang Jingwei regime. White, who later became one of the founders of the International Monetary Fund, was an extremely capable official, but he allegedly killed himself after the war, having been accused of being a Soviet spy. If he had indeed been a Soviet spy, it would have been only natural for him as a member of the international communist force that had hoped for a U.S.-Japan war—a war between two capitalist countries—to draft proposals that Japan could never have accepted.

Still, it was the team of experts on Far Eastern affairs under the leadership of Stanley Hornbeck, Hull's special advisor, that did all of the State Department's policymaking and policy implementation vis-à-vis Japan. Hornbeck was constantly at the heart of the State Department's Far Eastern policy, serving as chief of the Division of Far Eastern Affairs (1928–37) and a special advisor to the Secretary of State for Far Eastern Affairs

(1937–44). He was a China expert, having taught at a Chinese university before he joined the State Department, but he had never been stationed in Japan. Considering that the experience of actually living in the field could play a decisive role in understanding such foreign cultures as Japan and China, the fact that Hornbeck had never had the opportunity to learn first-hand about Japan's history and the Japanese people might have been one major factor behind the unsuccessful negotiations between Japan and the United States.

Hornbeck incorporated moral principles into U.S. diplomacy, refusing to make any compromise, and upgraded such traditional U.S. principles as the open-door policy and equality of opportunities to the level of quasi-law. It is not hard to imagine that behind Hull's blocking of the Konoe-Roosevelt talk, which could have led to a settlement, was the advice from experts of Far Eastern affairs, including Hornbeck.

If Hornbeck and White, the communist, teamed up to draft the ten proposals, it could explain the document's rigidity well. While there is no knowing why these ten proposals had been attached to Hull's preliminary counterproposal in the first place, the State Department officials, who had been secretly dissatisfied with Hull's compromising preliminary counterproposal, may well have deliberately attached the ten proposals originally drafted by the Treasury Department officials.

Yet Hornbeck continued to misjudge the situation at each step of the U.S.-Japan negotiations. He himself acknowledged as much in the days to come. Hornbeck consistently believed that Japan, unable to resist the pressure if the United States came down hard on the country, would give in.

A month before the attack on Pearl Harbor, a secretary at the U.S. embassy in Tokyo returned to the United States and visited Hornbeck to convey the concern of the diplomatic mission in Tokyo that Japan could start a war against the United States at any time. Hearing this, Hornbeck retorted, saying, "If you know of a single country in history that had started a war out of desperation, name one." As a matter of fact, half a month before this exchange, Tōjō had said, "Man sometimes has to close his eyes and jump in at the deep end."

On the day the Hull note was delivered to the Japanese side, Hornbeck announced that he would bet five to one that Japan will not start a war before December 15, three to one before January 15, and one to one before March 1.

If we summarize the history according to the extremely concise style of a Chinese classic, the lack of agreement in the runup to the U.S.-Japan war had been paved by Matsuoka's conviction that the United States would give in if Japan came down hard on the country, while the war was initiated by an ultimatum prepared by Hornbeck, who believed only power could restrain Japan.

Perhaps Hornbeck did not know that "Even a worm will turn." Moreover, I must say it was a superficial judgment by both Matsuoka and Hornbeck in believing that such proud major powers as Japan and the United States would back off obediently when pressured by an outside force.

Aside from these personal misjudgments, misunderstanding on the part of the U.S. side based on misinterpretation of the coded Japanese message also appears to have played a role.

Reviewing those coded messages today, we see that while there indeed were a few obvious misinterpretations, those portions that were regarded to have caused misunderstandings were simply a reflection of the limited capabilities of the U.S. code-breakers. After all, the accuracy rate is bound to be limited to 70 percent or 80 percent when it comes to code-breaking or simultaneous interpretation.

More salient here was the immaturity of American foreign policy, which depended too much on code-breaking.

In his memoirs, Shidehara Kijūrō, an early-Shōwa foreign minister of Japan about whom I have written another book in this series, revealed that the famed British foreign minister Edward Grey refused to read deciphered code messages. Grey believed that those broken codes were misleading and they could even cloud his own judgment. He adamantly refused to base his policy decisions on information that was stolen by such an unfair means.

Not only was code-breaking improper as a means to obtain information, it could also introduce inaccuracies. Diplomacy should never be conducted on the basis of inaccurate texts.

If Only I Could See President Roosevelt . . .

Putting those personal inclinations and misjudgments aside, do we see any chance of avoiding the catastrophe?

What if, for instance, the preliminary counterproposal had been delivered instead of the Hull note? Going back further, what if the Konoe-Roosevelt talks had actually taken place?

The preliminary counterproposal would only have delayed the crisis for three months. Because the content of the ten-proposal attachment, i.e., the Hull note, had already been circulated among countries concerned, it would have been difficult for the United States to make a compromise on those proposals. Thus bilateral negotiations would inevitably have been broken off. The United States would have utilized the three-month delay to strengthen its defense of the Philippines as originally planned, taken measures to protect the oil wells in the Dutch East Indies, and advanced its own naval construction program.

If that were indeed the case, pressure from Chiang Kai-shek and hardliners within the United States could have induced untimely U.S. participation in the war, leading to grand victories by Japan in the initial stage of the war. When Hull had to withdraw the preliminary counterproposal because it was rejected by Chiang Kai-shek, he said, "If we cannot dispatch the U.S. fleet to the Far East when the Japanese military advances southbound, that is not our fault." Hull recorded this comment in his memoir. Things turned out just as Hull had feared.

If Japan had accepted the U.S. preliminary counterproposal, would there have been a chance for Japan to abandon the war? December 8, the day Japan attacked Pearl Harbor, was the very next day after Hitler gave up on advancing into Moscow, having met extremely strong resistance from the Red Army in front of the city. In retrospect, it was the day when the outcome of the German-Soviet war became unpredictable. If Japan had revised its hitherto optimistic outlook in the subsequent three months, it might no longer have been possible for Japan to start a war against the United States. This was, however, still one full year before the decisive defeat of Germany in Stalingrad. Judging from the Japanese military's psychology in those days, which still placed high hopes on the German army's spring offensive, it was rather unlikely for the Japanese military to change its way of thinking.

Instead, the possibility of success was greater for the Konoe-Roosevelt talk.

It was still September–October of 1941 when the advance of the German troops was unstoppable and the fall of Moscow seemed to be only a matter of time. Thus, settlement with Japan through negotiations still had some strategic meaning for Britain and the United States.

The question was whether Konoe could have really controlled the military. Immediately after the September 6 cabinet meeting attended by the emperor, Konoe secretly met with U.S. Ambassador Joseph Grew and Counselor Eugene Dooman. In this four-person, closed-door meeting, Konoe said, "If only I could see President Roosevelt, . . . I have a proposition that he cannot resist."

To Dooman, who was serving as the interpreter in this meeting, Konoe said,

> I know you know Japan well. I am going to reveal a secret to you, but I'd like you to convey my true intention to Ambassador Grew instead of directly translating what I am going to say. As soon as I can reach an agreement with President Roosevelt, I intend to request the Emperor to order the Imperial Army to stop all of its aggressive action against the United States.

Konoe always wished to place the Emperor outside the responsibility for the war. This desire had been understood by the U.S. side, too. The special significance of Konoe's remark this time was, however, that he was prepared to ask the Emperor to take such a daring measure as the Imperial Rescript on the Termination of the War in 1945 at this early stage.

This kind of proposal could never have been offered if Konoe had to consult with the Imperial Army and Navy. It was a kind of proposal that Konoe could make only at a summit meeting with the U.S. president. Perhaps that would have been the only chance. A talk between heads of government can accomplish what working level meetings cannot.

Incidentally, the United States came very close to launching an attack on North Korea in 1994. On this occasion, former U.S. President Jimmy Carter visited Pyongyang to meet Chairman Kim Il-sung personally. An agreement was reached between the two sides and the war was prevented. Observing the U.S. negotiations with North Korea in the subsequent half year, it occurred to me that, had the United States negotiated with Japan with similar care before Japan's attack on Pearl Harbor, the Greater East Asia War could have been avoided. I am sure that there are others who share my reflection.

What would have happened if Konoe had met Roosevelt? There is no knowing what kind of proposal Konoe had in his mind. But, it would be natural to believe that "a proposition that President Roosevelt cannot resist" should at least entail something like the withdrawal of Japanese troops to the pre–Second Sino-Japanese War line by an Imperial Edict, facilitation of reconciliation between Chiang Kai-shek and Wang Jing-wei, abandonment of the scheme to separate northern China from China proper, and abolition of the foreign settlements in China.

Would the military have obeyed? Tōjō was a soldier perfectly loyal to the emperor. Hearing of the appointment of Tōjō to prime minister, the Ministry of War was excited about the birth of an Imperial Army cabinet, and its officials drafted its own list of cabinet members to hand to Tōjō. Having heard the Directive of the Emperor on Japan-U.S. Negotiations earlier, Tōjō turned around and walked away, murmuring something that sounded like "too much military interference."

Considering Tōjō's absolute loyalty to the Emperor as well as the Japanese people's orderly and respectful compliance with the Imperial Rescript on the Termination of the War, there was a significant possibility that the military would have backed off if an Imperial Edict had been issued.

And if this had really taken place, Hornbeck and White surely would have resented their premature compromise, in light of the collapse of the German military in Stalingrad a year later, while the Japanese leaders must have felt much relieved.

But the war started.

Although the Imperial Navy strongly wished for a surprise attack, Foreign Minister Tōgō stubbornly persisted with his own conviction and sent a telegram to the Japanese ambassadors to the United States, instructing them to "personally deliver the announcement on the termination of nego-tiations to the U.S. side at one o'clock in the afternoon of December 7."

In other words, Tōgō instructed to deliver the announcement 30 min-utes before the attack. It was, however, at 2:20 p.m., fifty minutes after the attack, that the announcement was actually delivered.

After the war, imprisoned war criminal Tōgō wrote, "Delinquency at the time of delivering of the announcement brought a great loss to the nation and it deserves to be punished with death."

Because the Imperial Navy had intended a surprise attack from the beginning and succeeded in launching it, accusations of a sneak attack would have been fully utilized in the opponents' war propaganda anyway, regardless of the time of delivering of the announcement. And because the United States from the beginning had endeavored to make Japan fire the first shot and succeeded in doing so—and, moreover, because the United States had known the content of the announcement well before Japan's "surprise attack"—the delay in the delivery of the announcement had no substantial meaning.

Nevertheless, the "sneak attack" on Pearl Harbor was thoroughly utilized in the war propaganda of the Allies. When Churchill suggested an honorable settlement for Japan, Roosevelt said, "After the attack on Pearl Harbor, Japan no longer has any honor to defend." Noting how much this delay in delivery was taken advantage of by Japan's opponent, it is undeniable that the delay caused Japan tremendous damage.

It was in November 1994, half a century after the attack on Pearl Harbor, that the Ministry of Foreign Affairs, at the initiative of Vice-Minister Saitō Kunihiko at that time, officially acknowledged that the delay was "truly regrettable and inexcusable." Although the acknowledgment was long overdue because all of those involved had already passed away, it was a commendable and highly appropriate announcement based on the continuity of the Kasumigaseki diplomacy and its sense of duty.

CHAPTER

12

Six Months of Phenomenal Glory

—Reminiscent of the Glorious Russo-Japanese War in Asia—

Japanese Strategy vs. U.S. Strategy

In the first half year of the Greater East Asia War, every one of Japan's military strategies came off well, as expected. Indeed, better than expected. In contrast, all the strategies of the British-U.S. forces fell short of expectations. As a result, the initial stage of the war was a complete victory for Japan.

This initial success made it possible for resource-poor Japan to continue the war for the next four years and provided Southeast Asian countries with ample time to prepare for their independence. Even though, as stated in the Imperial Rescript on the Start of the War, Japan had originally been forced to start a war by the economic blockade, these initial victories gave Japan the luxury to put up an idealistic slogan of "Establishment of the Greater East Asia Co-prosperity Sphere."

What, then, were Japan's military strategies?

First, in terms of the prospects of the war, let me quote Yamamoto Isoroku, commander-in-chief of the Imperial Navy's Combined Fleet and chief prosecutor of the war against the United States. At the time of the signing of the Tripartite Pact in September 1940, Prime Minister Konoe

Fumimaro asked Yamamoto about the prospects of a war with the United States. Urging Konoe to avoid war, Yamamoto answered by saying, "I can guarantee that we will put up a gallant fight in the initial six months to a year. Should the war linger for two or three years, however, I am not at all confident about our prospects."

In other words, Yamamoto deemed that Japan would lose the war if it lasted more than two years.

As far as oil for vessels was concerned, Japan had assiduously saved about 9.4 million tons by that time. This was believed to be the world largest oil reserve in those days. Setting aside 0.5 million tons for the final showdown, a minimum of 1 million tons for household uses, and 0.8 million tons deemed unusable because of sediment at the bottom of the reserve tanks, Japan would be out of oil for the operating vessels in 18 months as the Imperial Navy would consume 400,000 tons every month. While Yamamoto had given his word for "six months to a year," he revised it to a year and a half in January 1941, which was perfectly consistent with the above calculation.

If such were the case, the Japanese military would have to seize the oil-producing regions in the south and start transporting the oil to Japan as soon as the war started. Taking into account Japan's reserves of other strategic commodities as well, it was estimated that a constant standby of 3 million tons in vessels would be sufficient to transport commodities to Japan from Southeast Asia. Although Japan possessed a total of 6.5 million tons in vessels at the start of the war, 3 million tons of that had to be set aside for industrial purposes. It was also assessed that, even if Japan had to lose 1 million tons in vessels to the war every year, it could still retain the minimum requirement of 3 million tons by annually constructing 600,000 tons in new vessels.

In actuality, even though Japan lost only 1.2 million tons in the initial year, thanks to the successful near annihilation of the U.S. Pacific fleet in Pearl Harbor, it lost 2.56 million tons in the second year and 3.48 million in the third. Consequently, Japan fell into a vicious cycle of short supply of resources leading to lower-than-expected production of steel and, thus, fewer ships until Japan's defeat in 1945.

While the foregoing case was unique to Japan, it was obvious, given the American naval buildup capability, that the United States would become increasingly superior day by day regardless of Japan's success in securing resources from Southeast Asia.

In light of this situation, Yamamoto made the following observation on Japan's strategy:

> There would be no way that an ordinary strategy could work against the United States. In the end, we would have no other choice than to execute a plan similar to that of Oda Nobunaga's surprise attack at Okehazama, that of Minamoto Yoshitsune's downhill charge at Hiyodorigoe, and that of the battles of Kawanakajima simultaneously.

This logic was the basis for Japan's attack on Pearl Harbor. Because the United States continuously became more powerful even after Pearl Harbor, however, Yamamoto had to adopt the strategy of "successive all-out showdowns"—that is, challenging the opponent one decisive battle after another and crushing it completely each time. This strategy was crippled in only half a year in the Battle of Midway in June 1942: Japan suffered a devastating defeat.

Perhaps from Yamamoto's point of view, defeat at the Battle of Midway came as no surprise. It only it came a little earlier than expected. Pearl Harbor was a gamble and so was Midway. The only option left for Japan was to give everything it had and win every gamble. The war between Japan and the United States can be compared to a sumo match between a low-ranking wrestler and a grand champion. The only chance for the former to win is to catch the grand champion off balance at the beginning of the bout and confuse him at every turn without giving him a chance to recover from the initial shock. Because the Battle of Midway allowed the United States to bounce back, however, the chance for Japan was gone for good.

In a battle, sometimes you win and sometimes you lose. Strategy aimed at achieving constant victories was, therefore, an impossible proposition from the beginning. Had he been asked, Yamamoto must have said, "That was why I opposed the war. If I still had to fight the war, this would have been the only way."

In any event, the attack on Pearl Harbor was a military achievement that far exceeded initial expectations, and, at least tactically, it was a huge success for Japan.

Meanwhile, the primary operational goal of the Imperial Army was to seize the resource-rich regions in Southeast Asia. Once it had accomplished that, it had planned to prepare for a northbound advance, leaving defense of the seized areas in the south to the Imperial Navy.

Targets for occupation included Malay, the Dutch East Indies, the Philippines, part of Burma to the west, and Rabaul to the east. It was estimated that it would take about one hundred days to seize Singapore and about five months to occupy the entire region. Thanks to the Imperial Navy's success in the initial stage of the war that nearly paralyzed the British and American naval fleets, this occupation plan proceeded smoothly as initially planned.

American strategy for World War II was coded "Rainbow 5." While U.S. strategies had traditionally been color-coded according to the target country, including the War Plan Orange vis-à-vis Japan in the 1920s–30s, this time the United States used "rainbow" rather than any single color as it had to deal with Japan, Germany, and Italy simultaneously.

The core target of this multi-country strategy was, naturally, the most formidable opponent, Germany. As long as the United States could defeat this formidable foe, Japan was no match for the United States. Therefore, the United States took a strategic defense in the Pacific centered around a triangle connecting Alaska, Hawaii, and Panama. Beyond this basic posture, the U.S. operation was limited to the attack on the Marshall Islands to restrict Japan's offensive toward Malay, raids on Japan's maritime transports, and collaboration with the navies of the British Commonwealth to crush Japan's expeditionary force. The United States had no plan to send reinforcements to the Philippines, and Guam was to be abandoned from the beginning.

When Douglas MacArthur was recalled to active duty in late June 1941 to command the newly instituted United States Army Forces in the Far East, he learned about Rainbow 5 for the first time. Stunned by the plan to abandon the Philippines without any attempt at defending it, MacArthur demanded the strategy be revised. Consequently, a U.S. army-navy joint conference endorsed the revision of Rainbow 5 and ordered the strengthening of defenses in the Philippines. Had the U.S. provisional counterproposal, instead of the Hull note, been delivered to Japan and if Japan had accepted it, the defense of the Philippines in the subsequent three months would have been strengthened significantly.

Meanwhile, most of the U.S. operation plans came to nothing because the U.S. government failed to delay the start of the war and also because the U.S. Pacific fleet had been nearly annihilated in the initial stage of the war,. Instead, obstruction of Japan's maritime traffic by U.S. submarines achieved great results far beyond initial expectations, by disrupting Japan's maritime transportation, hastening Japan's defeat.

Successful Attack on Pearl Harbor

Attacking Pearl Harbor was Yamamoto Isoroku's idea. He had to suppress considerable opposition and cope with his colleagues' apprehensions about carrying out the plan, which eventually proved to be a huge military success.

The Japanese people began to associate the name Yamamoto Isoroku with near annihilation of the U.S. Pacific Fleet in the initial stage of the war. As a result, Yamamoto became Japan's greatest hero in World War II.

Yamamoto participated in the London Naval Conference in 1930 (5th Year of Shōwa) as a deputy delegate. Even in those days, Yamamoto was of the following view:

> Now that the Imperial Navy was forced to accept this disadvantageous ratio, we must first deliver a severe blow by air raid, to be followed with an all-out decisive battle with everything we've got when we have to fight against the highly capable U.S. Navy.

During a fleet drill in March 1940, 36 torpedo bombers of the aircraft carrier *Akagi* launched torpedoes at four target ships. Thirty-two of them hit the targets. Observing this from onboard the battleship *Nagato*, Yamamoto murmured to a nearby chief of staff, "I wonder whether an attack on Hawaii using aircraft carriers would be feasible."

Yamamoto instructed his staff to secretly study an attack on Hawaii in January 1941, the very year of the beginning of the war with the United States.

This study revealed that there were a number of technical difficulties. One of them was how to launch torpedoes from bombers flying at low altitude among the cluster of high-rise buildings after clearing the mountains. These technical problems were solved through intensive training.

By far the greatest challenge, though, was how to sail an armada of more than twenty vessels, including six aircraft carriers, two battleships, and two heavy cruisers, unnoticed for over 3,300 nautical miles (6,000 kilometers) across the Pacific. While frequent gales and high waves in the northwest Pacific in wintertime minimized the chances of being seen by merchant marines, the issue of refueling on the rough high seas was a concern. If the fleet was spotted by U.S. patrol aircraft near Hawaii, it would be intercepted and, in the worst case, be at the mercy of enemy aircraft stationed in the Hawaiian airbase.

Although the study commissioned by Yamamoto concluded that the chance of success would be fifty-fifty and recommended reconsideration, Yamamoto commanded the implementation of an attack on Pearl Harbor.

The result was a huge success, though there were also elements of good luck. For one thing, the U.S. side completely believed that Japan would raid the Philippines and Malay first. What also helped was that the policy to let Japan take the first shot and make it responsible for the eruption of a war had thoroughly permeated all parts of the U.S. military.

As a matter of fact, when the U.S. air force stationed in the Philippines prepared to take off to air raid the Japanese transport convoy spotted sailing southward, it was commanded to abort the interception. The United States could have sunk a few of the Japanese vessels that would have adversely affected Japan's Philippine invasion plan. But the U.S. chose not to attack. In a similar fashion, the U.S. military stationed in Hawaii could have spotted the Japanese fleet in the Pacific, and intercepted the Japanese aircraft over Pearl Harbor, but it would not have gone as far as to launch a preemptive strike at Japanese aircraft carriers.

In any event, the result was a huge success in military history.

According to the U.S. announcement after the attack on Pearl Harbor, four battleships and six cruisers and smaller vessels were sunk, and two battleships and four cruisers and smaller vessels were wrecked or severely damaged during the attack. It would not be an exaggeration to say that the U.S. Pacific Fleet was nearly annihilated except for its aircraft carriers and submarines.

It was those aircraft carriers and submarines that escaped damage during the attack on Pearl Harbor which later determined the direction of the war. Also, some of the sunken battleships were raised from the shallow Pearl Harbor water and repaired in the repairing dock that the Japanese bombers had failed to destroy. This allowed those battleships to be reactivated. For the time being, however, the attack on Pearl Harbor succeeded in eliminating the immediate threat to Japan's operations in Southeast Asia from the U.S. Pacific Fleet.

As a matter of fact, according to Rainbow 5, the U.S. Pacific Fleet was slated to sail to the western Pacific after a few months of the start of the war. Before that time, the British fleet stationed in Singapore was expected to be the principle impediment to Japan's operations in Southeast Asia.

On November 2, a few weeks before the eruption of the war, the British government released an announcement on the lineup of its newly formed Eastern Fleet. The *HMS Prince of Wales*, a jewel of the British navy that had provided the venue for the Roosevelt-Churchill talk in the summer, was appointed the fleet's flagship. Had this battleship been deployed in the South China Sea, the Imperial Japanese Navy's battleships *Kongō* and *Haruna* and its cruisers stationed in the region at that time would have been no match for it. The *HMS Prince of Wales* was such a formidable, state-of-the-art battleship that its deployment would also have isolated the Japanese troops that landed on Malay.

As expected, the *HMS Prince of Wales* sailed to the offing of Malay immediately after the start of the war. It was 95 Imperial Japanese Navy Air Service aircraft flying from the airbase in south French Indochina that spotted the small squadron headed by the *HMS Prince of Wales*. After waves of torpedo attacks and bombing, the flagship of the British Eastern Fleet (coded Force Z) was sunk together with another battleship, the *HMS Repulse*.

Although Vice-Admiral Sir Tom Philips, who commanded Force Z, had requested airborne cover at the start of the voyage, it was not granted. Still, it was out of the question for him to sit idly by and watch the Japanese troops advance. It was, therefore, during his reluctant voyage that his squadron encountered the attack by Japanese aircraft. When his staff officers begged him to leave the sinking *Prince of Wales*, Philips said, "No, thank you," and went down with the ship.

These sea battles in Hawaii and Malay were truly revolutionary incidents in the global history of sea battles. Gone were the days of big ships and big guns; the days of the air force had newly arrived. Although the possibility of this transition had been pointed out earlier, it was the first time that this transition was proven empirically.

And it was Yamamoto Isoroku who had the foresight to discern this transition and put it into practice earlier than anyone else in the world. In this sense, Yamamoto was a great naval commander whose name should go down in world history.

The task force that Yamamoto organized for the attack on Pearl Harbor was innovative in that it overturned conventional wisdom on fleet structure, centered as it was on aircraft carriers rather than battleships,. In no time, this idea was adopted by the United States, which built as many as 26 supercarriers and 110 escort carriers in four years during the war, overwhelming the Imperial Japanese Navy. Even today, the U.S. Navy commands the seven seas of the world with naval task forces centered around 12 supercarriers. This is a result of the naval strategic revolution inspired by Yamamoto's idea.

What kind of a person was Yamamoto Isoroku?

In light of his strategic insight that allowed him to predict Japan's demise, his judgment and determination in giving military air power the central role ahead of the rest of the world, and his courage to persevere with his own convictions unafraid of possible terrorism against him, Yamamoto must have been a man of extraordinary capabilities rising well above others.

What was truly amazing was that a man capable of bucking conventional wisdom could rise to the top of Japanese society. If people around him had not appointed him to commander-in-chief of the Combined Fleet to avoid assassination, Yamamoto without doubt would have assumed the post of a Minister of the Navy.

In his private life, Yamamoto was a master in all kinds of gambling, including bridge, poker, and Japanese chess (*shōgi*). In Japanese society, a good gambler often moves ahead in his career. Gambling is an intellectual game of sorts, but fortunately, no enemies come of it, only respect and admiration.

Yamamoto Isoroku

Moreover, for better or worse, one's personality tends to become transparent when gambling. Opponents are disarmed in their wariness. There have been countless cases, in fact, of master mahjong players getting ahead in officialdom and business thanks to their ability to gamble in the immediate postwar period, a time when people could not otherwise afford to indulge in sports and leisure activities.

In the case of Yamamoto, what became apparent through gambling was his lovable personality. According to military historian Hata Ikuhiko, had there been a popularity poll in the Imperial Japanese Navy, Yamamoto would have always been ranked top. He was well liked both by men and women, and had a few mistresses (in Japan, the more one had, the better, as it showed an ability to financially care for them). He was an extremely popular person, probably comparable to Admiral Horatio Nelson of the British Navy.

In the calligraphy that Yamamoto presented to the well-known Japanese restaurant *Komatsu* in Yokosuka frequented by navy officers, he wrote that, even though he could beat a million ferocious enemies, "I am totally defenseless against a pair of willowy arms." As this calligraphy clearly reveals, Yamamoto was adept in his leisure time activities. His handwriting was not only masterful but also straightforward and totally devoid of pretention.

Perhaps the capacity to distinguish people of genuine quality was part of the tradition of the Imperial Japanese Navy. It was also the Imperial Japanese Navy that had correctly judged that Yonai Mitsumasa, who at a glance gave a rather dull impression, was a man to whom the future of the navy could be entrusted. Aside from the environment in which navy personnel have ample opportunities to observe one another in the confined space of fleet duty, there must have been an excellent educational tradition at the Imperial Japanese Naval Academy and the Naval War College in teaching cadets how to discern the genuine value of a man.

Elite education certainly appears to have played an important role. In prewar Japan, there must have been something, not only in the Imperial Navy but also in the Imperial Army and in high schools under the prewar educational system, that enabled identification of the best and the brightest of society. These educational institutions must have instilled some form of modesty into the students' minds so that they could make a dispassionate assessment of others. They must have taught that men are not made equal and that the few truly excellent persons among them should be revered by everyone in the society.

Occupation of Singapore

The Imperial Japanese Army was also blessed with an opportunity to fully utilize its traditional battle capability, accomplishing complete victories one after another.

The absolute necessity for the Imperial Japanese Army's "Southern Operations" was to control all the key regions in Southeast Asia before the enemy could complete its preparation for a counteroffensive. Failing this, the United States would be able to dispatch its troops to the oil fields and build its own airfield in the southern Dutch East Indies, as it did on Guadalcanal a half year after the start of the war. This would wreck Japan's war objective of breaking the economic blockade to secure the nation's survival and self-defense.

As it happened, both the American and British fleets were annihilated by the Imperial Japanese Navy, rendering them incapable of recovering the Dutch East Indies as long as Japan's Combined Fleet remained active in the region. This allowed the Imperial Japanese Army to move forward as originally planned.

Consequently, Japan succeeded in conquering the oil field regions in the Dutch East Indies, which enabled the Imperial Navy to rely on oil supply from this region until Japan's defeat. And this provided Southeast Asian countries with ample time to prepare for their independence.

The British stronghold in Southeast Asia was Singapore. Although the Washington Naval Treaty of 1922 had prohibited fortification of Pacific islands, Britain exempted Singapore from the treaty's application and started fortifying the island. It was obvious that the fortification was to provide protection from Japan after the annulment of the Anglo-Japanese Alliance. Former British foreign minister Edward Grey criticized the fortification as "an act of eliminating noble memories of the Anglo-Japanese Alliance." Nevertheless, fortification was mostly completed by 1937, and Singapore became a great naval base equipped with the world's largest floating dock of 50,000 tons and 15-inch canons. Singapore at that time was believed to be impregnable.

Although the defense of Singapore's hinterland, i.e., the region along the Straits of Johor dividing Singapore from the Malay Peninsula, was thinly manned, a strategy to defend Singapore by separating it from the Malay Peninsula was unthinkable. It would bring about Singapore's sure death should it be severed from its supply of water from the Peninsula.

Almost the entire Malay Peninsula was so densely covered by jungle that it was considered impossible for large armies to traverse. Against invasion from the Thai side, Britain constructed a defense line called the Jitra Line, which was believed capable of withstanding enemy attack for three months. The east coast of the island had almost no spot suitable for enemies to land and, in any event, it was Britain's strategy to block any enemy landing with its navy and air force stationed in Singapore.

Because Britain's Eastern Fleet had been annihilated by the Imperial Japanese Navy in the early days of the war, allowing the Imperial Japanese Army to land on the Malay Peninsula and receive supplies, the Japanese troops were able to tramp across the 1,000-kilometer long Malay Peninsula and reach Johor Bahru on the other side of the Straits of Johor. The troops accomplished this in only in fifty-five days, fighting more than one hundred battles and skirmishes in the course of their march.

Like night battles, in which the Japanese army excelled, battles in the jungle brought a sense of fear to the opponent, because there was no knowing how much military force was behind the Japanese troops. Neither was there any means to keep an eye on soldiers' performance or desertion. Under these circumstances, the loyalties of individual officers and soldiers as well as their individual combat capabilities are the greatest decisive factors in determining the winner. When it comes to that, Japanese troops were unrivaled, leading to emergence of the myth that in a jungle battle the Japanese army was invincible.

Small groups of Japanese troops launched deadly attacks, forcing opponents unfamiliar with Japanese battle strategy to misjudge that they had been wedged apart by the vanguard of a massive Japanese force. This prompted opponents to retreat under the pretext of reorganizing the battlefront. The troops of British colonies, particularly Indians, were not loyal enough to risk their lives to hold their positions to the very end, and retreated without giving much resistance.

In those days, the Imperial Japanese Army had only three divisions equipped with automobiles, two of which were deployed to the Malay Peninsula and the third to the Philippines. Meanwhile, Japanese foot soldiers moved around on bicycles, allowing them to quickly break through the opponents' defensive lines one after another as the enemy tried to reorganize the battlefront in the rear. This enabled the Japanese troops to reach Johor Bahru in no time.

Then came the fall of Singapore. At the time, the main island of Singapore was defended by 100,000 British and Australian troops, about twice as many as the combined three divisions of the invading Imperial Japanese Army. There was also an overwhelming difference between the two sides in terms of ammunition. The ratio of shots fired was, initially, five to one in favor of the Singapore defenders; this was soon to rise to ten to one. The Japanese side was about to run out of ammunition when the British side was deprived of its water supply in Johor. The water reservoirs in Singapore were also jeopardized, forcing the British to surrender to the Japanese army.

As soon as the Japanese troops occupied Singapore, overseas Chinese who took part in the battle as volunteers were subjected to fierce interrogation and punishment, making their families resentful toward Japan even long after the war. Nevertheless, the occupation itself was highly orderly. The memoir of Lieutenant-General Arthur Percival, who commanded the forces of the British Commonwealth in Singapore, made special mention of the way that Japanese occupation forces refrained from disorderly conduct, one reason being that Japan made its troops stay outside the city.

Occupation of Palembang

On February 14, 1942, one day before the fall of Singapore, Japanese paratroops launched a surprise attack on oil refinery facilities and the airfield in Palembang, Sumatra. This was rather a bold and risky operation.

The Imperial Japanese Army simultaneously applied a more orthodox method of going up the Musi River for 100 kilometers from the coast. Parachute troops were used because a counteroffensive had appeared imminent as aircraft of the Royal Air Force began to flock at Palembang airfield after having been chased from airfields on the Malay Peninsula. Reinforcements from the U.S. Air Force also arrived. It was also feared that, had this situation not been attended promptly, the enemy force might destroy the oil refinery.

The first 300 paratroopers jumped into the jungle after flying 500 kilometers from the southern tip of the Malay Peninsula. Most of them were caught by the densely packed trees, but they managed to get down on the ground. They were ordered to attack the airfield and oil refinery as soon as they made a team of three. The combat capabilities of the Japanese soldiers displayed during this raid were again extraordinary.

A sergeant who landed alone was surrounded by some twenty enemies. He shot down eight of them single-handedly, receiving a few dozens of bullets himself. In the end, he sat straight to receive the last shot between his eyes. A Dutch lieutenant who was taken prisoner of war later stated that he had shuddered at this Japanese sergeant's valor.

A team of five, including Lieutenant Okumoto Minoru, intercepted the enemy's 500-man armored vehicle unit that was heading toward the airfield. The team not only put the enemy to rout after a fierce battle but also occupied the airfield before the enemy could destroy it. Team members were later granted individual testimonials for their distinguished military service.

Going through these and other battles, the Japanese airborne divisions succeeded in conquering two airfields and an oil refinery in Palembang. After a while, the division that had been advancing up the Musi River also arrived. By February 20, the Japanese troops had taken all the airfields on Sumatra.

Thus the military song *Sora no Shinpei* (released in April 1942) has the following passages:

> Bursting into full bloom in the sky which is bluer than blue
> Are hundreds of thousands of white roses
> Behold the paratroopers descending
> Behold the paratroops sailing the sky to attack

The bouncy and refreshing melody composed by Takagi Tōroku made this one of the most outstanding military songs of the Greater East Asia War. It was filled with unconditional optimism derived from initial grand victories and hope for the future.

Allow me to simply enumerate other Japanese military achievements in Southeast Asia around that time in the interest of saving time.

January 2, 1942
Fall of Manila. The Phil-Am forces fled to Bataan Peninsula and the fortress on Corregidor Island.

January 14, 1942
Japanese troops advanced to the territory of Burma.

January 23, 1942
Japanese troops invaded Rabaul.

February 15, 1942
Fall of Singapore

February 21, 1942
Occupation of Timor, severing its communication with the Netherlands and Australia.

February 27, 1942
Battle of the Java Sea, in which the Imperial Japanese Navy annihilated the combined fleet of American, British, Dutch, and Australian navies, paving the way for landing on Java.

March 1, 1942
Japanese troops landed on Java.

March 8, 1942
Japanese troops conquered Rangoon and landed on New Guinea at Lae and Salamaua.

March 9, 1942
Dutch East Indies troops in Java surrendered.

March 23, 1942
Japanese troops occupied the Andaman Islands on the Indian Ocean.

April 9, 1942
Japanese troops captured the Bataan Peninsula.

May 1, 1942
Japanese troops conquered Mandalay, Burma, severing the Burma route to assist Chiang Kai-shek.

May 7, 1942
Corregidor captured by Japanese troops.

Although the Japanese invasion forces were inferior to the garrison forces in terms of the number of troops and equipment, there was a huge gap in battle capabilities between the Japanese elite troops and the armies of the Southeast Asian colonies.

More significant, however, was the support from local residents. Everywhere in Indonesia, for instance, local residents guided the Japanese troops, cleared away obstructions on the road, and repaired bridges. Local residents welcomed the advancing Japanese troops, waving handmade Rising Sun flags, as if they were their own soldiers.

According to military historian Itō Masanori, the whole local population of Java—50 million people—allied itself with the Japanese troops. The Dutch troops must have felt that they were fighting on enemy land. It was the same thing in Burma, where the entire population was behind the Japanese troops.

These were just examples of the frenzy and jubilation that filled all of Asia. It was the same deep emotion that had run through the whole of Asia thirty-seven years earlier when Japan defeated Russia in the Russo-Japanese War.

While I wish to come back to this issue in the next chapter, let me point out here that whether Japan had had a genuine desire to liberate Asia has long been a controversial issue. Judging from the Japanese government's official announcements, it seems true that Japan's initial objective of war was to secure resources in Southeast Asia for national survival and defense. The liberation of Asia was added as a principle objective of the Greater East Asia War which was to be pursued after the above war objective was attained.

It would not do justice to categorically call it wartime propaganda.

After all, the liberation and reconstruction of Asia had been the banner that Japan had long raised since the Meiji era. And, witnessing the frenzy that went through all Asia after the Japanese occupation of Southeast Asian territories, the liberation and reconstruction of Asia became a grand policy from which Japan could no longer back off. Having seen how Japanese troops were welcomed by local residents, it became impossible to betray their expectations. At the same time, the Japanese leaders must have gained confidence that Japan would be able to continue the war with the help of local residents' trust and support.

Although some in the Japanese military and bureaucracy hoped for a continuation of the military administration in Southeast Asia, putting priority on securing supply of natural resources, the general atmosphere among the entire nation was overwhelmingly supportive of the liberation of Asia. Since around 1943 (18th Year of Shōwa), one year into the war, neither the Japanese government nor its people doubted that the liberation of Asia itself had been the objective of the war from the beginning.

But perhaps this is not the essence of the issue. The essence was the fact that the Japanese, a colored race, defeated the white race. This had a great impact on Asian peoples as it had done with Japan's victory in the Russo-Japanese War.

Particularly when British officials surrendered and were taken to the prison in Changi where they were closely watched by colored guards, it gave a strong impression to the Southeast Asian people that white supremacy had finally ended.

It was not that Japan had harbored the megalomaniac notion of deliberately changing the flow of world history. A war is a matter of great national importance that can determine the fate of a country. No country would risk its own fate for altruistic purposes—liberation of Asia in this case. Although Japan started a war out of desperation with its oil supply being cut off, it ended up playing a historic role of bringing irreversible changes to the white man's supremacy in Asia. (The same thing can be said about the Russo-Japanese War.)

Also, while Napoleon's conquest of the whole of western Europe had been motivated by France's nationalistic expansionism and Napoleon's personal greed for glory, the historic significance of the overturn of the entire *ancien regime* in the region in only thirty years after France's defeat is undeniable. This was a direct result of Napoleon's triumphant advance throughout the region waving the tricolor, a symbol of the revolutionary spirit. Incidentally, thirty-three years passed after the Battle of Waterloo before Europe experienced the final Revolution of 1848. It was also during the thirty years after Japan's defeat in World War II that countries in Asia and Africa obtained independence one after another until the Portuguese colonies in Africa, the last of the Western colonies, finally became independent in 1975.

Grand Victory and Aftermath

What would be the next step for Japan to take after those grand victories? Naturally, it would be how to end the war.

Tōgō Shigenori's memoir reveals that, compared with the strenuous amount of work before the start of the war, workloads at the foreign ministry became so scanty once the war started that officials did not quite know what to do with their time. This was only natural. Once a war starts, all the work is in the hands of the military and the only thing diplomats can do is to sit back and watch how circumstances unfold.

Particularly because the initial victories were much greater than expected, the majority of the Japanese people believe it unwise to pursue an early settlement of the war if Japan could continue to win at this pace. Even within the foreign ministry, some started saying that diplomacy was unnecessary during the war.

Taking this situation seriously, Foreign Minister Tōgō, in his New Year address in 1942, stressed the importance of wartime diplomacy to ministry officials, saying:

> Although we regrettably failed to prevent this war, we must put an end to it at a stage that is most advantageous to Japan. I expect all the members of the foreign ministry to devote their energy and time to study and prepare for the timing to end the war even at the expense of other tasks.

Even this rather mild statement was a dangerous one to make in Japan in those days as people were in an aggressive mood inspired by initial victories. In a House of Representatives deliberation in February 1942, Tōgō explained the intention of his address, saying, "It is only reasonable and necessary to put an end to this war and restore peace. And it takes thorough preparation as well as determination." Some Diet members criticized Tōgō's New Year address as inappropriate because "the goal of a war is to annihilate the enemy" and pressed him hard to take it back. Tōgō adamantly refused.

Again, a typically Japanese solution was applied to end this dispute. Prime Minister Tōjō decided to exclude Foreign Minister Tōgō's remarks from the stenographic record of the Diet session in order to settle the matter peacefully.

In other words, the prime minister withdrew his foreign minister's remarks, making it clear that his cabinet had absolutely no intention of seeking early peace.

Faced with this situation, Tōgō next attempted a peace settlement between Germany and the Soviet Union. He said, "The center of the diplomatic battle in the current war is the contest for the Soviet Union and I regard it a diplomatic Battle of Sekigahara[20]."

Theoretically, Tōgō was correct. With the Tripartite Pact on the one hand and the Britain-U.S. camp on the other, the only country that could affect the balance of power was the Soviet Union. This was also the logic that had been behind the conclusion of the Tripartite Pact. And in order to win over the Soviet Union, German-Soviet peace had to be accomplished at any cost. This conviction of Tōgō was passed on to his successor, Foreign Minister Shigemitsu Mamoru. Shigemitsu proposed a dispatch of special envoys to both Germany and Soviet Union to mediate a bilateral peace. Both countries turned down the proposal.

Objectively speaking, German-Soviet peace was no longer possible. The ultimate goal of Hitler had always been to overthrow the Soviet Union and he had no intention of changing it. On the Soviet side, around the time of the attack on Pearl Harbor, the Soviet Union had successfully stopped the advance of the German troops, which enabled it to pursue the strategy of reconstructing its war readiness with the help of Britain and the United

---

20   The Battle of Sekigahara was a decisive battle on October 21, 1600 that cleared the path to the Shogunate for Tokugawa Ieyasu, effectively ending the reign of the Toyotomi clan.

States and looking for the earliest chance for a counteroffensive. From the Soviet Union's point of view, it had just completed the ideal preparation for "making friends with distant countries to conquer those nearby" by joining hands with Britain and the United States, two of the greatest powers in the world. It had no intention of taking any action that could nullify this arrangement.

In those days, perceptions of Soviet communism were not yet that unrelenting in Japan or Britain or the United States: It was only during the Cold War days that studies of the Soviet Union began in earnest. Had it been understood that Soviet communism devoted itself to pragmatism, believing only in power and the ruthless pursuit of its own interest, Japan would not have sought Soviet mediation toward the end of the war.

Great Tactical Success, Miserable Strategic Failure

Looking back on the history of those days, it becomes clear that there was no longer any chance left for an early peace settlement.

Frankly, American and British leaders were ecstatic to hear the news of the attack on Pearl Harbor.

According to Winston Churchill's memoir, hearing of the attack on Pearl Harbor after a chain of bitter experiences since the Battle of Dunkirk, his first thoughts were, "So we had won after all! . . . Hitler's fate was sealed. Mussolini's fate was sealed. As for the Japanese, they would be ground to a powder." His memoir reveals that Churchill was able to go to bed at peace that night grateful for the turn of events.

On the cabinet meeting at the White House immediately following the attack on Pearl Harbor, Harry Hopkins, one of President Roosevelt's closest advisors, left the following observation:

> The atmosphere at the White House was not as tense as expected. That was because everyone must have felt "If the United States had to join the war sooner or later, Japan has given us the golden opportunity." Thanks to Japan, which in one fell swoop took such a provocative, rude and infuriating action, American public opinion, which hitherto had been split and undecided, was instantly unified and consolidated.

Some may still believe that the United States fell victim to the Japanese sneak attack when it had wished for peace, but this is propaganda that the U.S. government projected to its people. The truth of the matter is that both the United States and Britain were delighted that Japan attacked Pearl Harbor. They would no longer tolerate an early settlement. All that was left was to totally destroy Japan. And there was no third party that was willing to mediate and coordinate between the determined Britain-U.S. and Japan. The Soviet Union had already sided with the former.

If there were a third party that could have mediated between the two camps, that would have been American public opinion.

Today, nobody doubts that it was the oil embargo against Japan that triggered the war. When the League of Nations decided to impose economic sanctions on Italy that had occupied Ethiopia, it was unable to do so in light of Mussolini's following statement, "An oil embargo means a war with Italy." Had the Japanese government, too, made a similar announcement at an appropriate time, the U.S. government would not have been able to evade responsibility vis-à-vis American public opinion and the U.S. Congress for provoking a war. The U.S. government would also have continued to feel guilty even after it started.

What Churchill as well as the United States had feared most was the possibility that Japan would attack only Britain and the Netherlands first. Although the option had also been considered in Japan, the notion that the United States and Britain were inseparable prevailed in the end.

To judge that the United States and Britain had been united was correct. It was beyond doubt that the United States sooner or later would have found some excuse to join the war. Considering American public opinion, however, even if the U.S. government somehow succeeded in securing enough Senate votes to allow the United States to join the war, there would be a bad aftertaste. And this was where a chance lay to stop the war in the middle through compromise.

In any event, even if Japan had to fight a war with the United States, a surprise attack on Pearl Harbor was truly fatal for Japan from the viewpoint of the American public. While the delay in delivering of the announcement on termination of the negotiation became easy prey for American propaganda, the word "sneak attack" would have been used for a negative campaign anyway even if it had been delivered on time.

In fact, when the United States was criticized after the war for the Hull note, a de facto ultimatum, it refuted this criticism by stressing that the Combined Fleet of the Imperial Japanese Navy had already sailed out of Kasatka Bay (Pacific coast of Iturup Island, south Kurile Islands) on the very same November 26. In fact, Yamamoto Isoroku had given strict orders to abort the attack plan in the event of a peaceful agreement in the Japan-U.S. negotiations, suppressing opposition from Admiral Nagumo Chūichi, Commander in Chief of the First Air Fleet. But this conduct of Yamamoto's—continuing negotiations while moving toward a surprise attack operation—was criticized as being tantamount to a breach of trust.

If Japan had openly declared war after explicitly announcing earlier that the oil embargo could cause a war, making the Hull note public immediately after it was delivered, and demanding the lifting of the oil embargo through an ultimatum with a deadline, it is beyond doubt that the American public would have either opposed the war or, at least, split over the issue even after the start of the war.

In that case, it is quite doubtful whether the United States would have continued fighting after losing 20,000 men on Iwo Jima through death and injuries and another 60,000 men similarly on Okinawa.

Some 20 years after the end of the Vietnam War, I had a chance to spend an evening with Nguyen Co Thach who was North Vietnam's foreign minister during the war. When I said, "You must have had a tough time during the war," the former foreign minister replied as follows: "No, there cannot be a war that was easier than this one. While we only had to concentrate on fighting with the United States, our opponent had to deal both with us and its own public."

He added his observation that the American people could not put up with human losses. When I pointed out that the United States had lost 20,000 Marines (death and injury) on Iwo Jima, he repeated "Twenty thousand Marines!" and became speechless for a while. Obviously, he was pondering on why Japan nevertheless could not win the war.

In this sense, it stands to reason that the greatest mistake that Japan made in the Greater East Asia War was the attack on Pearl Harbor. And it must be the independence of military command that should be blamed for the fact that the foreign office had not known of the existence of a plan to attack Pearl Harbor until immediately before its implementation.

The valiant fight that the Japanese soldiers put up on Iwo Jima and Okinawa made the U.S. side wonder how many millions more it would lose when its troops landed on mainland Japan now that it had sacrificed so many lives just to control mere tips of the archipelago. This prompted the U.S. decision to drop the atomic bombs on Hiroshima and Nagasaki. It also made the Soviet Union join the war.

Had the valiant fight on Iwo Jima made the American public weary of the war and, thus, led to a peaceful settlement before air raids had burnt the entire land of Japan to the ground, the spirits of the Iwo Jima soldiers who had fought till death might have been able to rest in peace. If they learned that, on the contrary, their valor actually led to the horrible fate of the citizens of Hiroshima and Nagasaki as well as the Japanese residents in Manchuria and Sakhalin, their spirits could not attain eternal rest.

Everything depends on strategy. As long as the strategy is sound, bad tactics can be rectified. If the strategy is bad, however, you cannot win a war except by winning all the battles on tactics, a highly unlikely outcome. Moreover, the more tactically triumphant you become, the longer it takes for you to realize the defect of the strategy, eventually leading to irrevocable defeat.

The attack on Pearl Harbor was a huge tactical success, but I must say that, strategically, it was a fatal error.

Underneath all sound strategies are, without exception, good information and accurate assessment of the situation. In retrospect, Japan did not know the United States, particularly the danger of its public opinion. It was also ignorant of the reality of Soviet communism.

As the saying goes, "Know your enemy, know thyself, and you shall not fear a hundred battles." Japan, in contrast, was fighting World War II knowing nothing about its enemies.

CHAPTER
13

The Greater East Asia Co-Prosperity Sphere

—Conference Convened to Realize an Independent Asia—

Shigemitsu Mamoru and Tōgō Shigenori

Tōgō Shigenori and Shigemitsu Mamoru were the two leading figures in Japan's diplomacy during World War II.

From the start of the war until the signing of the surrender, Tōgō and Shigemitsu served alternatively as foreign minister except for a brief period in which Tani Masayuki assumed the post as a stopgap measure.

Both Tōgō and Shigemitsu were legendary prodigies of their hometowns, the elite of the elites who walked the royal road of the educational system and officialdom that modern Japan had developed since the Meiji era. This included high school under the prewar educational system, Tokyo Imperial University, and the Foreign Service Examination.

High schools under the prewar educational system have been the subject of nostalgia for the Japanese people, particularly among the elderly. The system underwent several historical phases. Of the total of 39 such high schools, the most legendary were the eight boarding schools—the so-called number schools—i.e. the First Higher School through Eighth Higher School—which predated Prime Minister Hara Takashi's educational reform of 1919 that established some 20 additional new schools. Graduates from these eight schools were truly the cream of the modern

Japanese educational system that had evolved since the Meiji era. Both Shigemitsu and Tōgō were the very products of this system.

But their family backgrounds were somewhat different.

Shigemitsu came from a family of distinguished scholars of the Chinese classics in Kitsuki-*han* (present-day Ōita prefecture), a reputable family of the region that had produced a number of other distinguished figures. In contrast, Tōgō was the descendent of a Korean potter who had been taken to Japan during the Japanese invasions of Korea in the sixteenth century. His family name was originally Park. Having built a fortune, Tōgō's father acquired a sufficient amount of tradable shares that entitled him to become a member of the samurai class. Nevertheless, in Kagoshima where honor and pride among former samurai were extremely strong, the Tōgōs were looked down on as descendants of Koreans immigrants.

This difference in family background was also reflected in the marriages of the two. As was the custom for those born into a prestigious family, Shigemitsu was married to a woman of class, the daughter of a former governor of Ōsaka Prefecture who was from a samurai family. Shigemitsu's marriage was so customary that his biography doesn't even mention it. Meanwhile, Tōgō's marriage was much more romantic, at least on the surface. He married a German widow—which was quite unconventional for the Japanese in those days.

These differences in family backgrounds notwithstanding, bureaucratic institutions in Japan had already become sophisticated enough by that time to evaluate a person only on his ability and intelligence, paying no heed to his social background. This is what allowed both Shigemitsu and Tōgō to reach the top of officialdom.

Nurtured deeply in traditional Japanese education, Shigemitsu's political judgment was deep and logical, based on historical and global perspectives. Tōgō was a literary enthusiast in his youth who had once devoted himself to German philosophy. His writing was sharp and straightforward, carrying an atmosphere of dauntlessness. Both men were precise and accurate in their analyses of international situations. Shigemitsu's *Shōwa no Dōran* and Tōgō's *Jidai no Ichimen* (An Aspect of the Times) were two of the greatest masterpieces of the time, demonstrating the level of intelligence of Japanese diplomats during a critical juncture that determined Japan's fate.

This was the very reason I decided to entitle the current volume *Shi-*

gemitsu/ Tōgō and Their Age. As a matter of fact, however, Japan no longer had any substantial diplomacy when Shigemitsu and Tōgō were at the helm of Japan's foreign policy.

By that time, the Japanese military had already deprived Japan of its diplomatic role. Yet it is common in any country for the military to be at the vanguard in place of diplomats in a time of war. In the case of Japan, especially after the attack on Pearl Harbor, the overriding issue became how to win the war militarily. Before that, considering that Foreign Ministers Hirota Kōki had inadvertently and Matsuoka Yōsuke had deliberately pushed Japan toward the attack on Pearl Harbor, diplomacy had indeed been in place. In the Shigemitsu-Tōgō days, however, no matter what kind of diplomacy was in place, there was not even the slightest chance of changing the course of events that led to Japan's defeat and its acceptance of the Potsdam Declaration.

This, however, did not stop the two from making their utmost effort to save Japan.

One significant difference between the two was the posts they had assumed. Tōgō had been appointed mainly to posts in the American and European Affairs Bureau. Having served as ambassador to Germany and the Soviet Union, his foreign policy thinking had been centered around Europe and the United States, which were then the power centers of the world. He had opposed the signing of the Anti-Comintern Pact (concluded between Japan and Germany in 1936) when he was Director-General of the American and European Affairs Bureau, believing that it would negatively affect Japan's relations with Britain and the United States. When he became foreign minister after the signing of the Tripartite Pact, Tōgō perceived that the Soviet card was the only available option that he could use for Japan's benefit, given the power balance at the time. Thus, although it all came to naught in the end, Tōgō tried to mediate peace between the warring Germany and Soviet Union. Toward the end of World War II, he tried to persuade the Soviet Union to mediate peace between Japan and the Allies.

On the other hand, Shigemitsu was a China expert, having served as minister to China for three years around the time of the Manchurian Incident and as Japanese ambassador to the Reorganized National Government of China (Wang Jingwei regime) after the eruption of the Greater East Asia War. Convinced that settlement of the China issue, the direct cause of the war, would be the starting point of everything, Shigemitsu thought that regardless of the outcome of the war, there was no other way to bring balance into the Sino-Japanese relations than to pursue a policy of equality and mutual respect. And in order to extend the same logic to all of Asia, Shigemitsu promoted the Greater East Asia Co-Prosperity Sphere scheme. However, the Greater East Asia Co-Prosperity Sphere, too, was lost forever with the defeat of Japan.

Meanwhile, in terms of the impact on history perhaps it should be said that Shigemitsu, an advocate of the Greater East Asia Co-Prosperity Sphere, had accomplished much more than Tōgō. This is because the independence of Asian countries became inevitable after the Greater East Asia War. One may argue that independence would have become a global trend sooner or later anyway, even without the Greater East Asia War. But history shows that the pace of change accelerates during the time of turmoil compared to peacetime. It seems undeniable, therefore, that the Greater East Asia Co-Prosperity Sphere scheme had indeed pushed the clock of history forward.

Reality of Western Colonial Rule

What was the reality of Western colonial rule in Asia before World War II?

The fact is that one cannot find too many testimonies on this issue. Like American racial discrimination, colonial rule during the era of modern imperialism is a disgrace to modern Western history, a past that former colonizers would like to erase by any means. For those who were colonized, on the other hand, that colonization was so humiliating that people would not dare to recall it even for a moment.

For those who had benefited from colonial rule in one way or another—both those in the Western powers and those in the colonies themselves—it was a sweet memory. Particularly for those who had experienced the colonial days in their infancy, it was a nostalgic and idyllic past, magnified further in its intensity because every memory of one's infancy would be sweet. Because of this sentimental drive, those people tended to look away from the negative aspects of their colonial experiences, a tendency also shared by the Japanese people who had experienced colonial rule in Asia as colonizers.

Indeed, up to a certain period of time in postwar Southeast Asia, people's resentment of Japan for having destroyed such a sweet life was stronger than their hatred of colonial rule itself. This resentment coupled with the historic view that the Japanese advancement into Southeast Asia was nothing but a vicious act of violence. Lee Kuan Yew of Singapore is an example of those holding such views.

Why, then, did the local residents in Indonesia and Burma enthusiastically welcome the advancing Imperial Japanese Army? In my view, this phenomenon cannot be explained without an accurate understanding of the dark side of Western colonial rule and local people's perception of that rule.

Here, let us first look into the case of the British rule of India. It seems highly appropriate to start with what is commonly regarded as the most successful model of Western colonial rule.

Indo ni Okeru Kokumin Undō no Genjō oyobi Sono Yurai (Current Status and Origin of the Nationalism Movement in India) is a classical masterpiece written by Ōkawa Shūmei (大川周明), a Japanese Pan-Asian writer, in the fifth year of Taishō (1916). This book is still highly regarded by the Indian people long after World War II.

According to Ōkawa, there were egregious cases of discrimination against the local people in India. For example, the flat and smooth center of a road was reserved for the colonial masters. Indians were obliged to walk on bumpy edges of a road and, failing this, violators were severely penalized with "unspeakable" punishments, including kicking and beating. There were also countless cases of Indians being beaten with fists just because they failed to lower their umbrellas when they passed a Briton on the road.

Furthermore, Indians were not allowed to share a train cabin with British citizens. Even with a ticket of the same class, a solitary Briton monopolized a cabin for six, while ten or even fifteen Indians were crammed into another cabin. When no vacant cabin was available for a British passenger, he was allowed to chase off Indian occupants as if they were dogs.

I do not think these episodes are exaggerated. In fact, these seem to be highly plausible when one recalls how vicious discrimination against the blacks was in the American south.

In order to intimidate local residents and make them accept such an unreasonable inequality, it was necessary for colonial masters to punish those who exhibited even the slightest sign of defiance with outrageous violence.

In the wake of the Indian Rebellion of 1857, a Briton who traveled around the rebellious region left the following observation:

> I had a very interesting experience travelling around India. We loaded cannons on a steamboat and fired them at both banks of the river as we sailed along. When we disembarked, we incessantly fired small guns. I killed several natives myself with my double-barrel gun. Life or death of the natives was in our hands. Those who were sentenced to death were bound by a rope around their necks and placed on the rooftop of a carriage. When the carriage moved forward, the accused lost their footing and hung themselves to death.

In day-to-day life, ordinary British residents in India gun downed the Indians quite frequently. The book revealed that the assailants who were formerly on trial claimed that they mistook humans for a fox (or a bear, a pig, or even a monkey), for which they were lightly fined.

Both the British people and the Indians must have been fully aware that mistaking a human for an animal was a sham. Nevertheless, it must have been the most effective way to teach the Indians what would happen to them if they disobeyed their colonial masters.

Meanwhile, British rule of Burma was even harsher than that in India because Burma had resisted Britain's control until the last minute in order to maintain its independence. While Indians were recruited to the colonial army and were allowed to form regiments composed solely by Indians, Burmese never received training in handling firearms and were not even allowed to possess cutlery. When Indian independence activists were captured, they were often sent to prisons in Burma instead of India, because in Burma they would receive harsher treatment. That explains why the Japanese occupying forces were welcomed so enthusiastically in Burma.

On the colonial rule in Indonesia, Dutch writer Rudy Kousbroek gave an insightful observation in his book, *Het Oostindisch Kampsyndroom* ("The East Indian Camp Syndrome" published in 2005). Being a victim of a Japanese detention camp himself, Kousbroek was not hesitant to criticize Japan. But he was conscientious enough to question in his book if the Dutch colonial rule in Indonesia was virtuous enough to entitle him to criticize the Japanese occupation during World War II.

This book quoted the following report of a Dutch prosecutor on the situation in Indonesia. Despite the efforts of a colonial official of the Dutch government who tried to block the disclosure of the report, the book revealed the following atrocities:

> The maid, Acina, was hit with a whip made of wicker and kicked in the back because she failed to collect a satisfactory amount of silkworms. She was eight-months pregnant at that time. There was a dent on the left side of her stillborn baby's head and the eyes were crushed.
>
> Meanwhile, a Dutch farm worker stripped two Indonesian women and lashed their buttocks with a leather belt until welts rose on their skin. After that, he ordered a local housemaid to rub red pepper chili on the two women's faces, breasts, and genitals and tie them to two underfloor pillars with their legs spread wide apart.

Descriptions of such sadistic conduct are also found in Ōkawa Shūmei's book on India. According to Ōkawa, an Indian woman was stripped naked and hung upside down from the ceiling; then peppered water was poured on her anus in order to force a confession out of her.

In the Dutch East Indies, the lives of local laborers were taken so lightly that they were beaten to death daily as if nothing had happened.

These laborers were not even allowed to take leave to attend funerals of their close relatives because their Dutch colonial masters thought there would be no end if they had to give laborers a break at every funeral.

In addition, the sick were placed in a ward inside the farm. But this so-called ward had iron-barred windows. A local administration inspector found the following atrocities during an unannounced inspection:

> Floating out of iron-barred windows was a piercing stench. Two males and eight females were packed in a space of a few square meters, and I found a dead corpse that had been lying on the floor for at least 24 hours. I found no drinking water or lavatory for the "patients." When they excreted, they had to cover it with dirt and pushed it out through a crack on the wall. When they were thirsty,

they had to obtain water from other laborers who happen to pass by in exchange for food they were given once a day. They received quinine every other week . . .

As is clear from description above, those who were unable to work due to illness were punished rather than treated medically.

Furthermore, in reality, laborers in the Dutch East Indies had to rely on rice imported from Burma and Thailand because Dutch-owned farms did not grow rice. Thus, laborers had no other choice than to work on a Dutch-owned farm to obtain rice.

Simply put, natives in the Dutch East Indies were not humanely treated.

According to Fusayama Takao, an officer of the Imperial Guard Regiment who took part in the occupation of Indonesia, Dutch colonizers resided in houses with elevated floors, while natives were forced to sleep on earthen floors. Moreover, Dutch males routinely picked their favorite local women as their sexual servants, who were then allowed to sleep on the elevated floor during night. Furthermore, because the Dutch colonial administration granted Dutch nationality to children born between a Dutch citizen and his native woman, it often happened that these mothers slept on the earthen floor at the back of the house while their mixed-breed children lived on the elevated floor, abusing and exploiting their mothers.

In those days, people in Java believed in what they called Jayabaya's Prophecy. According to the prophecy, the Javanese people would be ruled by whites for three centuries. The white race would be driven away by yellow dwarfs coming from the north for the life span of a maize plant prior to the return of the *Ratu Adit*. *Ratu Adit* in the Javanese belief system was the just king reborn in the dark age of suffering to restore social justice, order, and harmony in the world.

After the Russo-Japanese War, Javanese people began to believe that Japan was an inseparable part of this prophecy. The Javanese people's expectation of the arrival of a "yellow race from the north" coincided with the arrival of the Japanese military in Indonesia which drove the Dutch out of the region. No wonder the Japanese troops were welcomed enthusiastically by the Javanese people.

Viewed from a different perspective, though, colonial rulers were at the apex of their glory at the sacrifice of the misery and humiliation of those who were ruled.

The charm of the writing of Meiji Japan's educator/writer Fukuzawa Yukichi (福沢諭吉), whom I quote below, is his straightforward style, totally devoid of unnecessary discretion or hypocrisy. The following editorial he wrote for an 1882 issue of the daily *Jiji Shimpo* was a true reflection of the people's psychology during the age of imperialism,

During the Tokugawa period, shogunate officials who were directly under the shogun exercised great influence. Samurai from smaller *han* like ourselves, for example, had to wait for over four hours from early morning to cross the Ōi River. When our turn finally came, however, the shogunate's official courier arrived, ordering others around to stay low to show respect. We had to back off and let the courier cross the river first. Consequently, we ended up waiting for six hours to cross the river ourselves. . . .

Meanwhile, when I was touring in Hong Kong the other day, a Chinese merchant approached me with some shoes for sale. Having nothing else to do at that moment, I decided to entertain myself by bargaining with this shoe merchant in an unhurried manner. Perhaps mistaking our interaction for a case of a foreigner being bothered by a pushy Chinese merchant, a British gentleman nearby snatched the shoes from the merchant, shoved the pair at me, threw two dollars or so at the Chinese, and chased him away with a walking stick, all without uttering a single word.

I was simply envious of this British gentleman's highhanded attitude. Britons were walking freely in and out of Asia as if it were an uninhabited land, and their arrogance was no comparison to that of shogunate officials in olden days. I bet they must be feeling extremely jolly inside. As soon as Japan evolves into a country that can trade a few million yen worth of commodities, build a few thousand warships, and make its power felt abroad, perhaps we will be able to treat the Chinese in a similar way as the above British gentleman had done. Moreover, I could not control the bestial feelings inside me, hoping that we would even be able to treat the British tyrannically like our slaves.

While it is said that it is man's nature to detest tyranny, what it really means is that people do not like to be tyrannized. It is, in fact, the greatest pleasure for humans to tyrannize others. We in Japan complain about the conduct of the shogunate officials during the Edo period and, today, the conduct of foreigners because we are on the receiving end of tyranny from them. What I strongly wish to accomplish is to tyrannize all of those who tyrannize us today and, eventually, monopolize the world's tyranny.

This was a very candid and straightforward confession of a kind of desire that the Japanese and the Asian peoples must have developed at least once at the time.

By defeating the British and Dutch garrisons in the early stage of the war, Japan succeeded in humiliating the white race, satisfying the "bestial feelings" that Fukuzawa had referred to.

Incidentally, when the British and the Dutch accuse the Japanese of brutality during World War II, they mostly referred to the harsh living conditions in internment camps and the face-slapping they received from Japanese soldiers.

In reality, living conditions of the Japanese soldiers were as poor as those of the prisoners of war due to the dearth of food and other necessities during the war. In the case of the Europeans, however, the living conditions in Japanese war prisons must have been all the more unbearable because of the wider gap between their earlier comfort back at home and the poor living conditions at the time.

Meanwhile, face-slapping had an extremely bad reputation especially among the non-Japanese during the war. Face-slapping was a tradition in the Japanese military before and during World War II. Even in the context of the Japanese tradition since the Edo period, face-slapping must have been an utterly unthinkable insult. Nevertheless, it had become a habitual conduct in the Japanese military. Judging from Meiji army general Tanaka Giichi's testimony that he had banned face-slapping in his own regiment, it must have been common since the Meiji period. In a way, face-slapping can be interpreted as a means to thoroughly deprive new recruits of their pride in order to help them adapt to military life. Face-slapping is also the main reason that many former Japanese soldiers alive today hold a grudge against the military.

Moreover, senior officers showed no clemency. Whenever they slapped their subordinates' faces, they struck hard. A former Japanese soldier once said, "The trick was to satisfy the slapper just at the right moment by collapsing after two or three strikes. It is only an act of a tactless man to put up with the slapping until he really collapses."

While it might have been possible for a Japanese soldier to try the above trick, it is not hard to imagine that this face-slapping was an unbearable humiliation to the Caucasians who had up to then abused colored people, and sometimes even beat them to death, with a sense of racial superiority. To be treated so rudely by a yellow-skinned person must have been a dreadful kind of psychological oppression for them because it meant that they themselves could be beaten to death at any moment.

And this psychological oppression must be at the back of the habitual use of the phrase "brutal" whenever the Japanese military during World War II is referred to. Therefore, brutal Japanese conduct can hardly be substantiated even though this adjective is oftentimes reinforced by such adverbs as "hair-raisingly" and "unspeakably." From the viewpoint of Caucasians, what they received from the Japanese military must have truly been a "hair-raising" and "unspeakable" experience.

Actually, it was not only the Caucasians that found face-slapping oppressive. Peoples in Southeast Asia were equally offended by it. In places like Thailand and Burma, where god is believed to reside in one's head, even the childish act of touching another's head is strictly prohibited. In these cultures, face-slapping is such an offensive act that the killing of an offender is well justified among the locals. It is believed, therefore, that the Burmese army's rebellion against the Japanese military toward the end of the Greater East Asia War was the result of the latter's abuse of the Burmese people. In most cases, this "abuse" was likely a beating by Japanese soldiers.

The Acehnese are people with a free and independent spirit. Even though the Acehnese actively collaborated with the Japanese military for their independence in the early stage of the war, they rose in revolt against Japan toward the end of the war. It is believed that this change of attitude was also the result of face-slapping.

The negative effect of face-slapping can also be observed in the Burmese revolutionaries. Bo Min Gaung, the Burmese independence revolutionary who later served the country in various ministerial posts, fled Burma in April 1941. He later returned as a leader of the Burmese Independence Army with the Japanese troops from which he had received a military training. In his book *Aunsan Shōgun to 30-nin no Shishi* (General

Aung Sang and 30 Revolutionaries), Bo spent a few pages on his grudge against Japan, specifically referring to the face-slapping that even leaders of the Burmese revolutionaries had received from the Japanese during their training on Hainan island before the start of the Greater East Asia War.

The majority of the Japanese who were prosecuted as the so-called Class B and Class C war criminals at the International Military Tribunal for the Far East were accused of abusing prisoners of war and local residents. At a time when ill treatment was unavoidable due to the dearth of goods during the war, the Japanese military might not have been accused of being brutal, except for a few cases of criminal abuses, had it not been for the habitual use of face-slapping.

From the Japanese perspective, to whom face-slapping was nothing new, the act was merely a mode of mental discipline conducted routinely free of any sense of guilt. As such, the offender had absolutely no intention to kill or even harm the victim. Nevertheless, since it was such an unbearable humiliation to a victim that he could easily harbor a murderous intent, the Japanese side should have expected the accusation from the oppressed should Japan be defeated in the war.

This habitual use of face-slapping left a huge blot on the glory of the Japanese military, a scar that may not be eliminated over generations.

One exception among the Japanese commanders stationed in Southeast Asia was Lieutenant General Nakamura Aketo, who strictly prohibited his troops from face-slapping. Wise Siamese people had advised Nakamura as soon as he was stationed in Thailand that face-slapping could fatally damage Siam-Japanese relations. Nakamura complied with this advice. Consequently, he was adored by the locals as a benevolent commander. In later years after the war, he was invited to Thailand where he was treated like a state guest.

I have so far spent quite a few pages on the single subject of face-slapping. Given the impact it had on the image of the Japanese occupation forces during the war, however, I am confident that it was worth noting.

Shigemitsu's New China Policy

Setting aside the issue of the image of Japan's occupation in Southeast Asia for a while, let us look at Japan's official policy.

The chief architect of Japan's foreign policy in those days was Shigemitsu Mamoru. Because the liberation of Asia had long been Japan's slogan since the Meiji era, some may find it unacceptable to attribute everything to Shigemitsu alone. It was indeed Shigemitsu, however, who organized and theorized the concept of Asian liberation and, moreover, solidified views within the government and made Asian liberation the fundamental policy of Japan.

Shigemitsu had been appointed to become Japanese ambassador to China and stationed in Nanjing in early 1942. He reminisced in his memoir that, in those days, Japan's authority was at its apex, with Japan having won a series of earlier battles. Furthermore, because maritime transport had not yet been obstructed at the time, transportation of goods between China and Japan was also conducted smoothly.

In light of this favorable environment, Shigemitsu perceived the need to fundamentally reconstruct Japan's policy toward China while Sino-Japanese relations were still stable. This included (1) leaving all internal politics in China to the Nanjing government and refraining from any form of interference; (2) establishing an equal Sino-Japanese relations by abolishing all unequal treaties between the two countries; and (3) promising that Japan will withdraw all of its forces at the end of the war and return all concessions to China. Shigemitsu was convinced that regardless of the outcome of the war, the policy of equality and mutual respect was the only way to bring balance into the Sino-Japanese relations. As for Manchuria, as long as Japan dealt with the Nanjing government, which had already recognized Manchukuo, there would be no problem.

At this point, Shigemitsu returned to Japan to promote his new policy. He succeeded in obtaining approval of the Emperor, who instructed Prime Minister Tōjō to institutionalize the policy, which took Tōjō a good part of 1942.

Had Japan put forth the above conditions from the beginning, the Second Sino-Japanese War would have been settled many times over.

One of the reasons this new policy was endorsed by the Japanese government at this time was, according to Shigemitsu, that the

Shigemitsu Mamoru

Japanese had begun to "think big"—that is, "the Japanese perspective expanded since the start of the great war, making the Japanese realize that Japan's mission lies in Asia," that the mission "would require a joint responsibility from Japan and China," and that it "would be against the true mission of Japan to pursue short-term interests in China that would displease the Chinese people."

In fact, when Japan had already occupied Southeast Asian territories and started dreaming about the division of the world following Germany's victory, it was only natural for the Japanese people as well as the military to put more emphasis on mutual friendship and trust with China than on the Japanese interests in northern China, which had already become a trivial issue.

According to Shigemitsu, as Japan began to realize that it was the liberation and reconstruction of Asia that it had to pursue as its mission, Japanese people gradually awoke from a bad dream. And this "bad dream" referred to the "restless obsession with a trial issue in China."

This new policy was subsequently adopted by the cabinet meeting attended by the Emperor on December 21, 1943. During this cabinet meeting, Chief of the General Staff Sugiyama Hajime stated that this new policy was "akin to repentance" and "we must closely supervise our troops stationed overseas to comply with this new policy." Because Sugiyama had yielded to the trend of the times, tolerating all the arbitrary conduct of his subordinates, it must have been indeed an act of "repentance" to him.

This incident testifies to how far the thinking of Japanese leaders had evolved by that time.

Unfortunately, however, everything was already too late. From the viewpoint of Chiang Kai-shek, for instance, he had just succeeded in launching his grand strategy of making Japan clash with the United States so as to send the former to its doom, a goal that China alone could not have achieved. According to the January 29, 1942, telegram on Shigemitsu's meeting with Wang Jingwei immediately after the former was stationed in Nanjing, Wang observed that, "Japan's splendid military achievements notwithstanding, Chiang appeared to be convinced that Japan would be no match for the United States vis-à-vis manufacturing capabilities, and, therefore, that the United States would come off victorious in the end."

The Communist Party of China (CPC), for its part, had already attained a heavy influence in Chongqing, having formed the United Front with the Kuomintang. Seeing that its strategy of forcing Chiang Kai-shek to confront Japan had begun to show signs of success and, moreover, that its grand strategy of making two capitalist countries, the United States and Japan, fight a war had been accomplished, the CPC had no reason to respond positively to Japan's new stance.

It was too late from a shorter-term perspective too. It took a year for Shigemitsu's proposal of the new policy to be officially adopted by the cabinet meeting attended by the Emperor. During this one year, according to Shigemitsu, "the opportunity was about to be lost; but, at the same time, the time has ripened."

During this one year, Japan suffered a crushing defeat in Midway and it failed to withstand the U.S. counteroffensive in Guadalcanal, forcing it to withdraw from the island toward the end of the year. Japan's ally, Germany, also lost the battles in El Alamein in northern Africa in October, followed by a devastating defeat in the Battle of Stalingrad in November, which later proved to be a watershed in the war.

Had it not been for the crushing defeat in Midway or if this new policy had been launched in the spring of 1942 prior to Midway, the impact of the policy change would have been totally different.

At the time of the eruption of the war, Wang Jingwei had pursued peace settlements with such warlords as Yen Hsi-shan of Shanxi province and Li Jishen, Li Zongren, and Bai Chongxi of Guangxi province. He had already reached an agreement with Sun Liang-shi of Shandong province. Had Japan's new policy been adopted earlier, these negotiations would have been prompted much quicker.

As a matter of fact, the special envoy, Xiao Xuan, who had been dispatched to negotiate with the Chongqing government after the new policy was officially adopted, was shocked to hear of Italy's surrender in September 1943 and was forced to make a u-turn back to Japan.

Once a war starts, the only thing that matters is to seek victory. Even if various factions in China and Southeast Asian countries believed that Shigemitsu had proposed the new policy from the bottom of his heart and that Sugiyama had genuinely resented his past, it would come to nothing if they ended up being on the losing side of the war. Thus, it was only natural for them to observe the situation closely.

Shigemitsu had thought of the remote future, far beyond the outcome of the war. He came back to Japan in April 1943 to assume the post of foreign minister, a post which would allow him to implement his long-standing aspirations. In an opinion paper Shigemitsu wrote before assuming the post, he stated, "The aspiration of the entire Chinese people is nothing but the construction of an independent and autonomous united nation." Shigemitsu refuted those who voiced their concern that Japan could no longer control China once it obtained independence by saying, "[if Japan should win the war,] the only way for China to survive and prosper would be to collaborate with Japan. If, on the other hand, Japan should lose the war, all the Japanese interests in China would come to naught anyway." Using this logic, Shigemitsu proposed that Japan should accept all of China's requests.

This was a reasonable argument applicable to all the Southeast Asian countries that Japan had occupied, which was exactly where Shigemitsu's true intention lay.

In the Revised Japan-China Basic Treaty (改訂日華基本条約, sometimes referred to as the Japan-China Alliance Treaty, or 日華同盟条約) that was signed under this new policy, Japan did not request the right of stationing troops anywhere in China including north China, and it promised a complete withdrawal of Japanese troops once peace was attained. Had these conditions been presented earlier, there would have been no reason for China and Japan to fight a war from the beginning and there would have been no obstruction to the agreement between the two countries.

The Revised Japan-China Basic Treaty was signed in Nanjing on October 30, 1943. It became effective immediately.

Greater East Asia Conference Convened

Shigemitsu's scheme was to apply this new policy toward China to the entire Asian region that Japan had occupied and thereby clarify Japan's war objectives, which had hitherto been vague. Shigemitsu defined Japan's war objectives as follows:

> [Our goal should be] the liberation and reconstruction of Asia. Japan has no other ambition whatsoever. These are the objectives for

which Japan had waged the Greater East Asia War. As soon as these objectives are accomplished, Japan will be prepared to terminate the war at any moment.

Because the above is a quote from Shigemitsu's *Shōwa no Dōran*, which was published after the war, some may detect an element of self-vindication in it. The memorandum that Shigemitsu had written around May 1943 (*Shigemitsu Mamoru Shuki*), however, included a treatise entitled "Taiseiyō Kenshō to Taiheiyō Kenshō" (Atlantic Charter and Pacific Charter), in which Shigemitsu criticized the Atlantic Charter as an empty promise because it included the Soviet Union as a war ally. The Soviet Union had annexed the Baltic states despite the Charter's pledge to protect the minorities in the region and promote their independence. But Japan was, according to Shigemitsu, "in the position to give freedom to the Asian peoples and to protect their freedom, . . . which should be the Empire's national policy as well as its principle." After stressing that, "We should offer heart instead of goods. And we should resort to politics instead of arms," Shigemitsu concluded that, "While the Atlantic Charter has proven to be an empty promise which functioned as a means to wage a war, the Pacific Charter or the Greater East Asia Charter is very much valid. It is a real policy."

In the end, Shigemitsu's efforts came to naught due to Japan's defeat. But the above episode shows that he was indeed a diplomat with a broad perspective. Having carefully studied the Atlantic Charter concluded between the United States and Britain, Shigemitsu decided to compete with it squarely, including its underlying ideology.

Indeed, it was a sore spot for the United States and Britain that the Atlantic Charter included the Soviet Union, which had infringed upon the East European countries' right to self-determination, as their partner.

Before the signing of the Revised Japan-China Basic Treaty, Shigemitsu showed the draft privately to governments of Manchukuo and Thailand in order to promote a similar agreement with these countries. Adding, further, Burma and the Philippines, which were to become independent later, Shigemitsu envisioned a Greater East Asia alliance organization. According to Shigemitsu, the independence of Indonesia and the political participation and self-autonomy of Korea and Taiwan were contemplated.

And it was on November 5, 1943, that the Greater East Asia Conference (大東亜会議) was convened. It had been two years since Shigemitsu had first come up with his new policy toward China. He was right to predict that it would take a long time for the opportunity to ripen. But, as he had feared, it was already too late; the opportunity was indeed slipping away.

Between the fall of 1942 and the spring of 1943, the trend of the war reversed and a German defeat already appeared to be imminent. Japan had no chance of winning the war singlehandedly after the German defeat.

It is hard to imagine that the Thai people, who had weathered the rough waves of nineteenth-century imperialism, would overlook this reversal of the trend of war. When Japan showed goodwill toward Thailand by, for instance, returning the territories it had lost under British/French pressures, Thailand maintained a cautious stance.

Behind Thailand's signing of an alliance treaty with Japan immediately following the eruption of the war was, to be sure, an objective perception that it could never resist Japan's military pressure. On the other hand, it appeared that Prime Minister Luang Pibul Songgram was rather pleased to sign the treaty after hearing of Japan's initial victories. At the time, all of Asia including Thailand was in total euphoria celebrating Japan's victories over the white races. Therefore, Pibul's attitude was indeed not at all absurd. The reality was that Japan's initial victories were so remarkable that they exceeded the expectations of the Asian countries.

In 1943, however, Thailand refrained from joining the alliance with Japan proposed by Shigemitsu modeled after the Revised Japan-China Basic Treaty. Prime Minister Pibul did not participate in the Greater East Asia Conference and sent Prince Wan Waithayakon instead.

Needless to say, Thai leaders always assumed a courteous attitude toward Japan. They cited the commitment to existing alliance treaties as the reason for turning down Japan's proposal and attributed Prime Minister Pibul's absence to his ill health. Nevertheless, it was obvious that their attitude was a result of careful observation of the course of war.

Participants at the Greater East Asia Conference included Tōjō Hideki of Japan, Wang Jingwei from China, Prince Wan Waithayakon from Thailand, Zhang Jinghui from Manchukuo, Jose Laurel from the Philippines, and Ba Maw from Burma. Chandra Bose, head of the Provisional Government of Free India, also attended as an associate participant.

It was truly amazing that these Asian leaders participated in this conference with enthusiasm when Japan's defeat already appeared imminent. It was probably the universal value of national independence, which transcended the fear of life that participants would certainly have to face when Japan was defeated.

What participants at the conference commonly realized was that they had never seen the faces of their own neighbors before. Up until this conference, external relations of these Asian territories had been confined to that with colonial masters. Therefore, the participants were simply unaware of their neighboring countries. Similarly, when newly independent countries joined the United Nations one after another and were welcomed by their fellow newly independent countries after World War II, they claimed that they were having exactly the same experience as the participants of the Greater East Asia Conference.

At the Greater East Asia Conference, a sense of coherence was recognized for the first time among the participants. Prince Wan Waithayakon, for instance, looked back on the history of Asia and said, "Asia has long lost any function as a politically united continent and degenerated into a mere geographical name." Ba Maw stated that, "This kind of conference was utterly unthinkable [before the Greater East Asia War]. Asia as a homeland had never existed before. Asia was never cohesive, having been divided into multiple pieces which numbered as many as the enemies that had cut up Asia."

Laurel analyzed why Asia had been cut up, saying, "It was because the oppressive colonial policies of the Western powers had deprived Asian peoples of energy and aggressiveness. It was also because their divide-and-rule policies had prevented the unification of Greater East Asian peoples." Laurel's proclamation reflected his resolution that Asian peoples would never be broken up or victimized again by Western domination and exploitation.

Furthermore, participants declared that the Asian countries would not be able to enjoy freedom without Japan's victory (Laurel) and that accomplishment of the ideal of a free and prosperous Greater East Asia would "solely depend on the victory of this war" (Chandra Bose). Such was the determination of the participants to fight the war together.

The Greater East Asia Conference adjourned on November 6 after adopting the Joint Declaration of the Greater East Asia Conference, stressing the need to liberate the region from the yoke of British-American domination and construct an order for mutual co-existence and co-prosperity.

Liberation of Colonies and Japan's Contributions

As I have briefly touched on in the previous chapter, after more than half a century, conflicting views remain over the Greater East Asia War: some regard it as a war of invasion and some defend it as a war to liberate Asia.

As Sun Tzu (孫子) wrote in the opening of his book *Art of War*, "The art of war is of vital importance to the state. It is a matter of life and death, a road either to safety or to ruin." A country would not resort to war easily unless it has a very good reason to do so and a firm determination to see it through. A war of invasion must bring benefits to the invader. Unless victory is assured, no nation would dare to jump in at the deep end just to make a few profits. At the same time, no nation would risk its own survival for such an altruistic cause as facilitation of independence of other peoples.

After all, it appears that it was neither the will to conquer the world under the spirit of universal brotherhood (八紘一宇) nor the ideal to liberate Asia that motivated Japan to start the war. As concisely written in the Imperial Proclamation of War, which is believed to have been penned by Yasuoka Masahiro, the honest account of the Japanese in those days was that they had been pressured to start a war in order to survive.

It was, therefore, only natural for Japan to establish a governance structure that would allow it to utilize the natural resources of Southeast Asia freely at least as long as the war continued.

Indeed, when the commander of the 15th Army in Burma openly declared that his troops would "assist Burma's independence" (January 22, 1942), followed by Prime Minister Tōjō's similar remark at the Imperial Diet on February 16, Field Marshall Terauchi Hisaichi, Commander of the Southern Expeditionary Army Group, criticized the reference to Burma's independence as premature and instructed the 15th Army to continue military administration. Not surprisingly, the despair of the Burmese people was one of the reasons for them to believe that Japan's advocacy of liberation for Asia was nothing but a camouflage of imperialistic intention.

Furthermore, the Japanese military believed the independence of a country should be won by its own people. Bo Min Gaung's aforementioned book records a dialogue between Aung San and Colonel Suzuki Keiji, Commander of the Burma Independence Army, that took place around March 1942. Suzuki said,

> Independence is not given by others. You must win it with your own hands. I wouldn't be surprised at all if the Burmese people rise in revolt against the Japanese military. In fact, it would be only natural. I am warning you that you should not refrain from doing something you should do out of consideration for me. I cannot revolt against the Imperial Japanese Army because it would be an act to treason. If you think I am an obstruction to independence of your homeland, kill me with this military sword. Only then can you start your war for independence.

But readers should be reminded that these incidents took place in the period immediately after the occupation by the Japanese military. Around 1943 when Japan started preparing for the Greater East Asia Conference, the basic policy of Asian liberation had already become a consensus in Japan. The conflicting views that had been detected in the earlier days of the war was no longer seen. By that time, nobody opposed Shigemitsu's logic in launching a new policy toward China—that is, that Japan should support the independence of the Asian countries because, with Japan's victory, collaboration with Japan would be the only way for these countries to secure survival and development in any event.

Ironically, by that time, Japan's defeat appeared to be a matter of time, and Asian leaders now had to worry that Japan-supported independence might be written off after Japan's defeat. At this point, it appeared wiser to resist Japan for the sake of their national independence. And that was exactly what Burmese and Indonesian independence leaders opted for in the end. In the course of events, it became logically necessary for those independence leaders to criticize Japan's occupation policies and take an official stance that Japan-supported independence was nothing but a deception. Taking this stand was required for the independence leaders to be approved by the victorious side.

As one can detect from the above-quoted exchange between Aung San and Colonel Suzuki, however, both the Japanese and the Asian independence leaders knew it was a kind of mock quarrel based on mutual trust and understanding. This mutual trust and understanding between Japan and other Asian countries can be observed even today as the Burmese people still enthusiastically welcome the former Japanese associates of the Burmese Independence Army whenever they visit Burma. The Indonesian people have also shared a sense of affinity towards Japan to this day.

Although defeated countries are not allowed to leave their side of stories in written history, they can still leave their footprints in peoples' heart-to-heart relations.

To begin with, the role that the Greater East Asia War played in the liberation of Asia should not be discussed in conjunction with Japan's intention.

The intention of a war is one thing, while the result of a war is another.

While it is true that the Greater East Asia War facilitated the liberation of Asian countries, Japan's contribution to the liberation was limited to the following two.

First, for the second time in the twentieth century, the war proved that a colored race can beat white races.

It was in 1904 that Aceh, a region on Sumatra Island, Indonesia, that had resisted Dutch colonization until the very end, was finally conquered after proving unable to resist the bombardment by a Dutch Navy destroyer. When Acehnese witnessed Russia's Baltic Fleet sailing eastward in the offing of Sumatra, filling the entire Strait of Malacca, they thought that would be the end of Japan. Hearing later of the annihilation of the Baltic Fleet, however, the Indonesian people began to hope for liberation from the white man's rule with the help of Japan.

And, this time, they witnessed with their own eyes the annihilation of the Dutch military at the hands of the Imperial Japanese Army.

The second contribution that Japan made was that it taught the Southeast Asian peoples how to wage a war.

Western colonizers made sure that locals were not given a chance to learn how to use weapons, except for some minorities that were deliberately treated favorably for the purpose of divide-and-rule, e.g., the Karen in Burma and the Amboyna in Indonesia. In contrast, Japan's occupation administration restored a sense of nationalism through promotion of local languages, training of local elites, establishment of a self-government system and formation of troops composed of locals. All of this contributed to the foundation of management of an independent nation, which had been absent before the war.

Moreover, aside from the knowhow of fighting a war, the Japanese left the legacy of a fighting spirit to the Southeast Asian peoples. When I was sent to Cambridge University immediately after the signing of the Treaty of San Francisco in 1951, fellow students from Southeast Asia unanimously told me that what they had genuinely learned from the Japanese was its "tremendous fighting spirit."

Previously, even a few thousand local rebels could have been dispersed easily with the arrival of a few Caucasians and their mercenaries. The bravery that the Indonesian army showed against British and Dutch troops in the Battle of Surabaya in 1945, however, was such that British military referred to it as a sign of Indonesian metamorphosis.

Colonial control is possible only when the oppressed has an inferiority complex towards the oppressor. The moment the oppressed cease to fear the authority of the oppressor and defy it, it becomes impossible even to manage a single factory or a farm.

By the first anniversary of the start of the Greater East Asia War, it had already become meaningless to ponder the true intention of Japan itself. When the local people saw their former conquerors defeated easily by Japan and learned how to fight a war from Japan, the momentum toward their independence was already irreversible, even if it had been Japan's intention to subjugate those people in a similar way. And, without doubt, it was Japan that triggered this momentum.

Japan won the Russo-Japanese War, a war between a Caucasian nation and a colored nation. Japan opposed racial discrimination at the founding of the League of Nations. And Japan overwhelmed the white man's rule in Asia through the Greater East Asia War. Although Japan did none of these things from an altruistic aspiration, it seems undeniable that the impact of these Japanese achievements expedited the flow of history. And this born fruit after World War II when former colonies gained independence from the colonial powers.

CHAPTER

14

Lessons from the Defeat

—What Could Have Saved Japan from Catastrophe—

Wrong Country to Fight Against

I feel forlorn in trying to describe the details of all the battles during the Greater East Asia War.

When a country wins a war, as Japan did in the Russo-Japanese War, it boasts of its successful strategies and reminisces about the heroic conduct of fallen warriors. From the loser's side of the same war, however, as in the case of Russia, the war becomes the subject of scrutiny for causes of defeat, and its victims become a testimony to the futility and cruelty of war.

Unlike Russia, however, which could have won the Russo-Japanese War had it applied different strategies, Japan had no chance of winning the Greater East Asia War from the beginning, no matter what it did. This fact makes it all the more meaningless to discuss the rights and wrongs of individual strategies and tactics.

Take the Battle of Midway, for example. From the viewpoint of Japan, it was a crushing defeat that involved the loss of four of its main aircraft carriers all at once, while the American loss was limited to a single aircraft carrier. Had Japan won a complete victory as Yamamoto Isoroku had envisaged—sinking three U.S. aircraft carriers without any losses on the

313

Japanese side—the Japanese position would have been more favorable by seven aircraft carriers (four less vessels to lose and three more U.S. vessels to sink).

As a matter of fact, Japan built seven fleet aircraft carriers and seven escort carriers during World War II, while the United States built 26 fleet carriers and 110 escort carriers. This gap in the shipbuilding capabilities of the two countries, which resulted in a difference of 19 fleet aircraft carriers, was an almost insurmountable obstacle for the Japanese military to overcome. Specifically, in order to fill the gap, the Japanese side needed to achieve six consecutive complete victories by sinking three enemy ships each time while losing none of its own. The probability of such a chain of events would have been one out of tens of thousands, or effectively close to zero.

Shōwa Japan's military commentator, Itō Masanori, was correct when he said, "It was the wrong country to fight a war with. Japan was no match for the United States at all."

If so, it might be a total waste of time to examine the reason behind Japan's defeat at the Battle of Midway.

But the experience of failure is a precious lesson for both the people and the country of even the losing side. Because one rarely experiences utter failure, nor is one allowed to do so often, it would not be a waste of time to learn from that failure.

The leftist historic view in postwar Japan, however, has insisted that Japan had been destined to ruin anyway because of the autonomy of the military command and, moreover, because of the Meiji Constitution. This view completely ignores the need to obtain specific lessons from a war for which Japan and its people had exerted all their powers.

As a matter of fact, immediately after the end of the war, the Emperor said to Prime Minister Prince Higashikuni Naruhito, "We wish to study the cause of the Greater East Asia War and the causes of Japan's defeat so that the Japanese people would never have to repeat the same mistake."

Taking this Imperial wish seriously, Shidehara Kijūrō's cabinet, which succeeded the Higashikuni cabinet, agreed to explore the causes of Japan's defeat, a task of utmost importance for Japan's reconstruction. On December 20, 1945, Shidehara set up a board to investigate the Greater East Asia War and served as its chairman himself. At the Allied Council for Japan in July 1946, however, the participating countries took a strong position against the board. The Soviet representative, for instance, denounced the board as a basis for Japan's preparation for the next war, citing the participation of former military personnel on the board. Britain concurred with the view of the Soviets. Although Prime Minister Yoshida Shigeru, Shidehara's successor, attempted to obtain endorsement for the board from General Douglas MacArthur, Supreme Commander for the Allied Force, the board was abolished—much to Shidehara's indignation. If this board had functioned as Shidehara initially envisioned, Japan could have learned a number of lessons from the experience of the Greater East Asia War.

Subsequently, a certain historic view of the war developed a life of its own under the censorship of the occupation force. This view claimed that it was presumptuous for Japan to discuss the rights and wrongs of its past strategies because everything in the past was evil. In the extreme, this view even claimed that Japan was better off having lost the war.

Depending on how one looks at it, however, the outcomes of each battle had at least some effect on subsequent international situations.

Had Japan won the Battle of Midway, for instance, U.S. operations in the Pacific most probably would have been delayed for one year because the United States would not have been equipped with the power to fight the following Battle of Guadalcanal.

Meanwhile, Japan's strategies and political stand would have been very different depending on the point in time of the watershed event, i.e. the end of 1942 or one year later.

Since the eruption of the Second Sino-Japanese War, Japan had been fighting with no clear war objectives before it was dragged into a grand war with the United States. It was only after the beginning of 1943 that Japan finally realized that it had the great cause of liberating Asia with the enthusiastic support from the Southeast Asian people, something that Japan could be proud of in the face of world history.

The movement to support the liberation of Asia was originally led by the then Foreign Minister Shigemitsu Mamoru. In time, not only Prime Minister Tōjō Hideki and Army Chief of Staff Sugiyama Hajime but also the entire nation became convinced of this cause. The Japanese people who had first-hand memories of those days would have testified that they had experienced the shift in national mood from that of expansion-ism—i.e., "It would be a loss for Japan to let Southeast Asian territories become independent after striving so hard to conquer them"—to that of "doing what is righteous."

The Japanese military stationed in Southeast Asia became supportive of independence as the Japanese troops expanded their contacts with local residents. Local people, for their part, must have been able to sense that Japanese support and encouragement for their independence was not just mere wartime propaganda but true compassion stemming from fellow Asians.

The mood for independence also prevailed in China. This significantly affected the sentiment of the Chinese people as well as the fate of the war-lords around 1942–43.

Likewise, Japan's support for independence could also have borne fruit in India. A French historian testifies, "Had Japan and Germany collabora-tively pursued a joint strategy toward India by the first half of 1942, when Gandhi's anti-British struggle had reached its apex, the situation in India would have become totally unpredictable." As a matter of fact, Gandhi changed his strategy more toward cooperation with Britain after Japan's defeat in the Battle of Midway. Had Japan been able to devote itself fully to the liberation of India for the entire 1943, it might have achieved an out-come that would have left a mark on world history.

It is said that, although the Imperial Japanese Navy had initially schemed to conquer Colombo, Ceylon, instead of Midway, it had to switch its target to Midway because the Imperial Navy was unable to engage in Colombo alone. The Imperial Japanese Army could not afford to dispatch any of its troops to the Indian Subcontinent because it had to prepare for an operation against the Soviet Union.

It was in 1943 that the policy goal of liberation of Asia was firmly estab-lished in Japan. The war situation, however, had already been reversed in favor of the Allies both in Europe and the Pacific toward the end of 1942. Simply put, it was already too late for Japan to advance into India in any event.

In wartime, might is right. From the viewpoint of the Asian peoples, it would be against their interests to bet on a losing horse, even though they might have believed in Japan's sincerity in the end. It was obviously more beneficial for them to achieve their independence through resistance to Japanese rule. Thus, one of the reasons that Japan's goodwill failed to be recorded in history was its premature defeat.

Beginning of the End

Japan's fate in the Greater East Asia War was sealed at the Battle of Midway. The battle, which was fought only six months after the war began, marked the beginning of the end of Japan's glory.

More precisely, the state of the war had progressed exactly as Japan had initially envisioned, if not better, up until the Battle of Midway in June 1943.

What was hidden behind this initial success, however, was Japan's failure to develop a coherent military strategy between the army and the navy. The Imperial Japanese Army insisted on turning the war into a protracted war as the Imperial Japanese Navy had nearly annihilated American and British battleships in the Pacific and secured natural resources in the south,. The Imperial Japanese Army wanted to maintain a "long-term invincible defense posture" as originally planned. In contrast, the Imperial Navy argued for the need to continue its offensives. The Imperial Japanese Navy General Staff insisted on an operation to cut off Australia, the enemy's counteroffensive stronghold, from the United States, Commander-in-Chief of the Combined Fleet Yamamoto Isoroku argued for a series of brief but decisive battles. In other words, the strategies advocated by the Imperial Army and Navy were completely different.

Furthermore, the two resorted to empty words so as to strike a compromise. For example, *Sensō Shidō no Taikō* (General Principles in Waging the Future War) was written in a highly complicated manner. In a nutshell, it stated that Japan should "resort to aggressive measures at an appropriate timing while consolidating its long-term invincible defense posture."

This is a typical example of empty words, which are still seen in Japan even today. When asked which strategy was finally adopted after all, one could only read aloud the text and say, "It was decided as written here." As a result, both the Army and the Navy continued to separately pursue their own strategies.

Meanwhile, Yamamoto had predicted that the U.S. navy task force centered around its aircraft carriers would be dispatched to the front, if the Japanese military attacked Midway Atoll, because such a move by Japan would threaten Hawaii. By annihilating this task force, according to Yamamoto, Japan would deprive the United States of its will to fight a war, because it would have lost the aircraft carriers that had survived the Japanese attack on Pearl Harbor.

And, as Yamamoto had predicted, the U.S. aircraft carriers were dispatched—all three of them. But their purpose was not to recapture the Midway Atoll after it was conquered by Japan, but to ambush the Japanese fleet en route to Midway. The Americans had detected Japan's planned operation by deciphering the Japanese code.

However, there was still ample chance for the Japanese Combined Fleet to win the battle. At this point, the skills of the Japanese pilots far exceeded those of their American counterparts thanks to years of rigorous training. As a matter of fact, none of the bombs or torpedoes launched by American bombers flying from the airbase at Midway hit the mark, and they were put to rout in no time by the Japanese interceptors.

While the defeat at the Battle of Midway can be attributed to multiple factors, one of the main reasons was the inadequate reconnaissance on the part of the Japanese. Because the Japanese side was scheming to make a surprise attack and was unaware that its codes had been deciphered by the enemy, its reconnaissance was naturally inadequate.

Nevertheless, a Japanese reconnaissance plane spotted the American aircraft carriers immediately before the start of the Battle of Midway.

By that time, a wave of Japanese aircrafts was returning from the attack on Midway Atoll to their aircraft carriers. And this is when the fatal decision was made. Although, in principle, the Combined Fleet should have initially dispatched the attackers to bomb the enemy aircraft carriers that it had just spotted, it instead allowed the returning aircraft to land first. Those who made the decision explained later that they thought they still had time to spare. In an exercise, this was definitely a case in which precedence should be given to the offensive. Had there been awareness on the part of the Japanese that it was a matter of life or death, they surely would have let the attackers take off first. Even if returning aircraft ran out of fuel while waiting for the flight deck to be available, their pilots could still be saved from the sea.

While the first attackers were landing on the aircraft carriers, American torpedo bombers arrived. Due to their inadequate skills, however, they did not inflict too much damage on the Japanese side. Doubly unfortunate for the Japanese side, however, was the fact that the American bomber squadron happened to fly over the Japanese fleet on its way back, having lost its bearings.

When the American bombers flew over the Japanese fleet, the flight decks of the Japanese aircraft carriers were filled with fully fueled attackers about to take off. Torpedoes and bombs were also on deck ready to be loaded. Therefore, when bombs from the American bombers hit the flight decks, initial explosions immediately induced secondary explosions setting catastrophic fires all over the carriers. In no time, three of the four major aircraft carriers of the Combined Fleet were lost for good.

Although the only surviving aircraft carrier, the *Hiryū*, succeeded in sinking the American aircraft carrier *Yorktown*, it, too, was sunk by bombers launched from the two surviving aircraft carriers of the U.S. fleet.

Thus, Japan's aircraft carrier–centered task force, which was far superior to its American counterpart both in quality and quantity, was annihilated in a matter of hours due to several unfortunate misjudgments.

It was particularly damaging for the Imperial Japanese Navy to lose a great number of outstanding pilots whom it had trained and nurtured over many years. While the IJN constructed several more aircraft carriers after this battle, it was never able to fill the gap left by the top gun pilots who perished during the Battle of Midway.

Under normal conditions, it would have been only natural for Yamamoto to be forced to take responsibility for the defeat by resigning. It would also have been natural for the military to review its war strategies fundamentally. But not even the slightest sign indicated that these two actions had taken place. The defeat in the Battle of Midway was completely concealed from the eyes of the Japanese people and no punishment or reward was given.

When Winston Churchill was informed over the phone of the loss of Britain's state-of-the-art battleship *HMS Prince of Wales* off the east coast of Malaya, he was so shocked and terrified that he was thankful nobody was around him. The next morning, however, Churchill reported the loss to the House of Commons, adding, "We have no further details on this incident as of now aside from the Japanese official announcement."

This is a typical manifestation of British phlegm—the ability to stay calm and not get emotional or excited about things even in an extremely difficult or dangerous situation. Had there been an element of this phlegm in the Japanese culture and if the Imperial Japanese Navy had reported to the Imperial Diet about the defeat at the Battle of Midway immediately, what would have happened? It would have been only natural for Japan to readopt the strategy of a protracted struggle. It would have been utterly unthinkable to take the strategy of exhausting all of its remaining air power in the subsequent Solomon Islands campaign.

The traditional sense of solidarity inherent in Japanese society works toward covering up of each other's errors and tolerating lies. Eventually, this results in fatally unsound policy decisions. The history of Shōwa Japan is full of examples of this pattern, starting with the cover-up of the assassination of Zhang Zuolin. It is perhaps a defect deeply rooted not only in the Japanese military but in Japanese society and culture as a whole.

Battle of Guadalcanal

In July 1943, the Imperial Japanese Navy started constructing an airfield on Guadalcanal, the southernmost of the Solomon Islands. It was in line with the scheme to cut off Australia from the United States that had been decided before the defeat at the Battle of Midway.

Judging from the fact that, when the battle started on the island, nobody in the Imperial Japanese Army General Staff Office had even heard of its name, there must have been no prior communication whatsoever between the navy and the army.

A look at the map, however, reveals that Guadalcanal is obviously a strategic, make-or-break point in a contest in the South Pacific.

Guadalcanal is the last suitable spot to build an airfield along the archipelago, which runs southeastward from New Guinea. Beyond Guadalcanal lies the vast ocean area of the South Pacific. Because Japan already maintained a robust airbase in Rabaul, at the northern tip of New Britain Island, Australia-U.S. forces would have had a hard time launching a counteroffensive had another airbase been constructed in Guadalcanal.

Given the strategic importance of Guadalcanal, the Japanese side should have been fully prepared to defend it from the beginning. However, only 2,700 construction workers and 240 Imperial Japanese Navy guards defended Guadalcanal.

Grand victories in the initial stage of the war and the cover-up of the defeat at the Battle of Midway made the Japanese defenders carelessly relaxed. They believed it would be quite some time before the U.S. forces would be able to launch a counteroffensive.

The U.S. side, however, found itself with enough resources, having easily won the Battle of Midway. As the United States was contemplating a counteroffensive, it inevitably took note of the construction of a Japanese airfield in Guadalcanal. Construction had been nearly completed by August 5. On August 7, the U.S. side launched a full-scale landing operation with a grand force consisting of a battleship, two aircraft carriers, three cruisers, 15 destroyers, and 30 to 40 transport ships. U.S. troops overwhelmed the Japanese defenders, who were equipped only with two mountain guns. This airfield was occupied in no time.

In retrospect, the Battle of Guadalcanal was the last battle in which Japan still had the opportunity of winning with the necessary resources in hand.

Hearing of the U.S. counteroffensive, the Imperial Japanese Navy fully displayed its traditional capability since the days of the Battle of Tsushima in 1905. The 8th Fleet, composed of five heavy cruisers, sailed out immediately to launch a night raid on August 8. It won a decisive victory in this attack that lasted only half an hour, sinking four enemy heavy cruisers and setting two light cruisers ablaze. This surprise attack under the cover of darkness perhaps revealed that Japan at that time was still superior to the United States in terms of proficiency in fighting. But, surprisingly, the 8th Fleet withdrew after annihilating the escort ships without destroying the 30 to 40 anchored large transport ships.

This action has long since been a target of harsh criticism. While this withdrawal was implemented in light of the lessons learned from the Battle of Midway that fleet operations would be jeopardized without air cover, it cannot evade criticism of an absence of strategic thinking, at least as far as the result was concerned. After all, in war, might is right and the result is everything.

The strategic goal of this operation was to retake Guadalcanal and annihilate the enemy's landing party. Destruction of the escort ships was only a means to accomplish the goal. To allow landing parties to land from transport ships unharmed was tantamount to a complete defeat in the sea battle, even with the annihilation of the escort ships.

In the Battle of Pungdo in 1894, which triggered the First Sino-Japanese War, the Japanese cruiser *Naniwa* under the command of Tōgō Heihachirō sank the Chinese transport ship *Kowshing*, which was carrying the Chinese reinforcement troops bound for Asan. Tōgō chose to sink the *Kowshing* even at the expense of allowing the enemy cruiser, the *Jiyuan*, to escape. This strategic thinking was completely lost at the Battle of Guadalcanal.

It was said in those days that the distinct mission of the Imperial Japanese Navy was to sink enemy ships in fleet-to-fleet battles, It was also said, metaphorically, that it would tarnish a samurai's sword to kill a merchant with it. It is believed that at the root of the Imperial Japanese Navy's psychology was this kind of dandyism that had nothing to do with strategy.

The Imperial Japanese Army's defeat, in contrast, can be primarily attributed to inadequate military intelligence. Although the number of American troops that landed on Guadalcanal was 13,000 from the First Marine Division, the Japanese side had assessed the enemy strength to be approximately 2,000 men. This was the beginning of the crucial error of repeatedly deploying relatively small forces to Guadalcanal, where they were defeated one after another.

First, 900 troops led by the battle-scarred Colonel Ichiki Kiyonao launched a bayonet charge on August 18. Colonel Ichiki did not wait for the arrival of the following landing party, although his troops were equipped with only 250 rounds of ammunition and seven days of rations each. Consequently, his troops were wiped out completely. By that time, the runway of the Guadalcanal airfield became operational, allowing U.S. fighters to take off to strafe the Japanese attackers. The U.S. defenders also used tanks in this battle.

U.S. military history books state, "From that time on, U.S. Marines were invincible." This turned out to be a highly accurate description of what happened.

Subsequently, on September 13, the Japanese side mobilized 5,600 troops to launch an all-out attack on the 16,000-strong U.S. Marine forces.

This was indeed the last chance for Japan to have won the battle. Had the Japanese side waited a little longer for its troops to be well concentrated before launching the attack, it would have had a chance of winning. In fact, Japanese forces came so close to occupying the airfield that their officers lamented, "If only we had just one more regiment," and "If only we had two more rice balls."

But that was as far as the Japanese side could go. After the American side began to fully utilize the airfield, command of the air was always in U.S. hands. Although the Japanese side subsequently made a larger attempt at attacking Guadalcanal, it suffered tremendous loss in transporting the troops, equipment, and rations without the benefit of command of the air.

In November, the Japanese side attempted to reinforce its position by sending one division with war supplies on board eleven high-speed transport ships, but only four ships were able to land safely on the island. Moreover, those four ships were able to disembark only a portion of their cargo due to enemy fire. As a result, supplies never reached the troops who were dying to receive reinforcements, forcing them to suffer from starvation. Their predicament was so dire that a telegram said, "We have already been out of food for a week now." The situation on the island of Guadalcanal was so atrocious that the island came to be known as "Starvation Island."

The Battle of Guadalcanal developed into a bitter war of attrition.

The discussion among war leaders in Japan in those days focused solely on how to procure necessary vessels.

When the war broke out, the Imperial Japanese Army and Navy acquired a great number of vessels by requisition from the private sector. In time, this strategy began to have grave effects on the domestic economy in Japan, including steel production. Initially, it was planned to return some of the ships to the private sector when the initial battle operations had achieved their major aims.

It was at this time that the Battle of Guadalcanal erupted, making it all the more necessary for the military to acquire more private vessels. Divided between two opposing needs, opinions within the government and the military remained split. A cabinet decision was required to settle the issue.

At this point, therefore, it was already obvious that a protracted struggle and advance into the Southeast Pacific were no longer compatible.

When it came to a war of attrition, Japan was no match for the United States from the beginning in terms of resources. Japan still might have had a slight chance had the war been fought near Japan, letting the enemy come as close to Japan as possible. But the Battle of Guadalcanal took place in a location that was most disadvantageous to Japan.

Guadalcanal was 1,000 kilometers away from the airbase in Rabaul. Because of this distance, even the Japanese Mitsubishi A6M Zero (the "Zero"), which boasted the longest range in the world in those days, was able to engage in the battle over Guadalcanal for only 15 minutes. This put the Japanese side at a critical disadvantage compared with the U.S. side, whose aircraft were flying from the airfield on Guadalcanal.

In the end, the Japanese side was forced to withdraw, leaving 20,000 corpses behind. The Imperial Japanese Navy exhausted a total of 2,076 operational aircraft, degrading the glorious Rabaul Air Squadron, which had been proudly labeled "the southern battlefront of silver wings." Subsequently, air capabilities continued to be extracted gradually from Manchuria and Burma in order to wage battles on New Guinea. This worsened the balance of Japan's air capabilities throughout all the battlefronts. In subsequent battles, the Japanese military was forced to fight in absolutely disadvantageous conditions with command of the air constantly in the hands of the enemy.

Exactly as the U.S. Side Envisaged

From the Battle of Guadalcanal until its final defeat, Japan had absolutely no chance of winning the war. With its manufacturing capabilities dwindling day by day, Japan was unable to make up for the daily loss of its military equipment.

Meanwhile, the U.S. side advanced through two routes. One was that taken by the army-centered force led by General MacArthur, whose plan was to advance along the reverse route that the Japanese military had taken, starting from the Solomon Islands to eastern New Guinea, to western New Guinea along the island's north shore, and finally to the Philippines.

The second route was taken by the U.S. Navy and Marines under the command of Fleet Admiral Chester Nimitz. They occupied the Pacific islands one after another to reach Saipan, Iwo Jima, and, finally, Okinawa.

This dual-route operation completely confused the Japanese defenders, who were unable to figure out what the next U.S. target would be.

When the U.S. side gathered all of its naval capabilities in the Pacific (eventually raiding Saipan, for instance), the Japanese Combined Fleet could not figure out the enemy's intention. Assuming that the areas around Biak Island in northwest New Guinea, the very place where MacArthur's troops had started their operations, would be the main battlefield, the Combined Fleet had already sailed out toward this destination. When it learned of the U.S. plan to attack Saipan, therefore, it had to sail northward for 700 nautical miles to intercept the enemy forces.

This dual-route operation, however, was not the outcome of a well-co-ordinated U.S. military strategy. The difference of opinion over the operation plan between MacArthur and Nimitz forced the United States to adopt both plans simultaneously. From Nimitz's viewpoint, it would be far easier to conquer the isolated islands on the Pacific one by one, considering the tremendous cost required for a frontal attack on Japan's stronghold in Rabaul. MacArthur, on the other hand, believed that occupation of the Philippines would cut off Japan's access to natural resources in the south, thus expediting Japan's eventual defeat. One may suspect, though, that MacArthur's pride may also have played a role in his plan, seeing as he once declared, "I shall return" when evacuating from the archipelago in March 1942.

In Japan's case, the failure to coordinate between the army's protracted struggle strategy and the navy's continuous offensive strategy led to the defeat at the Battle of Guadalcanal. If the U.S. operation, too, had turned out to be a failure due to the division of resources, somebody would have been blamed for having failed to coordinate a coherent plan between the army and the navy. But at this point, the difference in the military strengths of the two countries was already so great that the U.S. failure to concentrate its military did not make a difference.

At the Casablanca Conference in early 1943, U.S. Fleet Admiral Ernest King, dissatisfied with the allocation rate of the Allied troop strength and war materials which was set at only 15 percent for the war with Japan, insisted that the ratio should be elevated to 30 percent. However, he was unable to change the allocation rate which heavily favored the European front.

This means that Japan was almost overwhelmingly outplayed in all the battlefields by only 15 percent of the entire Allied military strength—and that strength was further divided into the above two routes. This goes to show that the differences in the military strength between the two sides was already so decisively large that it really makes no sense to argue the rights and wrongs of Japan's strategies and tactics.

In particular, the difference in air power was overwhelming.

Admittedly, the entire world was astonished by the extraordinary performance of the Japanese fighter planes at the start of World War II. Only 12 days into the war, British Foreign Secretary Anthony Eden, who was visiting Moscow at the time, told Stalin that based on British experience and assessment, the pilots flying Japanese fighters must have been either Germans or German-trained Japanese.

Fighter pilots were the heroes of World War II. A number of sons of the British high society volunteered to be pilots during the Battle of Britain which was fought in the sky above England after the defeat in the Battle of Dunkirk. The number of casualties among them was so great that their deaths became one of the causes of the British Empire's later decline. Perhaps Eden did not wish to believe that it was the Japanese pilots who demonstrated incredible capabilities that appeared to be superior to those of the heroic British youths.

Furthermore, the Mitsubishi A6M Zero was indeed a world-class masterpiece among fighters in the earlier days of World War II. The plane was superior to all of its contemporaries in terms of range, speed, climbing power, and maneuverability. Along with the battleship *Yamato*, the Zero was the culmination of the modern technology that Japan had laboriously developed since the Meiji Restoration. It was when Japan's military technology had finally caught up with and, in some areas, even overtaken the Western technology that the war erupted.

In the world of technology, even if you succeed in surpassing an opponent on one occasion, you will be overtaken soon if you indulge in self-complacency.

In June 1942, a Zero made an emergency landing on Akutan Island in the Aleutian Islands. Because the pilot died instantly of a broken neck, the U.S. military was able to obtain the Zero nearly intact. After studying the Zero thoroughly, American engineers developed their own fighter that could well compete with the Zero, i.e., the Grumman F6F Hellcat. Eventually, the Hellcat superceded the Zero in its ascending and descending performance. The Hellcat was also more heavily armed and armored than the Zero.

In contrast, by this point weak defense capabilities had always been the sore spot of the Zero. Because its designer had been requested to limit its body weight to the minimum for the benefit of performance—its range in particular—many, many pilots lost their lives from enemy fire which penetrated the thin steel plate protecting the cockpit.

Moreover, the performance of American fighter pilots had become superior to their Japanese counterparts by 1943. According to American nonfiction writer John Toland, American fighter pilots had much improved their flying and fighting skills by the time of the Battle of the Philippine Sea in June 1944, due to two years of intensive training with more than 300 flight hours.

In contrast, the Japanese pilots had been trained only for six months with only a few flight hours. Much more serious for Japan, though, was that it had lost the majority of excellent pilots that it had laboriously trained before the eruption of the war during the battles of Midway and Guadalcanal. As a result, the Japanese pilots in June 1944, according to Toland, were "utterly incomparable to those who had fought in Pearl Harbor and Midway. And they flew the already antiquated Zero with minor modifications from the days of Pearl Harbor."

In modern warfare, command of the air is an absolutely decisive factor.

In the Pacific, Nimitz's troops conquered the Pacific islands one after another by defeating the selected target after establishing command of the air with carrier-based aircrafts. Whenever the Japanese side decided to send reinforcements, it simply lost its transport ships without the command of the air. It was only a matter of time for the isolated Japanese ground troops to fall.

The U.S. forces captured the islands of Makin and Tarawa in November 1943 and Kwejalein in February 1944. The U.S. forces bypassed major bases of the Imperial Navy's Combined Fleet, instead destroying them completely with massive air raids. U.S. forces went on to capture Saipan in July, Guam in August, and, finally, Iwo Jima in March 1945.

Meanwhile, MacArthur's southbound advance had originally targeted Rabaul. However, it was soon discovered that that was no longer necessary. Had the Rabaul Air Squadron remained intact, it would have been difficult for MacArthur's forces to advance westward on the north shore of New Guinea because that area would have been under Japanese air command. But such a concern was no longer necessary. It made more sense to MacArthur to simply bypass Rabaul and advance further north.

Had the U.S. forces attempted a frontal attack on Rabaul, they would have needed ten times more time and may have incurred ten times more casualties than the raid on Iwo Jima because the 100,000-strong Japanese defending force under the excellent command of General Imamura Hitoshi had been well prepared in terms of equipment, morale, food (obtained through complete self-sufficiency), and fortification. Because MacArthur bypassed Rabaul, however, these elite troops became an idle force and saw the end of the war without fighting.

Before the end of 1943, MacArthur's troops conquered the Japanese Army's defensive strongholds in northern New Guinea one after another. In May 1944, MacArthur's troops captured the island of Biak near the western end of New Guinea. Using Biak as a base, MacArthur's troops landed on the island of Leyte, Philippines, in October.

Although the Japanese resistance against these U.S. advances proved futile in the end, the Japanese troops nevertheless waged heroic fights that upheld the glorious tradition of the Imperial Army and Navy since the days of the First Sino-Japanese and Russo-Japanese Wars. I wish to touch on this in the next chapter. As heroic and gallant as their resistance might have been, however, the best the Japanese troops at each defensive strong-hold were able to achieve was to delay U.S. advances for a few weeks.

It would be too cruel to claim that all of the Japanese troops' resistance was completely useless. After all, defenders on New Guinea alone endured for 22 months. That must have had the effect of delaying U.S. operations at least that much. It might well have delayed U.S. landing operations on mainland Japan until the U.S. use of atomic bombs and the Soviet partici-pation in the war against Japan in August 1945.

Had the Japanese defenders allowed an earlier U.S. invasion of main-land Japan, the level of catastrophes would have been entirely different from that caused by air raids or even the atomic bombings.

Fighting a War with American Public Opinion

In retrospect, what else could Japan have done?

A war was inevitable after the U.S. oil embargo against Japan and the failure to avert war at the Konoe-Roosevelt talk. Even if some kind of temporary agreement had been struck between Japan and the United States, it would only have allowed Japan to receive a small quantity of low-quality oil from the United States until the latter completed its war readiness. In sum, unless Japan yielded completely to U.S. demands, war would have been inevitable anyway.

Was there, then, any other way for Japan to fight the war?

Indeed there was. The one and only way would have been to implement the strategy used by the Vietnamese during the Vietnam War. In a nutshell, Vietnam forced the United States to fight simultaneously on two fronts; the war with Vietnam and the battle with the U.S. public opinion.

The postwar, leftist historical view in Japan has argued that, as long as Japan possessed Manchuria with its troops deeply advanced in mainland China, the United States would never have tolerated Japan's conduct. This view, however, ignores the reality of the American public opinion at the time.

The American public had no intention to fight a war with Japan only for the sake of curbing Japan's conduct in Asia. A Gallup survey taken in the United States seven months prior to the eruption of the Greater East Asia War indicated that 79 percent of respondents opposed fighting a war because of problems in the Far East. Another survey taken six months before the war showed that 34 percent were against a war even to defend the Philippines from the Japanese attack.

In my view, two factors could have forced the United States to fight two wars simultaneously—military battles with Japan on the one hand and a war with domestic public opinion on the other.

One factor was the U.S. isolationism that had been deeply rooted in American history. In effect, the U.S. Congress passed two neutrality acts between 1935 and 1937. Meanwhile, President Roosevelt continued his attempt to drive the United States into a war with Germany in order to save Britain. In sum, Japan was only a secondary consideration for both the Congress and the President.

On December 8, 1941, however, Roosevelt strongly denounced Japan's attack on Pearl Harbor, calling it "a date which will live in infamy" in what was later called the Infamy Speech.

It was Hamilton Fish, Congressman from the state of New York, who made a speech in full support of Roosevelt ahead of anyone else. Informed of the presence of the Hull note in later days, however, Fish wrote as follows in his *Tragic Deception: FDR and America's Involvement in World War II* (1983): "Today, now that I am aware that President Roosevelt had coerced Japanese leaders to start a war by sending a shameful ultimatum, I am ashamed of this speech by Roosevelt."

The atmosphere in the U.S. Congress at that time was such that, had the Hull note been disclosed, it would have been obvious for the majority of the Congress, including Hamilton Fish, to vote against the war.

What would have happened if Japan had not resorted to such a measure as to launch an attack on Pearl Harbor and, instead, openly demanded an immediate lifting of the oil embargo, with an ultimatum attached, after disclosing the Hull note to the public? Even if the United States had rejected the Japanese demand and started the war, it would have forced Roosevelt to deal immediately with two battlefronts—Japan and the U.S. Congress—much the same situation as President Richard Nixon had to face during the Vietnam War.

Another factor that could have forced the United States to fight the two battlefronts simultaneously was Japan's intention to liberate Asian colonies.

To begin with, the American public opinion was antagonistic or, at least, unsympathetic to the idea of joining a war in order to help Britain and the Netherlands protect their colonies in Asia. Had Japan succeeded in giving an impression to the American public that Japan's actions were solely for the sake of liberating the Southeast Asian peoples, it could have had a very good chance of weakening the will of the American public to fight a war with Japan.

To be sure, China's will to fight a war with Japan put the U.S. government in a favorable position. This is because whenever the importance of assistance to Chiang Kai-shek was debated during the war, the U.S. government was able to refer to the risk of a racial war in which all of Asia became America's enemy once China yielded to Japan's pressure. In fact, it is believed that Chiang himself secretly threatened to conclude an agreement with the Japanese government for the sake of "Asia for Asians" if the United States discontinued its assistance to him.

Had it not been for the "sneaky attack on Pearl Harbor" and if Japan had championed the liberation of Asian colonies, to which the United States could have hardly opposed, it would have been impossible for the Roosevelt government to persuade the American public opinion to continue the war only for the sake of assisting Chiang Kai-shek. Should this situation have actually occurred, the excessiveness of the Hull note's demands would have had adverse affects.

Thus, the only reason for continuing the war that the United States could have mustered was the cruelty of Japan at war. And it was the Bataan Death March that the U.S. government frequently used to stress the inhumanity of the Japanese. What happened in Bataan was something that was bound to happen in a battlefield, and it should not necessarily be interpreted as evidence of the evil will of the Japanese. It has been pointed out that it was actually the fully armed Japanese guards rather than the unarmed prisoners who suffered more from the march.

In fact, the lack of a strategic goal cornered Japan during the war. If Japan had had an explicit strategic goal of cornering the United States into a "dual war" from the beginning, it would have deliberately treated the prisoners far better than under ordinary conditions. And the situation would have become a reenactment of the strategic thinking that was manifested in the deliberate hospitality shown by the Japanese toward the Russian prisoners-of-war during the Russo-Japanese War.

With the "dual war" strategy in hand, Japan would have been able, with a good chance, to win a peace agreement with the United States before air raids reduced mainland Japan to ashes by putting up such brave fights as those on Iwo Jima and Okinawa or, more precisely, by showing the degree of human loss the United States had to be prepared to withstand.

In sum, Japan could have been saved from a devastating defeat if it had acted based on common sense: that is, starting the war fairly and squarely in compliance with the procedures stipulated by international laws; raising morally high war objectives and carrying them out steadily; treating prisoners-of-war chivalrously according to the way of the samurai so as not to leave any space for criticism; and impressing opponents with its military power and showing it has the potential to inflict massive casualties.

In this regard, one can hear the echo of the Wang Yang-ming philosophy—it is best for man to conduct himself in a way that does not go against the way of heaven.

This, however, does not necessarily apply to all wars. Against opponents whose actions are firmly predetermined no matter what one does or does not do, including the Mongol armies in the 13th century and the determined communist forces of the Soviet Union, winning would be the only thing that matters.

Instead, the strategy which Japan should have taken as stated above would be effective only against such a unique opponent as the United States, which is bound by its own public opinion and moral principles.

If this indeed is the case, then the genuine cause of Japan's defeat must have been its failure to acknowledge the importance of intelligence. Neglect of intelligence consistently remained a critical shortcoming of Japan in the runup to as well as during the war. If only Japan attached some importance to intelligence, it would have been able to understand that the United States was a unique nation bound by its public opinion and moral principles.

Sun Tzu said, "If you know the enemy and you know yourself, you need not fear the result of a hundred battles." This is a classic that should be quoted over and over. The fundamental cause of Japan's defeat was that it fought the United States without knowing the enemy. Had Japan known the United States better, it would not have experienced such a devastating defeat, even though defeat itself might perhaps have been inevitable.

In a way, Japan was forced to pay the price for having abrogated the Anglo-Japanese Alliance twenty years earlier, which resulted in Japan's isolation from the intelligence of the Anglo-Saxon which had always been the mainstream of the world.

In the more than 70 years since Japan's defeat, there have been a variety of economic frictions between Japan and the United States, some of which could have shaken the foundation of the bilateral alliance that developed after the war and continues today. However, through the experiences of the war, occupation, and near 70-year-long alliance relations, Japan has learned how it should associate itself with the United States, which so far has been successful in fending off all possible crises.

CHAPTER
15

The Epic of the Fall of an Empire

—Japanese Warriors Proved Their Worth on Iwo Jima—

New Guinea: General Imamura, a Man of Integrity, and General Adachi, A Man of Compassion

By October 1942, the defense of Guadalcanal had already become utterly hopeless. For the United States, this meant that the time had come to launch the next operation. In no time, General MacArthur started to advance his troops into eastern New Guinea.

Because the Japanese side had been totally tied up with defending Guadalcanal, it was unable to respond to this new U.S. move. By the time Japan realized that the U.S. was launching a full-scale attack, the Americans had already constructed an airfield nearby, which enabled it to gain command of the air. As a result, Japan's attempts to send supplies were crippled as practically every transport vessel was being sunk en route by American air power. This left local Japanese garrisons isolated in the face of an opponent with an overwhelming advantage.

Nevertheless, the Imperial Japanese Army troops stationed in Buna, New Guinea, fought gallantly for two months against an opponent with three times more forces and ten times the fire power. They put up such a good fight, killing some 10,000 American and 5,000 Australian troops, that the battle was marked as the world's fiercest battle in the official U.S. military history document.

The bravery shown by Taiwan's Takasago Volunteers during this battle was particularly noteworthy.

In the end, in January 1943, eight soldiers who could still move out of some dozen survivors charged at U.S. tanks, completing a banzai attack.

In Girua adjacent to Buna, a Japanese battalion constructed a strong fortification that endured fierce enemy attacks for 20 more days before it was ordered by headquarters to withdraw. All the troops who could still walk did so. Major General Oda Kensaku, commander of the Girua garrison, righteously stayed behind with the seriously injured. In the end, Major General Oda committed suicide, facing northward toward Japan, the mother country, together with Lieutenant Colonel Tomita Yoshinobu, who insisted on sharing his last moment with Oda.

There were countless examples of heroic conduct such as these in each and every battle. As a result, it took U.S. forces more than twenty months to advance from east to west on New Guinea and complete their preparation for the attack on the Philippines.

Such conduct was basically a product of intense patriotism found among Japanese soldiers since the Meiji period as well as virtuous officers who acted in a spirit of *noblesse oblige* in carrying out their missions, taking the initiative, and setting good examples. These traits were generally seen in the Japanese military not only in New Guinea but also in other subsequent battles. In fact, each and every soldier fought in his own courageous way.

Success in maintaining the morale and discipline of the troops for such a long time stems largely from the presence of outstanding leadership. In the battles in the South Pacific, troops' morale and discipline owed much to General Imamura Hitoshi, the "saintly general" who commanded the Eighth Area Army including Rabaul, and Lieutenant General Adachi Hatazō, the "compassionate general" who commanded the Eighteenth Army in New Guinea under Imamura.

Both were transferred as soon as the battle of Guadalcanal began, Imamura from Java and Adachi from north China. Both assumed their respective new posts in November 1942.

Imamura was an elite in the Imperial Japanese Army. At the time of the Manchurian Incident, Imamura held the important post of director of operations. But as he remained critical of the arbitrary conduct of the military, he was alienated from the central military leadership for quite some time. Nevertheless, Imamura's capability as well as his temperate and fair nature led him to assume important military posts one after another. At the opening of the Greater East Asia War, Imamura was assigned to command the Sixteenth Army in Java.

In Java, anticipating a protracted battle with the U.S., Imamura endeavored not to provoke antipathy among local residents. He restrained his men from acting self-indulgently by tightening up the military regulations and, at the same time, implemented an administration that was compatible with the practices of the old Dutch colonial rule as well as local people's sentiment. In doing so, Imamura deliberately ignored criticism that his military rule was too soft.

After the end of World War II, Imamura was first tried by the Australian war criminal court in Rabaul. Imamura was later transported to Java because the Netherlands insisted on the death penalty for Imamura, who was the first commander of the Japanese occupation forces in Java. To the surprise of the Dutch, however, the court found him not guilty.

While Imamura was imprisoned in Java, Sukarno of the Indonesian Independence Army (and later president of the Republic of Indonesia) confided to Imamura his plan to raid the prison and free Imamura to repay him for his benevolent administration during the occupation of Java. Imamura declined with thanks.

When Imamura was transported to Sugamo Prison, Tokyo, to serve the ten-year sentence determined by the Australian war criminal court, he pleaded to be sent to Manus Island where his subordinates were imprisoned. Hearing this, MacArthur was moved by what he regarded as "the first genuinely samurai-like conduct that I have encountered in Japan" and granted Imamura's wish.

After completing his term in Manus Island together with his former subordinates, Imamura returned home to Tokyo, where he resided until his death in a tiny shack he built in his yard as his own way of taking responsibility for his part in the war. This is the very reason that Imamura is still revered as a holy general long after his death.

Lieutenant General Adachi Hatazō was also a man of character. At the time, Adachi's Eighteenth Army was in New Guinea under the command of General Imamura. However, communications with and supplies

Imamura Hitoshi in Java

from Rabaul had been severed because command of the air was in enemy hands. Completely isolated, Adachi commanded the battle in New Guinea until Japan's defeat with a spirit of compassion for his men.

Adachi shared the military spirit with his fellow Imperial Japanese Army officers, but he was distinct from others in openly professing his faith in Christianity.

Adachi constantly preached to his subordinate officers that they "should refrain from giving soldiers unreasonably harsh orders or orders that are inappropriate to real situations. We should also refrain from doing things that could harm soldiers' honor." It must have been excruciatingly painful for Adachi to witness his beloved men die of sickness or malnutrition (starvation, to be exact) one after another.

Hearing of Japan's surrender, Adachi murmured, "I do not know how to apologize to my men." The Eighteenth Army, which had boasted 140,000 troops, had shrunk to a mere 13,000 ghostly and starved soldiers by the time of Japan's surrender.

Adachi killed himself after the Australian war criminal court was completed. It was also after the schedule for the return of his surviving soldiers was confirmed. Although his military sword had been confiscated, Adachi was able to conceal a rusty knife. Sitting upright and facing north, he disemboweled himself with the knife. Unable to die, Adachi clenched his carotid artery with his own hands to end his life.

One can't help wondering how a man could kill himself that way.

It was exactly as Adachi had repeatedly avowed: "Once a man is determined to kill himself, he can do it no matter what."

Adachi left five suicide notes addressed to General Imamura, his officers and men, as well as his family members, all of which were written in beautiful Japanese. In these notes, Adachi apologized for having lost more than 100,000 promising youths by starvation. Even though he had demanded hardship of the exhausted and starved men that was well beyond and above what a man could endure, all of them accomplished their missions without complaint. "Even though they died for the Emperor's country, only God knows what passed through my mind as I watched them fall and perish like falling cherry blossoms with my own eyes," wrote Adachi. He concluded, "Even though I have escaped death in battle, I cannot possibly return home alive. I am determined to be buried in New Guinea together with my 100,000 fellow warriors."

To his family, Adachi left a note saying imminent destitution was only to be expected in any country under the defeat and prayed that all the surviving members of his family would behave honorably as Japanese people throughout the rest of their lives.

Hearing these suicide notes, all the officers and soldiers who were waiting for the vessels to take them home cried uncontrollably.

Tragedy in Imphal

In his instruction immediately following the surrender, Adachi said to his men:

> The gallant fight that the troops of the Eighteenth Army put up in New Guinea with total disregard for their own lives will remain in history forever as a demonstration of the true worth of the Japanese people as long as the nation exists.

This message should be remembered as an epitaph for all the officers and soldiers who sacrificed their lives in pursuit of their duties not only in New Guinea but also in all the other battlefronts including Leyte, Luzon, and Okinawa.

Nevertheless, the noble self-sacrifice of warriors could become the object of remorse and resentment, depending on the quality of the leadership. The Battle of Imphal was indeed a case in point.

Much has been discussed and written about the tragedy that happened in Imphal. The debate between critics and defenders of Lieutenant General Mudaguchi Renya who commanded the battle has lingered even for decades after the end of the war.

Simply put, the Battle of Imphal was an operation in which Mudaguchi's hardliner argument prevailed even though its feasibility had been seriously questioned from the beginning.

By that time, Japanese military aircraft had already been mostly deployed and lost in New Guinea. Command of the air had been in the enemy's hands. Before the supply corps were fully prepared, however, Mudaguchi's Fifteenth Army took the gamble of attacking Imphal, hoping vainly that conditions might improve if Imphal could be occupied in three weeks. The operation, however, turned out to be a total failure, with 80,000 officers/soldiers out of 100,000 killed or injured. It was also a highly unusual battle in that the commanders of the three participating divisions were dismissed and replaced during the operation, an extremely rare case in world military history.

To be sure, though, this operation was not totally unreasonable.

At the Casablanca Conference in early 1943, the United States insisted on the recapture of Burma in order to prevent, for one thing, Chiang Kai-shek from dropping out from the front. Under this strategy, the Allies had already started counteroffensives from the north, west, and south. It was, therefore, militarily reasonable to attack one of the three counteroffensives first and prepare for the subsequent counteroffensives from two other directions.

The tremendous fights that the Japanese side had put up in Iwo Jima and Okinawa testify to the superhuman capabilities of Japanese troops in defensive battles. Had Mudaguchi concentrated all of his troops solely on defense, perhaps the operation could have endured the allied attacks a little longer. As a matter of fact, the defense of Burma crumbled in no time after the defeat in Imphal, which deprived the Japanese military of its capabilities to put up a strong fight thereafter.

If there was any positive significance for Japan in the Battle of Imphal, it must have been the participation of the Indian National Army.

As soon as Japan captured Singapore in February 1942, Prime Minister Tōjō Hideki announced his policy for supporting the Indian independence movement.

Although Chandra Bose, India's independence revolutionary and former president of the Indian National Congress, had fled to Germany after he had been repeatedly imprisoned in India, he declared that he would promote India's independence movement in collaboration with Japan, having learnt of Tōjō's announcement. After being escorted to Japan by an Imperial Japanese Navy submarine, Bose established the Provisional Government of Free India in October 1943 in Singapore, which Japan recognized immediately.

Itō Masanori, Shōwa Japan's leading military commentator, once wrote that the Imperial Japanese Army might not have launched a campaign in India without the very existence of Chandra Bose.

Certainly, it is not hard to imagine that, when Tōjō made the final decision on the Imphal operation, over which many had voiced their concerns, he must have harbored a strong desire to respond to Boze's patriotic feeling.

In March 1944, when the Indian National Army crossed the Chindwin River and reached Indian territory, they knelt down to kiss the ground of their homeland. When they advanced, they chanted, "Jai Hind (Hail India)! Jai Hind!" I personally wish they were at least given a chance to raise the flag of independent India in Imphal. It was a pity that their dream was so short-lived and that they met a miserable end due to the totally irrelevant military operation in Imphal.

It would not be an overstatement to say that the failure in Imphal was caused more by Mudaguchi's forceful personality than problems in tactics or strategies.

This, however, does not mean that Mudaguchi was a particularly incompetent or vicious man. If anything, he was such a mundane, stereotypical military man that it would have been too much for him to be entrusted with the lives of a hundred thousand officers and soldiers at this critical juncture.

Mudaguchi himself had become elated with overconfidence, which came from his war record ranging from the Marco Polo Bridge Incident to the Battle of Singapore. His overconfidence made him believe in such a cliché as "Where there's a will, there's a way." He rejected voices of caution as cowardly argument lacking faith in victory. He firmly believed that subordinates would blindly obey commanders' orders and gladly sacrifice their lives for their country.

Undoubtedly, Mudaguchi's soldiers were patriotic enough that they were able to endure much more hardship than ordinary people. But in order for them to put up with that degree of hardship, they had to have a shared sense of comradeship and mutual trust among themselves and with their commanders. Mudaguchi, however, was not the type of commander who could inspire this kind of unit cohesiveness among his men.

Mudaguchi's personality defect becomes even clearer when he is compared to Lieutenant General Adachi Hatazō, the commander of the Eighteenth Army in New Guinea. Adachi made it a rule to stop his officers from giving soldiers unreasonably harsh orders or orders that were inappropriate in light of the real situation. Under this type of commander, soldiers would find it in their hearts to fight above and beyond the human limit even when circumstances inevitably made the task extraordinarily demanding. But none of the three division commanders under Mudaguchi trusted him. They did not have the same compassion for Mudaguchi as they would have had for Adachi. It would not be an overstatement to say that the problem of the Imphal operation comes down to this.

One anecdote about Mudaguchi goes like this. After the wretched defeat in Imphal, Mudaguchi said to his staff officer, "Now that I have caused so many of my men to lose their lives, I believe I should apologize for the defeat as their commander by disemboweling myself. I'd like to hear your candid opinion." Without even turning his face toward Mudaguchi, the staff officer replied, "Those who publicly declare that they will commit suicide rarely do so. If you do feel responsible for the defeat, disembowel yourself without uttering a word. There is no one to stop you. Actually, your misjudgments in the current operation deserve much more atonement than that." Having half expected that his staff officer would try to dissuade him from killing himself, Mudaguchi walked away crestfallen.

Compare this glimpse of Mudaguchi's character with Adachi's character. As I have written, Adachi always said, "Once a man is determined to kill himself, he can do it no matter what"—and then Adachi did exactly as he had said. On the other hand, Mudaguchi was an ordinary, successful military bureaucrat. He was not endowed with the insight to the deep realities of a war or a man's life beyond such clichés as "resolve to secure a victory at any cost" or "in defiance of death." Nor did Mudaguchi have a philosophy or conviction about life and death. Mudaguchi's tragedy, thus, was that of an ordinary man who had to assume and failed to live up to his heavy responsibility for the lives of tens of thousands of men.

There may have been countless other tragedies during the Greater East Asia War in which officers and soldiers were given similar inhumane tasks by mundane commanders who were only good at repeating clichés even at moments of life and death. And this has been a cause of the war-weariness still prevalent among the Japanese people who lived through the Greater East Asia War.

The Battle of Imphal also left behind many other anecdotes. Lieutenant General Satō Noriyuki, commander of the Imperial Japanese Army 31st Division, first evacuated 2,000 sick and wounded soldiers from the front, and subsequently ordered a complete withdrawal in defiance of Mudaguchi's order. Satō confided to his senior officers that "since Mudaguchi and the headquarters of the Fifteenth Army are degrading themselves by forcing the soldiers to work and starve to their death, I intend to remedy the situation immediately at the risk of my own life." His decision saved the lives of 10,000 men under his command who would otherwise have been annihilated. For a division commander to ignore army orders was a serious offense worthy of the death penalty. But Satō requested a court martial so that he could openly condemn Mudaguchi's imprudent operations. The Imperial Japanese Army decided not to rock the boat and instead declared Satō mentally ill and transfered him to the first reserve.

Upon the withdrawal of Satō's division, Lieutenant General Miyazaki Shigesaburō was assigned to command the covering force. He was the commander of a regiment that remained the only unbeaten force during the Nomonhan Incident in 1939. He had also achieved a brilliant victory at the early stage of the Battle of Imphal. With only 600 troops under his command, Miyazaki succeeded in blocking the advance of two British infantry divisions and a tank division for two weeks. It was only after all the dead were buried and the injured retrieved that 420 survivors under his command retreated in an orderly manner. Because of his conduct and the way he fought, Miyazaki still enjoys the honor of being lauded as one of the great commanders during the Greater East Asia War even today.

The "True Victor" on Iwo Jima

The United States advanced toward Japan via two different routes. The troops under Fleet Admiral Chester Nimitz, which took the northern route along the Pacific islands, launched an attack on the Mariana Islands in June 1944. The Mariana Islands, which include Saipan and Guam islands, were a stronghold for Japan in the inner South Pacific. From the viewpoint of the Japanese strategy, an enemy advance to the Mariana Islands would present Japan with a golden opportunity to intercept and annihilate their forces.

As a matter of fact, the Combined Fleet of the Imperial Japanese Navy countered Nimitz's fleet with everything it had. Nimitz also deployed all of its fighting vessels to the Pacific to fight this decisive battle, creating a situation the Japanese side had long hoped for. Unfortunately for the Japanese side, however, by that time, U.S. military power had become overwhelmingly superior to that of Japan. In terms of the number of fighting vessels alone, the American side had three times as many vessels. In order to win this fight, the Japanese side had no other choice than to mobilize all of its remaining air power. But the Japanese side was also overwhelmingly inferior in terms of the number of aircraft. Much more detrimental to the Japanese side was the lack of proficient pilots who had been hastily trained after the loss of veteran pilots during the Battles of Midway and the Solomon Sea, while the skills and experience of American pilots continued to grow. As a result, the Japanese side suffered a crushing defeat in the Mariana Islands, losing almost all of its remaining aircraft carriers. Soon thereafter, Saipan was captured by the United States. This defeat cast doubt on Prime Minister Tōjō's capability to lead the war, forcing him to resign in July.

Meanwhile, MacArthur's troops at last passed through New Guinea and invaded Leyte Island of the Philippine Archipelago in October 1944. Here too, the Imperial Japanese Navy encountered the U.S. troops with all its remaining naval vessels, including battleships. With command of the air in the enemy's hands, however, Japanese vessels became easy targets of the U.S. aircrafts one after another. After these naval battles off Mariana and Leyte, the Combined Fleet of the Imperial Japanese Navy, which had reigned over the East Asian seas for half a century, was effectively annihilated.

Subsequently, MacArthur's force advanced from Leyte to Luzon, by which time it had become clear that the United States intended to directly attack Okinawa and Japan's mainland. It was more or less predictable to observers that the next target of the U.S. forces would be Iwo Jima, which, if taken, would provide a relay point for U.S. aircraft.

Iwo Jima is situated just about halfway along the 2,500 kilometer route between Mariana and Tokyo. Although it became possible for the U.S. side to launch strategic bombings on mainland Japan after the invasion of Saipan, the distance restricted the amount of bombs each bomber could carry due to limited fuel consumption. Also, because the distance was too great for bombers to be protected by fighters, the United States suffered heavy losses each time the bombers flew. Thus, it wasn't until after the seizure of Iwo Jima that the United States was able to bomb major Japanese cities as it wished. In fact, many Japanese cities were burnt to ashes by U.S. bombers from Iwo Jima.

General Kuribayashi Tadamichi, commander of the Iwo Jima garrison, had long judged that the next target of the U.S. forces would be Iwo Jima. Kuribayashi believed that the task given to his garrison was to "restrict the enemy" in such a way that the "Combined Fleet of the Imperial Japanese Navy would be able to slap the enemy forces in the face."

Newly arrived Major Horie Yoshitaka, Kuribayashi's staff officer, was well informed about the true conditions of the Imperial Navy. Horie briefed Kuribayashi on the war in detail, saying, "Your Excellency, the Combined Fleet no longer exists. On June 19 (the day when the task force of the Imperial Japanese Navy was annihilated off the Mariana Islands), both the Combined Fleet and Empire of Japan died." Kuribayashi lamented, "Ah, I knew none of these things."

Horie continued, "If each one of us can take down ten enemies before being killed, the world will acknowledge that we are the true winner of the war." This was Horie's way of telling Kuribayashi that he no longer believed in the chance for Japan to win the war. Horie added, "Personally, I am ready to die" and showed Kuribayashi a packet of cyanide.

Perhaps contemporary Japanese who have been able to indulge in peace would find it hard to understand what Horie meant by "the true winner." It is an expression that refers to a man's true value and to the criterion used to judge whether such value has been realized in the face of one's inevitable death.

Perhaps the sentiment of Xiang Yu, a prominent military leader and political figure in the 3rd century B.C. China, can be found in what Horie referred to as "the true winner." When Xiang Yu had lost all but 28 men, he declared, "I have never lost any of the some 70 battles in which I have engaged. I have been cornered into the current situation not by my own mis-handling of the battle but by heaven's will. To prove it, I will break the enemy's blockade and kill its commander." After doing exactly what he had declared, Xiang Yu killed himself by slitting his throat by the Wu River.

In the case of Iwo Jima, it was not entirely meaningless for the Japa-nese garrison to fight to the end. The better it fought, the longer the time it could buy for Japan to prepare its defense on the mainland. Nevertheless, it was a war that was destined to be lost sooner or later.

Horie's "true winner" remark must have been a way to refer to a com-petition between the Japanese and the U.S. sides with regard to command-ers' leadership and the troops' fighting capabilities.

The superiority of Japanese patriotism over American patriotism was another area of competition. Horie's "true winner" remark was meant to encourage Japanese officers and soldiers to be proud of themselves and their country as the winner.

Yamanashi Katsunoshin, one of the most outstanding persons of culture in the Imperial Japanese Navy and later president of Gakushuin University after his retirement from the Navy, had long wondered uneasily whether "the death of Japanese youths during the Greater East Asia War, includ-ing those who flew kamikaze missions, was nothing but a sacrifice wasted away." One day after the war, Yamanashi happened to hear someone say, "Americans do not think the Japanese people are the losers. They are well aware of the real worth of the Japanese." According to his memoir, the remark made Yamanashi think, "Although the Japanese were defeated on the battlefield, spiritually the Japanese were not beaten at all. I have never heard anything more pleasing or gratifying before." Beneath this comment was Yamanashi's own conviction of the "true winner."

Hearing Horie's debriefing, Kuribayashi must have made up his mind. Now that the Imperial Combined Fleet no longer existed and there was lit-tle, if any, chance for Japan to win the war, all he had to care about was how to accomplish his true value as a warrior and as a man. At this stage of the war, it was not only Kuribayashi but also many Japanese officers and soldiers who had to fight and die under this resolution. About a month before the U.S. attack on Iwo Jima, Kuribayashi wrote a letter to his wife, forbidding her to pray for his safe return. The letter said, "Although my remains will not return to Japan, my spirit will come back to where you and our children are. I pray that you will live long to take care of our children."

Having been stationed in Japanese embassies in the United States and Canada earlier in his career, Kuribayashi was an elite in the Imperial Japanese Army who was appointed to regimental commander earlier than any one of his classmates (Army Academy's 26th class). He was also endowed with literary talent. *Aiba Shingun-ka* (Cavalier's March), to which he contributed the lyrics based on his experience as a cavalryman, was one of the most popular military songs during the Greater East Asia War. To introduce its third verse:

> In the midst of a shower of bullets
> I was able to cross the muddy stream on your back
> After I accomplished my task
> I gave fodder to you with tears of appreciation

This was a masterpiece, expressing a cavalryman's deep affection for his beloved horse with soldier-like simplicity and straightforwardness.

In another, relatively unknown work, *Akatsuki ni Inoru* (Prayer at Dawn), Kuribayashi wrote,

> I see in breaks of remote clouds
> Flags that my wife and children waved
> Wishing for my distinguished service to my country
> With faces and voices that I can recall vividly

> On board a magnificent transport ship
> I bid farewell to my motherland
> May my country flourish
> I pledge my resolve to the distant sky over the Imperial Palace

Reciting this song with the feeling of how Lieutenant General Kuribayashi fought and died in Iwo Jima, we are overwhelmed by a flood of emotions. This was not a mere patriotic propaganda song. It was filled with the genuine feelings of Kuribayashi, the poet.

Before constructing his Iwo Jima defense strategies, Kuribayashi thoroughly studied the tactics the U.S. military had used in battles in the Pacific islands. Kuribayashi tenaciously followed his strategies until the end.

One of the strategies was to have Japanese batteries refrain from opening fire until the enemy force made some headway after landing on the island. Hitherto, the Japanese strategy had been a traditional "shoreline defense" based on Sun Tzu's teaching: "When an invading force crosses a river in its onward march, . . . it will be best to let half the army get across, and then deliver your attack." If this strategy had been adopted, as was the case in Saipan, the enemy side would have learned the location of Japanese batteries and garrisons, which could then be totally annihilated by the enemy's naval gunfire. This strategy would have forced the Japanese troops to lose tactical sustainability. If, instead, batteries open fire after enemy troops come close to the defense line, the enemy must hold off on its naval bombardments so as not to harm its own troops.

In sum, Kuribayashi's tactic was to damage the enemy forces by initially concentrating fire after they had landed. Then he would have his garrisons retire to the northern hillside, from which they would engage in a protracted battle.

Iwo Jima was full of natural caves. Kuribayashi instructed his men to dig underground tunnels some ten meters below the surface to connect these natural caves. The caves were extremely hot and the level of carbon monoxide and sulfur gas was so high that soldiers had to wear gas masks when digging the tunnels. Despite these and other difficulties, Kuribayashi's men managed to complete an underground network of some 18 kilometers of tunnels in six months. By New Year's Day of 1945, all 20,000 troops went underground to await the enemy raid.

Almost all of Kuribayashi's predictions were proven to be accurate. His battle plans outmaneuvered the U.S. military, which had been familiar with the traditional tactics of the Japanese side.

Before the U.S. Marines landed on Iwo Jima, they launched a heavy naval bombardment, showering as many as 7,500 tons of shells on February 19 alone. The U.S. side expected the Japanese side to have incurred tremendous damage from the bombardment, but it actually did little more than stir up a tremendous amount of sand because all the Japanese defenders had hidden themselves deep underground.

The only thing that went wrong in Kuribayashi's plans was when the naval batteries stationed on Mount Suribachi in the south of the island fired prematurely at the enemy vessels. While this firing naturally inflicted considerable damage on U.S. forces, it revealed the location of the naval batteries, which were destroyed by the enemy's concentrated fire. This loss weakened the sustainability of the Mount Suribachi defense, undermining the overall plan to launch a pincer attack against the enemy landing parties from batteries situated in the north and south of the island.

The loss of some of the batteries at the initial stage of the battle notwithstanding, the reserve troops stationed on Mount Suribachi put up a respectable resistance for three days and nights. After the war, a statue depicting the U.S. Marines raising the Stars and Stripes on the top of Mount Suribachi was erected adjacent to Arlington National Cemetery (just outside of Washington, D.C.), the home of the Tomb of the Unknowns, to commemorate the fiercest battle in World War II.

Meanwhile, the Japanese batteries in the north remained completely silent, faithfully following Kuribayashi's order. After the U.S. troops advanced some 450 meters inland, the batteries opened fire at the enemy, instantly killing and injuring 25 percent of the Marines and destroying 28 tanks, or 50 percent of the total. This created pandemonium. Furthermore, Japan's newly deployed rocket mortars were launched at the advancing U.S. Marines. The loud blasts and high lethality terrified the American forces. The situation was exactly how it was described in the record of the U.S. side, which said, "The first night on Iwo Jima can only be described as that of hellish terror."

At night, the U.S. side prepared against the traditional Japanese night raids. Kuribayashi, however, strictly prohibited his men from committing suicidal attacks and instead ordered a small number of troops armed with hand grenades to raid U.S. ammunition/gasoline storages. These raids achieved outstanding results that once again caused chaos on the U.S. side.

The U.S. side had originally intended to occupy Iwo Jima in one fell swoop by landing a massive force of three divisions and 600 tanks with the help of 600 vessels on February 19. It intended to finish the mission by February 23 so that it could start launching the Okinawa operations. In reality, however, what the U.S. Marines managed to accomplish by February 23 was "only" the capture of Mount Suribachi. They still had to advance north to confront Kuribayashi's full-scale resistance.

Having installed triple defense lines, the Japanese side put up fierce resistance each time the U.S. Marines approached these lines, just as it had demonstrated during the earlier battle on the beach. On Byobu Iwa, hand-to-hand combat lasted three days, during which time the U.S. side captured the site six times only for it to be retaken by the Japanese side five times. At the battle on Nidan Iwa, a 1,000-strong U.S. battalion was annihilated with 990 of its troops either killed or injured.

American newspapers started to criticize the U.S. Marines operations, stating, "If this type of battle goes on, our forces will be exhausted before they reach Japan." Dealt a heavy blow by the Japanese, Nimitz even contemplated the use of poison gas. President Roosevelt, however, rejected the idea because Britain opposed the use of poison gas in fear of Hitler's retaliation. The last guarantee of international law is power. The bombing of Dresden, which was the precursor to the non-discriminatory bombings of Tokyo, Hiroshima, and Nagasaki, was launched only after Germany lost its capability to retaliate. Before Nimitz died, he deplored the restriction on the use of poison gas, saying, "I lost a tremendous number of outstanding Marines because of this ban on poison gas."

Meanwhile, Kuribayashi constantly reported to the Imperial General Headquarters on the progress of the battle in detail, including data on enemy's tactics. Kuribayashi's estimate of damages inflicted on the U.S. side was so accurate that there was only some ten percent difference from the U.S. documents.

To no one's surprise, true to their image, the U.S. Marines continued to attack relentlessly. In an effort to prevail against the Japanese military at its own game, they launched a grand night raid on March 3, perhaps the only one during the Pacific War, leading to several heroic stories.

While the three U.S. divisions alternately attacked the Japanese troops, the same Japanese defenders had to deal with the raid without sleeping or resting. Knowing the Japanese troops must have been at the end of their strength, the U.S. side prepared itself for the "banzai attack" that the Japanese troops were known to resort to when they were at the end of their rope. Kuribayashi's operation, nevertheless, remained unchanged.

Both sides continued to fight face to face with hand grenades, the Japanese side attacking from the caves and the U.S. Marines from the trenches. By that time, however, the Japanese side had run out of water to the extent that soldiers were unable to eat the remaining dry bread rations because they were unable to salivate.

Finally, on March 16, Kuribayashi invited surviving senior officers to a banquet as a last farewell. After thanking his officers for their long and selfless services, Kuribayashi personally led the final all-out attack on March 17.

In the morning of March 17, Kuribayashi sent the following final telegram to Tokyo before the last all-out attack:

> . . . The gallant fight that officers and soldiers under my command have put up since the enemy's attack would have made even devils weep . . . Now that we are completely out of ammunition and water, we are about to make a last charge at the enemy . . . We are determined to be a vanguard in the renewed attack of the Imperial Army even if we ourselves are already dead spirits by then. Praying for the final victory and security of our homeland, I wish to bid an eternal farewell . . .

At the end of the telegram, Kuribayashi added two *tanka* poems:

> It saddens me to run out of ammunition
> And perish
> Before accomplishing heavy duties for my country

And:

> Soldiers who fell before avenging fellow warriors
> Decaying in the fields
> Will resurrect seven times and rise in arms

Lieutenant General Holland Smith, commander of Task Force 56 in the Battle of Iwo Jima, instructed his men to look for Kuribayashi's remains so that the brave enemy commander could be given a proper burial. The search was in vain. As a matter of fact, after the all-out attack, Kuribayashi moved to another cave and sent a telegram to the general headquarters, pledging, "We intend to continue our resistance until the very last minute."

True to his words, Kuribayashi continued to fight yet for ten more days, rejecting surrender, before he died on March 27. There was no survivor who could tell with certainty whether Kuribayashi was killed in battle or killed himself. In appreciation of Kuribayashi's outstanding accomplishments, Imperial Japanese Army Headquarters promoted him to a full general on March 21, an honor understandably unknown to Kuribayashi himself.

Colonel Baron Nishi Takeichi, a tank unit commander, had been an Olympic Gold Medalist in the individual show jumping competition in the 1932 Summer Olympics in Los Angeles. Leading 300 soldiers under his command, Nishi charged at the enemy day in and day out until, at 10 o'clock in the evening on March 17, he reached a cliff in the north of Iwo Jima with fifteen surviving men. Hearing the U.S. military's appeal for him to surrender—"Baron Nishi, please come out"—Nishi just smiled and killed himself.

By the end of the battle, the 21,000 strong Japanese garrison had been nearly annihilated. Casualties on the U.S. side totaled 29,000 (of which 7,000 lost their lives), making it the only battle during the Pacific War in which American casualties exceeded those of the Japanese.

For the Sake of International Justice and Peace

Prior to the last all-out attack on March 17, Rear Admiral Ichimaru Rinosuke, the commander of the Imperial Japanese Navy in Iwo Jima, recited his personal letter addressed to U.S. President Roosevelt in the cave of the navy headquarters.

Declaring at the outset that, "At the end of the current battle, this is the last word I am sending to Your Excellency," Ichimura in summary wrote as follows:

> Although you have harbored a unilateral prejudice against Japan, calling us a yellow peril and using the attack on Pearl Harbor in war propaganda against Japan, I believe that the world knows that the Japanese have been fighting this war in order to save their country from peril. We, the Japanese, are by nature peace-loving people.
> Emperor Meiji's poem, "I wonder why there is trouble, even

though all the countries overseas in all directions are considered to be brothers and sisters in the world" had deeply moved your uncle President Theodore Roosevelt. And it was in the spirit of this poem that we took our arms. Even though material inferiority may have made it appear as if we were in a disadvantageous position in the war, we are spiritually overjoyed and enjoying immense peace of mind.

Here, by way of pitying your spiritual weakness, allow me to point out one or two things.

The Caucasians, particularly the Anglo-Saxon people, have attempted to monopolize the world's wealth at the sacrifice of the colored races. The birth of the Greater East Asian Co-prosperity Sphere will contribute to the realization of the world's peace. Why, then, should the United States, an already prosperous power under Your Excellency's command, obstruct the Oriental peoples' attempt at retrieving the Orient for themselves?

One more thing. From our viewpoint, it is extremely bizarre for Your Excellency, who has adamantly denounced Hitler, to collaborate with the Soviet Union under Stalin.

If it were only violence that dominates the world, wars would be endlessly repeated and the world would never experience peace or happiness.

This letter of protest was later discovered in Iwo Jima by an American soldier, and it is now stored in the museum of the U.S. Naval Academy in Annapolis. It did not reach Roosevelt, who died himself the following month in April 1945.

This letter is testimony to the fact that the Japanese military did not fight solely for the glory of the Empire of Japan and the Emperor. The Japanese military was also convinced that it had been fighting a right war for international justice and peace.

While a rather long quote, I wish to emphasize that the Japanese in those days had been fighting the war convinced that they had a moral position. I believe that the above letter helps explain it.

White races had been enjoying prosperity at the sacrifice of the colored races. The Greater East Asia War was fought to liberate Asia from domination by the white races. Why should Britain, which already possessed affluent spheres of influence, obstruct Asian peoples' attempt at retrieving Asia for themselves? Why should the United States, an already prosperous power under President Roosevelt's command, obstruct the Oriental peoples' attempt at retrieving the Orient for themselves? The Greater East Asia War is a war of self-defense that Japan was cornered into waging. So goes the logic.

Any nation or any man strives hard to pursue its own/his own interest. A nation's conduct can never be 100 percent right or 100 percent wrong.

It makes me wonder, though, if Japan believed in this logic, why it did not implement a strategy of trying to convince the world, particularly the American public.

Here, I must conclude that the attack on Pearl Harbor is to blame for everything.

In terms of tactics alone, there was no need for Japan to achieve its aims by attacking Pearl Harbor. In light of the supremacy of the Japanese naval air capabilities, which were the best in the world at the beginning of the war, Japan would have been able to accomplish military achievements similar to those of the naval battle off Malaya if the Combined Fleet of the Imperial Japanese Navy had confronted the American battleships off the Marshall Islands, following a conventional battle plan. In terms of the overall results of the series of battles, including that of the Battle of Midway, it might have been more advantageous to Japan to have taken this option.

But, more than anything else, it was indiscrete of Japan to take on the clear and simple responsibility of being the party that had launched the first assault by attacking Pearl Harbor.

It is beyond doubt that all of Rear Admiral Ichimaru's arguments would have become points of contention within the United States had Japan made the Hull note public and declared war openly with an ultimatum of 24 hours.

To begin with, Japan and the United States are separated by the Pacific Ocean and, as a point of common sense, it would not be possible for the two countries to fight a war.

When Vice Minister of Navy Suzuki Kantarō, who later became Prime Minister of Japan at the end of World War II, led a training squadron to the United States in 1918 (7th Year of Taishō), he made the following comment in San Francisco:

The Japanese would not surrender even if Japan's naval fleets are defeated. Should that happen, the Japanese will fight on the ground, which would make the United States suffer the loss of a few hundred-thousand to a few million lives. What good would it be for the United States if it could gain only a territory the size of the state of California at the expense of such heavy sacrifice? Japanese troops, on the other hand, would not be able to cross the Rocky Mountains to reach Washington, D.C., even if they landed on the United States mainland. Thus, the Pacific Ocean is truly a sea of peace. If either Japan or the United States dares to sail out their respective military transport ships in this Pacific Ocean, it would be punished by heaven.

Suzuki was completely correct as proven in the following events.

It is not hard to imagine how the American public and the Congress would have reacted to the desperate struggles in Iwo Jima and Okinawa as well as to the sacrifice of so many young American lives as reported daily, if the Americans knew that Japan had been provoked by Roosevelt to start a reckless war. It would have been impossible for the United States to continue the war any further.

As it turned out, the brave fight put up by the Japanese warriors in Iwo Jima made such a strong impression on the American leadership that the participation of the Soviet Union in the war and the use of atomic bombs against Japan were absolutely imperative. This brought indescribable suffering to the citizens of Hiroshima and Nagasaki as well as Japanese residents in Manchuria and Sakhalin.

Unquestionably, the warriors of Iwo Jima who had done their very best are not to be blamed. Had the basic strategy been a sound one, their bravery could have saved their homeland from being ruined by air raids. However, the fact is that the better the Japanese warriors fought, the more miseries their prowess brought to Japan. And all of this should be attributed to the fault of Japan's basic strategy.

CHAPTER
16

This War Must End

—Fifty Years of Glory Perish Like a Bubble—

Bloody Battle on Okinawa

Space does not allow me to describe in detail the battle in the Philippines or the bravery demonstrated by the Japanese warriors in Okinawa. Knowing how patriotically and competently each and every Japanese soldier fought in those battlefields, I feel urged to appease the souls of the brave warriors by devoting a few pages here to mark down how they fought.

However, both of these battles lasted for a few months in battlefields that were much broader in scope than Iwo Jima. As such, it would be simply impossible to elaborate the noble deeds exerted by the Japanese warriors in the current volume. It is my hope that my description of the battle in Iwo Jima in the preceding chapter would enable readers to understand how valiantly Japanese troops must have fought in the Philippines and Okinawa.

To briefly summarize the strategic significance of the battle in the Philippines, the defeat in Luzon severed Japan's communication with the regions rich in natural resources in Southeast Asia. After this defeat, every time Japan dispatched transport ships to retrieve natural resources, the ships were inevitably sunk by U.S. aircraft. The exhaustion of Japan's military capability was now a matter of time. It was around this time that

Japanese leaders began to think that Japan could not endure the war any longer.

The battle of Okinawa was, from the U.S. perspective, no longer an attempt to expel the Japanese troops from the occupied areas; it was an integral part of the U.S. plan to invade and occupy mainland Japan. The first target of the plan was Iwo Jima, which was to be followed by Okinawa and, eventually, Kyūshū.

On the other hand, Japan's preparation for the battle in Okinawa had not been consistent. The elite 9th Division, which had been stationed in northern Manchuria against possible attack by the Soviet army, was initially dispatched to Okinawa, but was subsequently relocated to Taiwan because the Imperial Japanese Army Headquarters was unable to determine what the next U.S. target would be—Taiwan or Okinawa. This raveled the Japanese battle plan. Some say that had the 9th Division remained in Okinawa, the U.S. invasion of Okinawa would not have been successful.

Nevertheless, Japanese garrisons in Okinawa endured enemy attacks for three long months, inflicting a loss of approximately 65,000 American troops. This bought time for Japan to prepare the defense of its mainland. By way of praising the extreme efforts exerted by the Japanese troops in Okinawa, allow me to quote a paragraph from Churchill's memoir on World War II. Churchill was relieved when he received news of the success of the nuclear testing on July 17, 1945:

> Up to this moment we had shaped our ideas towards an assault upon homeland of Japan by terrific air bombing and by invasion of very large armies. We had contemplated the desperate resistance of the Japanese fighting to the death with Samurai devotion, not only in pitched battles, but in every cave and dug-out. I had in my mind the spectacle of Okinawa island, where many thousands of Japanese, rather than surrender, had drawn up in line and destroyed themselves by hand-grenades after their leaders had solemnly performed the rite of *hara-kiri*. To quell the Japanese resistance man by man and conquer the country yard by yard might well require the loss of a million American lives and half that number of British—or more if we could get them there: for we were resolved to share the agony. Now all this nightmare picture had vanished. In this place was the vision—fair

and bright indeed it seemed—of the end of the whole war in one or two violent shocks. I thought immediately myself of how the Japanese people, whose courage I had always admired, might find in the apparition of this almost supernatural weapon an excuse which could save their honour and release them from their obligation of being killed to the last fighting man.[21]

Hearing of the successful nuclear test, Churchill told Foreign Secretary Anthony Eden that participation by the Soviet Union in the war was no longer necessary. But, unbeknownst to Churchill, it was already too late to stop the Soviet participation.

Two facts about the battle in Okinawa merit special attention.

First, it should be noted that the battle was the first defensive battle fought on Japanese territory. At that time, anyone who was capable of fighting or engaging in work participated, directly or indirectly, in the battle. The elderly and children, along with their female caretakers, on the other hand, were evacuated beforehand to the northern region of the island.

The battle required combat readiness throughout all of Okinawa. Imposition of martial law, which would grant full authority to the military commander, was considered. However, because citizens in Okinawa would not hesitate to fight until death, just like any other Japanese at the time, and because the prefectural government as well as every local government in Okinawa were fully cooperative, martial law was found unnecessary. Thus, the civilian administration in Okinawa was retained, and the military and civilians fought together hand in hand.

Rear Admiral Ōta Minoru, the Imperial Navy Commander in Okinawa, and Shimada Akira, who had in January bravely assumed the post of Governor of Okinawa that nobody wished to take (not so much because it was a dangerous post but simply because it was off the career track), became comrades with total respect for each other. At times, Ōta reported on the situation in Okinawa to Tokyo via the Ministry of Navy upon the request of Governor Shimada.

---

21   Winston Churchill. *The Second World War and An Epilogue on the Years 1945 to 1957: Abridged Edition*. (London: Cassell & Co. 1959), p. 940.

Once the battle began, however, this peacetime administrative structure inevitably collapsed. While those who evacuated to the north of the island were unharmed, many of those who had run south in the midst of the confusion were victimized. Also, as demonstrated in Imphal, there must have been a number of cases in which Japanese officers and soldiers were unnecessarily wasted by mundane leaders who were obsessed only with such a fixed concept as "faith in victory."

The number of local conscripts was estimated to be at around 35,000 civilians. Underage children over 12 years old were mobilized as well—boys to provide non-combatant assistance as members of the *Tekketsu Kinnotai* (Student Units of Blood and Iron for the Emperor) and girls to act as military nurses.

Rear Admiral Ōta left a detailed note on the situation on the island in his farewell telegram on June 6, 1945. Poor communication conditions made some portions of the note illegible, but let me introduce the gist of this telegram:

> While it is the duty of the prefectural governor to report on the conditions of the Okinawa citizens, there exists no available means for communication. The headquarters of the 32nd Army [Imperial Japanese Army defending Okinawa] does not seem to have enough communication capabilities to spare, either. I feel compelled to report on the conditions in Okinawa, although I am not requested to do so by the governor. I do not have the heart to let the situation in Okinawa go unknown to others.

> Since the beginning of the battle on Okinawa, both the Imperial Army and Navy have been totally devoted to the defense of the island, so much so that we have hardly had time to pay attention to its people.

> As far as I can tell, however, all male youths and adults in Okinawa have responded fully to the call-up for military service. The remaining elders, children, and women, having lost their houses to enemy bombing, are exposed to the harsh elements of nature and are forced into hiding in underground shelters which are located in areas that would not hamper the military operations.

> Young women have devoted themselves to nursing and cooking

for the military. They even carried ammunition and joined the volunteer corps to attack the enemy.

Volunteer nurses stayed behind even when the military including the medics were transferred, and took care of the seriously injured soldiers who were left behind. This conduct must have come from their sincere compassion. I do not think they were merely driven by transitory emotion. . . .

In sum, ever since the Imperial Japanese Army and Navy were stationed in Okinawa, local people have continued to serve with sincerity [illegible character which might be "sincerity," "pride," or "commitment"] in spite of the constant demand on their labor and frugality (while, admittedly, there were a few cases of complaints.) [Following fifteen illegible characters.] The true conditions of Okinawa toward the last stage of the battle were . . . [six illegible characters].

Okinawa will be burnt to the ground, every stick and stone of it. The island will be out of food by the end of June.

This is how Okinawa's citizens have fought the war.

For this reason, it is my sincere hope that special consideration be given to the citizens of Okinawa in days to come.

In a battlefield, everyone is requested to devote any and all available time and energy for the sake of winning the battle. Thus, the very act of sending such a lengthy telegram could have been criticized as an unnecessary waste of resources. This fact alone demonstrated the depth of Ōta's determination to leave an account for future generations to truly understand the conditions of the Okinawa people at the time.

The so-called Okinawa problem, which still haunts Japan today, is part of a larger problem of not having settled the issues of the Greater East Asia War and those who sacrificed their lives in the war.

Until the first years of Meiji, it had been unclear to which suzerainty Okinawa belonged. Judging from its linguistic structure, however, it was beyond doubt that Okinawa was an integral part of Japan. In fact, during the Greater East Asia War, people in Okinawa willingly devoted their lives to their country out of their desire to serve as Japanese. It is this Okinawa that was occupied by the United States like a colony for a quarter of a century after the war, even after mainland Japan obtained its independence. Okinawa has long suffered from a sense of alienation during postwar times.

The criticism that Okinawa, the fourth smallest prefecture in Japan, has been burdened with 70 percent of the U.S. military bases stationed in Japan is based on the logic that represents only one aspect of the issue. There are regions in Japan that have supported American military bases, appreciating their significance and, more positively, enjoying their economic value. Yokosuka, headquarters of the U.S. 7th Fleet, is one such region. Behind the one-dimensional interpretation of the presence of U.S. military bases to be a burden and sacrifice for Japan—which ignores their significance for Japan's security as a whole—I detect the influence of the Cold-War anti–military base, anti–U.S.-Japan Security Pact, and anti-U.S. leftist propaganda.

I do not deny the existence of a military base problem in Okinawa. The issue was closely associated with the Okinawan's anger over the absence of understanding, respect, and sympathy on the part of the people in mainland Japan about the history of Okinawa. Okinawans want mainland Japanese to truly recognize that Okinawa is the only region in Japan that had put up a united military-government-citizen fight against the invading enemy, that Okinawa was put under U.S. military occupation until long after the end of the war, and that it still has the highest concentration of U.S. military bases in Japan.

After the end of World War II, there was a prolonged period during which the mood throughout Japan was unsympathetic toward anything military. Furthermore, while the heroic fight that Okinawa's people had put up was not unknown to the Japanese, everyone in Japan in those days was too busy worrying about his or her own life. Nobody could afford to sympathize with others. And this was not only in regard to the people in Okinawa.

Now that everyone in Japan is enjoying immense prosperity, it is high time that every Japanese starts considering how he or she can honor the contributions made by the people of Okinawa spiritually at the very least.

A spiritual settlement of the Okinawa problem would become possible only when all Japanese people learn to sympathize with the people of Okinawa with the same or even deeper intensity than that with which they remember Yasukuni Shrine, kamikaze pilots, and bereaved families of the war dead. The final settlement of the Okinawa problem can be reached when Rear Admiral Ōta's last wish for special considerations for the people of Okinawa is sincerely carried out in an acceptable way for the Okinawans.

Oh, Falling Cherry Blossoms! Remaining Cherry Blossoms to Follow Shortly

Another distinctive feature of the battle in Okinawa was the frequent use of suicide attacks.

Also used literally in English, *"kamikaze,"* or the suicide attack, is a well-known tactic employed in the battle in Okinawa. Kamikaze sank 36 American vessels, damaged as many as 368 vessels (number of hits), and killed/injured a total of 4,907 U.S. naval personnel, according to American records. Some American officers/soldiers became so completely weary of the round-the-clock suicide attacks that they complained that they could not continue to fight.

The idea of the suicide attack emerged and evolved gradually as battles became increasingly fierce.

Even before the Battle of Okinawa, there had already been countless suicide attacks in earlier battles. Quite a number of Japanese pilots flew into enemy ships in battles in the South Pacific. Once their aircraft were hit and caught fire, the pilots chose to die by making their aircraft themselves weapons, realizing they had no chance to survive.

As the war situation became more and more unfavorable for Japan, there were increasing cases of individual pilots sacrificing their lives on their own judgment in pursuit of military achievement. In the case of the Imperial Japanese Army, quite a number of soldiers armed themselves with explosives and charged at enemy tanks. During the Formosa Air Battle, Rear Admiral Arima Masafumi, who led an attack against U.S. Navy Task Force 38, personally set an example of sinking an enemy ship single-handedly by crashing his aircraft into a vessel. He had realized that the Japanese side had no chance of winning the battle by use of conventional means.

As the situation worsened even more, everyone in the Japanese military prepared themselves to die sooner or later.

Cherry Blossoms of the Same Class, the military song from the Greater East Asia War that is still sung most frequently even today, depicts the atmosphere of those days well.

(first verse)
You and I are cherry blossoms of the same class
Blooming in the yard of the same military school
A cherry blossom, once it blooms, is bound to fall inevitably
We'll fall splendidly for the motherland

(third verse)
You and I are cherry blossoms of the same class
Blooming in the yard of the same flying corps
At the evening glow on the southern sky—we look up
The first fighter has yet to return

The first fighter was flown by an ace pilot who was the squadron leader. The term, the first fighter, thus makes people think of a gallant young man filled with a sense of mission. And it was this young leader in the formation that flew south to carry out his mission in the sky over Okinawa and never returned in the dusk. He must have charged at an enemy ship.

(fifth verse)
You and I are cherry blossoms of the same year
Blooming in the yard of the same military school,
Let us meet again as blossoms in the same vernal cherry tree
Of the Yasukuni Shrine in the flourishing capital city

It was a time when everyone came to have the same frame of mind, as expressed in these words:

Oh, falling blossoms,
Remaining blossoms [himself]
Will soon be falling blossoms

Under these circumstances, technology also reflected the mood of the time. Because military aircraft had not been designed to crash into an enemy in the first place, it would be more efficient to develop a weapon that could be used for that very purpose. It was this thinking that was behind the development of Ōka (桜花), a rocket-powered human-guided anti-ship suicide attack plane carried underneath a mother airplane; *Kaiten*

(回天), a manned torpedo for suicide attacks, and *Shin'yō* (震洋), a suicide motorboat.

These weapons were designed for suicide attack missions from which no one was expected to come back alive. Nevertheless, there were such a large number of volunteers that the military had to select the crews from among them. In other words, military morale was still so high in those days that there were countless volunteers for suicide attacks. Particularly, pure and outstanding youths with a fervent sense of duty rushed to volunteer ahead of others. Thus, after the war, it was often said, "Good men died ahead of others who were first in order," by way of regretting the loss of invaluable human resources.

As death became a regular daily event, everyone in the military was expected to participate in suicide attacks without exception. By that time, volunteers were in name only, and I suspect the atmosphere was such that it would have been difficult for them to refuse when their turn came.

Perhaps the majority of kamikaze attackers accepted their fate with pleasure. While their determination moves us to tears, we cannot help but feel sorry for those youths who lost their young lives, wondering for what purpose they were sacrificing themselves.

Meanwhile, the departure of the Imperial Japanese Navy's battleship *Yamato* for Okinawa was filled with dilemmas.

The pride of the Imperial Navy, the world's largest battleship displacing more than 70,000 tons, was destined to head for Okinawa with fuel enough for a one-way voyage. Upon reaching Okinawa, it was to run aground so as to function as a gigantic battery.

As a safe passage to Okinawa was by no means guaranteed, the Imperial Japanese Army General Staff Office opposed this reckless battle plan. Even General Ushijima Mitsuru, commanding general of the 32nd Army stationed in Okinawa, was against the plan.

Fleet command of the Imperial Japanese Navy's Combined Fleet, however, carried out the plan against all opposition, saying, "Because all of the Navy's aircrafts have already been mobilized for suicide attacks, the only way the Imperial Navy can serve the nation is to employ all of its remaining vessels and cannons to the end." The Navy also stated, "The Imperial Japanese Navy would not be able to look the Japanese people in the eye if it were to preserve its battleships."

As people feared, *Yamato* became the target of intensive torpedo attack and air bombing by some 250 U.S. aircraft almost as soon as it left Kyushu. The ship was sunk in no time together with its 3,000 crew members.

This operation was no longer within the bounds of military rationality.

Author Yoshida Mitsuru, one of *Yamato*'s few survivors, recorded in his memoir an argument among *Yamato*'s officers immediately before the ship sailed:

We were on the brink of death. What was our death for? What would we accomplish and how would we be rewarded?

Sub-Lieutenants 1st Class and 2nd Class, who were graduates of the Imperial Japanese Naval Academy said unanimously, "We will die for the country and for the Emperor. I am happy to do so. What more do we need? We should rest in peace knowing we have served the country and the Emperor."

Turning red at this remark, an officer, who had been drafted when in college, refuted, "I agree with you that we are going to die for the country and the Emperor. . . . Nevertheless, I can't help but hope to find a proper value for my death, as well as the defeat of Japan as a whole. What is the deeper meaning of all of this?"

It Has to Be Stopped

What the last officer in the above argument asked was a question that must have been on everyone's mind.

On the very day that the *Yamato* sailed to Okinawa, Suzuki Kantarō completed forming his cabinet. According to his memoirs, Suzuki posed exactly the same question to himself when he looked out of the window to see the cherry blossoms in full bloom, some of which were already starting to fall,.

All the military officers wish to "die with good grace like the cherry blossoms" and "live for an eternal cause." But I wonder what this "eternal cause" means. When Japan itself is ruined, what will survive? When Carthage was ruined, where did the brave Carthaginians go, and where are they today? They are nothing but a speck of dirt today, are they not?

"It has to be stopped." That was the conviction that Suzuki felt that day.

It was truly commendable that Suzuki gave such a deep historical perspective to Japan's fate and actually acted on it. It was a perspective that never occurred to the leader of Japan's remaining ally, Hitler.

On the other hand, was the death of so many young kamikaze volunteers totally meaningless?

Judging from the rationality of the ordinary world, including military rationality, it is no longer possible to find any meaning in the suicide attacks that occurred toward the end of the Greater East Asia War. In offering prayers for the souls of those youths, we have to apply values that exist in a totally different dimension than that of the world we normally live in.

Shōwa-Heisei writer Kōsaka Jirō, who was himself an Imperial Army juvenile aviator, quoted the following two paragraphs in his work:

> I have never seen such beautiful youths before. They were almost divinely pure. (Togawa Yukio)

And,

> The measure taken by those youths who perished in this conduct [suicide attack] was horrifying. These Japanese heroes, however, presented a lesson to the world on the great value of purity. They have dug out from a 1,000-year-old past the long-forgotten value of being a great human being. (Bernard Millot)

The cherry blossoms in Edajima, where the Imperial Japanese Naval Academy was located, are still gorgeous today. The naval museum there displays farewell notes of the suicide attack volunteers. Visitors would be deeply touched and shed tears by reading them one after another.

This is no longer a matter of strategy or military rationality.

> Go tell the Spartans, stranger passing by
> That there, obedient to Spartan law, we lie

This epitaph of Simonides commemorates 300 Spartan warriors who fought bravely, not giving an inch to a massive Persian force, in the Battle of Thermopylae some 2,500 years ago. All of them perished in the battle.

Likewise, honoring the sincere motives of the kamikaze pilots may in itself be the greatest service to the deceased.

I wish to add that the commanders who led the suicide attacks also honored the kamikaze pilots. When the number of Japanese aircraft was about to touch the bottom during the Battle of Leyte Gulf, , Vice Admiral Ōnishi Takijirō resigned himself to his fate and became the first commander to officially order a kamikaze attack. On a later occasion when he had to send off another group of his men on a suicide attack, he said to them, "I will not let you die alone." True to his word, Ōnishi killed himself by disembowelment in the evening of Japan's surrender. In order to fulfill his full responsibility to the youths that he had sent to their death, he strictly prohibited people around him from calling for a doctor. Ōnishi passed away after long hours of excruciating pain.

In his suicide note, Ōnishi wrote:

> Allow me to speak to the souls of the departed war heroes. You have all fought well and I am deeply grateful to all of you . . . I wish to make compensation to the souls of heroes and their families with my own death.

> Farewell Poem

> Having done what I should have done
> I am now going to take
> A nap of one million years

In attaining spiritual peace, Ōnishi thought of nothing but leaving a testimony to the greatness of a man for the people to acknowledge one million years later.

No one in Japan by that time could have had any hope for the present. They could but look forward to the remote future.

General Ushijima Mitsuru, who committed suicide in accordance with ancient ritual at the end of the battle in Okinawa, left the following farewell poem:

Young grasses of the island
Withering before the arrival of autumn
Must sprout again in the spring of the Emperor's land

"Young grasses" here must be a metaphor for the young lives that were lost.

When the building of the Ministry of Navy in Tokyo was burned down by an air raid about a month earlier, Admiral Yamanashi Katsunoshin, an outstanding man of culture in the Imperial Navy, visited the ruins and cited the following poem by the Tang Dynasty poet Bai Juyi:

Wildfire may burn the field
But it will never end the life of the field
Which will revive with the arrival of the spring breeze

This must be the hope that everyone in Japan in those days shared. While Ōnishi killed himself after learning about the defeat of Japan, it was then their only hope that a thaw would come in the remote future, giving birth to new life.

Hell Caused by Nondiscriminatory Bombings

The bombing of Japanese cities that the U.S. Army Air Forces launched toward the end of World War II was conducted in a nondiscriminatory manner by deliberately targeting noncombatant citizens.

At the bottom of Americans' anti-fascism sentiment was their antipathy toward the massacres of noncombatant citizens that occurred during the Spanish Civil War and the Second Sino-Japanese War. In fact, when World War II broke out in Europe, U.S. President Franklin Roosevelt put out a message that such an act of barbarity as bombing on noncombatant citizens should be forbidden.

Subsequently, however, the United States introduced "an unannounced and unrecorded policy change" (John Toland) to "destroy anything that assists enemy war efforts."

As Ronald Schaffer discussed squarely in his book *Wings of Judgment: American Bombing in World War II*, it appears that there was no

Nondiscriminatory Bombings

particular point at which the U.S. policy toward bombing was changed. In the case of Germany, the United States initially targeted German military facilities specifically, but gradually resorted to so-called carpet bombing to cripple the enemy's morale. Although there was occasional skepticism within the military that nondiscriminatory bombing would be a disgrace to the U.S. Army Air Forces, those voices never developed into an effective opposition.

It should also be noted that U.S. nondiscriminatory bombings both in Germany and Japan started in 1945 when the general trend of the war had already been determined. Looking at the flip side of the coin, the U.S. policy change occurred after it no longer had to worry about enemy retaliation.

The bombing of Dresden in February 1945 and the bombing of Tokyo in March in the same year each killed about 100,000 civilians. Getting a taste of success from these experiences, the U.S. Army Air Forces bombarded Tokyo, Nagoya, Ōsaka, and Kōbe between March 10 and March 19. With each attack the air force mobilized a huge squadron composed of 300 B-29s, killing or injuring more than 200,000 citizens, and depriving 2 million people of their houses.

Subsequently, the U.S. military carried out a plan to burn down 50 percent of the houses in major Japanese cities. This was followed by another plan to burn down four local cities per one sortie. By the end of the war, U.S. bombers had bombarded 61 Japanese cities and succeeded in burning down more than 50 percent of the houses in half of the target cities. With the improvement of its incendiary bombs, the U.S. military further planned to increase the gross number of aircraft to be used per month to 6,700 after September 1945 (from 1,600 in March) in order to destroy all the remaining cities in Japan. It is horrifying to imagine what would have happened had Japan not decided to surrender on August 15.

By that time, Japan's defeat was already only a matter of time. Having secured an airfield in Okinawa that could be used freely and having surrounded Japan's coastal seas with 20 aircraft carriers, the United States was now in a position to simply torture Japan to death.

In later days, when questioned by his junior officers about the morality of nondiscriminatory bombardments of Japanese cities, Colonel Curtis LeMay, commander of the XXI Bomber Command in the Marianas who led the operation, answered, "Killing Japanese didn't bother me very much at that time. . . . all war is immoral and if you let that bother you, you're not a good soldier."

The dropping of the atomic bombs was only an extension of this thinking. Although voices of concern were heard from many corners, none of them evolved into an effective opposition. The final decision on the atomic bomb was in the hands of President Harry Truman. Referring to the attack on Pearl Harbor and to Japanese cruelty against prisoners-of-war, the president said, "This is the only language that the Japanese seem to understand."

Here, again, one can detect the effect of the blunder of attacking Pearl Harbor.

Peace Effort with Absolutely No Hope of Success

From the beginning of the Greater East Asia War, when the entire nation was elated by the victories in initial battles, Foreign Minister Tōgō Shigenori had sought an early peace settlement. His efforts were subsequently pursued by his successor Shigemitsu Mamoru. It would be fruitless, however, to trace his efforts in this chapter, because, realistically, there was no chance of success.

Anticipating that isolated Germany would end up fighting single-handedly against Britain, the United States, France, and Russia as it had done during World War I, Tōgō became convinced that "the center of the diplomatic battle in the current war is the contest for the Soviet Union, and I regard this as the ultimate battle of Japanese diplomacy. With Germany and the Soviet Union already at war against one another, however, it would have been extremely difficult to entice the Soviet Union to join the Japanese side. Thus Foreign Minister Tōgō was forced to pursue a peace settlement between Germany and Soviet Union.

In order to realize a German-Soviet peace at the time when Germany remained dominant, Tōgō tried to arrange a settlement before the scheduled German offensive in 1942. Germany, however, demanded Japan's participation in the war against the Soviet Union instead. Unfortunately, before the scheme for German-Soviet peace showed any progress, Foreign Minister Tōgō left the cabinet of Prime Minister Tōjō Hideki.

Although Shigemitsu, who succeeded Tōgō as foreign minister, adopted the same line, the Soviet Union expressed its adamant refusal of a peace settlement with Germany.

The Soviet Union had already expressed its intention of joining the war against Japan after defeating Germany at the Teheran Conference in November 1943. At the Yalta Conference in February 1945, Stalin committed himself to participating in the war against Japan within two or three months after the end of the war against Germany on condition that southern Sakhalin and the Kuril Islands be conceded to the Soviet Union. The secret agreements reached between Churchill, Roosevelt, and Stalin in Yalta were kept so secret that even President Truman was surprised to find the official documents in Roosevelt's safe after his death. Having no way to know about these secret agreements, Japan continued to place its hope on the Soviet mediation of peace with the United States. There was no sign at all, however, that the Japanese approaches had appealed to the Soviet leadership even a little bit.

The only outcome from this attempt was a series of lengthy telegrams exchanged between the Japanese Ambassador to the Soviet Union Satō Naotake, who had consistently maintained a cool assessment of the infeasibility of Soviet mediation, on the one hand, and Foreign Ministers Shigemitsu and Tōgō, who had nevertheless continued to exert their efforts in spite of slim chance of success, on the other. Although space does not permit me to go into details, these telegrams were full of a subtle charm that is to be quietly appreciated from the angle of national strategy in those days.

Shigemitsu placed his last hope on the possible clash of interests between the United States/Britain and the Soviet Union in the Balkans, the Middle and Near East, and China. Had such a clash of interests actually occurred, it could have presented a good opportunity for convincing the Soviet Union that a compromise with Japan would be better than cooperation with Britain/United States as a means to protect its interests in Asia.

Theoretically speaking, this was not necessarily an unrealistic idea. But the reality of U.S.-Soviet relations under the leadership of President Roosevelt was far more solid than an outsider could imagine.

Even today, it has not been fully explained why Roosevelt was so accommodating toward Stalin. It is said that Roosevelt personally had some Marxist sympathies, while it has been confirmed that some of Roosevelt's aides had strong pro-Communist inclinations. In any event, Roosevelt was extremely soft toward the Soviet Union, even to the extent that he could be described as naïve.

In contrast to what Stalin anticipated, Roosevelt gave the Soviet Union an almost perfectly free hand as far as East Europe was concerned. As for Asia, at the time of the Teheran Conference, Roosevelt had already recognized the Soviet need for securing warm water ports. Roosevelt paid no attention to China's intentions. Warm water ports in this context meant the ports of Dalian and Lüshun.

Under these circumstances, chances were slim, if any, for Japan to win the support of Stalin.

As anticipated by the Allies, the Soviet Union declared war on Japan three months after Germany's surrender, violating the neutrality pact that was still valid at that time. Within a month, the Soviet Union's act brought unspeakable miseries and hardships to the Japanese civilian residents in Manchuria, Sakhalin, and the Kuril Islands. Moreover, the Soviet Union violated Article 9 of the Potsdam Declaration—that is, that "Japanese military forces, after being completely disarmed, shall be permitted to return to their homes with the opportunity to lead peaceful and productive lives." The Soviet Union captured as many as 570,000 Japanese officers and men and forced them to work. More than 70,000 died from starvation and cold.

I had a chance to talk about the incident with a Russian one time. He replied, "We are not responsible for the conduct of the Soviet people who are from a different generation with different ideas." He also added, "In those days, fellow Russians also met a similar fate."

He may well have been right. Roosevelt, Japan, and the Russians at the time of the Russian Revolution may have committed the common error of harboring an illusion about the Communist Soviet Union without knowing its true nature.

Japan Surrenders

Everything was in vain, from kamikaze attacks by young volunteers of the Imperial Japanese Army and Navy to the diplomatic peace engineering with the Soviet Union. None of these efforts even slightly affected the general trend of the war toward Japan's ruin and surrender.

Among all of the abortive attempts, there was only one act that could change the future of Japan. And that was the decision to end the war.

And this decision required a tremendous amount of human effort. In retrospect of the entire Shōwa history, if only the efforts to suppress hard-liner arguments within Japan had been successful at critical junctures, Japan could have taken advantage of countless opportunities for avoiding the nation's crisis. As it turned out, however, the attempts never succeeded even on one occasion until the last moment.

For Japan, acceptance of surrender was much more difficult than any other task at earlier turning points of the war.

The Japanese people were firmly made to believe in their final victory, and they had sacrificed everything to cooperate with the war effort, believing it would be for their country. In the battlefield, too, Japanese warriors demonstrated their courage on countless occasions, sacrificing themselves because they believed they were paving the way for fellow warriors to follow. They were taught that a Japanese would never surrender but would fight it out to the very end.

Accepting surrender would entail a 180-degree reversal of the values the Japanese had hitherto believed in. I was fifteen years old when the war ended, and I personally heard from most of the Japanese youth that I met at that time comments such as this: "If Japan had to lose the war anyway, I wonder why our leaders didn't decide to fight more thoroughly."

During the Greater East Asia War, all the power as well as public order in Japan were in the hands of the military. Needless to say, the Japanese military was an advocate for continuing the war. Those were the days when even a slight reference to the unfavorable war situation would attract the strict supervision of the military police. The atmosphere was such that the moment any leader spoke of surrender, he had to be prepared for a mutiny and/or death at the hands of his subordinates.

Under these circumstances, a quartet of individuals helped bring about Japan's surrender. These four paid no attention whatsoever to their own lives, as if death were as natural as a night that comes after daytime. Prime Minister Suzuki Kantarō was a man with a broad perspective and sincere loyalty; Foreign Minister Tōgō Shigenori was a man of reason and conviction who would never compromise objective observation and logical consistency; Minister of Navy Yonai Mitsumasa was a samurai who never misjudged the key currents of the times and remained unaffected by any peril; and Emperor Shōwa was the one who made the final decision to surrender.

An outstanding accomplishment can only be made by an outstanding individual. Yet even an outstanding individual cannot accomplish something outstanding singlehandedly. Such an accomplishment is possible only when equally outstanding individuals who maintain deep mutual trust and communication occupy every strategic post. Had one of the quartet been missing or replaced by the likes of Konoe Fumimaro and Hirota Kōki, who were prone to go along with the general trend, it would have been quite uncertain if such a major decision could have been made. In fact, it would have been more likely for the leadership to have compromised with the Imperial Army and added unnecessary conditions to the terms of surrender that would have prolonged the war for weeks, months, or even a year. Meanwhile, the northern part of Japan, including Hokkaido, would have been invaded by the Soviet Union. And the Japanese people would have been forced to suffer from air raids, hunger, and, eventually, the miseries and hardships of a ground war on mainland Japan.

Suzuki Kantarō was born and bred as a navy man to the core. During the First Sino-Japanese War, Suzuki participated in the Battle of Weihaiwei in January/February 1895. This battle is well known as the first naval battle in the world's war history in which torpedo boats were employed in night raids. Suzuki was commander of one of the torpedo boats. Ten years later,

Ryōgoku area, Tokyo, nothing but burnt-out ruins

during the Russo-Japanese War, Suzuki contributed to Japan's victory in the Battle of Tsushima as commander of a destroyer flotilla. He was an officer who fought in every critical phase during the rise of the Empire of Japan, risking his own life.

Within the Imperial Navy, Suzuki assumed all the key posts, including Vice-Minister for Navy, Commandant of the Imperial Japanese Naval Academy, Commander in Chief of the Combined Fleet, and Chief of the Naval General Staff. At the time of the February 26 Incident in 1936 (11th Year of Shōwa), he was Grand Chamberlain to Emperor Shōwa.

According to Suzuki's memoir, he at first firmly declined when he was appointed as Grand Chamberlain. On second thought, however, he realized that being appointed Grand Chamberlain was actually a demotion by 20 or 30 ranks from Chief of the Naval General Staff in terms of the Imperial Court's precedence. Finding it against his conscience to decline a demotion, Suzuki decided to accept the appointment. Of course, Suzuki must also have detected Emperor Shōwa's strong wish behind the nomination. In any event, this episode confirmed that Suzuki was a man with the self-respect of a samurai, knowing what was the right thing to do.

As a professional military individual, Suzuki had been consistently against the military's interference with politics. His stance made him a target of the so-called reformist officers. As such, at the time of the February 26 Incident, he was shot four times by the rebel force led by Captain Andō Teruzō. He narrowly escaped the jaws of death when Andō restrained one of his men from delivering the finishing shot, believing Suzuki had had enough.

Andō had visited Suzuki at his private residence a year earlier and requested Suzuki's views on political reforms. After listening earnestly to Suzuki's view, Andō left Suzuki's resident saying, "Now, all my doubts have been dispelled."

Nevertheless, a year later Andō ordered his men to shoot Suzuki. After Suzuki was gunned down, Andō said to Mrs. Suzuki, "We have no personal grudge against His Excellency. We have come to this only because of a difference in our views on Japan's future." Then he explained the outline of their national reform plan. Murmuring that he had to kill himself since he had murdered Suzuki, Andō aimed a shot at his own throat after he led his men back to their headquarters in the Sannō Hotel. But he failed to die, and he later ended up being sentenced to death by court martial.

Let me quote one of Suzuki's arguments in persuading Andō a year earlier as described in detail in Suzuki's autobiography. In response to Andō's argument for political reform based on his concern for impoverishment of rural villages and its implications for the future of Japan, Suzuki quoted an example of French soldiers after the French Revolution. Despite their own families' suffering from hunger and fear of execution by guillotine, these soldiers fought bravely for the homeland against invading enemies. Suzuki said,

> Are the Japanese a race that cannot fight an enemy because of concern over personal futures as you claim? I do not think so . . . I do not think so because during the First Sino-Japanese and Russo-Japanese Wars many parents in Japan encouraged their sons to fight bravely for the country even though they themselves were in their sick beds.

Since Suzuki had personally experienced both the First Sino-Japanese and the Russo-Japanese Wars, his argument was persuasive.

Having survived all kinds of dreadful situations himself, Suzuki no longer paid any attention to life and death. When asked why he did not commit suicide after Japan's defeat, he explicitly declared, "I shall not die," and continued:

For someone to whom life or death does not matter from the beginning, death is the easiest way out. To him, death is nothing. A royal vassal in ancient China, facing the need for self-immolation, entrusted state affairs to his colleagues upon his death, saying, "I am taking an easier choice. I regret that I must beg you to take the difficult option." Since I might well have been dead at the time of the February 26 Incident, I am now determined to live as long as I can to witness with my own eyes how Japan will recover.

Again, Suzuki was already 79 years old when he was nominated as prime minister. At first he firmly declined the nomination; in the end, however, he made up his mind to accept it. This was because Suzuki was able to "perceive what His Imperial Majesty's true intention was" through his long experience as Grand Chamberlain and President of the Privy Council. According to Suzuki,

In a word, I humbly detected that His Majesty's true intention was to end the war in which the outcome had already become obvious and to nurture the chance for peace so that people would not have to suffer from unnecessary misery and that further sacrifices on both sides would be prevented.

Prime Minister Suzuki appointed Tōgō Shigenori as his cabinet's foreign minister. As for this appointment, Suzuki said, "I did not know Tōgō well, but, hearing that he had tendered his resignation to Tōjō and given up the foreign ministership, I decided he must be a man of strong will."

In response to the appointment, Tōgō stressed the primary importance of Suzuki's judgment on the current situation and firmly declined the nomination, saying,

Tōgō Shigenori

Although I judge it would be impossible for Japan to continue the current war for more than one year, the prime minister declares that Japan can go on for another two or three years. Given this discrepancy, I find it difficult to render my full support to the cabinet.

It is commendable that Tōgō firmly maintained the iron rules in diplomacy that policy should only follow the objective assessment of a situation and that such assessment should be given priority.

Suzuki reassured Tōgō, saying, "I have no objection to going along with your view on the future of the war, and I wish to leave all diplomacy at your discretion." Hearing this, Tōgō finally accepted the nomination.

This actually completed the groundwork for Japan's surrender. History would show later that, as Suzuki had expected, Tōgō's indomitable will displayed his real value in the days to come.

As I have already written, Suzuki, upon completing the formation of his cabinet, made up his mind that the war had to be stopped as he looked out of the window to see the cherry blossoms in full bloom.

Details about the process toward the eventual surrender of Japan are of little importance. Both Suzuki and Tōgō secretly harbored a wish to explore the chance to end the war, but the time for doing so was not yet ripe in Japan as a whole even at the time of Germany's surrender or the Potsdam Declaration.

On August 6, an atomic bomb was dropped on Hiroshima that caused unspeakable suffering and misery to noncombatants, male and female, young and old. Field surveys confirming that the weapon of mass destruction was indeed an atomic bomb were reported on August 8, the very day that the Soviet Union declared war on Japan.

The Supreme Council for the Direction of the War was convened in the evening of August 9. (Earlier that day, a second bomb had been dropped on Nagasaki.) Attendees were Prime Minister Suzuki, Foreign Minister Tōgō, War Minister Anami, Navy Minister Yonai, Chief of General Staff Umezu, and Chief of Naval General Staff Toyoda. Views were split among them on the conditions to be attached when accepting the Potsdam Declaration. These "conditions" were in fact measures to save face for the Japanese military. They included the refusal of U.S. forces landing on mainland Japan and the stipulation that the surrender of the Japanese forces stationed overseas be treated as a "voluntary withdrawal" requested by the Imperial Army. These conditions were, naturally, unacceptable to the U.S. side. In that sense, then, they were effectively arguments to continue the war.

Finding it a waste of time to argue among themselves in the face of a critical situation in which every second counted, Suzuki decided to convene the Supreme Council for the Direction of the War once again, this time in the presence of the Emperor. The second meeting was held at 11:50 p.m. on the same evening.

Regarding developments from this point on, I believe it best to rely on descriptions found in Prime Minister Suzuki's memoir. Suzuki was concurrently the chairman of the Supreme Council for the Direction of the War. The following remarks in quotation marks are direct quotes from this memoir.

First, Foreign Minister Tōgō briefed attendees on the background of the Potsdam Declaration and stated that unconditional acceptance of the Declaration would be the best option for Japan, "logically and in a clear tone." Suzuki expressed his deep respect for Tōgō, who had "explained the significance of the Potsdam Declaration calmly but resolutely when facing those who opposed it, and always argued with conviction."

This was the last glow of diplomacy of the Empire of Japan that had been nurtured by Mutsu Munemitsu, Komura Jutarō, and Shidehara Kijūrō.

In response, War Minister Anami insisted on the need to continue resistance, saying, "I am against the Foreign Minister's opinion," and "We should wait and attack the enemy until the bitter end when it raids mainland Japan. Through this, a more favorable path to peace should open itself."

The atmosphere was, according to Suzuki, "highly strained and earnest, truly appropriate for a conference in the presence of the Emperor." It was this atmosphere that "made me decide strongly that we should directly submit this crucial matter for imperial decision from the standpoint of head of state." Thus, approaching the Imperial Throne, Suzuki addressed the Emperor, saying, "With all due respect, now that things have come to this impasse, allow me to approach Your Imperial Majesty to request your imperial decision to conclude this council."

No one in Japan's modern history had dared to act this way before. Perhaps I will not be the only one to wonder what would have happened if the prime minister of the time also had requested an Imperial decision at one of the many critical junctures leading to the war.

To continue to quote from Suzuki's memoir, Emperor Shōwa replied to Suzuki, saying, "We agree with the advice of the foreign minister." Suzuki marveled at Emperor Shōwa's reasoning for his decision, saying, "His Imperial Majesty's persuasion was extremely logical and reasonable, based on a highly appropriate perception of the situation. One can tell how accurately His Majesty has constantly perceived the war situation. This left all the Council members speechless and inspired us with a feeling of awe."

The Council meeting lasted until two o'clock in the morning of August 10. At seven o'clock Prime Minister Suzuki instructed that a telegram be dispatched telling the Allies that Japan was prepared to accept the terms of the Potsdam Declaration.

A formal reply arrived from the Allies on August 13. The reply was, however, unclear about the fate of Japan's national polity (国体の護持), rekindling the argument for a continuation of the war. This required the convening of another council in the presence of the Emperor on August 14. Emperor Shōwa's determination, nevertheless, remained unaffected.

And, finally,

> His Imperial Majesty said, "It breaks our heart to consider the sorrow that Imperial officers and soldiers, fallen soldiers and their bereaved families, and all the other war victims must be feeling. But the direction of the tide of the times is beyond our control. Therefore, we find it unavoidable to request our people to endure the unendurable and to suffer what is unsufferable . . . ," upon which His Majesty's imperial voice temporarily broke off. Looking up at His Majesty, alas I found the Emperor was weeping.
>
> Hearing His Majesty's remarks, everyone present collapsed in tears despite the Imperial presence. Some even cried uncontrollably."

In the dead of night on August 14, after the Supreme Council for the Direction of the War broke up, War Minister Anami apologized to Prime

Minister Suzuki for "the uncompromising argument I made on behalf of the Imperial Japanese Army." Suzuki in reply said, "I do not mind what you said because it all comes from your patriotic ardor." When Suzuki told Anami that he was not altogether pessimistic about the future of Japan, Anami said, "I have no doubt in my mind that the Emperor and the people will work together to rebuild Japan." The two men shook hands firmly and parted.

Suzuki later wrote,

> Had Anami been a narrow-minded warrior arguing nothing but the continuation of resistance, he could have easily caused the collapse of my cabinet by walking out of the Council meeting and tendering his resignation. But he remained in the Council until the last minute, while expressing his opposition. It was only after he countersigned the Imperial Rescript of Surrender that he killed himself magnificently. Great conduct indeed.

Two or three hours after Anami shook hands and parted with Suzuki, Anami performed a splendid ritual disembowlment that was perfectly faultless as the conduct of a samuai. His farewell poem reads:

> Having bathed in deep blessings of the Emperor
> I have nothing to say now at my death

Anami ended his life in a magnificent way that symbolized the end of the Empire of Japan.

As such, the Empire of Japan, which our predecessors had laboriously and strenuously constructed since the Meiji period, perished like a bubble.

After the surrender, Tōgō and Shigemitsu were imprisoned on allegations of war crimes. For those politicians with diplomatic backgrounds who were not imprisoned, including Shidehara Kijūrō and Yoshida Shigeru, the days of enduring the humiliation of an occupation were waiting. They turned their efforts to exploring ways for the defeated Japan to survive.

REFERENCES

Abe Makirō (1993). *Kiki no Gaishō Tōgō Shigenori* (Tōgō Shigenori: Foreign Minister in the Midst of Crisis). Tokyo: Shinchōsha.

Andō Tokuki (1941). *Ō Seiei Jijoden* (Wang Jingwei Autobiography). Tokyo: Dai-Nippon Yūbenkai Kōdansha.

Aritake Shūji (1986). *Saitō Minoru.* Vol. 14 of *Nippon Saishō Retsuden* (Lives of the Japanese Prime Ministers), edited by Hosokawa Ryūgen. Tokyo: Jiji Tsūshin-sha.

ASEAN Center, ed. (1988). *Ajia ni Ikiru Daitōa Sensō: Genchi Dokyumento* (The Living Greater East Asia War: Documentary from the Ground). Tokyo: Tentensha.

Ashida Hitoshi (1995). *Dai-2-Ji Sekai Taisen Gaikō-shi* (Diplomatic History of World War II). Tokyo: Jiji Tsūshin-sha.

Bo Min Gaung (1990). *Aunsan Shōgun to 30-nin no Shishi* (General Aung Sang and 30 Revolutionaries), translated by Tanabe Toshio. Tokyo: Chūkō Shinsho.

Butow, Robert Joseph Charles (1961). *Tōjō Hideki,* translated by Kinoshita Hideo. Tokyo: Jiji Tsūshinsha.

Chihaya Masataka, et al. (1994). *Nippon Kaigun no Kōzai: 5-nin no Sakan ga Kataru Rekishi no Kyōkun* (Merits and Demerits of the Imperial Japanese Navy: Lessons of History as Told by Five Former Imperial Navy Officers). Tokyo: President-sha.

Churchill, Winston S. (1948). *The Second World War.* London: Cassell.

Coox, Alvin D. (1998). *Chōkohō Jiken: Mō Hitotsu no Nomonhan* (Battle of Lake Khasan: Another Nomonhan Incident), translated by Iwasaki Hiroichi and Iwasaki Toshio. Tokyo: Hara Shobō.

Dōdai Keizai Konwa-kai, ed. (1995). *Kindai Nihon Sensō-shi* (Military History of Modern Japan). Tokyo: Dōdai Keizai Konwa-kai.

Domon Shūhei (1982). *Saigo no Teikoku Gunjin: Kakaru Shikikan Ariki* (The Last Imperial Warrior: There Once Was Such a Commander). Tokyo: Kōdansha.

Fish, Hamilton (1985). *Nichibei Kaisen no Higeki* (Tragic Start of the U.S.-Japan War), translated by Okazaki Hisahiko. Tokyo: PHP Kenkyūsho.

Fujioka Taishū (1986). *Kaigun Shōshō Takagi Sōkichi: Kaigunshō Chōsaka to Minkanjin Zunō Shūdan* (Imperial Japanese Navy Rear Admiral Takagi Sōkichi: Research Department of the Ministry of Navy and a Private Think Tank). Tokyo: Kōjinsha.

Fukunaga Misao (1978). *Kyōsantōin no Tenkō to Ten'nōsei* (Defection of Communist Party Members and the Emperor System of Japan). Tokyo: San'ichi Shobō.

Fusayama Takao (1992). *Indoneshia no Dokuritsu to Nipponjin no Kokoro* (Indonesian Independence and Japanese Heart). Tokyo: Tentenha.

—(1998). *Murudeka: Indoneshia Dokuritsu to Nippon* (Murdeka: Indonesian Independence and Japan). Tokyo: Zenponsha.

Gaimushō Hyakunen-Shi Hensan Iinkai, ed. (1969). *Gaimushō no Hyakunen* (One Hundred Years of Japan's Ministry of Foreign Affairs). Tokyo: Hara Shobō.

Grew, Joseph C. (1944). *Ten Years in Japan*. New York: Simon & Schuster.

Hagiwara Nobutoshi (1985). *Tōgō Shigenori: Denki to Kaisetsu* (Tōgō Shigenori: Biography and Commentary). Tokyo: Hara Shobō.

Hagiwara Tōru (1950). *Taisen no Kaibō: Nippon Kōfuku madeno Bei-Ei no Senryaku* (Anatomy of World War II: American/British Strategies to Lead Japan to Surrender). Tokyo: Yomiuri Shimbunsha.

Handō Kazutoshi (1998). *Nomonhan no Natsu* (A Summer in Nomonhan). Tokyo: Bungei Shunjū.

Hata Ikuhiko (1986). *Nankin Jiken: "Gyakusatsu" no Kōzō* (Nanking Incident: Structure of the So-called Massacre). Tokyo: Chūkō Shinsho.

—(1996). *Rokōkyō Jiken no Kenkyū* (A Study of the Marco Polo Bridge Incident). Tokyo: University of Tokyo Press.

Hatano Sumio (1996). *Taiheiyō Sensō to Ajia Gaikō* (Pacific War and Japan's Asia Diplomacy). Tokyo, University of Tokyo Press.

Hattori Takushirō (1965). *Daitōa Sensō Zenshi* (Complete History of the Greater East Asia War). Tokyo: Hara Shobō.

Hiraizumi Shūichi (1971). *Ishihara Kanji wa Kō Katatta* (Thus Spoke Ishihara Kanji). Tokyo: Taiyōsha.

Hirota Kōki Denki Kankōkai, ed. *Hirota Kōki*. Tokyo: Ashi Shobō.

Hosaka Masayasu (1996). *Rikugun Ryōshikiha no Kenkyū: Miotosareta Shōwa Jinbutsu-Den* (A Study on the Sensible Element in the Imperial Japanese Army: Inventory of Overlooked Showa Characters). Tokyo: Kōjinsha.

Hosokawa Ryūgen, ed. (1985–87). *Nippon Saishō Retsuden* (Lives of the Japanese Prime Ministers). Tokyo: Jiji Tsūshin-sha.

—(1986). *Tanaka Giichi*. Vol. 12 of *Nippon Saishō Retsuden* (Lives of the Japanese Prime Ministers), edited by Hosokawa Ryūgen. Tokyo: Jiji Tsūshin-sha.

Hosoya Chihiro, et al. eds. (1971–72). *Nichibei Kankei-shi: Kaisen ni Itaru 10-nen (1931–41)* (History of U.S.-Japan Relations: A Decade toward the War, 1931–41). Tokyo: University of Tokyo Press.

Hull, Cordell (1949). *Kaisōroku: Kokusai Rengō no Chichi* (Memoir: "Father of the United Nations"), translated by Miyaji Kenjirō. Tokyo: Asahi Shimbunsha.

Ikeda Michiko (1992). *Tainichi Keizai Fūsa: Nippon wo Oitsumeta 12-Nen* (Economic Blockade on Japan: The 12 Years That Cornered Japan). Tokyo: Nippon Keizai Shimbunsha.

Inoue Toshikazu (1994). *Kiki no Naka no Kyōchō Gaikō* (Cooperative Diplomacy in the Midst of Crisis). Tokyo: Yamakawa Shuppansha.

Irie Akira (1978). *Nichibei Sensō* (U.S.-Japan War). Tokyo: Chūō Kōronsha.

Ishibashi Tanzan (1971–80). *Ishibashi Tanzan Zenshū* (Complete Works of Ishibashi Tanzan). Tokyo: Tōyō Keizai Shinpō-sha.

Ishibashi Tsuneki (1979). *Shōwa no Hanran* (Rebels in Shōwa). Tokyo: Takagi Shobō.

Ishii Itarō (1950). *Gaikōkan no Isshō* (Life of a Diplomat). Tokyo: Yomiuri Shimbunsha.

Itō Masanori (1956). *Rengō Kantai no Saigo* (Last Days of the Imperial Japanese Navy Combined Fleet). Tokyo: Bungei Shunjū.

—(1957–58). *Teikoku Rikugun no Saigo* (Last Days of the Imperial Japanese Army). Tokyo: Bungei Shunjū.

—(1958). *Gunbatsu Kōbō-shi* (Rise and Fall of Warlords). Tokyo: Bungei-Shunjū.

Itō Musojirō (1983). *Manshū Mondai no Rekishi* (History of the Manchurian Issue). Tokyo: Hara Shobō.

Iwabuchi Tatsuo (1986). *Inukai Tsuyoshi*. Vol. 13 of *Nippon Saishō Retsuden* (Lives of the Japanese Prime Ministers), edited by Hosokawa Ryūgen. Tokyo: Jiji Tsūshin-sha.

Izumiya Tatsurō (1996). *Biruma ni Saita Yūjō to Shinrai no Hana: Inpāru Sakusen/Irawaji Kaisen Gaishi* (Blossoming Friendship and Mutual Trust in Burma: Unofficial History of the Battle of Imphal/Battle of Meiktila and Mandalay). Tokyo: Omokagebashi Shuppan.

Kaigun Rekishi Hozon-kai, ed. (1995). *Nihon Kaigun-shi* (History of the Japanese Navy). Tokyo: Kaigun Rekishi Hozon-kai.

Kajima Kenkyū-sho, ed. (1970–73). *Nihon Gaikō-shi* (Diplomatic History of Japan). Tokyo: Kajima Kenkyū-sho.

Kanahele, George S. *Nippon Gunsei to Indoneshia Dokuritsu* (Japan's Military Administration and Indonesia's Independence), translated by Gotō Ken'ichi, Kondō Masaomi, and Shiraishi Aiko. Tokyo: Ōtori Shuppan.

Kazami Akira (1951). *Konoe Naikaku* (Konoe Cabinet). Tokyo: Nippon Shuppan Kyōdō.

Kissinger, Henry A. (1994). *Diplomacy*. New York: Simon & Schuster.

Kitaoka Shin'ichi (1978). *Nippon Rikugun to Tairiku Seisaku* (Imperial Japanese Army and Japan's Policy toward China). Tokyo: University of Tokyo Press.

—(1987). *Kiyosawa Kiyoshi: Nichibei Kankei eno Dōsatsu* (Kiyosawa Kiyoshi: His Insight into U.S.-Japan Relations). Tokyo: Chūō Shinsho.

Komatsu Shigerō (1989). *Ai no Tōsotsu Adachi Hatazō: Dai-18 Gun Shireikan Nyūginia Senki* (Adachi Hatazō's Command by Love: How the 18th Army Commander Fought in New Guinea). Tokyo: Kōjinsha.

Konoe Fumimaro (1946). *Heiwa eno Doryoku: Konoe Fumimaro Shuki* (Efforts toward Peace: Konoe Fumimaro Memorandum). Tokyo: Nippon Denpō Tsūshinsha.

Kōsaka Jirō (1995). *Tokkō Taiin no Inochi no Koe ga Kikoeru: Sensō, Jinsei, Soshite Waga Sokoku* (Hearing the Voices of the Kamikaze: War, Life, and Our Homeland). Tokyo: PHP Kenkyūsho.

Kurasawa Aiko (1992). *Nippon Senryō-ka no Jawa Nōson no Hen'yō* (Transformation of Javanese Rural Villages under Japanese Occupation). Tokyo: Sōshisha.

—(1997). *Nanpō Tokubetsu Ryūgakusei ga Mita Senjika no Nippon* (Japan at War as Seen by Scholarship Students from Southeast Asia). Tokyo: Sōshisha.

—(1997). *Tōnan Ajia-shi no Naka no Nippon Senryō* (Japanese Occupation in the History of Southeast Asia). Tokyo: Waseda Daigaku Shuppanbu.

Kurusu Saburō (1952). *Nichibei Gaikō Hiwa: Waga Gaikō-shi* (Unknown Episodes in U.S.-Japan Diplomacy: My Diplomatic History). Tokyo: Sōgensha.

Liddell, Hart and Basil, Henry (1971). *History of the Second World War*. New York: Putnam.

Lu, David John (1967). *Taiheiyō Sensō eno Dōtei: Rokōkyo yori Shinjuwan e* (Milestones toward the Pacific War: From the Marco Polo Bridge Incident to Pearl Harbor), translated by Tajima Kaneko. Tokyo: Hara Shobō.

Mainichi Shimbunsha translated and edited. (1975). *Taiheiyō Sensō Hishi: Bei Senji Shidōsha no Kaisō* (Anecdotes from the Pacific War: Memoir of a U.S. War Leader). Tokyo: Mainichi Shimbun-sha.

Matsushita Yoshio (1993). *Mizuno Hironori: Kaigun Taisa no Hansen* (Mizuno Hironori: Anti-War Conduct of an Imperial Naval Officer). Tokyo: Yūzankaku.

Mikuriya Takashi (1997). *Baba Tsunego no Menboku* (The Honor of Baba Tsunego). Tokyo: Chūō Kōron-sha.

Miwa Kimitada (1971). *Matsuoka Yōsuke*. Tokyo: Chuō Kōron-sha.

Miyazawa Toshiyoshi (1970). *Ten'nō Kikansetsu Jiken: Shiryō wa Kataru* (Emperor-as-Organ-of-the-State-Theory Incident: The Documents Speak). Tokyō: Yūhikaku.

Nakagawa Yatsuhiro (1995). *Konoe Fumimaro to Rūzuberuto* (Konoe Fumimaro and Roosevelt). Tokyo: PHP Kenkyūsho.

Naruse Yasushi (1991). *Yugamerareta Kokubō Hōshin: Shōwa Ten'no to Rikukaigun* (Distorted National Defense Policy: Emperor Shōwa and the Imperial Japanese Army and Navy). Tokyo: Saimaru Shuppankai.

——(1997). *Senken no Mei: Kakusareta Shōwa-Shi* (Farseeing Intelligence: Hidden History of Shōwa).Tokyo: Futaba-sha.

Nomura Kichisaburō (1946). *Beikoku ni Tsukai Shite: Nichibei Kōshō no Kaiko* (Serving as Japanese Ambassador to the United States: U.S.-Japan Negotiations in Retrospect). Tokyo: Iwanami Shoten.

Ogata Sadako (1966). *Manshū Jihen to Seisaku no Keisei Katei* (The Manchurian Incident and the Process of Policy Formulation). Tokyo: Hara Shobō.

Ōkawa Shūmei (1975). *Ōkawa Shūmei Shū* (Collected Writings of Ōkawa Shūmei). Tokyo: Chikuma Shobō.

Okuda Masahiko (1997). *1941-nen no Nichibei Kōshō* (U.S.-Japan Negotiations in 1941). Tokyo: Asahi Shimbun Shuppan Sābisu. Okumura Fusao, ed. (1996). *Daitōa Sensō no Honshitsu* (Essence of the Greater East Asia War). Tokyo: Dōdai Keizai Konwakai.

Ōsugi Kazuo (1996). *Nicchū Sensō 15-nen Sensō-shi: Naze Sensō wa Chōkika Shitaka* (History of the 15-Year War between Japan and China: Why Was the War Protracted?). Tokyo: Chūkō Shinsho.

Ōta Shūji (1997). *Pagoda no Kuni no Samurai-tachi Dokyumento* (Documentary on Samurais in the Country of Pagoda). Tokyo: Dōhōsha.

Rekishi Kentō Iinkai, ed. (1995). *Daitōa Sensō no Sōkatsu* (Summing up the Greater East Asia War). Tokyo: Tenkaisha.

Ritsumeikan Daigaku Saionji Kinmochi-den Hensan Iinkai (Ritsumeikan University Editorial Committee on Saionji Kinmochi's Biography) (1990–96). *Saionji Kinmochi-den* (Biography of Saionji Kinmochi). Tokyo: Iwanami Shoten.

Sankei Shimbun (1985). *Shō Kaiseki Hiroku* (Secret Memoir of Chiang Kai-shek). Tokyo: Sankei Shimbun.

Schaffer, Ronald (2007). *Amerika no Nippon Kūshū ni Moraru wa Attaka: Senryaku Bakugeki no Dōgiteki Mondai* (Were the U.S. Air Raids on Japan Moralistic?: Ethical Questions of Strategic Bombings), translated by Fukada Tamio. Tokyo: Sōshisha.

Sherwood, Robert E. (1957). *Rūzuberuto to Hopukinsu* (Roosevelt and Hopkins), translated by Murakami Mitsuhiko. Tokyo: Misuzu Shobō.

Shigemitsu Mamoru (1952). *Shōwa no Dōran* (Showa: A Time of Upheaval). Tokyo: Chūō Kōron-sha.

—(1986–88). *Shigemitsu Mamoru Shuki* (Personal Accounts by Shigemitsu Mamoru). Tokyo: Chūō Koronsha.

Shin Jinbutsu Ōrai-sha, ed. *Yamamoto Isoruku no Subete* (A Complete Picture of Yamamoto Isoroku). Tokyo: Shin Jinbutsu Ōrai-sha.

Shinobu, Seizaburō (1974). *Nihon Gaikō-shi* (Diplomatic History of Japan). Tokyo: Mainichi Shimbun-sha.

Sorimachi Eiichi (1956). *Ningen Yamamoto Isoroku* (Yamamoto Isoroku, the Man). Tokyo: Kōwado.

Suzuki Kantorō (1971). *Suzuki Kantarō Jiden* (Autobiography of Suzuki Kantaro). Tokyo: Jiji Tsūshinsha.

Suzuki Seihei (1999). *Nippon Senryō-ka Bari-tō kara no Hōkoku* (Report from Bali under Japanese Occupation). Tokyo: Sōshisha.

"Taiheiyō Sensō Meishō Yūshō Sōran" (A Source Book on Great and Brave Generals during the Pacific War), September 1996 Extra Edition of the Monthly *Rekishi to Tabi* (History and Journey).

Takahashi Masae (1965). *2.26 Jiken: Shōwa Ishin no Shisō to Kōdō* (February 26 Incident: Philosophy and Conduct in the Shōwa Restoration). Tokyo: Chūkō Shinsho.

Takamiya Taihei (1973). *Shōwa no Shōsui* (Great Generals and Admirals in Shōwa). Tokyo: Tosho Shuppansha.

—(1986). *Yonai Mitsumasa.* Vol. 16 of *Nippon Saishō Retsuden* (Lives of the Japanese Prime Ministers), edited by Hosokawa Ryūgen. Tokyo: Jiji Tsūshin-sha.

Takeda Kunitarō and Sugawara Kazutaka (1996). *Ishihara Kanji: Eikyū Heiwa no Shito* (Ishihara Kanji: An Apostle of Eternal Peace). Tokyo: Tōseisha.

Takeda Taijun and Takeuchi Minoru (1965). *Mō Takuto: Sono Shi to Jinsei* (Mao Tse-tung: His Poetry and Life). Tokyo: Bungei Shunjū Shinsha.

Tamura Kōsaku (1968). *Taiheiyō Sensō Gaikō-shi* (Diplomatic History of the Pacific War). Tokyo: Kajima Kenkyūsho Shuppankai.

Thorne, Christopher (1995). *Bei-Ei ni Totte no Taiheiyō Sensō* (The Pacific War in the Eyes of Britain and the United States), translated by Ichikawa Yōichi. Tokyo: Sōshisha.

Tobe Ryōichi, et al. eds. (1984). *Shippai no Honshitsu: Nippon-Gun no Soshikiron-teki Kenkyū* (Essence of Failure: Organizational Study of the Imperial Japanese Military). Tokyo: Diamond-sha.

Tōgō Shigehiko (1993). *Sofu Tōgō Shigenori no Shōgai* (Life of My Grandfather Tōgō Shigenori). Tokyo: Bungei Shunjū.

Tōgō Shigenori (1985). *Jidai no Ichimen: Tōgō Shigenori Gaikō Shuki* (An Aspect of the Times: Diplomatic Memoranda by Tōgō Shigenori). Tokyo: Hara Shobō.

Toland, John (1971). *The Rising Sun: The Decline and Fall of the Japanese Empire, 1936–45.* New York: Random House.

—(1982). *Shinjuwan Kōgeki* (Attack on Pearl Harbor), translated by Tokuoka Takao. Tokyo: Bungei Shunjū.

Toyoda Jō (1979). *Matsuoka Yōsuke: Higeki no Gaikōkan* (Matsuoka Yōsuke: A Tragic Diplomat). Tokyo: Shinchōsha.

—(1986). *Meishō Miyazaki Shigesaburō: Fuhai, Saizensen Shikikan no Shōgai* (Great Commander Miyazaki Shigesaburō: Life of an Invincible Commander at the Forefront). Tokyo: Kōjinsha.

Tsunoda Fusako (1984). *Sekinin: Rabauru no Shōgun Imamura Hitoshi* (Responsibility: General Imamura Hitoshi of Rabaul). Tokyo: Shinchōsha.

Tsunoda Jun, eds. (1966). *Ishihara Kanji Shiryō—Kokubō Ronsaku-hen* (Ishihara Kanji Documents—Compilation of Ishihara's Treatises on National Defense). Tokyo: Hara Shobō.

—(1987). *Seiji to Gunji: Meiji/Taisho/Shōwa-shoki no Nippon* (Politics and the Military: Japan in Meiji/Taishō/Early-Shōwa Periods). Tokyo: Kōfūsha Shuppan.

Uchida Yasuya Denki Hensan Iinkai, ed. *Uchida Yasuya*. Tokyo: Kajima Kenkyūsho Shuppankai.

Ujita Naoyoshi (1987). *Shidehara Kijūrō*. Vol. 17 of *Nippon Saishō Retsuden* (Lives of the Japanese Prime Ministers), edited by Hosokawa Ryūgen. Tokyo: Jiji Tsūshin-sha.

Umemoto Sutezō (1976). *Riku-Kai Meishō 100-Sen* (100 Top Army/Navy Generals). Tokyo: Akita Shoten.

—(1983). *Shōgun no Shiki: Saigo no Kantōgun Sō-Shireikan Yamada Otozō Taishō* (A General's Four Seasons: General Yamada Otozō, the Last Commander-in-Chief of the Kanto Army). Tokyo: Kōjinsha.

Usui Katsumi (1974). *Manshū Jihen* (Manchurian Incident). Tokyo: Chūkō Shinsho.

Waldron, Arthur (1992). *How the Peace Was Lost: The 1935 Memorandum "Developments Affecting American Policy in the Far East"*. Stanford: Hoover Institution Press.

Wan Feng (1989). *Nippon Fashizumu no Kōbō* (Rise and Fall of Fascism in Japan). Tokyo: Rokkō Shuppan.

Watanabe Kyōji (1978). *Kita Ikki*. Tokyo: Asahi Shimbunsha.

Wedemeyer, Albert Coady (1967). *Wedemeyer Kaisō-roku: Dai 2-ji Taisen ni Shōsha Nashi* (Memoir of Albert Wedemeyer: There Is No Winner in World War II), translated by Senō Sakuratō. Tokyo: Yomiuri Shimbunsha.

Wohlstetter, Roberta (1962). *Pearl Harbor: Warning and Decision*. Stanford: Stanford University Press.

Yabe Teiji (1952). *Konoe Fumimaro*. Tokyo: Kōbundō.

—(1986). *Konoe Fumimaro*. Vol. 15 of *Nippon Saishō Retsuden* (Lives of the Japanese Prime Ministers), edited by Hosokawa Ryūgen. Tokyo: Jiji Tsūshin-sha.

Yoshino Sakuzō (1975). *Yoshino Sakuzō Hyōron-shū* (Collected Critiques by Yoshino Sakuzō). Tokyo: Iwanami Bunko.

APPENDIX

Chronogical Table of Outstanding Events in the Period Covered by the Current Volume

Year	Japanese Era	Age of Person in Events Column	Events in Person's Life	Domesitic/Overseas Incidents
1878	Meiji 11th		Hirota Kōki born in Fukuoka Prefecture. Entered the Ministry of Foreign Affairs in 1906 (39th Year of Meiji).	
1880	Meiji 13th		Matsuoka Yōsuke born in Yamaguchi Prefecture. Entered the Ministry of Foreign Affairs in 1904 (37th Year of Meiji).	
1882	Meiji 15th		Tōgō Shigenori born in Kagoshima Prefecture. Entered the Ministry of Foreign Affairs in 1912 (1st Year of Taishō).	
1887	Meiji 20th		Shigemitsu Mamoru born in Ōita Prefecture. Entered the Ministry of Foreign Affairs in 1911 (44th Year of Meiji)	
1931	Shōwa 6th	60	Shidehara Kijūrō appointed to foreign minister of the Wakatsuki Reijirō cabinet	Liutiaohu Incident erupts, marking the beginning of the Manchurian Incident (Sept. 18)
				Japanese government announces its policy not to escalate the Manchurian Incident (Sept. 24)
				Bombing of Jinzhou (Oct. 8)
				Ousted Chinese Emperor Puyi flees Tianjin (Nov. 18)
				The Wakatsuki cabinet resigns (Dec. 11)
		58	Yoshizawa Kenkichi appointed foreign minister	Formation of the Inukai Tsuyoshi cabinet (Dec. 13)
1932	Shōwa 7th			Occupation of Jinzhou by Japanese forces (Jan. 3)
				January 28 Incident erupts (Jan. 28 until Mar. 2)
				Manchu State (Manchukuo) proclaimed (Mar. 1)
				Puyi installed as Manchukuo's Head of State (Mar. 9)

Year	Japanese Era	Age of Person in Events Column	Events in Person's Life	Domesitic/Overseas Incidents
1932	Shōwa 7th			Prime Minister Inukai assassinated (May 15)
		75	Foreign Minister Saitō concurrently serves as prime minister (until July 26)	Formation of the Saitō Minoru cabinet (May 26)
				House of Representatives unanimously approves recognition of Manchukuo (Jun. 14)
		68	Uchida Yasuya appointed foreign minister (Jul. 26-)	Foreign Minister Uchida's so-called "until we are all reduced to ashes" speech at House of Representatives (Aug. 15)
		46	Ishii Itarō appointed to the Japanese Consul General at Shanghai (Sept. 1932-July 1936)	Japan recognizes Manchukuo (Sep. 15)
				Lytton Commission's report presented to Japan's Ministry of Foreign Affairs (Sep. 30), then made public on Oct. 1
		53	Matsuoka Yōsuke to head Japan's delegation to the League of Nations	
1933	Shōwa 8th			Hitler appointed to chancelor and forms his cabinet (Jan. 30)
		52	Tōgō Shigenori appointed Director-General of the European and American Affairs Bureau (Feb. 1933-Oct. 1937)	The Kanto Army invades Manchuria (Feb. 23)
				League of Nations adopts Lytton Commission's report. Japan's chief delegate Matsuoka delivers a speech condemning the League and announcing Japan's withdrawal (Feb. 24).
				Franklin Roosevelt sworn in as U.S. President (Mar. 4)
				Japan withdraws from the League of Nations (Mar. 27)
				The Kanto Army advances beyond the Great Wall (Apr. 10)
				The Kanto Army ordered to return to the Great Wall line (Apr. 19); withdrawal completed by April 23.

Year	Japanese Era	Age of Person in Events Column	Events in Person's Life	Domesitic/Overseas Incidents
1933	Shōwa 8th	47	Shigemitsu Mamoru appointed Vice-Minister for Foreign Affairs (May 1933-April 36)	The Kanto Army once again invades beyond the Great Wall (May 3)
				Tanggu Truce signed between the Republic of China and Japan (May 31)
		56	Hirota Kōki appointed Minister for Foreign Affairs (Sep. 14-)	
		54	Matsuoka Yōsuke resigns as member of the House of Representatives (Dec. 8)	Crown Prince Akihito born (Dec. 23)
1934	Shōwa 9th			Manchuko becomes the Great Manchurian Empire and Puyi becomes its first emperor (Mar. 1)
				Amau Statement (Apr. 17)
				Admiral Tōgō Heihachiro passes away (May 30)
				The Saitō cabinet resigns due to the Teijin Incident (Jul. 3)
		57	Hirota Kōki appointed to foreign minister of the Okada Keisuke cabinet	Okada Keisuke cabinet formed (Jul. 8)
				Hitler becomes president cum chancellor of Germany (Aug. 2)
				Preliminary negotiations at London Naval Conference commence (Oct. 24)
				Japanese government announces abrogation of Washington Naval Treaty (Dec. 3)
				* Serious famine all over Japan this year
1935	Shōwa 10th			Foreign Minister Hirota stresses friendly relations with China (Jan. 22)
				Foreign Minister Hirota announces at Diet that there will be no war during his tenure (Jan. 25)
				Germany announces its rearmament (Mar. 16)
				Japan-Manchukuo-Soviet agreement on acquisition of the Chinese Eastern Railway (Mar. 23)
				Republic of China bans anti-Japanese movement (Jun. 10)
				He-Umezu Agreement signed (Jun. 10)

Year	Japanese Era	Age of Person in Events Column	Events in Person's Life	Domesitic/Overseas Incidents
1935	Shōwa 10th			Chin-Doihara Agreement signed (Jun. 27)
				7th Comintern convention convened (Jul. 15-Aug. 20)
				Communist Party of China proposes united front with the Nationalists against Japan (Aug. 1)
		56	Matsuoka Yōsuke appointed President of the South Manchuria Railway	The Nutrality Pact of 1935 passes the U.S. Congress (Aug. 31)
				Italy starts invading Ethiopia (Oct. 3)
				The Hirota Three Principles for Japan-China collaboration, i.e. (1) suppression by China of all anti-Japanese movements; (2) establishment of economic cooperation between China, Japan, and Manchukuo; and (3) joint defense by China and Japan against communism. Chinese ambassdor to Japan Chiang Tso-ping basically accepts the three principles (Oct. 7).
				Japan's Ministry of Foreign Affairs unofficially announces its opposition to Frederick Leith-Ross's proposal for a joint loan with Britain to promote reform of China's monetary system (Nov. 9)
				East Hebei Autonomous Anti-Communist Council established, later to be renamed East Hebei Autonomous Council (Nov. 25)
				Hebei-Chahar Political Council estalished (Dec. 18)
				*This year witnesses the issue of the theory of the Emperor as an organ of government; resignation of the theory's chief advocate, Minobe Tatsukichi, from the House of Peers; and the government's declaration of proved national polity.
1936	Shōwa 11th			Japanese government endorses the First Administrative Policy toward North China to keep north China separate from the Nationalist government (Jan. 13)

Year	Japanese Era	Age of Person in Events Column	Events in Person's Life	Domesitic/Overseas Incidents
1936	Shōwa 11th			Japanese government announces its withdrawal from the London Naval Treaty, marking the resumption of the naval armaments race among world powers (Jan. 15)
				Hirota's speech on the three principles vis-a-vis China, i.e. (1) suppression by China of all anti-Japanese movements; (2) establishment of economic cooperation between China, Japan, and Manchukuo ; and (3) joint defense by China and Japan against communism, delivered (Jan. 21)
				February 26 Incident erupts (Feb. 26)
		59	Hirota Kōki becomes prime minister cum foreign minister	Formation of Hirota cabinet (Mar. 9)
		53	Arita Hachirō appointed foreign minister (April 2-)	Cabinet meeting decides to send 3,000-strong reinforcement to China, making the Japanese troops stationed in China 5,000-strong (Apr. 17)
				The system by which only active-duty army or navy officers could serve in the cabinet posts of war minister or navy minister revived (May 18)
				Spanish Civil War started (Jul. 17-March 28, 1939)
		50	Shigemitsu appointed ambassador to the Soviet Union (Aug. 1936-Oct.1938)	Hirota cabinet decides Standard of National Policies (Aug. 7)
				The Second Administrative Policy toward North China endorsed (establishment of anti-Communist, pro-Japan/Manchukuo zones in five north China provinces) (Aug. 11)
				President Roosevelt re-elected (Nov.3)
				Suiyuan Campaign (Nov. 14)
				Anti-CommunistPact concluded between Japan and Germany (Nov. 25)
				Xian Incident erupts (Dec. 4)
				*A number of terrorist attacks and armed conflicts erupt this year all over China, including Chengdu Incident
1937	Shōwa 12th			The Hirota cabinet resigns (Jan. 23)

Year	Japanese Era	Age of Person in Events Column	Events in Person's Life	Domesitic/Overseas Incidents
1937	Shōwa 12th			Imperial appointment to Ugaki Kazunari to form a cabinet (Jan. 25) which Ugaki has to decline due to opposition from the Imperial Japanese Army (Jan. 29)
		62	Foreign Minister Hayashi Senjūrō appointed prime minister	The Hayashi Senjūrō cabinet formed (Feb. 2)
		56	Satō Naotake appointed foreign minister (March 3-)	Prime Minister Hayashi dissolves House of Reprentatives ("Eat and Run" dissolution) (Mar. 31)
				The Third Administrative Policy toward North China endorsed (abandonment of separate government of north China) (Apr. 16)
		51	Ishii Itarō appointed Director-General of East Asian Affairs Bureau of Ministry of Foreign Affairs (May 1937-November 1938)	German Luftwaffe air raids on Guernika, Spain (Apr. 26)
		60	Hirota Kōki appointed foreign minister	The Hayashi cabinet resigns (May 51)
				First Konoe Fumimaro cabinet formed (Jun. 4)
				Marco Polo Bridge Incident erupts (Jul. 7)
				Verbal on-site truce reached between the Japanese and Chinese sides. The Japanese government names the incident North China Incident and decides on dispatch of troops from Manchuria and Korea (Jul. 11)
				Langfang Incident (Jul. 25)
				Guanganmen Incident (Jul. 26)
				The Imperial Japanese Army in China initiates military actions in Beijing and Tianjin (Jul. 28 - 30)
				Tungchow Mutiny (Jul. 29)
				The Kanto Army launches Operation Chahar (Aug. 7)
				Lieutenant Ōyama Isao of the Imperial Japanese Navy Land Forces shot dead by Chinese Peace Preservation Corps troops in Shanghai (Aug. 9)

Year	Japanese Era	Age of Person in Events Column	Events in Person's Life	Domesitic/Overseas Incidents
1937	Shōwa 12th			Japanese government decides on dispatch of Imperial Japanese Army troops to Shanghai, where Chinese troops assault Japanese Navy Land Forces (Aug. 13)
				Chiang Kai-shek sends 600,000 of his best-trained and equipped soldiers to defend Shanghai. (Aug. 15)
				Imperial Japanese Army starts landing in Shanghai (end of August)
				Japanese government decides on formation of the Japanese Northern China Area Army and its dispatch to North China (Aug. 31)
				The North China Incident renamed the China Incident (Second Sino-Japanese War) (Sep. 2)
				The Japanese Northern China Area Army starts the North China Operation (Sep. 14)
				War-containment advocate Ishihara Kanji resigns as the Kanto Army's director of war planning (Sep. 28)
				The Japanese Northern China Area Army starts an offensive which becomes the Battle of Taiyuan (Oct. 2)
				U.S. President Roosevelt's Quarantine Speech (Oct. 5)
				The Japanese Northern China Area Army occupies Shijiazhung (Oct. 10)
				The Nine-Power Treaty Conference condemns Japan's violation of the treaty (Nov. 3-15)
				Mediation attempt by German Ambassador to China Oscar Trautmann commences (Nov. 5)
				Japanese 10th Army lands near Hangzhou Bay (Nov. 5)
				Chinese troops withdraw from metropolitan Shanghai, while the Japanese military captures Taiyuan (Nov. 8)
				Japan's Imperial General Headquarters reestablished (Nov. 20)

Year	Japanese Era	Age of Person in Events Column	Events in Person's Life	Domesitic/Overseas Incidents
1937	Shōwa 12th	56	Tōgō Shigenori appointed Japanese Ambassador to Germany (December 1937-October 1938)	Nanjing falls (Dec. 13)
1938	Shōwa 13th			Japanese government announces, "From now on the Empire of Japan would not regard the Kuomintang Government as its negotiation partner" (Termination of Trautmann mediation attempt)(Jan. 15)
				Austria annexed to Nazi Germany (Mar. 18)
				National Mobilization Law (Japan) enacted (Apr. 1)
		73	Ugaki Kazunari appointed foreign minister (May 26-)	The Kanto Army occupies Suchow (May 19)
				Battle of Lake Khasan (until Aug. 10)
			Prime Minister Konoe concurrently serves as foreign minister (Sept. 30-)	Munich Agreement signed (Nazi Germany's annexation of "Sudetenland") (Sept. 29)
				The Kanto Army occupies Canton (Oct. 21)
			Arita Hachirō appointed foreign minister (Oct. 29-)	Wuchang, Hankow, and Hanyang cities occupied by Japanese forces (Oct. 27)
			Shigemitsu Mamoru appointed Japanese Ambassador to Britain (Oct. 1938-Jun. 1941)	
			Tōgō Shigenori appointed Japanese Ambassador to the Soviet Union (Oct. 1938-Oct. 1940)	
				Prime Minister Konoe announces a vision for a New Order in East Asia (Nov. 3)
				Wang Jingwei flees Chongqing, stressing peace, anti-Communism, and national salvation (Dec. 20)
				Prime Minister Konoe announces three principles in coordinating relations with China (neighborly friendship, anti-Communist cooperation, and economic partnership) (Dec. 22)
				*Burma Road to transport supply to Chiang Kai-shek completed this year, connecting Burma with Kunming, China

Year	Japanese Era	Age of Person in Events Column	Events in Person's Life	Domesitic/Overseas Incidents
1939	Shōwa 14th			Konoe cabinet steps down (Jan. 4)
		56	Arita Hachirō appointed foreign minister	Hiranuma Kiichirō cabinet formed (Jan. 5)
		49	Ambassador to the United States Saitō Hiroshi passes away (Feb. 26)	Hainan Island occupied (Feb.10)
				Nanchang, Jiangxi, occupied (Mar. 27)
				Nomonhan Incident (May 11-Sept. 15)
				Imperial Japanese Army blockades British concession in Tientsin, worsening Anglo-Japanese relations, resulting in British military's withdrawal toward the end of the year) (Jun. 14)
				United States gives notice that it will abrogate the Treaty of Commerce and Navigation with Japan (Jul. 26)
				German-Soviet Nonagression Pact signed, while ongoing negotiation toward a tripartite alliance (Japan, Germany, Italy) is terminated (Aug. 23)
				Hiranuma cabinet steps down (Aug. 28)
		65	Foreign Minister Abe Nobuyuki to concurrently serve as prime minister	Abe Nobuyuki cabinet formed (Aug. 30)
				Yamamoto Isoroku appointed to commander-in-chief of the Imperial Japanese Navy Combined Fleet (Aug. 30)
				Britain and France declare war on Germany, marking the beginning of World War II (Sept. 3)
				Headquarters of the China Expeditionary Army established in Nanjing, commanding all the Japanes troops stationed in China (Sept. 12)
			Nomura Kichijirō appointed foreign minister (Sept. 25-)	Soviet troops advance into Poland (Sept. 17)
				Nanning, Guangxi, occupied (Oct. 24)
				Foreign Minister Nomura requests French ambassador to Japan to terminate transport of supplies to Chiang Kai-shek via French Indochina (Nov. 15)
				Soviet troops invade Finland (Nov. 30)
				*U.S. embargoes export of eleven items to Japan, including rubber and tin, on moral grounds this year

Year	Japanese Era	Age of Person in Events Column	Events in Person's Life	Domesitic/Overseas Incidents
1940	Shōwa 15th			Abe cabinet resigns (Jan. 14)
		57	Arita Hachirō appointed foreign minister	Yonai Mitsumasa cabinet formed (Jan. 16)
				U.S.-Japan Treaty of Commerce and Navigation abrogated (Jan. 26)
				Saitō Takao makes a historical, so-called anti-military speech at the House of Representatives (Feb. 2), for which he is expelled from the House together with a few who oppose Saito's expulsion (Mar, 7)
				United States provides China with a new loan of $20 million, collateralizing China's tin (Mar. 7)
				Resolution on "Carry through the Holy War" passes House of Representatives (Mar. 9)
				Wang Jingwei regime established, accompanied by the Nationalist government's relocation of its capital to Nanjing (Mar. 12)
				German troops accomplish bloodless occupation of Denmark, followed by their excursion to Norway (Apr. 9)
				German troops start attacking the Western Front (May 1)
				Imperial Japanese Army Air Service starts bombing China's inland cities, including Chongqing (May 13)
				British Expeditionary Force and French Army evacuate from Dunkirk (May 27-Jun. 4)
				U.S. government condemns Japan's bombing of Chongqing (Jun. 14)
				France surrenders to Germany (Jun. 22)
				Minister of War Hata Toshiroku resigns singlehandedly followed by resignation of the Yonai cabinet (Jul 4)
				German Luftwaffe starts air raids on Braitain proper (Jul. 10 - late Nov.)
		61	Matsuoka Yōsuke appointed foreign minister	Second Konoe Fumimaro cabinet formed (Jul 22)
				Japanese government decides Basic Outline of National Policy (construction of new order in East Asia and a military state) (Jul. 26)

Year	Japanese Era	Age of Person in Events Column	Events in Person's Life	Domesitic/Overseas Incidents
1940	Shōwa 15th			Imperial General Headquarters-Government Liaison Conference decides on southern expansion policy including use of force (Jul. 27)
				Massive counteroffensive by Communist Party of China's National Revolutionary Army (including the Hundred Regiments Offensive and north China front) (Aug. 20)
				Japan starts economic negotiation with Dutch East Indies (Aug. 30)
				Imperial Japanese Army advances to French Indochina (Sept. 22)
				U.S. government provides China (Chiang Kai-shek government) with a loan of $25 million (Sept. 25)
				Tripartite Pact concluded among Germany, Italy and Japan
				Launching ceremony of Taisei Yokusankai (Imperial Rule Assistance Association) (Konoe Fumimaro, President) (Oct. 12)
				Celebration of the Empire's 2,600th anniversary (Oct. 12)
				Treaty on Basic Relations between Japan and China signed (Nov. 13)
				U.S. government provides China (Chiang Kai-shek government) with an additional loan of $50 million (Nov. 30)
				U.S. Congress passes an act to provide China (Chiang Kai-shek government) with a loan of $100 million (Dec. 2)
				British government provides China (Chiang Kai-shek government) with a loan of £10 million (Dec. 10)
				U.S. President Roosevelt delivers a radio speech, declaring that the United States would be an armory for democratic countries (Dec. 29)
				*Imperial Japanese Navy's fighter A6M "Zero" deployed in the Chinese theater for the first time this year
1941	Shōwa 16th	65	Nomura Kichijirō appointed Japanese ambassador to the United States (Feb. 11-)	Soviet-Japanese Neutral Pact signed (Apr. 13)

Year	Japanese Era	Age of Person in Events Column	Events in Person's Life	Domesitic/Overseas Incidents
1941	Shōwa 16th	65	Foreign Minister Matsuoka visits Germany, Italy, and Soviet Union (March 12-April 22)	Agreement reached between U.S. Secretary of State Cordell Hull and Japanese Ambassador Nomura to put U.S.-Japan Draft Agreement, a private initiative, on the agenda for governmental negotiations between the two countries (Commencement of U.S.-Japan negotiation to coordinate the bilateral relations) (April 16)
				Foreign Minister Matsuoka expresses his opposition to the U.S.-Japan Draft Agreement (Apr. 22)
				Revision to the U.S.-Japan Draft Agreement submitted by the Japanese government to the U.S. government (May 12)
				U.S. Secretary of State Hull presents U.S. revision to the U.S.-Japan Draft Agreement (May 31)
				U.S. Secretary of State Hull hands Ambassador Nomura the above May 31 revision to the U.S.-Japan Draft Agreement as well as an oral statement denouncing Foreign Minister Matsuoka (Jun. 21)
				German forces start advancing into Soviet territory, upon which Foreign Minister Matsuoka submits to the Emperor a proposal to immediately start war with the Soviet Union (Jun. 22)
				The Japanese government decides on advance into southern French Indochina (Jun. 25)
				Cabinet meeting in the presence of the Emperor decides to prepare for a war with the Soviet Union and announces that Japan would not hesitate to enter a war with Britain and the United States (Jul. 2)
				Foreign Minister Matsuoka instructs the Japanese embassy to the United States to demand the U.S. government to withdraw Hull's oral statement (Jul. 14)
				Foreign Minister Matsuoka instructs the Japanese embassy to the United States how to respond to U.S. proposal on June 21, which Ambassador Nomura does not convey to Hull (Jul. 15)

Year	Japanese Era	Age of Person in Events Column	Events in Person's Life	Domesitic/Overseas Incidents
1941	Shōwa 16th			Second Konoe cabinet resigns (Jul. 16)
		57	Toyoda Teijirō appointed foreign minister	Third Konoe Fumimaro cabinet formed (Jul. 18)
				United States freezes Japan's assets in the United States (Jul. 25)
				Britain freezes Japan's assets in Britain (Jul. 26)
				Dutch East Indies freezes Japan's assets within its territory (Jul. 27)
				Imperial Japanese Army advances to southern French Indochina, while Dutch East Indies imposes oil embargo against Japan (Jul. 28)
				United States oil embargo against Japan (Aug. 1)
				Foreign Minister Toyoda suggests a talk between Konoe and Roosevelt (Aug. 7), to which the U.S. emphasizes the need for prior consultations, de facto rejecting the proposal (Sept. 3)
				U.S. President Roosevelt and British Prime Minister Churchill announce the Atlantic Charter (Aug. 12)
				Cabinet meeting in the presence of the Emperor decides to complete preparation for a war with Britain, the Netherlands, and the United States before the end of October (Sept. 6)
				Ozaki Hidemi and Richard Sorge arrested on spying charges (Oct. 15-16)
				Third Konoe Fumimaro cabinet resigned (Oct. 16)
		60	Tōgō Shigenori appointed foreign minister	Tōjō Hideki cabinet formed (Oct. 18)
		56	Ambassador Kurusu Saburō dispathed to the United States to assist Ambassador Nomura. Kurusu departs for the U.S. on Nov. 4.	Cabinet meeting in the presence of the Emperor decides on two proposals concerning the negotiations with the United States (Proposals A and B); it also decides that diplomatic efforts would be terminated at midnight on December 1 and that Japan would open war with the United States in early December (Nov. 5)

400

Year	Japanese Era	Age of Person in Events Column	Events in Person's Life	Domesitic/Overseas Incidents
1941	Shōwa 16th			Ambassadors Nomura and Kurusu submitt Proposal B to U.S. Secretary of State Hull (Nov. 20)
				Secretary Hull delivers the Outline of Proposed Basis for Agreement between the United States and Japan (the Hull note) to the Japanese side (Nov. 26)
				Imperial General Headquarters-Government Liaison Conference decides that the Hull note is indeed an ultimatum (Nov. 27)
				A cabinet meeting attended by the Emperor decides that Japan would start a war with Britain, the Netherlands, and the United States (Dec. 1)
				Imperial Japanese Navy task force launches a surprise attack on Pearl Harbor (Dec. 8)
				Naval Battle off Malaya (Dec. 10)
				Imperial Japanese Army occupies Hong Kong (Dec. 18)
1942	Shōwa 17th	56	Shigemitsu Mamoru appointed Japanese Ambassador to China (Wang Jingwei regime, Jan.-Nov. 1942)	Imeperial Japanese Army occupies Manila (Jan. 2)
				Imeperial Japanese Army occupies Rabaul (Jan 23)
				Imeperial Japanese Army occupies Singapore (Feb. 15)
				Imeperial Japanese Army occupies Rangoon (Mar. 8)
				Dutch East Indies forces in Indonesia surrender (Mar. 9)
				American and Filipino forces in the Philippines surrender (May 7)
				Battle of Midway (Jun. 5)
				U.S. forces land on Guadalcanal (Aug. 7), after which Battle of Guadalcanal lasts until January 1943, resulting in withdrawal of Japanese troops from the island
		59	Prime Minister Tōjō concurrently serves as foreign minister (Sept. 1-)	Ministry of Greater East Asia established, against which Foreign Minister Tōgō resigns in protest (Sept. 1)

Year	Japanese Era	Age of Person in Events Column	Events in Person's Life	Domesitic/Overseas Incidents
1941	Shōwa 16th			U..S. forces commence a massive counteroffensive on Solomon and New Guinea (June)
				State of Burma proclaims independence (Aug. 1)
				Italy surrenders (Sept. 8)
				Cabinet meeting in the presence of the Emperor decides on an Absolute National Defense Sphere (Sept.. 30)
				Republic of the Philippines declares independence (Oct. 14)
				Alliance Treaty between Japan and China (Wang Jingwei regime) signed, upon which the Treaty on Basic Relations between Japan and China is abrogated (Oct. 30)
				Greater East Asia Conference convened (Nov. 5)
				Cairo Conference convened (Nov. 6)
				Teheran Conference convened (Nov. 28)
1944	Shōwa 19th			The Battle of Imphal commences (Mar. 8-Jul.)
				The Allies start the Invasion of Normandy (Jun. 6)
				U.S. forces land on Saipan (Jun. 15)
				Battle of the Philippine Sea (Jun. 19)
				The last Banzai attack by the Japanese garrison on Saipan (Jul. 7)
				Tōjō cabinet resigns (Jul. 18)
		58	Shigemitsu Mamoru appointed foreign minister	Koiso Kuniaki cabinet formed (Jul. 22)
				U.S. forces land on Leyte (Oct. 20)
				Battle of Leyte Gulf (Oct. 23-26)
				Kamikaze suicide attacks started (Oct. 25)
				President Roosevelt re-elected for a fourth term (Nov. 8)
				Wang Jingwei passes away (Nov. 10)
				First air raid of Tokyo by B29 bombers flying from Mariana (Nov. 24)
1945	Shōwa 20th			U.S. Forces land on Luzon, Philippines (Jan. 9)

Year	Japanese Era	Age of Person in Events Column	Events in Person's Life	Domesitic/Overseas Incidents
1945	Shōwa 20th			U.S. forces regain Manila (Mar. 3)
				Bombing of Tokyo (start of nondiscriminatory bombing on Japanese cities) (Mar. 10)
				U.S. forces land on Okinawa, in the midst of Kamikaze suicide attacks that were started a few days earlier (apr. 1)
				Koiso Kuniaki cabinet resigns (Apr. 5)
				Suzuki Kantarō cabinet formed/Imperial Japanese Navy's battleship Yamato sunk en route to its mission in Okinawa (Apr. 7)
				U.S. President Roosevelt passes away. He is succeeded by Vice President Harry Truman (Apr. 12).
				Hitler kills himself (Apr. 30)
				Germany surrenders (May 7)
				Potsdam Declaration released (Jul. 26)
				Atomic bomb dropped on Hiroshima (Aug. 6)
				Atomic bomb dropped on Nagasaki. The Soviet Union declares war on Japan. (Aug. 9).
				Imperial decision to accept the Potsdam Declaration (Aug. 9)
				Imperial decision to accept the Potsdam Declaration repeated and its acceptance is officially decided (Aug. 14)
				Emperor Shōwa reads the Imperial Rescript on the Termination of the War over the radio at noon (Aug. 15)

INDEX

（英文版）重光・東郷とその時代
Shigemitsu and Togo and Their Time

2019年3月29日　第1刷発行

著　者　　岡崎久彦
訳　者　　野田牧人
発行所　　一般財団法人出版文化産業振興財団
　　　　　〒101-0051 東京都千代田区神田神保町3-12-3
　　　　　電話　03-5211-7282（代）

ホームページ　http://www.jpic.or.jp/

印刷・製本所　　大日本印刷株式会社